T4-ACW-300

This Little Boy is Master of His Pets (p. 204)

DON MANUEL OSORIO DE ZUNIGA
by Francisco de Goya

The Bookshelf
for Boys and Girls

Prepared under the Supervision of
THE EDITORIAL BOARD
OF THE UNIVERSITY SOCIETY

VOLUME VI

Art and Music

THE UNIVERSITY SOCIETY, INC.
Educational Publishers since 1897
NEW YORK

1962

© *Copyright, 1958, by The University Society, Incorporated*

In addition to its wealth of new material THE BOOKSHELF FOR BOYS AND GIRLS combines the very best features of its highly successful predecessors: namely, Boys and Girls Bookshelf, copyright 1912, 1915, 1920; Young Folks Treasury, copyright 1909, 1917, 1919; Father and Son Library, copyright 1921; Modern Boy Activity, copyright 1921, 1923; The Mother's Book, copyright 1919; The Child Welfare Manual, copyright 1916; The Home Kindergarten Manual, copyright 1921; Bible Stories and Character Building, copyright 1915; The Home University Bookshelf, copyright 1927, 1938, 1945; The Bookshelf for Boys and Girls, copyright 1948; 1955.

All rights are reserved. Reproduction in any form or part is prohibited unless written consent is received from the Copyright owner, The University Society, Incorporated.

Manufactured in the U.S.A.

ACKNOWLEDGEMENTS   Volume VI

Credits for Photographs

(in addition to photographs furnished by private owners, museums, or representatives of foreign nations)

A. C. L. BRUSSELS: p. 80, 81
ALINARI: p. 13, 14, 21, 36, 39, 41, 42, 48, 50, 51, 52, 55, 69, 72, 76, 77, 79, 88, 98, 99, 103, 104, 107, 109, 112, 113, 121, 124, 139, 142, 144, 152.
ANDERSON: p. 89a, 89b, 90, 91, 96, 97, 108, 120, 150, 151.
ARCHIVES PHOTOGRAPHIC: p. 7, 56, 57, 58, 62, 63, 64, 68, 180, 181, 182, 198, 212, 213, 214, 225, 240.
OLIVER BAKER: p. 7.
BOARD OF EDUCATION, CITY OF NEW YORK: p. 2.
BRAUN & CO.: p. 118.
BRUCKMANN, MUNICH: p. 32.
ENCYCLOPEDIA BRITANNICA: p. 8.
PHILIP GENDREAU: p. 2, 258.
GERMAN ARCHAEOLOGICAL INSTITUTE, ATHENS: p. 15, 34.

FOTO G. F. N.: p. 44.
GUNDERMANN: p. 185.
HEGE: p. 22, 23, 26, 27.
PHOTO HOUVET: p. 58, 66.
HURON PRODUCTIONS: p. 5.
PROF. CLARENCE KENNEDY: p. 30.
KLINGHARDT & BIERMAN: p. 35.
LYTT: p. 4.
FOTO MARBURG: p. 59.
METROPOLITAN MUSEUM OF ART, N. Y.: p. 8c.
BARBARA MORGAN, SCARSDALE, N. Y.: p. 6.
NATIONAL GALLERY, LONDON, ENGLAND: p. 193.
JOHN REWALD: p. 3.
SCHROLL: p. 199.
UNITED NATIONS: p. 253.
WILDENSTEIN: p. 231.
WOLFRUM: p. 189.

A Word to Parents about this Volume

THE STORY OF ART
and
THE STORY OF MUSIC

FOR its illumination of painting, sculpture, architecture, and music, as well as for the richness of its illustrations, this is by far the most valuable volume in this set.

Actually it contains *two complete books:* THE STORY OF ART and THE STORY OF MUSIC. Together they are of priceless educational value, not only for children with artistic or musical leanings but for anyone, young or old, who would like to understand more about the nature of beauty as an expression of man's deepest emotions.

THE STORY OF ART

The main purpose of THE STORY OF ART is to show children how to look at a work of art intelligently. In these pages they will learn that in art every shape, every color, every grouping *means* something. And armed with such understanding, they will come to recognize these meanings whenever they look at *any* work of art.

After an explanation of how to approach art in general, THE STORY OF ART begins with the art of ancient Greece and Rome, for that was the fountainhead of most European and American art as we know it today.

From those primitive beginnings, as our author shows us, came the changes made by artists representing successive schools of thought and styles of art. Therefore (with the exception of Oriental art which appears in a small separate section near the end) the pictures are arranged in *historical order*. This has been done not so much to teach children the history of art as to show them the *logic* of its development. Like everything else, art changes with time. Artists with new approaches experiment with new ideas and change the old established forms, often introducing exciting new styles.

The growth of art can be compared to a tree-trunk on whose growing boughs new buds and leaves and flowers and fruits spring forth as the earth turns.

Not every bough on the tree of art is here, of course. But you can see the tree itself and all the really important branches—also the direction the twigs have taken and the *kind* of blossoming that is characteristic at each stage of the tree's development.

A child who looks at the successive pictures here, reads the stories that go with them, and then looks at the pictures again, should be familiar with the general trend of European and American art and able to put paintings and statues in their proper place on the growing tree of art when he sees them.

Our author, Dr. Elizabeth Gutman, has an impressive background of art study and art teaching in her native Budapest, in Vienna, and in New York. She has written original treatises on art for adults and has also had great success in explaining art to children so as to arouse their interest and deepen their understanding.

She uses the same method here—beginning with simple stories about the simple pictures made long ago by the ancient Greeks, suggesting similarities to other pictures made at the same time, and going on logically to the next stage of art development and so on.

Her first emphasis is on the *story* to be seen in a picture, her second on the forms and colors and techniques the artist used to bring out that story. Her main objective has been to enable the child to look at a painting or a sculpture or a piece of architecture and *read the story in it for himself*. Any child who finds himself able to do that as the result of THE STORY OF ART will be immeasurably enriched.

THE STORY OF MUSIC

THE STORY OF MUSIC is presented on the same historical principles as THE STORY OF ART, but it takes up far less space in this book. That is certainly not because it is in any way less important. But music is something to be *listened to* rather than looked at, and melodies and harmonies cannot be reproduced in a book as pictures can.

To be sure, for those who can play the piano there are musical notations and musical themes to highlight the story. But except for these and the little sketches illustrating the text, THE STORY OF MUSIC has to depend on what the *words* say.

In the opinion of the editors, the words here tell the story of music more simply, more delightfully, and with more illumination than we have ever seen the story told for young readers. From an enlightening beginning that tells the child exactly what music is—and how to distinguish it from mere noise—the story traces music from its origins up through ancient times, the Dark Ages, and all the fascinating phases that music passed through until it became *great* music. There are stories here about the great composers, about why each wrote the kind of music he did, and about both early religious music and entertaining modern music.

For the child who is really interested in music, there is an illuminating section on how to read music, one on harmony, one on musical instruments and orchestras, and one on how to listen to music with understanding and above all, enjoyment.

Ruth Goode, the teller of the story, is not only a music appreciator of great sensitivity and intelligence but, more important, she has so fired her two children with an understanding of music that they have bettered her instruction. Mrs. Goode's ability to teach and inspire her children to proceed musically on their own seems to us an ideal quality for the writer of our STORY OF MUSIC. She has long been a professional writer on children's learning. That she can write about music as charmingly as she does is an added delight for our young readers.

Mrs. Goode's hope—and ours—is that THE STORY OF MUSIC will enable more children to get more pleasure and enjoyment from music than they ever before imagined they could.

For those pursuing music seriously, there is a glossary of common musical terms at the end of the book, and for those collecting a record library a list of recommended recordings.

A word is in order, too, about the illustrations adorning THE STORY OF MUSIC. They are by Rafaello Busoni, son of the famous pianist, Ferruccio Benvenuto Busoni, and we think they add as musical a sparkle as any drawings could.

Table of Contents for The Story of Art

A NOTE ABOUT THE PARTICULAR USEFULNESS OF THIS TABLE OF CONTENTS

This *Table of Contents* does more than merely list the contents of the book. It is in itself a guide to the successive styles of art in Europe and America. With the exception of the separate section on Oriental art near the end, the works of art pictured and described in this **"Story of Art"** appear in historical order—and they are so arranged in the *Table of Contents*. But, in addition, here they are also *grouped under the periods of art history they exemplify*. Thus the *Table of Contents* may in itself be studied as a quick outline of the history of art.

And now a word about the spelling of artists' names and the dates of their lives and works. These sometimes vary in different reference books. They are, indeed, sometimes entirely unverifiable. We have therefore used the spellings and the dates for which we found authority in the best American biographical dictionaries and encyclopedias.

	PAGE
DON MANUEL OSORIO DE ZUNIGA, *By Francisco de Goya*	*Frontispiece*
(Story on p. 204)	

General Approaches to Art … 1-10
- ART SPRINGS FROM A FEELING FOR FORM … 2-3
- ART SPRINGS FROM A FEELING OF RHYTHM … 4-5
- THE DIFFERENCE BETWEEN PRACTICAL ORDER AND ARTISTIC ORDER … 6-7
- PEOPLE ARE DIFFERENT IN DIFFERENT CLIMATES … 8-8a
  - In Arctic Greenland … 8
  - In the Tropics … 8a
  - In Temperate North America … 8a
- PEOPLE ARE DIFFERENT IN DIFFERENT PERIODS … 8b-8c
  - In Ancient Greece (ORPHEUS AND EURYDICE, fifth century B.C.) … 8b
  - In the Middle Ages (THE OFFERING OF THE HEART, Tapestry early 15th century) … 8b
  - In Modern Times (LE BAL À BOUGIVAL, *By Auguste Renoir*) … 8c
- EVEN THE SAME PERSON IS DIFFERENT AT DIFFERENT TIMES … 8d-9
  - Self-Portrait of YOUNG REMBRANDT … 8d
  - Self-Portrait of MIDDLE-AGED REMBRANDT … 9
  - Self-Portrait of OLD REMBRANDT … 9
- THIS IS A PICTURE BOOK … 10

The Art of the Ancient Greeks and Romans … 11-47
- "THE GLORY THAT WAS GREECE" … 11
- VIEW OF THE ACROPOLIS IN ATHENS, GREECE … 12
- ATHENA PARTHENOS, between 447-432 B.C. … 13

VI

	PAGE
Geometric Vase, eighth century	14-15
The Francois Vase, *By Ergotimos* and *Klitias*	16-17
Hector Prepares for Battle, *By Euthymides*	18
Theseus Visits Amphitrite, *By Euphronios*	19
Harnessing Horses for a Chariot Drive, *By Psiax*	20
Charioteer, about 480 B.C.	21
The Parthenon, *By Iktinus*	22
The Erechtheum, about 420 B.C.	23
The Doric Style	24
The Ionic Style	25
Corinthian Capital	25
Riders on the West Frieze of the Parthenon, about 450 B.C.	26-27
Caryatid Hall	28
Caryatid from the Erechtheum, about 415 B.C.	29
Head of the Athena Lemnia, *By Phidias*	30
Wounded Amazon, *By Polyclitus*	31
Discus Thrower, *By Myron*	32
Niké Fastening Her Sandal, about 415-408 B.C.	33
Hermes with Little Bacchus, *By Praxiteles*	34
Head of Hermes and Aphrodite, *By Praxiteles*	35
Apollo of the Belvedere, fourth century B.C.	36
Venus De Milo, first century B.C.	36
Demosthenes, *By Polyeuctus*	37
Laocoon and His Sons, *By Agesander, Athenodorus, and Polydorus*	38-39
"The Grandeur that was Rome"	40
Trajan's Column, *By Apollodorus*	41
The Arch of Titus, about the end of the first century A.D.	42
Roman Arches	43
The Colosseum, about 80 B.C.	44
The Pantheon *(Painting by Pannini)*	45
Mummy Portrait of a Man, first century A.D.	46
Mummy Portrait of a Little Girl, fourth century A.D.	47

Christian Art in the Earlier Middle Ages — 48-57

Christian Art Is Spiritual	48
Colossal Head of Constantine, fourth century A.D.	49
St. Apollinare in Class 560 A.D.	50
St. Apollinare Nuovo 504 A.D.	51
The Holy Women at the Sepulcher, sixth century A.D.	52-53
Tournay Cathedral, 12th century	54
Pisa Cathedral, 12th and 13th centuries	55
Doorway in Fontgomboult, 12th century	56
Side of a Doorway, about 1150	57

Art in the Later Middle Ages — 58-75

- St. Theodore, 13th century — 58
- St. Modeste, 13th century — 58
- Ekkehard and Uta, about 1260 — 59
- Chartres Cathedral, 12th to 13th centuries — 60-61
- Rheims Cathedral, 12th to 15th centuries — 62
- Amiens Cathedral, (Interior) *By Robert de Luzarches* — 63
- Flying Buttresses, about 1220-1240 — 64
- Roof of the Cathedral of Notre Dame, 12th and 13th centuries — 64
- Cologne Cathedral, (Interior) *By Gerhard von Rihle* — 65
- St. Eustache Hunting, (Stained Glass 13th century) — 66-67
- The Ste. Chapelle, (Interior) *By Pierre de Montereau* — 68
- The Arena Chapel, (Interior) *By Giotto* — 69
- The Flight into Egypt, *By Giotto* — 70-71
- The Nativity, *By Giovanni Pisano* — 72-73
- The Annunciation, *By Simone Martini* — 74-75

Art of the Early Renaissance — 76-103

- St. George and the Dragon, (Relief) *By Donatello* — 76
- St. George, *By Donatello* — 77
- The Toll Money, *By Masaccio* — 78-79
- The Ghent Altar-Piece, (closed) *By Hubert van Eyck* and *Jan van Eyck* — 80
- The Ghent Altar-Piece, (open) — 81
- The Arnolfini Couple, *By Jan van Eyck* — 82-83
- Portrait of a Young Lady, *By Roger van der Weyden* — 84-85
- Christ Appears to His Mother, *By Roger van der Weyden* — 86-87
- Room of the Bride and Groom, *By Andrea Mantegna* — 88-89
- The Battle of Constantine, *By Piero della Francesca* — 90-91
- The Madonna of St. Job, *By Giovanni Bellini* — 92-93
- Portrait of a Young Man, *By Giovanni Bellini* — 94-95
- Gattamelata, *By Donatello* — 96
- Colleoni, *By Andrea Verocchio* — 97
- Palazzo Rucellai, *By Leon Battista Alberti* — 98
- Palazzo Vendramin-Calerghi, *By Pietro Lombardo* — 99
- Giuliano Medici, *By Andrea Verocchio* — 100
- The Madonna of the Lilies, *By Sandro Botticelli* — 101
- The Birth of Venus, *By Sandro Botticelli* — 102-103

Art of the High Renaissance — 104-137

- The Last Supper, *By Leonardo da Vinci* — 104-105
- Mona Lisa, *By Leonardo da Vinci* — 106-107
- David, *By Michelangelo* — 108-109
- St. George and the Dragon, *By Raphael* — 110-111
- Philosophy, *By Raphael* — 112-113

	PAGE
THE SMALL COWPER MADONNA, *By Raphael*	114-115
SELF-PORTRAIT, *By Albrecht Dürer*	116
THE HARE, *By Albrecht Dürer*	116
ST. EUSTACHE, *By Albrecht Dürer*	117
ST. ANTHONY AND ST. PAUL, *By Matthias Grünewald*	118-119
THE SISTINE CHAPEL, (Interior) *By many artists*	120-121
THE TRIBUTE MONEY, *By Titian*	122-123
EARTHLY AND HEAVENLY LOVE, *By Titian*	124-125
GANYMEDE, *By Correggio*	126-127
LANDSCAPE, *By Albrecht Altdorfer*	128-129
MOSES, *By Michelangelo*	130-131
HIERONYMUS HOLZSCHUHER, *By Albrecht Dürer*	132-133
HENRY VIII, *By Hans Holbein*	134
EDWARD, PRINCE OF WALES, *By Hans Holbein*	134-135
KINGS HENRY VII AND VIII, *By Hans Holbein*	136-137

Art of the Late Renaissance (Mannerism) 138-149

PIER LUIGI FARNESE, *By Titian*	138-139
VENICE RULING, *By Paolo Veronese*	140-141
THE LAND OF COCKAINE, *By Pieter Brueghel*	142-143
ST. GEORGE AND THE DRAGON, *By Jacopo Tintoretto*	144-145
ST. MARTIN, *By El Greco*	146-147
VICTORY, *By Michelangelo*	148
FLYING MERCURY, *By Giovanni da Bologna*	149

Art in the Earlier Baroque Period 150-166

DAVID, *By Gian Lorenzo Bernini*	150
SCIPIONE BORGHESE, *By Gian Lorenzo Bernini*	151
ST. MATTHEW, *By Michelangelo Caravaggio*	152
AURORA, (Dawn) *By Guido Reni*	153
VENUS AND ADONIS, *By Pieter Paul Rubens*	154-155
THE HAPPY VOYAGE OF CARDINAL INFANT FERDINAND, *By Pieter Paul Rubens*	156-157
LORD JOHN AND LORD BERNARD STUART, *By Anthony van Dyck*	158-159
THE NURSING OF BACCHUS, *By Nicholas Poussin*	160
THE HERDSMAN, *By Claude Lorrain*	161
THE PASTRY-EATERS, *By Esteban Murillo*	162-163
PRINCE PHILIP PROSPER, *By Diego Velazquez*	164-165
THE LANCES, *By Diego Velazquez*	166-167

The Golden Age of Dutch Art 168-179

LAUGHING CHILD, *By Frans Hals*	168
PORTRAIT OF A COUPLE, *By Frans Hals*	169
TITUS READING, *By Rembrandt van Rijn*	170

	PAGE
THE THREE TREES, *By Rembrandt van Rijn*	171
JACOB'S BLESSING, *By Rembrandt van Rijn*	172-173
THE STUDIO OF THE PAINTER, *By Jan Vermeer van Delft*	174-175
THE EVE OF ST. NICHOLAS, *By Jan Steen*	176-177
WATERING CATTLE, *By Aelbert Cuyp*	178
THE BIG FOREST, *By Jacob Ruisdael*	179

Art in the Later Baroque Period — 180-186

VERSAILLES PALACE, *By Louis Le Vau and J. Hardouin Mansard*	180
LOUIS XIV, *By Gian Lorenzo Bernini*	181
COMPANY IN THE PARK, *By Antoine Watteau*	182
THE ALLEGORY OF PAINTING, *By François Boucher*	183
COUNT SINZENDORF, *By Hyacinth Rigaud*	184
STAIRCASE OF WÜRZBURG PALACE, (ceiling) *By Giovanni Baptista Tiepolo*	185
TIMOCLEA AND THE THRACIAN COMMANDER, *By Giovanni Baptista Tiepolo*	186-187
GOODBY BEFORE SCHOOL, *By Jean Simeon Chardin*	188-189

Art in the Time of Revolutions — 190-214

THE GRAHAM CHILDREN, *By William Hogarth*	190-191
MASTER CREWE AS HENRY VIII, *By Sir Joshua Reynolds*	192-193
THE BLUE BOY, *By Thomas Gainsborough*	194-195
CHARLES I, *By John Singleton Copley*	196
BENJAMIN FRANKLIN, *By Antoine Houdon*	197
MADAME RÉCAMIER, *By Jacques Louis David*	198
NAPOLEON CROSSING THE ALPS, *By Jacques Louis David*	199
THE PEACEABLE KINGDOM, *By Edward Hicks*	200
STAIRCASE GROUP, *By Charles Wilson Peale*	201
THE HAY-WAIN, *By John Constable*	202-203
DON MANUEL OSORIO DE ZUNIGA, *By Francisco de Goya*	204
THE AMERICAN MARIANO CEBALLOS RIDING A BULL, *By Francisco de Goya*	205
THE FIGHTING TÉMÉRAIRE, *By William Turner*	206-207
THE LION HUNT, *By Eugene Delacroix*	208-209
THE WASHERWOMAN, *By Honoré Daumier*	210-211
IN REMEMBRANCE OF MORTEFONTAINE, *By Camille Corot*	212
THE GLEANERS, *By Jean François Millet*	213
THE WAVE, *By Gustave Courbet*	214

Art in the Time of Impressionism — 215-231

BREEZING UP, *By Winslow Homer*	215
ARRANGEMENT IN GRAY AND BLACK, *By James McNeill Whistler*	216-217
CHILD WITH SWORD, *By Edouard Manet*	218
IN THE BOAT, *By Edouard Manet*	219
RACE HORSES, *By Edgar Degas*	220
FOUR DANCERS, *By Edgar Degas*	220-221

	PAGE
GIRL WITH WATERING CAN, *By Auguste Renoir*	222-223
THE CITIZENS OF CALAIS, *By Auguste Rodin*	224-225
ROCK OF ETRETAS, *By Claude Monet*	226
PALAZZO MULA, *By Claude Monet*	227
THE BATH, *By Mary Cassatt*	228-229
MOUNT STE. VICTOIRE, *By Paul Cézanne*	230
THE BLACK CLOCK, *By Paul Cézanne*	231

Art in the Time of Post-Impressionism 232-242

CLAUDE AT THE EASEL, *By Auguste Renoir*	232-233
CYPRESSES, *By Vincent Van Gogh*	234-235
SIEGFRIED AND THE RHINE MAIDENS, *By Albert Pinkham Ryder*	236-237
THE WHITE HORSE, *By Paul Gaugin*	238-239
ADAMS MEMORIAL, *By Augustus Saint Gaudens*	240-241
THE GRAND JATTE, *By Georges Seurat*	242-243

Art in Modern Times 244-257

HOMAGE TO CÉZANNE, *By Aristide Maillol*	244
PICADOR, *By Pablo Gargallo*	245
EQUATORIAL JUNGLE, *By Henri Rousseau*	246-247
PAUL REVERE'S RIDE, *By Grant Wood*	248-249
GOLDFISH AND SCULPTURE, *By Henri Matisse*	250-251
UNITED NATIONS BUILDING	252-253
THE LOVERS, *By Pablo Picasso*	254-255
THE WHITE SEAL, *By Constantine Brancusi*	256-257

Art of the Orient 258-262

THE SEVEN WONDERS OF THE ANCIENT WORLD	258-259
THE PYRAMIDS	258
THE TAJ MAHAL	260
HINDU TEMPLE	261
INDIAN BUDDHA	261
CRAG WITH MISTY VALLEY, Chinese Landscape, Ming Period	262
THE WAVE, Japanese Woodcut, *By Hokusai*	262

Stories of Changing Trends in Art 263-268

A GREEK LEGEND: HOW DID ART BEGIN	263
BISON FROM ALTAMIRA and Copy	263
LION, *By Villard de Honnecourt*	264
ANNUNCIATION, *By Giovanni da Fiesole (Fra Angelico)*	265
THREE GREAT RENAISSANCE ARTISTS	266
ST. PETER'S CATHEDRAL IN ROME	267
THREE STORIES ABOUT ARTISTS	268

What is the Use of Art?

Some of you may ask, "What is the use of art?"

Let's pretend your father has bought a new house. Everything you need seems to be in it: the beds to sleep in, the chairs to sit on, and the table where you can eat your meals. There are lamps to give you light and heat to keep you warm, closets and cabinets for storing the things you need.

But as long as the walls are without pictures, they look bare and uninteresting.

Your eyes get hungry for something pretty or gay. You wish you had a picture of a story or a place or people. You might like to look at a quiet landscape to give your mind a rest, or something cheerful to brighten you up. This is what pictures can do for us in the home. This is one of the uses of art.

In the Town Hall or the Court House, we like to have pictures showing the important events in our country's history. In the Public Library we want portraits of great writers and poets whose works we read. In the parks and main squares of a city we like to see statues of the great men and heroes who fill our hearts with pride. This is the use of art in public places.

The magic power of art can arouse all kinds of emotions in us, from simple joy to much deeper feelings. And artists are great people whose works of art can gladden our eyes, enrich our thoughts, and deepen our feelings.

Those artists who are sculptors make shapes or statues out of shapeless stone or clay. Painters make pictures out of lines and colors. There is order and rhythm in their work, and it takes great skill to do it well. Our highest praise for anything that is beautifully done is:

"This is a real work of art!"

The Story of Art

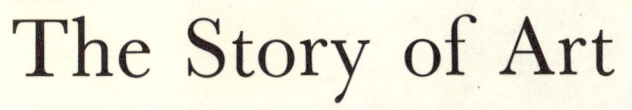

By Elizabeth Gutman

Art Springs from a Feeling for Form

Small Children Make Mud-pies

Betty loves to make shapes out of the sand on the beach. Betty is a very little girl, and her mother is helping her press the sand into her pail and then turn it out. See—delightfully clean-shaped mud-pies!

Bigger Children Model in Clay

Bill models with clay. He can make any shape he wants to out of it. He can make people or animals. Right now he is modeling a sturdy animal. It will be a great joy to him when he has made it look right.

2

The Sculptor Maillol in His Studio

    An artist makes shapes of clay and casts them in a bronze or brass or lead. Or he carves figures in stone. This is the work of a sculptor. To become a sculptor requires talent, imagination, and many years of practice and study.
    Here we see the great sculptor Maillol finishing one of his sculptures. He has given the woman's figure the radiant life and beauty created by his imagination.

Art Springs from a Feeling of Rhythm

Some Motions are Merely Practical

When Vicky goes to school in the morning she just walks along. It is something she does on every ordinary day.

Rhythm is the First Step Toward Art

After school Vicky feels full of joy. It is her birthday and on her way home she expects happy surprises. She feels like hopping and dancing and swinging her bag in rhythm, because she feels so gay.

Dancing is the Art of Rhythmic Motion

The art of a dancer is to express feeling in graceful rhythmic motion. To become an artist a dancer must have special talent and years of training. Finally the performance will be so exquisite that the dancer gives artistic joy to those who watch.

The Difference Between Practical Order and Artistic Order

A Festive Table

It is Johnny's birthday and his friends have been invited for supper. Mother has decorated the table for the festive occasion. She has made place cards, tucked the napkins into the forks to make them look pretty, and made a centerpiece of moss and fir branches. The table is neatly set—everything in its proper place. The silver and the glasses, bread and butter, cream and sugar are all within easy reach. The table looks very pretty, but the main purpose for setting it was a practical one: to make Johnny and his friends comfortable and happy as they eat their supper.

When you look at this painting of a table by the old Dutch painter De Heem you see great disorder among the food and dishes. Even the tablecloths are in disorder. But the picture pleases us just the same. The reason is that this table was not set for practical purposes. It was arranged and painted to satisfy the *eye*, not the *stomach*. The fragrant-looking fruit, the meat, the shimmering decanters and goblets, the velvety dark table cover and the crumpled linen tablecloth were arranged in a rhythmic artistic order.

When the modern French painter Henri Matisse painted his *Variation* of De Heem's picture he was interested *only* in the arrangement, the artistic order. Matisse did not care to make the objects look pretty and appealing in any way.

His only interest was in the rhythmic order of their shapes and colors. The value of Matisse's art lies in the rhythmic beauty and artistic order of his paintings.

Still-Life
by De Heem

Variation of
De Heem's Still-Life
by Henri Matisse

People are Different in Different Climates

IN TROPICAL AFRICA

This tall dark-skinned African Princess and her little boy are wearing very light clothing. The sun burns hot in Africa and heavy clothes would be unbearable. This mother is giving her child the love all mothers feel for their children.

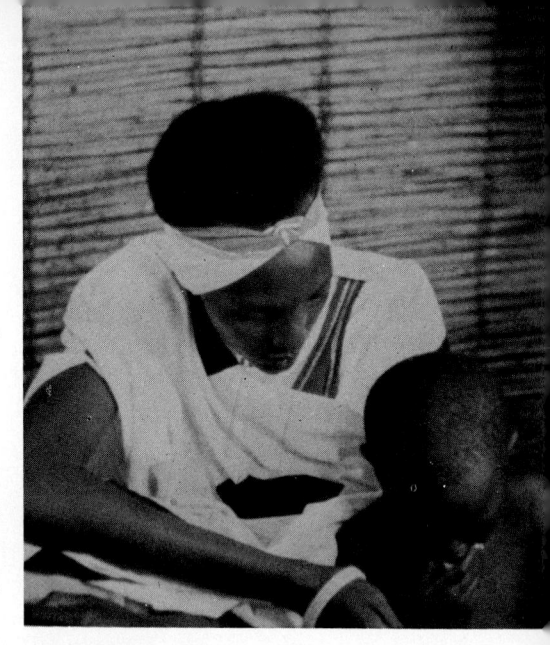

Eskimos, who live in cold Arctic climates, are short, stocky, and yellow-skinned. This Eskimo mother and her baby are all bundled up to keep themselves warm. The little boy is wearing a fur hood. The Eskimos are different in many ways from people who live in other climates. But the love of the Eskimo mother for her baby in the cold north is just like that of the black mother under the hot sun of equatorial Africa.

North, South, East, West—you will find the same love and tenderness between mother and child everywhere. But people look different, have different customs, and speak different languages according to where and how they live. Art is a language too, and the art of different countries is as different as the speech of their people.

IN ARCTIC GREENLAND

Courtesy Royal Danish Ministry for Foreign Affairs

IN TEMPERATE NORTH AMERICA

In temperate climates people wear heavier clothes than they do in the Tropics but lighter than would be necessary in the Arctic. This white mother differs in many ways from her Negro and her Eskimo sisters, but she is like them in many ways too, especially in her love for her little son.

People are Different in Different Periods

IN ANTIQUITY

The ancient Greeks lived a simple life. They had beautiful and healthy bodies and they moved freely in their loose flowing garments. Their faces and their gestures were gently expressive, as we know from the ancient Greek sculptures that have survived.

ORPHEUS AND EURYDICE, fifth century B.C.

In mediaeval times fashions were different and people looked different too. In their tight clothing the natural shapes of their bodies were hidden. But, different as this was from the Greeks, these people with their elaborate rich garments had their own quaint kind of prettiness.

The figures are unnatural, to be sure, and so are the animals and trees around them. But the young man offering his heart to the lady he loves is no doubt expressing the same feeling the Greeks had for their loved ones.

The people in these three pictures are as different as the widely separated times in which their creators made them. But different as they are, the old feeling of love, which they all share, has remained the same throughout the ages.

IN THE MIDDLE AGES

THE OFFERING OF THE HEART, Tapestry early 15th century

IN MODERN TIMES

In recent centuries garments changed again to more natural shapes, as we can see in this nineteenth century French painting. Here are a man and a woman in love—dancing. Fashions change and people change too, but the old feeling of love remains the same.

LE BAL A BOUGIVAL, *By Auguste Renoir*

Even the Same Person is Different at Different Times of His Own Life

YOUNG REMBRANDT

The great Dutch painter Rembrandt was only a young man when he painted this portrait of himself. He drew his face with simple outlines smoothly melting into the shadow. A sudden light lets us see the shape of his cheek, eye, nose, and mouth. The rest is lost in darkness. Rembrandt is wearing a jaunty cap that goes well with the daring expression on his young face.

As he did in the earlier painting, Rembrandt highlighted only the most important part of this self-portrait painted when he was in his middle years. This time he faces us fully. We can see both eyes, his nose and mouth—all carefully painted with subtle shades. The features of Rembrandt, saddened in middle age, are lined by unhappy years. His searching expression tells of the depth of his mature thought and feeling.

MIDDLE-AGED REMBRANDT

OLD REMBRANDT

Old Rembrandt smiles at us and at himself—because this picture is reflected in a mirror, as all self-portraits must be. Turning his face in the same way, only in the opposite direction, his smiling mouth is half-open as in the portrait of his youth. But here the active daring expression is gone. Instead of tossing his head in a cocky way he can now hardly straighten his head above his shoulders, bent as they are by old age. The light plays around his face, his cap, and his scarf with equal brightness, because the old artist does not want to emphasize his person any more. But we can see the painter's joy in the rhythm of his brushstrokes.

This is a Picture Book

In a way, looking at this picture-book is like looking at an album of some friends' family photographs. The pictures of your friends—we'll call them Ellen and Joe—begin when they were very small, probably when they were tiny babies. You see them later taking their first steps. By this time they may have been living in another town. Then they are in nursery school with their friends. Here Joe is just starting out on his tricycle. There Ellen has her first try at swimming.

A few years later, when Joe and Ellen have traveled to more distant and more interesting places, the pictures tell you all about their trips.

Some pages later, you see a bigger Joe riding his bicycle. He is more skillful now. And here is Ellen, who started to swim a few years ago, winning a swimming contest.

But then, all of a sudden, she has become a bookworm. In all the pictures of her at this time she is surrounded by books.

When she began to be interested in dancing, the album is full of pictures of her at dances.

Meanwhile, as you can see, Joe has become interested in airplanes—making them fly, putting them together or taking them apart, even designing them.

You will know a great deal about Ellen and Joe when you have turned all the pages and looked at all the pictures of them in their family album.

The Art section of this book is like the photograph album in many ways. The pictures that follow tell stories about the people who made them. They tell about different places and about the changing interests of people very much like Joe and Ellen who like to do one thing at one time and something else at another time or in another way.

The pictures start with the works of the ancient Greeks because we think of their art as the true beginning of our art today.

Of course there was great art in other countries of the world too, notably the Egyptian, the Indian, the Chinese and Japanese, and the largely lost ancient arts of the Americas.

But because most African and Asiatic art had but little influence on our art today, we give you only a few glimpses of those distant wonders of the world. (You will find them on pages 258-260). But the story of *our* art begins with the art of Ancient Greece.

The Glory that was Greece

Our art—that is, American art—is derived from the art of Europe.

Most American families are descendants of European people. That is why American buildings and sculpture and painting styles are closer to the European than to the rest of the world.

Because Europe was almost entirely separated from the other continents for many hundreds of years, European art developed largely without being influenced by countries beyond Europe.

The story of European art begins with the art of the Greeks.

About a thousand years before the birth of Christ, a new people, the Greeks, invaded the land that became Greece after they conquered it. The battles and adventures of their gods and heroes have come down to us in poems and pictures, in buildings and sculptures. These superb creations of the Greeks mark the true beginning of European art.

The Greeks had a special gift for creating beautiful things.

VIEW OF THE ACROPOLIS IN ATHENS, GREECE

Courtesy of the Royal Greek Consulate

A Sacred Citadel of White Marble

ONE OF the Greek legends tells a story about the people of Athens when they were about to choose their protector from among the gods. Pallas Athena, the armored goddess of wisdom and the arts, competed for this honor with Poseidon, the powerful god of the sea.

Pallas Athena won the contest by producing an olive tree, a symbol of peace, while Poseidon produced a salt water spring, a symbol of war-like sea power.

A temple, called *The Parthenon,* was built to honor the victorious Pallas Athena. This temple was built on the top of the Acropolis, the sacred district of ancient Athens. It is a shining white beautiful sight even today, as you can see in our picture. A statue of the goddess, called Athena Parthenos, was put up inside the temple.

Made of gold and ivory, the statue was adorned with precious stones and vivid painting. It was as tall as seven tall men one above the other. It was made by Phidias, the noblest of all Greek artists.

This magnificent statue was lost long ago, but we know about it from books and from copies that remain. These copies are much smaller than the original, not quite exact, and much less beautiful. But they help us to imagine what the original masterpiece must have been like.

It stood on a base of dark marble decorated with half-raised sculptures, called *reliefs,* of gold and ivory. They showed the birth of Pandora, who, according to Greek mythology, was the first woman.

A Statue of Gold and Ivory

The ivory-white statue of the goddess, clad in purest gold, stood erect on the base, with her left foot slightly forward. Her left hand rested on a shield that sheltered the serpent-protector of Athens, Erichtonius by name.

The outside of the shield showed the head of the Gorgon—a female monster so terrifying that anybody who looked at her was supposed to have turned to stone.

In her right hand Athena held a statue of Niké, the goddess of victory, itself seven feet tall. Thus Athena was shown bringing victory with one hand, and with the other shielding her devoted people, the Athenians. There was a kindly expression in her jewel-eyes.

Pallas Athena, the goddess of wisdom and the arts, was a well-chosen symbol for the glorious people of Athens because the most brilliant of all Greek artists were Athenians. Under Athenian leadership Greek wisdom and art reached its highest peak.

ATHENA PARTHENOS
sculptured between
447-432 B.C.
(Marble copy)

GEOMETRIC VASE made in the eighth century B.C. by unknown artist

National Museum, Athens, Greece

Rhythm Makes the Design of this Vase

MOST of the architecture, sculpture, and painting created by the early Greeks is now lost. But many decorated pottery vases known to have been made by them have been found. Some of these vases were used for storing food and water, some for drinking out of. There were very small flasks for holding ointments and salves and some very large vases for monuments.

The one you see here is as tall as a man. It was put on a grave as a monument to someone well-beloved and mourned by many. We see this in the picture painted shoulder-high between the two handles of this richly decorated vase.

In the middle of the picture we see someone lying on a bier. The bier is surrounded by people wailing and tearing their hair in sorrow.

We cannot tell whether the dead person is a man or a woman, or whether the mourning people are men or women. The picture does not give particulars. It does not show the features of the faces, or real figures or clothes.

Detail: PICTURE OF FUNERAL

The bodies of the people are simple triangles, with mere suggestions of heads, necks, arms and legs. We know by signs, rather than by pictures, that they are people. We can see what is being done, but we are not shown by whom or when or where.

The very early Greek artists did not know how to make their pictures look any more real than this. They painted as if they were in a primary class of art. That is why their work is known as "primitive" art.

The picture is set into the general decoration of strips around the vase. The strips are ornamented by ribbons, winding in and out like the winding Greek river Meandros, and this pattern is therefore called the "meander" pattern

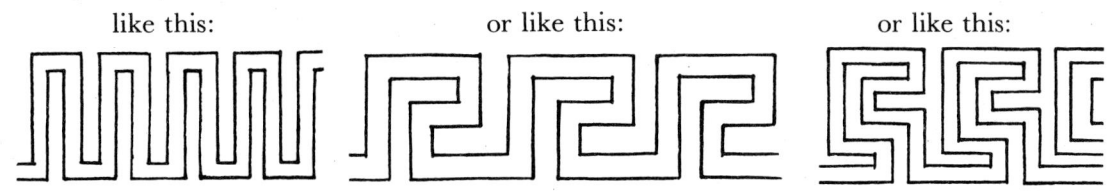

like this: or like this: or like this:

Triangles and squares are also part of the decoration on our vase. So are the shapes that look as if they had been drawn with the help of a compass. The ribbons looks as if they had been drawn with a ruler. Compasses and rulers are tools we use in geometry, the science that measures squares, triangles, and circles. That is why we call this style of decoration the "geometric style."

The Greeks had a wonderful gift for measurement and for proportions that please the eye. The order and variety of the simple patterns on this vase are like the rhythm of simple music.

To make the rhythm of this design more lively, the artist put in two rows of animal figures. One row, at the base of the vase's neck, repeats the shape of a goat at rest. Higher up, another row repeats the shape of a deer grazing.

The picture of mourning set into this general decoration is emphasized by darker coloring.

The geometric ornament is beautifully even. It is very hard to draw as evenly as this. An artist must be skilled to do it so well. But it is even more important that he be able to arrange shapes in clear and rhythmic order so pleasing to the eye.

THE FRANCOIS VASE (Front) made about 570 B.C.
by the potter Ergotimos and by the painter Klitias

Archeological Museum,
Florence, Italy

This Vase Tells Us Many Stories

THIS early Greek vase was probably a wedding present, for a picture of a wedding adorns the main strip, between the two handles, on the body of the vase.

The front of the vase shows the story of the Greek hero, Peleus, and his son, Achilles, who fought in the Trojan war. The wedding parade of Peleus and his bride, the goddess Thetis, with the carriages and the march of the gods toward the palace of Peleus, goes all around the vase.

Above this we see the chariot races at the funeral of Achilles' best friend, Patroklos. In faithful friendship Achilles arranged these races to honor the dead Patroklos.

Below, Achilles is about to commit a crime. He is going to kill the enemy, Prince Troilus, in the sanctuary of the god Apollo.

Beneath this scene we see wild beasts fighting.

At the foot of the vase, a funny picture shows pygmies fighting cranes, those birds that eat the crops.

All the stories on the front of the vase are taken from the sagas of the war in ancient Troy known as the Trojan War. Many of the sagas are told by the Greek poet, Homer, in his great epic poem, the *Iliad*. This poem was so named because Ilion was the ancient name for Troy. The main hero of the *Iliad* is Achilles. The events that led up to the Trojan War started at the wedding of Achilles' parents, Peleus and Thetis.

We are led to the other side of the vase by the top row telling of a famous hunt for a colossal wild boar. Peleus and Theseus are among the fighting Greek heroes. The back of the vase, that you see below, tells part of Theseus' story.

Theseus was the son of the King of Athens, who owed tribute to Minos, the King of Crete. Each year seven young girls and seven young boys had to be sent to Crete to be fed to the horrible Minotaur, a creature half man and half bull. Theseus made up his mind to free his country and kill the Minotaur. He succeeded with the help of the gods who were friendly to him, and of Ariadne, the daughter of King Minos. After he killed the Minotaur, Theseus married Princess Ariadne.

On the vase we see the boys and girls Theseus has saved. They are dancing gaily with Theseus and his Princess beside the ship that took them back to Athens.

This vase is known as the *François Vase,* so named after the man who dug it up. It is one of the most elaborately shaped and most richly decorated of Greek vases. It was shaped by the potter Ergotimos, and painted by Klitias, as the lettering on the vase shows.

On this vase we see various people and animals, houses and chariots, all drawn with exact precision. The figures are simple and seem to be flat, but they all have grace and dignity. The right distribution of light and dark colors gives exquisite beauty to the surface of the vase.

In the *Geometric Vase* (p. 14-15) the figures are dark brown against a light background. On the *François Vase* the figures are painted in glossy black. We call such vases "black-figured." They were most popular in the middle period of Greek vase-painting. The most famous of them all is this *François Vase*.

THE FRANCOIS VASE (Back)

HECTOR PREPARES FOR BATTLE
Picture on a vase made about 500 B.C.
by Euthymides

Antiquarium, Munich, Germany

This Style is
Simple and Direct

Two Styles of Greek Art

THIS picture shows the Trojan hero, Hector, getting ready for his battle with the Greek hero, Achilles.

Hector's father, the King, warns his son not to fight Achilles. The contest, he assures him, would be too one-sided because Achilles, as you know, was invulnerable.

But Hector pays his father no heed. His mother, the Queen, brings him his helmet and his spear. His shield leans against the wall.

The Greek artist, Euthymides, who made this vase, not only signed his name to it but also wrote on it, "This work is better than anything Euphronios can do." Euphronios was his greatest competitor.

What made Euthymides so boastful? The fact that he used light figures against a dark background? Or that he suggested the outlines of the bodies under the garments? Or that he drew the garments so well that we can see the difference between the heaviness of the King's and Queen's mantles and the lightness of the Queen's dress?

No, it was for none of these reasons. All these things Euphronios did too. But Euthymides could well be proud because he gave real expression to his simple figures. There are wisdom and thoughtfulness in the eyes of the King. Hector's features show that he is listening while he fastens his armor. We see in his expression, too, that he is not going to obey.

All the figures are simple and direct and have quiet dignity.

In the picture below we see the young Greek hero, Theseus, asking for help from the goddess of the waters, Amphitrite (p.16). He has been carried down by Triton, a creature half man and half fish.

The dolphins we see swimming around here show us that we are under water. Amphitrite is seated on her throne. The magic wreath she is going to give Theseus is ready in her hand. Pallas Athena, the protecting goddess of Athens, introduces Theseus with a wave of her hand. Amphitrite extends hers to the young visitor, and he in turn reaches out his hand to clasp hers. He raises his left hand as if embarrassed by so much honor.

Just the interplay of these expressive hands is enough to tell us that a great artist was at work here. The composition is well rounded: Nothing is straight except Athena's spear that divides the picture to show us that Athena is on Theseus' side. Otherwise, soft motions fill the flowing circle of the frame so that you can turn the picture around slightly and it will still look right.

In this picture the people's manners are most graceful, and their grace is matched by the painter's style.

It is hard to believe that the slender youth in the picture, with his elaborate hair-do, perfectly pleated garment, and fragile hands, could possibly kill the Minotaur.

Mighty Pallas Athena is most delicately built too. Her armor is more like an ornament than like fighting gear, and she holds the spear in her hand as though it were a flower. Amphitrite wears even more ornate clothes.

The style of the painter is almost over-elaborate. And this is where the older master, Euthymides, won out. For in later Greek art you will see more of quiet dignity than of graceful manners.

This Style is Graceful and Mannered

THESEUS VISITS AMPHITRITE
Picture on a vase made about 500 B.C.
by Euphronios

The Louvre, Paris, France

HARNESSING HORSES FOR A CHARIOT DRIVE
Picture on a vase made about 500 B.C.
by Psiax

Antique Department of the State Museums, Berlin, Germany

The Greeks Loved Horses and Chariots

IN THIS picture we see how horses were harnessed in ancient Greece.

A youth named Simon (we know his name from the inscription) stands behind the chariot. He holds the goad that spurs the horses on, and he has a firm grip on the reins. He needs to hold them firmly, for the horses are restless. They bare their gleaming teeth and one of them sets his foot forward, ready to go. But he has to wait. The groom has not even finished harnessing the two pole-horses, and only one of the trace-horses has been led up.

The dappled horse, held by another youth, Sikon, raises his head and taps the ground impatiently. Sikon has turned back to quiet the horse because the bearded chariot-driver is far from ready. He is still overseeing the harnessing. He is wearing a simply folded, shirt-like garment.

Simon and Sikon wear garments of fine embroidered material, slung around their strong and slender bodies in well-arranged folds. Even the groom's loincloth has a rich design. We can see by the way the horses are drawn that they must be swift-footed in motion. Their slim legs and small heads are those of thoroughbreds. They are carefully groomed. We can see by the daintiness of their manes and tails, and by their ornate gear, how much their master values them.

The painter of this vase, Psiax, was able to show us all this because he was a wonderful draftsman. Here he used the old-fashioned black-figured style. In other vases he painted in what was then the modern way, with red figures. But the old-fashioned black-figure painting was never quite abandoned by the Greeks.

On this silver coin of ancient Syracuse, coined in 479 B.C., we see a chariot driven by a charioteer with a Winged Victory flying above it.

By permission of the Trustees of the British Museum, London, England.

CHARIOTEER sculptured about 480 B.C.
by unknown sculptor

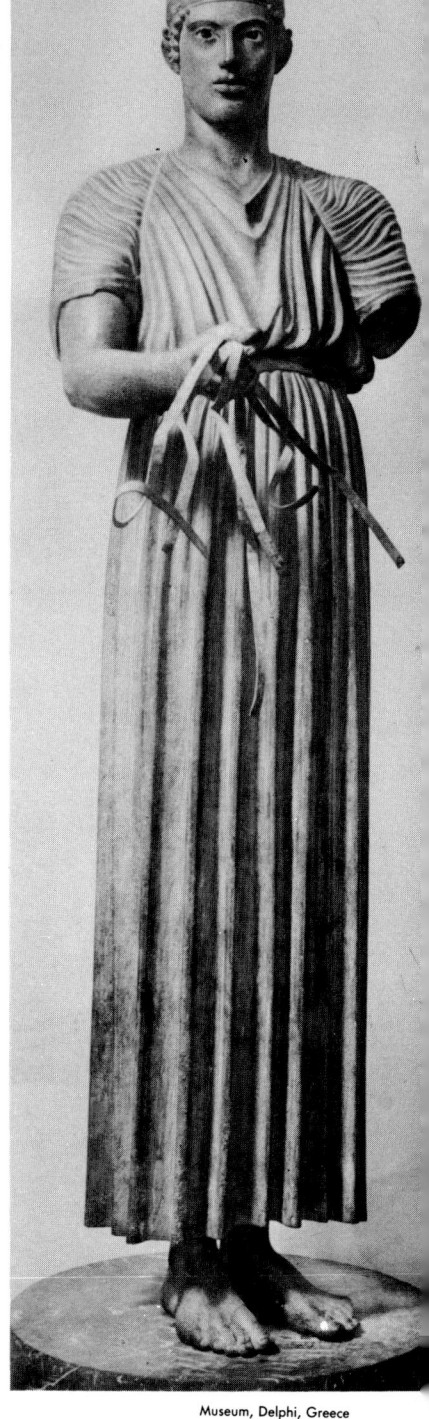

Victorious Charioteer

FROM distant Syracuse, a city at the southern tip of Italy, many centuries ago, a young Prince came to the Delphic festivals to prove his prowess in chariot-driving. He won the race, and his uncle, the King, erected a bronze monument to celebrate his victory.

The statue of the Prince is one of the few original Greek bronzes that has come down to us reasonably well preserved. It lacks only a left arm, and though only the reins in one of the driver's hands remain, they are enough to show us that originally there was a chariot with horses attached.

The young Prince stands erect in his simple driver's garment. With attentive eyes he watches the road. His lips seem to move as he urges his horses on. He is full of energy and intent on what he is doing. He looks so spirited that at first he seems perfectly real. We forget to notice that his form is not really natural after all. We have to examine him to see that his head is very simple in shape, almost egg-like. The forceful body, clothed in the even folds of a belted robe, is not much more than a fluted column (p.23).

The simple nobility of the *Charioteer* reminds us of *Hector Putting on his Armor*, by Euthymides (p.18). He is earnest and quiet and simple. These qualities will be seen in statues made by later Greek artists who represented human beings in more natural detail.

Museum, Delphi, Greece

THE PARTHENON built about 450 B.C.   by Iktinus   Acropolis, Athens, Greece

This Doric Temple, the *Parthenon,* is Strong and Simple

THE *Parthenon* was built by the ancient Greek architect Iktinus. It is a temple made entirely of white marble. It has been praised throughout the ages as the most perfect building in the world.

The temple was built to contain the gold and ivory statue of the goddess Pallas Athena known as Athena Parthenos. (p.12). The best artists of Athens decorated the temple with sculptures showing important events of the goddess's life. In the triangle that we see below the roof, her miraculous birth was shown as she sprang fully armed from the head of Zeus, the King of the gods. In the triangle at the other end of the temple the story of her competition with Poseidon was sculptured.

The *Parthenon* was once resplendent with colors, but it has been bleached by age. Today only the ruins stand. Most of the fabulous marble figures are now in the British Museum in London. Only a few remain in their former place, and those few are badly mutilated. Still, the view of the *Parthenon* is awe-inspiring even today.

A simple experiment can show you how wisely it was built. If some day you should go to see this beautiful temple yourself, put a hat on one corner of the base. Then go to the opposite corner, and at the same level, try to see the hat. You won't be able to see it, for the base, that seems to be a straight surface, is actually curved. This curve softens its harshness. That is what makes it so pleasing to the eye.

The *Parthenon* was built in the Doric style which is strong and simple (p.24).

THE ERECTHEUM built about 420 B.C. (NORTH HALL) Acropolis, Athens, Greece
by unknown architect

This Ionic Temple, the *Erechtheum,* is Slender and Refined

ANOTHER white marble temple on the Acropolis is the *Erechtheum*. It was built to hold an older statue of Pallas Athena than the statue known as Athena Parthenos.

The *Erechtheum*, like the *Parthenon*, was dedicated to Pallas Athena, but the *Erechtheum* was also dedicated to her competitor, the sea-god Poseidon, and also to Erechtheus, the fabulous ancient King of Athens. Hence the name Erechtheum.

The *Erechtheum* was built by men who were children at the time when the *Parthenon* was built. Meanwhile the fashion in building had changed. A new style had come to the Greek mainland from the Ionic islands, and this style was therefore called the Ionic style.

The Ionic style is similar to the Doric, but the Ionic forms are finer and more slender, as you can see in this picture of the Ionic *Erechtheum*.

Before it was damaged, it looked richer because a band of sculpture adorned the flat strip above the columns. But just the same, even as it looks today, this hall of the Erechtheum is perhaps the most perfectly graceful building in the world (p.25).

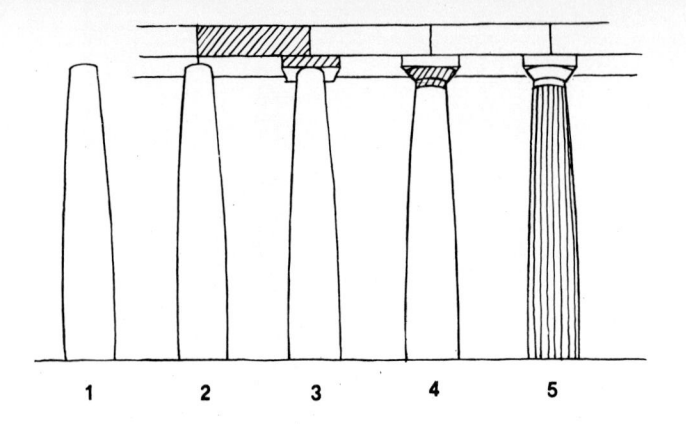

What Makes the Doric Style so Simple and Strong?

Let's pretend we are building the *Parthenon* ourselves.

1. We must have a solid base to build our row of columns on. To make our columns pleasing to the eye we taper them in a carefully measured curve.

2. To make a base for the roof we put marble beams across the tops of the columns. But we find that this makes for too great a contrast.

3. So, to lessen the contrast, we slip a square marble slab between the top of the column and the beams.

4. Then, to further soften the contrast, we insert another marble slab—a rounded one. The bottom of this slab is no wider than the column underneath, but the top is as wide as the square slab above it. The two slabs together look like a head to the column's body, and are therefore called the head or *capital* of the column. Below the head, on the column's body we cut a groove to mark a neck.

5. Now, to break the harshness of the sunlight on the body of the column, we carve lengthwise grooves into it. These grooves make a *fluting*. These columns are *Doric* columns.

6. Now let's put another row of beams *crosswise* above the first row. The ends of the beams will show at the front of the building, and we carve two grooves into them for a more pleasing effect.

7. Now we close the openings between these beams with marble slabs and decorate them with sculptures.

8. Finally we put up the roof, like two cards balanced against each other. Then we close the triangle with a wall, and decorate it with sculptures.

We have now built the Parthenon in the *Doric style:* strong, simple, and pleasing.

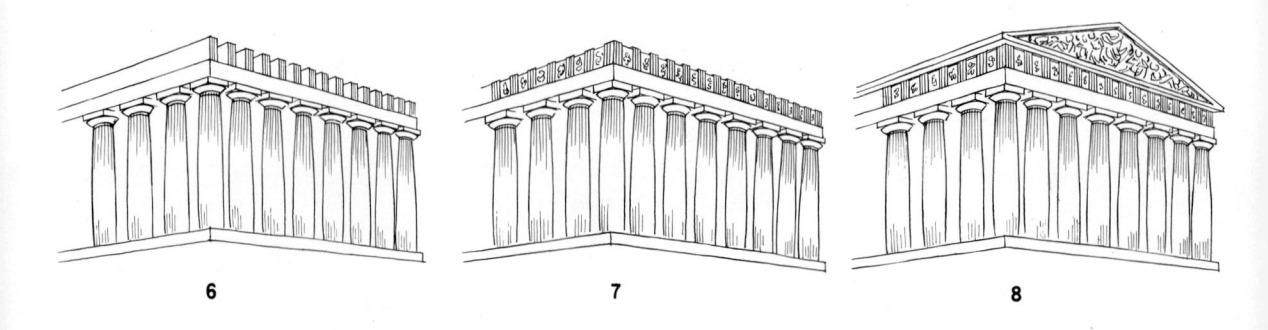

What Makes the Ionic Style so Graceful and Gentle?

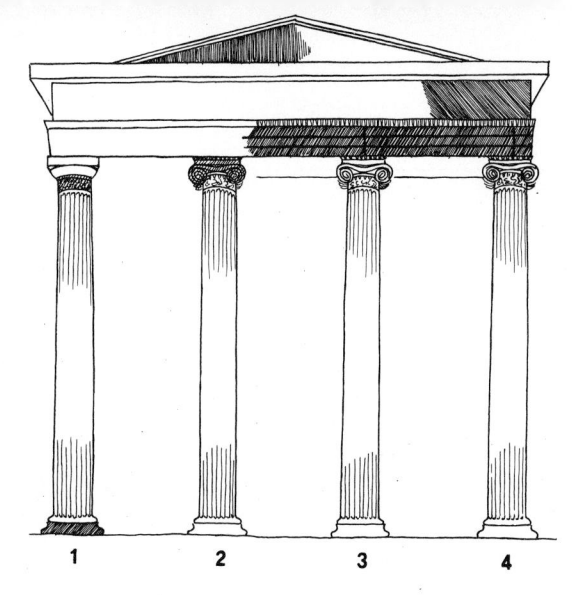

N OW let's pretend we are building this gentler-looking temple, the *Erechtheum*. Here too we must begin at the base where the columns stand.

1. To ease the sharp angle of the starkly rising columns, we slip a round pedestal between the columns and the base. We call this pedestal a *foot*. From this foot a column more slender than the Doric rises and tapers upward in a curve. The curve is so gentle that we can hardly see it. Remember the hat on the Parthenon base (p.22)? We get only the pleasing effect. We mark the neck on this column with a finely carved ornament.

2. Now we carve and flatten the simple round part of the Doric column's capital and curl it back toward the column. We divide the square slab in two and carve ornaments into the top part. Now we have an *Ionic column*.

3. To finish the building we put up the first row of beams, and to make it look more delicate we divide it into three slender parts. In the Doric style the second row had alternating sculptured plates between the two-grooved beam-ends. Here, in the Ionic style, we cover this entire part with sculptures. (The sculptures originally on the Erechtheum have been lost).

4. Now we put up a roof similar to the one on the Parthenon.

We have now built the Erechtheum in the *Ionic style* which is softer and gentler than the strong simple Doric style.

CORINTHIAN CAPITAL

A richer version of the Ionic style is the Corinthian. The Corinthian capital that we see here, a third type of capital, is the richest and softest of the three. Here profusely carved leaves spring in two rows, one above the other, from the top of the column. The rolled scrolls look like tendrils of a plant with flower-buds.

RIDERS ON THE WEST FRIEZE OF THE PARTHENON sculptured about 450 B.C.
by unknown artists

Greek Art Does Not Imitate Nature But Glorifies It

IN ANCIENT Athens a big parade took place every fourth year. And as a permanent tribute to the goddess, this parade was carved in marble on the frieze of the *Parthenon*.

Pallas Athena herself is shown here receiving a gift from the women of Athens. The other eleven chief Greek gods and goddesses are carved there too, but only as spectators.

The parade was indeed a spectacle worthy of the gods. The noblest citizens of Athens, the most important officials and their families, all took part in it.

The main feature of the parade was the procession of the horsemen. In the Western part of the frieze they are shown in front as they gathered to form their cavalcade. We see them here in our picture although it shows only four of the many carved tablets of the frieze.

The tablets are equal in size and shape. They give a measured order to the whole frieze, much as the time-beat does in music. Within this order a great deal of action takes place.

The first two riders seem to be in pretty good control of their prancing horses.

In the second tablet, however, we see a restless horse rearing high in the air, and his rider, who has been thrown off, has to make a great effort to get back into the saddle. We cannot see the saddles here because they were painted and not sculptured and the paint has faded away. The reins of the horses are missing too.

But let's have another look at this tablet. Here the artist meant to show the horse above all. The richly-shaded folds of the rider's garment have been used mainly as a background to make the horse stand out more clearly. The large gesture of the man trying to remount shows us how hard it was for him to do so.

Acropolis, Athens, Greece

In the next tablet the next rider has mastered his horse and forced it to stand still. His neighbor, who is nearer to us, is also well in control but his horse is still rearing. We see him holding the reins with firm hands. With his head bent down he talks to the animal to quiet it.

In the following tablet, again, horse and rider seem to be in difficulties. One rearing horse has to be held by a very short rein. Indeed the youth in front has to grip the mane of his fiery horse to keep from being thrown off. His prancing horse has all four feet in the air. The horse looks so natural and so excited that we imagine we can hear him neigh. Yet, in spite of the violence of the action, these two horsemen are blended into a perfectly harmonious group.

In each tablet horses and horsemen match their forces against each other, and this theme is varied from tablet to tablet. Damaged though it is, the frieze still has plenty of interest for us. The rising and falling lines of the figures tell us a great deal about the characters of the men and the horses.

We may look for a long time and perhaps not realize that the animals are unnaturally small compared to the men. Why does this not disturb us? We do not notice it because the artists did it with such perfect skill. **Men were more important** to the artist than horses. That is why he made them bigger. He was so successful at this that he made us forget about real proportions and we notice only the beauty and spirited action of horses and men.

The young people of this frieze have softer and more richly modelled bodies and features than those we see in *The Charioteer* (p. 21). Their clothes have different shapes. The folds vary. Some are large and fly out in big curves; others are small and cling to the bodies in close ripples. They seem to be different even to the touch. While in *The Charioteer* we feel only the expression of the charioteer's lively eyes and mouth, in our Parthenon frieze we feel the quality of flesh in both men and beasts.

CARYATID HALL
by unknown artist

How to Tell the Difference Between an Original and a Copy

Erechtheum, Athens, Greece   Courtesy of the Royal Greek Embassy

THE South Hall of the *Erechtheum* is supported by six Caryatids made to look like six beautiful maidens. Each one carries a basket on her head. These baskets, with the square slab above them, resemble Doric capitals (p.24). When we approach the Caryatids from the corners of the building, we can see the even folds of their garments. They look like the fluting on a column. In this way the Greek artist who made these figures was able to add the firm solidity of a column to the charm of human beauty.

The Caryatids of the *Erechtheum* were famous for their beauty and were often copied. Let us compare one of the original Caryatids (on the left) with a copy (on the right), and find out how they differ.

In both statues the figures stand erect. Both figures support their weight on the right leg and relax the left. That is why the right hip curves out and is somewhat higher than the left. Both hold their shoulders straight, and their heads and necks too, as they support the beams of the Caryatid Hall.

But notice the differences. The original is serene, spirited; the copy is stolid, dull. The original head carries the weight with ease under a lively crown of curls. In the copy stringy waves of hair bear down on a sullen face. Both wear the same kind of garment. It is fastened at the shoulders and belted at the waist under a bloused fold. An overfold falls from the shoulder to the waist.

But this garment looks very different in the two statues. In the original the drapery reveals the way the maiden stands. The folds, falling from the shoulder, curve out over the higher hip and swell ever so slightly on the relaxed side. The rest of the fine cloth clings to the bust, to the torso, and to the leg at ease and unites these parts into one whole active body.

In the copy, the parts of the body are shown too, but without making us feel how these parts hang together, because the curves of the folds do not follow the curves of the body clearly. There is no noticeable difference between the right side and the left, and this is why we feel that the figure does not actively support the building. The folds are coarser too.

In the original the folds fall straight over the firmly supporting leg. The resemblance of these folds to the fluting of a column gives a look of firmness to this Caryatid.

In the copy, the imitator thought he would be improving on the original if he varied the folds. So he made them deeper here, shallower there. He made smaller folds cut into larger ones, as we see in the folds over the stomach. As a result, the column-like strength of the original is lost.

CARYATID FROM THE ERECHTHEUM sculptured about 415 B.C.
by unknown sculptor   British Museum, London, England

CARYATID (Roman copy)
The Vatican, Rome, Italy

The copyist was unable to give the feeling of a spirited body. He did not understand how the parts of the body were connected. Finally, his copy does not give the impression of a column, for he did not understand that the creator of the original wanted to suggest a column. In the original each shape serves a purpose, and is made according to the artist's intentions. The copyist did not understand these intentions; hence his failure to make his copy as impressive as the original.

HEAD OF THE ATHENA LEMNIA
sculptured about 440 B.C.
by Phidias

The Sculptor's Own Favorite

Pinakotheka, Bologna, Italy

PHIDIAS, the noblest of the Athenian sculptors, made three figures of the goddess Pallas Athena for the city of Athens: the gold and ivory *Athena Parthenos* (p. 13); the bronze figure of the fighting *Athena Promachos;* and a third statue, the *Athena Lemnia,* so called because it was a gift from the Lemnian people to the Athenians.

Ancient writers praised the lovely expression of the *Lemnia,* her delicate cheeks and finely proportioned nose.

This is the one statue on which Phidias inscribed his name. He thought it the most beautiful of all his Athena statues.

In this picture we can see why the nobility of Greek art can still move and charm us.

WOUNDED AMAZON sculptured about 440 B.C.
by Polyclitus (Copy)

This Artist Measured the Beauty of the Human Body

IN OLD Greek tales the Amazons were a tribe of warring women. They were a horseback-riding, spear-throwing lot. They imitated men and wanted to live without them. They never married.

Once four of Greece's foremost artists each sculptured an Amazon for a group. All four statues seemed equally beautiful to the judges. So, to find out which was really the best, the judges asked each sculptor to say which statue *he* ranked first, then second, then third, then fourth. The judges thought the artists would know best, but they also thought that each artist would rank his own work first. They therefore decided to give the prize to the one each artist ranked *second* best.

The statue made by the sculptor Polyclitus won. It was a statue of a wounded Amazon, and the picture you see here shows a copy of it.

The Amazon stands leaning her left arm on a pillar. Her right is raised over her head, as if to ease the pain of her wound.

Antique Department of the State Museums, Berlin, Germany

The original statue probably showed an arrow-head or a spear-head in her side, but it is not shown in the copy. The body rests on the right leg and the left foot is at ease, so that her right foot and left arm support her while the left foot and right arm are at rest. This way the Amazon's posture has an interesting X-shape—and is perfectly balanced. This was a new sort of balance that became famous through the ages.

Polyclitus created a beautiful statue not only by figuring out the Amazon's posture, but also by carefully calculating the measurements of her body. For example, the length of the head is one-seventh the entire length of the figure. The length of the foot is just as long as the head. Those Greeks who preferred the sturdy Doric style thought that these sturdy proportions were the most beautiful.

DISCUS THROWER sculptured about 450 B.C.
by Myron (Copy)

This Artist Shows Us Motion in an Undraped Figure

Glyptothek, Munich, Germany

DISCUS throwing was part of the Olympic Games in which the Greek nations took part every fourth year, just as the nations of the world do today.

In ancient Greece the winners were often immortalized in statues. One of the most famous of these statues was *The Discus Thrower* by the Greek sculptor, Myron. We know it from marble copies only; the original was probably cast in bronze. This was usual for statues representing violent motion.

The discus thrower seems to be in full motion indeed. But is he really? Not yet. We see him here wound up and compressed like a spring. All his muscles are taut as he contracts his body. Bending his knees, his right foot grips the ground, while with toes pressed against it, his left foot gathers momentum for a swing forward.

He has swung back his right arm, the one with the discus, and he looks back to it seeking balance with his left hand. We feel that in a moment he will swirl about, straighten up, and whirl around like a released spring. He will bring the discus first down, then up, and then let fly in an expanding circle—a sure winner.

Athletes have tried to throw a discus as the discus thrower does in this statue. But they discovered that it could not be successfully done that way. It is not the right position for throwing a discus. But the artist was right to form his figure like this because it was his way of making us *feel* the discus thrower's motion. Artistic truth often differs from practical reality—and this is an excellent example of just that.

NIKE FASTENING HER SANDAL
sculptured about 415-408 B.C.
by unknown sculptor

This One Shows Us Motion in a Draped Figure

Temple of Athena Nike, Athens, Greece

THE Athena Parthenos held Niké, the goddess of victory, in her right palm (as we saw on p. 12). But to bring even more homage to victorious Pallas Athena, the Athenians erected a little temple to the goddess called Athena Niké. This little temple was surrounded by a balustrade, adorned by many Nikés each on a different errand.

One of the Nikés has stopped to fasten her sandal. She balances her supple body with ease. Half bending down, half raising her leg, she adjusts whatever it was that went wrong. The softly flowing folds of her garment cover and reveal the gentle curves of her body. The figure of the goddess is framed by majestic wings.

We can almost share the artist's delight in hammering this miracle of delicate softness out of the hard stone.

The folds of Niké's garment are not copied from reality. They have been shaped to follow the motions of her figure. A few large folds between her legs show great contrasts of light and shadow. These folds call attention to the difference in position of the two legs. Many more folds modeled in playfully changing light and shade, follow the curve of the gracefully stooping body, and branch out over the balancing elbow. These folds bring to life the subtle shapes under the gossamer garment. But they are not really *true* to life. There are far more folds here than there would be in any real garment. If Niké were to straighten up, all the folds would fall to her feet. She wouldn't be able to take a step.

Here the sculptor used drapery to explain motion, and again, he succeeded, in making the figure *look* true, even though we would never find drapery like this in real life. But artistic truth has nothing to do with practical reality, as we saw on the opposite page, and we see it again in this lovely figure.

HERMES WITH LITTLE BACCHUS sculptured about 350 B.C. by Praxiteles

This Artist Made Sculptures Look Alive

LITTLE Bacchus was a motherless orphan. His father, Zeus, the King of the gods, decided that the nymphs of the woods should take care of the little boy. Zeus summoned another son, Hermes, the swift messenger of the gods, to carry the baby to the nymphs.

This statue by the great Greek sculptor, Praxiteles, shows Hermes with little Bacchus at a moment of rest on their journey to the nymphs. Hermes leans lightly against a tree-trunk, with the child on his arm. His mantle hangs over the tree-trunk. He holds up a bunch of grapes to Bacchus who eagerly reaches for the fruit.

The grapes are not shown here. They have been lost. But we know from a copy of the group that they were once part of the sculpture. They belong there for they show us that Bacchus is the god of wine. Wine is made of grapes, and therefore grapes are the symbol of Bacchus.

The scene is playful and at the same time full of meaning. Here Bacchus is a baby, but some day he will dwell on Mt. Olympus among the twelve chief Greek gods.

Museum, Olympia, Greece

There is a dreamy mood in Hermes' face that seems to change as the light that falls on it changes. When a passing cloud darkens the sky, Hermes seems almost to smile. When the sun comes out, the smile seems to melt away. His parted lips seem to smile when the space between them is filled with shadow. When more light makes the shadow vanish, the smile vanishes with it.

The sculptor, Praxiteles, also softened the definite outlines of Hermes' eyes into indefinite rounded shapes to make their expression change too. In fact, all the shapes of the face and body are rounded and melt into one another. The play of light and shade seems to bring gentle life to the marble. The only exception is the straight line that comes down from the forehead to the tip of the nose, the line of the famous Grecian profile.

This group is one of the very few original marble statues by a great artist that has come down to us in fairly good condition. It was dug up at the exact spot where an ancient guide-book tells us it stood originally.

It is not Praxiteles' most famous work. His Venus was more famous, but of that statue we have only copies. A head of Venus was recognized as a work of this artist by the soft tender shapes and lovely expression of the features.

You can see in these pictures that Praxiteles made the face of a god or a goddess almost alike. The artist brought to life a gentle spirit in a gentle body in all his sculptures.

This is the charm that the sculptor Praxiteles added to the noble figures of Greek art that were made before his time.

HEAD OF HERMES AND APHRODITE sculptured about 350 B.C.
by Praxiteles

VENUS DE MILO
sculptured in the first century B.C.
by unknown sculptor

The Goddess of Beauty

⟵

The God of the Sun and of Poetry

⟶

APOLLO OF THE BELVEDERE
sculptured in the fourth century B.C.
by unknown sculptor

Vatican Musuem, Rome, Italy

The Louvre, Paris, France

OUR picture shows one of the best-known statues of Venus. It is called the *Venus de Milo* because the Greek island of Melos or Milo is where it was unearthed.

The *Venus de Milo* is larger than life-size. There is a certain magnificence in the way she stands that makes us recognize her as a goddess rather than just a woman.

The *Venus de Milo* is larger than life-size. Yet in spite of her noble greatness, her expression is one of gentle serenity.

We do not know exactly what Venus was doing, because the statue was damaged and she has no arms. What remains of them makes us believe that they were extended toward someone and that Venus was part of a group.

Incomplete as it is, this Venus is still considered the world's most beautiful woman.

THE STATUE called the *Apollo of the Belvedere* is so named because it stands in the Belvedere garden of the Vatican Museum. Apollo is shown here as the sun-god. He has just released his bow (not seen here, for it has been lost). His eye follows the flight of his arrow as he continues his walk in another direction. His mantle is fastened around his neck, the end slung lightly over his arm.

The drapery is not very natural, but as it winds around Apollo's neck and arm it has a grace of its own. It frames the beautiful head of the god, and the shadows of the folds make a perfect background for the smooth beauty of his body, so slender and tall.

Something new about this Apollo is the way the artist makes us feel motion by contrasting the direction of Apollo's glance and action with the direction in which he is moving.

Above all, the *Apollo of the Belvedere* is known as the perfect model of manly beauty.

DEMOSTHENES sculptured about 280 B.C
by Polyeuctus (Plaster reconstruction)

A Portrait is More than a Mere Photographic Likeness

THE GREAT Greek orator, Demosthenes, had never stopped warning his people against Philip, King of Macedon, who had planned to conquer Greece. But Demosthenes' speeches were not listened to and Philip succeeded: Greece was conquered by Macedon.

It was forty years after Demosthenes' death that the Greeks erected a monument to this great man. They put an inscription on the statue saying that if Demosthenes had had as much power to fight Philip as he had determination, Greece would not have lost her freedom.

The statue shows the great orator standing simply as any ordinary man would. The crumpled mantle around his lean figure tells us how little he cared about his looks. His head is slightly bent. His lower lip is withdrawn showing his effort to concentrate. His deep-set eyes under the furrowed brow all speak of the same effort.

The sculptor of this statue, Polyeuctus, brought Demosthenes' two hands together in a firm grip to show his singleness of purpose. The lines of his arms are straight and square to show us what a straight and square man Demosthenes was.

Metropolitan Museum of Art, New York, N. Y.

It is unlikely that the sculptor knew at all what the great orator who had died forty years earlier looked like. He made the statue fit Demosthenes' personality as it was known to all the Greeks so that it could not be mistaken for anybody else and became Demosthenes forever after.

This is much more than a photograph can do. By the force of their imagination the Greeks were able to form a true picture of their great man: a pure portrait of character.

An Expression of Deathly Suffering

IN THE Trojan War the Greeks made a wooden horse to give to the Trojans as a present. Laocoön, the Trojan priest, warned his people not to accept the enemy's gift because he knew it would be fatal. But the gods, who were resolved to destroy the city of Troy, stopped Laocoön's warning voice by sending two powerful serpents to strangle him and his two sons.

The three Greek sculptors, Agesandros, Apollodoros, and Polydoros, made a marble group showing Laocoön and his two sons as they struggled with the serpents.

Laocoön is writhing with pain from the vicious bite of the serpent in his loin. But the expression on Laocoön's face tells us of another pain too. His wailing mouth and sorrowful eyes speak of the tortures of his soul as he sees his children suffering.

Both sons are unnaturally small compared to the mighty figure of their father. It is believed that they were made so small for a purpose. The artist wanted us to give special attention to the most important, the central figure, Laocoön himself.

The children only mirror the father's double pain. The younger boy points to the bodily struggle of the father. He tries, as his father does, to ward off the snake's bite.

The younger seems entirely lost in the coils of the snake. The older boy is not yet so hopelessly entangled.

The older boy, who is less entangled by the snake, is hindered, hand and foot, from helping his father. He mirrors the father's pain at being unable to help his sons.

The sculptors have given greatest attention to the figure of Laocoön himself. They created an ideal human form. It seems to be a model for nature rather than a copy of it. The *Laocoön* has indeed served as a model for artists throughout the centuries.

All the shapes are hewn out of the marble with clarity and vigor.

See how the groove along the body accentuates the tortured writhing of Laocoön.

Deep shadows between the eyeballs and the eyelids mark the expression of the eyes. A dark shadow in the open mouth makes us feel the man's deep sigh. We read pain in the furrowed face surrounded by a crown of noble locks. Deathly suffering is written all over this magnificent group.

At the time of Greece's greatest glory, such pain had not been considered a worthy subject for art. By the time the *Laocoön* group was made the Romans had already conquered Greece. The ancient Greek ideal of serenity and quiet dignity had long since been forgotten.

The *Laocoön* group could have been made only in this period when deadly fights between men and beasts were common in Rome. (The Greeks never found pleasure in such sights.)

This group bespeaks the great art and the high spirits of the Greeks because, in spite of the deathly pain of Laocoön and his sons, human dignity is written all over this late monument of Greek sculpture.

LAOCOON AND HIS SONS sculptured about 50 B.C.
by Agesander, Athenodorus and Polydorus

The Vatican, Rome, Italy

The Grandeur that was Rome

While Greece gloried in the poetic world of wisdom and beauty on one side of the Adriatic sea, on the other shore the Romans founded their empire on the Italian peninsula.

The foremost thought in the Roman mind was grandeur. Huge columns of stone had stories of their victorious wars hewn in strips running around them from the bottom to the top. Although the Romans were the ones who ordered the columns to be built, the actual work was usually done by Greek artists.

Colossal arches were erected to commemorate the Roman emperors. Like the columns, they were adorned by sculptures showing their history. Here too most of the sculptures were made by Greeks.

The Roman spirit was mainly practical. The Romans were wonderful builders. Their roads were excellent. Ancient Roman arches still support the water pipes that brought fresh mountain water into their distant cities. They are an impressive sight even today.

The Romans' skill in building and love of grandeur enabled them to make their greatest contribution to the world of art— (p.42-43).

TRAJAN'S COLUMN erected about 111-114 A.D.
designed by Apollodorus

A Monument of Conquest

Rome, Italy

THE Roman people erected this monument to their Emperor Trajan. A sculptured picture-strip that winds from the bottom to the top of the column shows the stories of two wars. One is the story of Emperor Trajan's conquest of Dacia (now Romania), the other his victorious war in Germany.

The sculptured strip is more than a yard wide so that you can actually read the stories when you walk around the column as you would in a comic strip. The column rises 100 feet and can be seen from far over the rooftops of the city. It is an imposing monument that proclaims far and wide the bravery of Emperor Trajan and the great power of the Roman Empire.

THE ARCH OF TITUS erected about the end of the first century A.D. by unknown artist

Rome, Italy

The Triumphal Arch is Another Kind of Monument

WHENEVER a victorious general of the Roman army returned to Rome, he entered at the head of a big parade marching into the city through richly decorated arched doorways. These doorways were made of flimsy material because they were meant for the day's celebrations only.

But when such arched doorways, called simply "arches," were meant as monuments commemorating the victories of Roman Emperors, they were built of stone and marble.

An arch of this kind was erected in Rome in memory of Emperor Titus's conquest of Jerusalem.

Here we see a picture of this famous arch. It is not complete, because there was originally a statue of the victorious Emperor standing on his four-horse chariot on top of the arch.

The doorway, the actual arch, is flanked by thick stone walls decorated with columns. In each of the triangular spaces between the columns and the arch there are sculptured stone figures of goddesses of victory. Within the arch, on the wall, sculptured pictures of Titus's victory-parade adorn one side, and on the other we see the precious loot of the Temple of Jerusalem.

On the piece of wall above the arch, an inscription hewn in marble tells us that the arch is dedicated to the Emperor Titus.

How did the Romans Make Their Arches So Imposing?

WHEN you look at this drawing of the *Arch of Titus,* you will see that the decoration on the arch above the doorway has been taken away. This has been done so that we can see how the arch was actually built or "vaulted": wedge-shaped stones were put together next to one another to form it.

But stones are heavy and they press against one another and drift to the sides. A big stone arch would fall apart if it were not held together in some way. It would never remain an arch.

But big stone arches are imposing and the Romans were determined to find a way of making theirs hold together. They decided it could be done if they put up big stone walls at both sides of the vaulting. This they did, as you can see in our picture. They liked to build these big walls because big walls look imposing too, and the chief aim of the Roman people was to make their buildings look grand and powerful.

In this the Romans were different from the Greeks. The Greeks built their temples by putting up vertical columns and connecting them with horizontal cross-beams. But the cross-beam could not be wider than the piece of marble it was made of.

The Romans wanted to span a much bigger space than was possible in the Greek manner. Therefore they developed their supreme skill in vaulting.

Roman vaulting became the most important feature in Roman art and, indeed, in all monumental building for many centuries after.

THE COLOSSEUM built about 80 B.C. by unknown architect

The Most Colossal Circus of Ancient Rome

CIRCUSES have been popular ever since the Roman Republic became an Empire. But the Roman circus was very different from ours. In our circuses we have highly skilled performers, and trained animals do tricks.

In the Roman circuses fights were the main attraction. Pugilists and wrestlers or sword-fighters fought one another, or sword-fighters fought with wild beasts. This was the main amusement of the Roman people at the time of the Empire. They asked for nothing better than "bread and circuses."

The most colossal circus, the Colosseum, was built by the Emperor Titus. The Colosseum has an oval shape. The free place in the middle of the building where the fight went on is called the "arena." Around the arena there are tiers of seats for the spectators. The Colosseum could seat 50,000 people.

The entire building is surrounded by a high wall divided into four stories. The three lower floors have vaulted Roman arches. Between the arches there are decorative columns. On the first floor the columns are in the Doric style (p.24); on the second in the Ionic (p.25). On the third floor there are half columns with Corinthian capitals (p.25), and on the fourth floor there are flattened columns we call *pilasters*. Pilasters are like shadows of a column. They have the same height and width but they are almost flat against the wall.

This variety of columns suggests that the building has a solid foundation and solid support. As it becomes lighter and lighter with its growing height, it gives us the feeling of a well-balanced building. This variety also gives heightened interest to the huge walls.

The Colosseum is the biggest of all Roman circuses and the most imposing building that has come to us from ancient Rome.

THE PANTHEON built second century A.D.
(Painting by Pannini 18th century)

The Greatest Achievement in Roman Vaulting

Rome, Italy
National Gallery of Art, Washington, D. C.
Samuel H. Kress Collection

THIS picture shows a painting of the inside of the *Pantheon*. It is a Christian Church now, called St. Maria Rotonda. But when it was built it was dedicated by the Romans to all their gods. The word *pantheon* means *all gods*.

The picture we show you here is a painting, not a photograph, since photography cannot do justice to space at all. Even painting falls somewhat short, because any picture is flat and space is all around us.

But look at this picture anyway. Compare the lofty height of the building with the size of the people in it. Or see how small the people look in the opposite doorway because they are so far off compared with those in the foreground.

The *Pantheon* measures 150 feet in both width and height. To support this huge vaulted cupola the surrounding walls had to be made very strong. They are seven yards wide!

When you enter the *Pantheon* through the thick wall and find yourself within the great round space you have a sense of freedom rarely felt inside a man-made building. You feel as if you were breathing in the free and open air.

The *Pantheon* indeed makes you feel "the grandeur that was Rome."

MUMMY PORTRAIT OF A MAN painted first century A.D. by unknown artist

A Mummy's Face Made Vivid with Quick Deft Strokes

Courtesy of the Ny Carlsberg Glyptothek
Copenhagen, Denmark

AFTER the Romans had conquered Greece, many Greek artists found their way into Egypt which was then a part of the Roman Empire.

It was a custom of the Egyptians to do everything they could to save their loved ones from destruction after they had died.

They worked out elaborate methods for this. They wrapped up the bodies in swaddling clothes and put a portrait of the dead person over the face, as you can see in this picture.

Here we see a man in middle life. His eyes are so vivid that we almost feel the thought behind them. His mouth all but moves with energy as if expressing the same thought we see in his eyes.

The unknown artist who painted this picture got this effect with quick bold strokes of color. He put the right colors into the right places so that they melt together. The artist's skill with his brush adds much to this portrait's freshness and liveliness.

This is the ENTIRE MUMMY

MUMMY PORTRAIT OF A LITTLE GIRL painted fourth century A.D. by unknown painter

Another Mummy's Face Has Simple Outlines

Courtesy of the Brooklyn Museum, Brooklyn, N.Y.

WOULD you ever imagine that this over-simple portrait of a little girl mummy was painted about three centuries later than the life-like portrait of the man on the opposite page?

The man's face is so full of life that you feel he is going to change his expression the next minute. The little girl's expression seems to be one of steady wonder. She seems to be thinking of something deep in her heart.

We cannot tell whether her cheeks are soft or firm. There is not even a proper connection between her face and her neck because the outline of her egg-shaped face is simply set above her neck. Her eyes are outlined by two simple strokes of the brush and so are the lids. Each of her lashes is drawn with thin brush-strokes and they look very different from real lashes. A child could have drawn them. The same is true of the brows, the nose, the mouth, and the ears. The hands look as if they were made of wood.

Just the same, although we can't tell why, the child's expression makes this simple picture very striking. The look of wonder in her too-big eyes goes well with the way she holds her hands.

The painter who made the face of the man mummy, about three hundred years earlier, was more interested in life than this one was.

Instead of making a more perfectly natural portait the later artist seems to have gone backward and become more primitive, as if he had gone back to first grade after college.

Christian Art is Spiritual

THE face alone of this colossal head of the Roman Emperor Constantine is one whole story high. The head is a remnant of a marble monument made in his honor. Constantine was the Emperor who made Christianity the official religion of the Roman Empire.

In this sculpture the Emperor's face looks thoughtful. We feel that he is not thinking of anything practical, or of any action. His eyes are turned upward and look into the distance as if thinking of a better world beyond.

His mouth has no particular interest for us; it has not much expression. His features are modeled sparingly. His entire being seems to center in his enormous eyes. They are carved with great vigor and strong effects of light and shadow.

The eye is often called the mirror of the soul, and Christianity cared more for the soul than for the body.

Since the birth of Christ the old interest in beautiful things had begun to wane and an interest in spiritual expression increased. Artists no longer tried to make portraits look life-like but rather to make human expression stirring.

COLOSSAL HEAD OF CONSTANTINE sculptured fourth century A.D.
by unknown sculptor

Capitol Museum, Rome, Italy

DENTE CLEMENTE X PONT OPT MAX
S P Q R

ST. APOLLINARE IN CLASSE built 560 A.D.
by unknown architect

Ravenna, Italy

The Early Christian Church Looks Simple on the Outside

CENTURIES ago, when Christianity began, people did not care about outward appearances. They were interested only in inner beauty. The way they built their Churches shows this. They were resplendent with gold and precious stones inside, while the outside walls remained simple and without decoration.

The very early Christian Churches were called *basilicas*. They got their name from the old Roman basilicas, indoor market-places. These had big halls where many people could gather. The early Christians gathered there to worship.

Later they built Churches on the same pattern and kept the name *basilica*.

A good example of an early Christian basilica, *St. Apollinare in Classe,* is pictured here. The walls and roof are quite plain. On the street side there is an entrance hall. A plain arched opening in the center is the door. Arches, supported by columns, serve as windows. A second door opens from the entrance hall into the sumptuous interior.

ST. APPOLLINARE NUOVO built 504 A.D.
by unknown architect

Ravenna, Italy

The Inside of the Church Shines with Gold and Jewels

THE main place of worship in a Church is the *nave*. The nave is a long hall ending in a rounded part called the *apse*. The aisles are on either side of the nave.

Between the nave and the aisles columns support the walls.

In this Church, *St. Apollinare Nuovo,* the columns are connected by arches in the Roman way; but in some places the walls rest on cross-beams laid on top of the columns, Greek fashion.

The walls of the nave are built higher than those of the aisles. Set into the upper part of these walls are large windows. Small windows admit a little light into the aisles, but the main light for the entire Church comes from the large windows above.

On the high walls of the nave light-colored pictures on a gold background add to the nave's light and splendor.

In the early time of Christianity sculpture was banned because it reminded people of the old idols. Christianity broke with the old pagan tradition so as to be able to build the new faith firmly in the people's hearts.

THE HOLY WOMEN AT THE SEPULCHER made sixth century A.D. (mosaic)
by unknown artist

St. Apollinare Nuovo, Ravenna, Italy

Here We See a Miracle

THE Bible tells us that Christ was buried in a new tomb, or sepulcher, that belonged to Joseph of Arimathea. After Christ had been buried, a big stone was placed in front of the entrance to the sepulcher.

At sunrise of the first day of the week of Christ's death, Mary Magdalen and another holy woman, also named Mary, went to visit the grave. When they arrived they saw that the big stone had been rolled aside and the grave was open. On the stone sat an Angel in white robes. The Angel told the holy women that Christ had arisen from death and was no longer in the grave.

This is the great religious story we see in the picture here.

In the center the sepulcher, in the form of a little temple, is very simply designed. It is just a base with four columns topped by a small dome or cupola. In the middle of the sepulcher we see the door, off its hinges, lying in the doorway. At the left the Angel is seated on the stone. At the right stand the holy women. They extend their hands as if asking a question.

The figures do not look very natural. They do not seem to be of flesh and blood. We do not see how the parts of their bodies hang together. We cannot tell of what material their clothes are made. We cannot even tell where they actually stand, for the background of the picture is plain gold, with merely a narrow strip of green as a base.

But this was all done with a purpose. The early Christians had abandoned the ways of the ancient non-Christian Greeks and Romans whose art showed the beauty of the world they saw around them. Christians did not care about earthly things. They yearned for the golden splendor of heaven. Therefore they set their figures against a background of gold. It was an entirely new way of making pictures.

In this picture the Angel's eyes are unnaturally large, yet they seem to be speaking. The Angel's mouth is formed by two lines only, but with just these two lines the artist has made us see his smile as really angelic.

When we look back to the two Marys, we can see that the faces of these two women are different. The one in the background seems to be questioning the Angel about the empty grave. The other seems to know the answer. As she lifts her eyes up to heaven, she seems to be looking into her own soul too. She understands that a miracle has happened.

After we have noticed this, we also notice that the puppet-like motions of the two women's hands are different. The first Mary points at what she sees; the other raises her hands as if to worship Christ's miraculous resurrection. The artist was able to make us feel, also, the gesture of her other hand, even though it is covered by her garment. She stands there rapt in wonder at God's miracle.

Christian artists did not show people the way they really looked. They were interested only in expressing the world of the spirit.

• • •

This picture was made in what we call *mosaic*. That is, it was not painted with a brush, but painstakingly put together out of tiny pieces of colored glass. The gold background is made of glass covered with real gold leaf. In this particular Church, *St. Apollinare Nuovo,* precious stones were added to the glass and to the gold to give even greater brilliance to the inside of the House of God.

Romanesque Cathedrals

In Northern Europe They Express Power

TOURNAY CATHEDRAL built 12th century by unknown architect
Tournay, Belgium
Courtesy of the Belgian Consulate

TO BUILD a mighty Cathedral to the glory of God—this was the aim of the people of northern Europe in the Middle Ages. The House of God, they felt, should tower above any castle that even the mightiest noble might build for himself. A powerfully built Cathedral expressed, also, the power of the Christian Church which was firmly established by the year 1000.

For instance, the Cathedral of Tournay, that we see in this picture, looks like a mighty fortress in the middle of the town.

In this Romanesque Cathedral there are many windows with round Roman arches. Hence the name "Romanesque."

The floor looks similar to that of the basilica, (p.51), with one difference. In the Romanesque Cathedral the transept is built across the nave and aisles in front of the apse. The transept is shorter than the nave, and on the floor it looks like the cross-bar of a cross. Where the transept crosses the nave—the *crossing*—a big tower arises. At each end of the transept stand two other towers, one on each side.

The Cathedral overshadows the town like a mountain and rises high toward Heaven.

In Italy
They
Express Beauty

PISA CATHEDRAL built 11th to 13th centuries by unknown architects

Pisa, Italy

IN ITALY a baptistry was usually added to the Cathedral as a separate building.
    In our picture on the left we see the round building which is the baptistry of the Cathedral of Pisa. The bell-tower stands separately too. There is a cupola over the crossing instead of a tower. The baptistry is also covered by a cupola.
    The cupola is a heritage of Roman times. We saw the mighty cupola of the Pantheon (p. 45). But the cupola of the Pantheon was open on top. Here it is covered by a little building called the *lantern.* The lantern has openings on the side to let in light and is covered by another cupola, a small one. In later times most big Christian Churches had and still have cupolas.
    In all three of the buildings we see here, graceful rows of arches, supported by columns, have been put up in front of the walls. Between the columns and the walls a little passage has been left open, except on the first floor. There the columns and the arches stand directly next to the wall to give the buildings a more solid base.
    The baptistry differs from the Church and the tower in that it has little triangles built above each pair of its rounded Romanesque arches. These triangles were put up at a later time, when Gothic art became stylish (pp.60-65).
    The tower is lop-sided. It was difficult to build a tower this way. It was an extra touch of artfulness of which Italian builders were very proud.
    To the builders of Romanesque Cathedrals in Italy, beauty was more important than the expression of power. This group of white marble buildings on the green velvet lawn shines to testify to this love of beauty under the cerulean sky of Italy.

DOORWAY IN FONTGOMBOULT
built 12th century
by unknown architect

Doorways Pierce the Walls Step by Step

Fontgomboult, France

TO GET inside the thick walls of a Romanesque Church you have to pass through a doorway or portal shaped like a wedge. The doorway is wider at the front of the thick wall, narrower at the back.

The wall is built of stone blocks, one layer behind the other. The door pierces these layers one by one and becomes narrower with each step we take toward the inside of the Church. That is why these portals are called step-portals.

If these steps had been left just steps, they would have looked harsh and angular. To soften this effect and to make the doorway look richer, columns were put between the steps.

The Romanesque doorway had a Roman arch on top. The step-portal was also used in the Gothic Style of architecture, although the rounded Roman arch was changed into a pointed Gothic arch as you will see in the picture of Rheims Cathedral (p.62). By that time figures had been added to the columns.

But the solid strength of the Romanesque arch fits the powerful style to perfection.

SIDE OF A DOORWAY
built and sculptured about 1150
by unknown artists

Figures of Saints are Made to Look Like Columns

Chartres Cathedral, Chartres, France

A ROUND the middle of the twelfth century life-size figures were put up in front of the columns of the step-portals to make them look more ornate.

By that time the Christian religion was firmly established and there was no longer any fear that the people would mistake the carved figures for the ancient idols the Greeks and Romans had worshiped. Besides, these figures were put up only on the outside of the Churches, at least for a hundred more years.

Also, the figures do not look life-like at all; they look like columns. The folds of their garments are like the fluting of columns (p. 24). Their flat sleeves fall from their arms as if they were the sides of the stone slab of which they are hewn. They look rigidly ahead so that their noses and the book or scroll they hold in their hands are in a straight line.

These figures are symbols of Saints. We know they were meant to be Saints because they all have halos, in the form of round flat pieces of stone, behind their heads. Their feet point downward to show that they are not resting on them. They are soaring in Heaven.

① ST. THEODORE sculptured about the middle of the 13th century by unknown sculptor

② ST. MODESTE sculptured before the middle of the 13th century by unknown sculptor

In France Gothic Figures Look Gentle and Refined

① Chartres Cathedral, Chartres, France
② Chartres Cathedral, Chartres, France
E. Houvet, Rep. Int.

ST. THEODORE was a soldier of a pagan Emperor of Rome, but he was converted to Christianity and lived and died for his newly-won faith.

Here he stands at the door of the Cathedral of Chartres as a pious champion of the Church. He wears the complete armor of the Knights of the sainted King Louis IX of France. Under his surcoat his entire body is covered by chain mail. In his right hand he holds his lance. His left hand holds his shield. His sword hangs from his belt.

But even in all his armor he does not look warlike. He looks gentle, like a man who is devoted to God rather than to fighting. His feet do not stand firmly on the ground. His whole figure seems to be swaying gently as Gothic figures always do.

STE. MODESTE was the daughter of the Roman Governor of France who was a pagan. Modeste was converted to Christianity and when she was threatened with death if she did not renounce her new faith, she said she would rather die than betray her religion.

She seems, in this statue, to sway gently as she rises from the drapery at her feet. With one hand she holds her Bible, while with the other she seems to be expressing her faith in it. Her eyes smile shyly. It is the mood we find in so many Gothic sculptures. Her figure still has something of the look of a column, but softly flowing lines and gentle motion give life to the statue.

EKKEHARD AND UTA sculptured about 1260
by unknown sculptor

In Germany Gothic Statues Look Sterner and Heavier

Naumburg Cathedral, Naumburg, Germany

THESE two remarkable figures stand in the choir of Naumburg Cathedral among the statues of the other founders of the Cathedral. These men and women lived a long time before their statues were made, but the stories of their lives were known, and the sculptor made their likenesses to fit these stories.

The serious look and imposing head of the man, Ekkehard, above his squarely built body, are impressive. So are the dreamy eyes and gentle features of his wife Uta, the frail woman at his side. Her face seems almost to tremble with deep feeling. He looks powerful and bold. His figure is forcefully outlined within the straight folds of his cloak made by deep cuts into the stone. Equally straight and heavy folds hide Uta's slender body. She holds the rough cloth against her tender cheek. Her beautiful hand, with its softly curving fingers, tell us she has a sensitive and shy soul.

Within the heavy masses of their cloaks these figures seem amazingly natural. Yet neither Ekkehard nor Uta seems to stand firmly on the ground.

As in Gothic sculptures made somewhat earlier (p.58), rounded outlines smooth the joints of their legs and feet. But by that time the German sculptor was cutting deeply into stone, and so were the sculptors of France. Their figures no longer remind us of columns at all.

The Gothic Cathedral was Built for the Queen of Heaven

THE Cathedral of Chartres is one of the most important Gothic Cathedrals ever built because it has served as a model for so many others.

We don't know when the first building of Chartres Cathedral was begun, for it was destroyed several times by fire. But we do know that in the middle of the twelfth century building was started anew, and the Cathedral was finished in the early part of the thirteenth. The new building was consecrated in the presence of the King Louis IX who was made a Saint after his death.

Chartres Cathedral, like most great French cathedrals of this period, was dedicated to Notre Dame (which is French for Our Lady). They were all called Notre Dame with the name of the town added. Chartres Cathedral is known as Notre Dame of Chartres.

Chartres Cathedral was built by the people in the true sense of the word. Everybody wanted to contribute to the rebuilding: the King, the Queen, noblemen and ordinary citizens, rich and poor. Clergymen were willing to go without their income for three years so that the money could go to the rebuilding of the Cathedral.

The stone for the building was taken from a quarry many miles away. It was very hard to transport the huge blocks. But, as the Norman abbot, who saw it being done, wrote: "Powerful Princes... nobles, men and women have bent their proud and haughty necks to the harness of the carts. Like beasts of burden they dragged to the abode of Christ these wagons, loaded with all that is necessary for the construction of the Church... Thousands of persons, and more, are attached to the chariots—so great is the difficulty. Yet they march in silence, that not a murmur is heard... At the voice of the Priest who exhorts their hearts to peace, discord is thrown aside; unity of hearts is established."

The finished Cathedral looks almost as if it had come down from Heaven. The slender body seems to float aloft in contrast to the Romanesque Cathedral (p.56) that seems to grow from the ground like a mountain.

The Gothic Cathedral is supported by many arches. There are practically no walls because they have been entirely replaced by windows. The arches reach to a height of 120 feet, and because they are so tall, they need firm support. Some way had to be found to support them—and it was.

The builders made arches at a right angle to the wall—that is, what remained of it between the windows. These arches reach out far from the sides of the Cathedral's body. They are called *flying buttresses* because they support (or buttress) the wall (p.64), and because they look as if they were flying out from the sides of the building, down to earth. They are like legs reaching down to hold up the body of the Cathedral, and at the same time they make the Cathedral look more ornate from the outside.

Richly decorated and graceful, the Cathedral looks worthy of the Queen of Heaven to whom it is dedicated and whose name it bears.

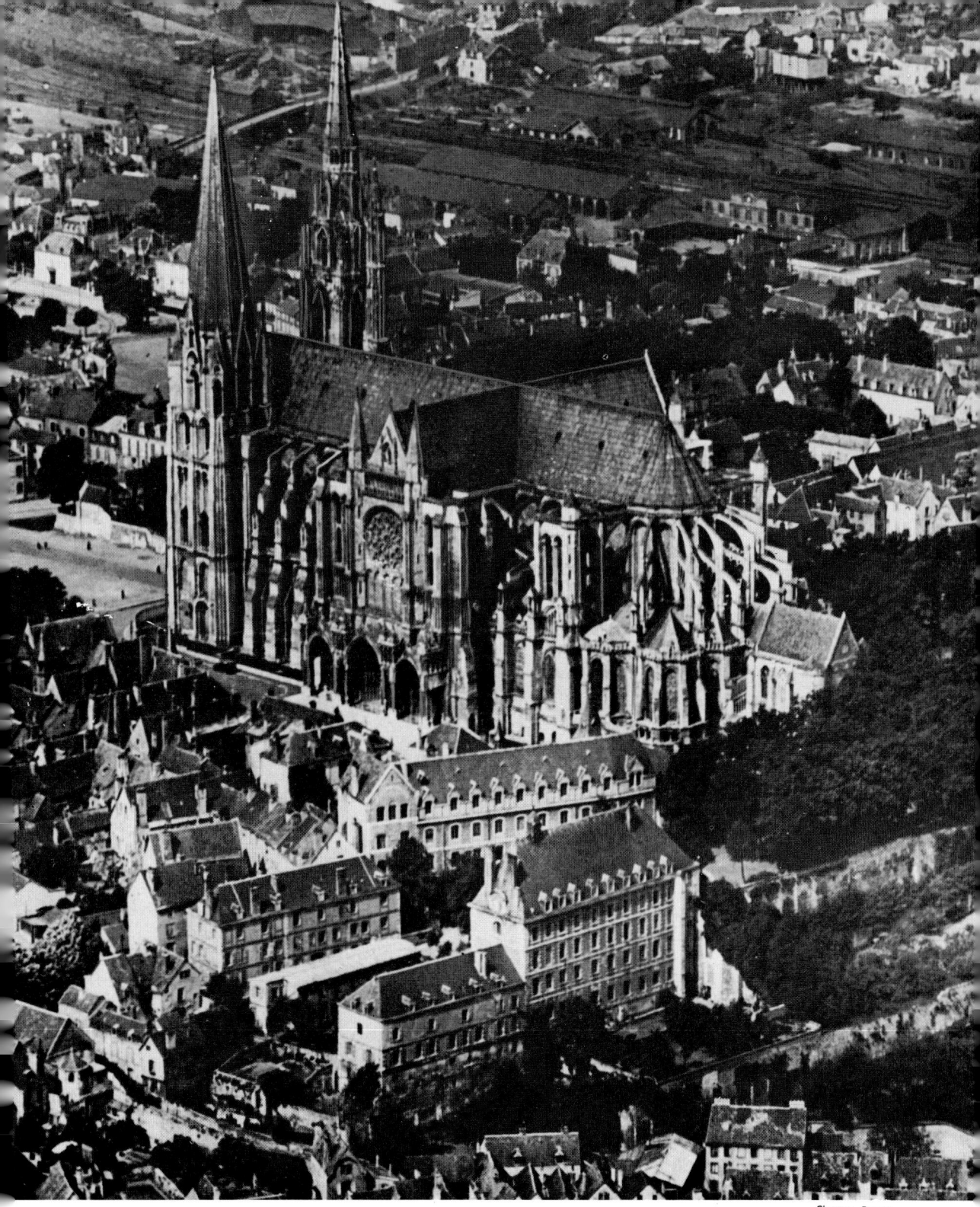

CHARTRES CATHEDRAL built 12th to 13th centuries
by unknown architects

Chartres, France

RHEIMS CATHEDRAL built 13th to 15th centuries by Jean d'Orbais, Jean de Loup, Gauchet de Rheims, Bernard de Soissons, and other architects

The Front of a Gothic Cathedral is Strong and Imposing

Rheims, France

THIS is the front view of the French Cathedral where the Kings of France were crowned. The first King of France, Clovis, was baptized here. He was still a pagan when he won his victory over the last Roman Governor of this part of Europe, which later became France.

That ancient Church burned down some time after the old Chartres Cathedral was also destroyed by fire (p.61), but the people of Rheims began to rebuild their Cathedral soon afterwards. The building got its finishing touch in 1492, the year Columbus discovered America. It took generations of architects hundreds of years to finish just the front of the building, even though they did not put up turrets on top of the towers as the builders of Chartres Cathedral had done.

Here the arches are all pointed, in the Gothic manner. Notice how the arches become more pointed, narrower, and lighter from story to story. The triangles on top of the arches make them look even more pointed. Like the spirit of the Church itself, the entire building points toward Heaven.

AMIENS CATHEDRAL (Interior)
built 1220-1236
by Robert de Luzarches

The Inside is Lofty and Solemn

Amiens, France

AMIENS Cathedral was built about the same time as the Cathedrals of Chartres and Rheims but it was started last. Fire destroyed an early version of this Church. But the people of Amiens began to plan their new Church immediately. They were rich manufacturers and merchants or wealthy land-owning noblemen.

Everyone agreed with the Priests that the new Cathedral should be bigger than any Cathedral anywhere else. The King of France gave a helping hand, and only two years after the destruction of the old Church, the French architect, Robert de Luzarches, started the new building.

One hundred and twenty-six pillars support the lofty vaults of the Cathedral sanctuary. The vaulting (p.43) of the nave is 144 feet high.

Originally the nave was flooded with colored light streaming through the stained-glass windows which have since been destroyed. From the entrance to the apse you walk 475 feet in glory and splendor. It makes you feel that Heaven has indeed come down into the House of God.

Detail of NOTRE DAME CATHEDRAL
built 12th and 13th centuries
begun in the 12th century by unkown architects,
continued in the 13th by Jean de Chelles

Most Cathedrals are built in the shape of a cross. Here, in the great Cathedral of Notre Dame, we see the cross-shaped roof that covers the nave and the highest part of the transept (p.54). The picture also shows us the Cathedral's flying buttresses as seen from above.

Paris, France
Courtesy of the French Embassy

Detail of COUTANCE CATHEDRAL
built about 1220-1240
by unknown architect

The flying buttresses are built at just the right angle to the rounded apse (p.51) so as not to get in the way of the picture windows. They reach out in a slender arch from the top of the pillars between the windows of the nave. Another row of arches reaches out from the pillars around the aisles (p.54). Each arch is supported, as the Roman arch was (p.43), by a firm wall at the side. Here the supporting walls at the end of the arches are crowned by turrets.

Coutance, France

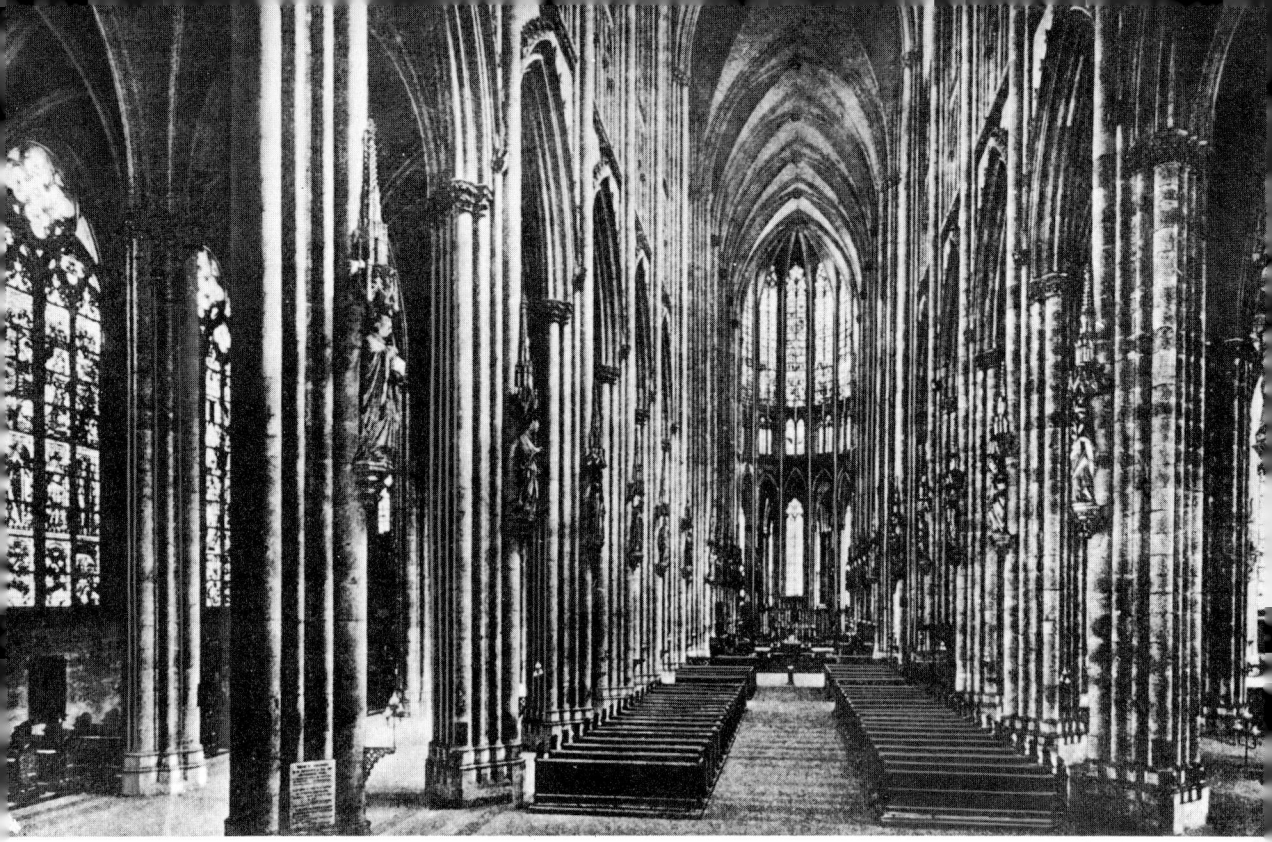

COLOGNE CATHEDRAL (Interior) built 1248-1313
by Gerhard von Rihle

Cologne, Germany

The French Cathedrals Became Models

THE German Cathedral of Cologne was started when children born at the start of Amiens Cathedral were grown up. The German architect, Master Gerhard of Rihle, built the famous Cathedral of Cologne on the Rhine. He found a French model for his building in the Cathedral of Amiens.

In Cologne Cathedral there are two aisles on each side of the nave. As in the early Christian basilicas (p.50-51) the aisles are not as high as the nave. As time went on, the builders took pride in building the nave higher and higher, and lighter and lighter.

The stained-glass windows look like a wall of transparent pictures.

Cologne Cathedral has a wealth of stained-glass windows. In a fashion then new, statues are attached to the pillars of the nave. Each statue has an elaborate canopy above it, in the shape of a turret. All these ornaments make the inside of Cologne Cathedral particularly rich and beautiful.

ST. EUSTACHE HUNTING
  Stained Glass of the 13th century
  by unknown artist

E. Houvet, Rep. Int.

Chartres Cathedral, Chartres, France

Why This Picture is Not Clear in Black-and-White

IN A black-and-white picture of stained-glass we cannot see the shapes clearly. There are too many black lines. These black lines are the frames made of lead that hold the bits of colored glass together.

Only some of these lines are part of the design and form the outlines of shapes in the picture. It is only when we see color within these outlines that the shapes become clear. We cannot see the horses or the dogs or the deer in the black-and-white picture. Only the color makes the animals stand out against the blue background or against one another. The people are a little easier to see because a little shading makes their figures clearer.

The picture is made of plain stained-glass pieces. That is why it is called stained-glass. But because of the lead that holds the pieces together, it is also called leaded-glass.

The glass pieces are colored through and through and look like precious jewels. The art of making beautifully colored glass was a secret of the masters of the Middle Ages.

The light sifting through this stained-glass picture makes it glow in jewel-like beauty. The story is clear and easy to understand—but only because of the colors.

Same as on opposite page in colors

Colors Make Stained-Glass Pictures Clear

AN old legend tells us this story of St. Eustache, the hunter. Eustache was a military officer at the time of the Emperor Trajan. He was a pagan but a man of great kindness with a charitable heart.

One day, as he went hunting with his groom and dogs, he came upon a group of deer. One of them, unusually beautiful, leaped into a thicket and Eustache followed. The deer sprang onto a rock. As Eustache stood wondering how he could catch it, he suddenly saw a cross appear between its horns. This miraculous appearance converted Eustache to Christianity. From that time on he lived for his religion, and he finally died for it. After his death he was made a Saint.

In this picture we see St. Eustache galloping gaily on his brown horse, blowing his horn. Four of his dogs follow closely behind the deer. St. Eustache is in the center of the picture because he is the most important figure. The groom, the dogs, and the deer surround him like a frame. There is no sign of a landscape except for a large mushroom next to the groom's foot.

THE STE. CHAPELLE (Interior)
consecrated 1248
built by Pierre de Monterau

These Walls
—All Windows—
Tell Sacred Stories
in Stained Glass

Paris, France

THIS exquisite little French chapel was built by St. Louis, King of France. It is a miracle of building, the high walls being almost entirely made of glass.

Inside the chapel there are only narrow pillars of stone left between the huge windows. These slender pillars could not possibly support the vaulting of the ceiling, but we know that the pillars are buttressed on the outside (as we saw on p. 64). Figures of Saints carved in stone are attached to each pillar.

The windows are made of leaded-glass pictures, such as we saw on the previous page. These windows are not meant to look through. Colored-glass is translucent enough to let light in, but we cannot see through it.

But the stories of Saints shown in these stained-glass paintings glow in light that shines on them from the outside whether it is the warm sunlight or the cold light of snow. We cannot see them at all when it is dark outside. As the light changes with the passing hours, or even with a passing cloud, the pictures keep changing too. Because of these constant changes, the sacred stories seem to have a magic life of their own.

THE ARENA CHAPEL (Interior)
built about 1305
painted by Giotto
(about 1270-1338)

These Walls
—All Solid—
Tell Sacred
Stories in Painting

Padua, Italy

WHEN we enter the Arena Chapel in Padua, we feel the radiant blue Heaven all around us. There are only a few small windows to let in light, but it is enough to make the blue sky of the pictures all around the walls look radiant.

Here, in Italy, sacred stories were told in paintings on the walls, not in stained-glass. These wall paintings, called frescoes, are painted on the fresh, still damp wall. The entire inside of the Arena Chapel is decorated with frescoes by the great Italian painter Giotto.

In the Sainte Chapelle we see stone pillars between the windows. Here in the Arena Chapel we have painted pilasters (p.44) between the pictures. But here the wall is divided crosswise by painted narrow ledges, so that each picture-story stands by itself, and each has a frame to separate it from the next one. The pictures—thirty-eight in all—make one story. The story starts with the miraculous birth of the Virgin Mary and her life, continues with the life of Jesus, and ends with the miracles He performed after his death.

We feel that all the light in the chapel comes from these painted stories just as it came through the colored-glass windows in the Sainte Chapelle.

Here too, as in the Sainte Chapelle, we feel that we are in an enchanted world.

A Great Painting of a Great Bible Story

THE Bible tells us that, soon after the birth of Christ, St. Joseph dreamed he saw an Angel who said to him: "Take the young Child and His Mother and flee into Egypt."

Joseph wrapped their few belongings into a bundle, hung it on a stick, and put it over his shoulder. He poured water into a jug and carried it in his hand. Then, helping Mary to mount a little donkey, they set off with Baby Jesus on their journey.

In this picture—one of the thirty-eight in the Arena Chapel (p.69)—the Italian painter Giotto shows us the Holy Family as they follow a winding path among the mountains. St. Joseph heads the little group, but he is not really guiding them, for he looks back at the boy leading the donkey. The boy has his head raised as if listening to an inner voice.

We can see where the voice comes from. It is the voice of the Angel above. This Angel points the way with his hand while his face is turned toward the boy who leads the donkey. Three more boys follow. They seem to be discussing the strange happenings.

In the center of the picture we see the noble figure of Mary sitting straight on the donkey's back. She looks ahead with a calm and earnest expression. Her hands fold around little Jesus who is tied to her by a cloth. In Italy, even now, children are often tied to their mothers in this way.

Mary's cloak was originally painted blue, but today only specks of the color remain. We see the warm red of Mary's dress beneath her cloak.

There is not much detail painted in her garments. The painter arranged the folds of her cloak to explain the way she sits: with one knee near the donkey's neck. The shading of the folds gives a well-rounded modelling to her entire figure. We can all but feel the air that surrounds her and the other figures in this picture too.

This is not true, though, of the landscape. The mountains are unnaturally small compared to the figures, and so are the scanty trees. They don't look natural at all. The mountain in the foreground is painted entirely in one light color. The one behind it is painted darker to show us that it is farther away. A small part of a third mountain, even more distant, is painted in an even darker color.

In nature the colors would melt together. But the painter did not care to show us what the landscape really looked like. He wanted to tell his *story* clearly, that was all. To tell us that the figure of Mary with the Baby Jesus is the most important in the picture, he painted the first mountain like a frame around her. The curving slope of the mountain surrounds the figure of the Angel in Heaven. This curve also connects Mary with the Angel who is there to guide her and her small Son so that they may arrive safely in Egypt.

Giotto was a Florentine artist. In Florence people were interested mainly in stories, and Florentine painters told the stories they painted plainly and clearly. When they painted landscapes, it was only to make their stories clearer. They modeled figures as strongly as if they were sculptured. Giotto was the greatest painter of democratic Florence in the Middle Ages.

THE FLIGHT INTO EGYPT painted about 1305
by Giotto (about 1270-1338)

Arena Chapel, Padua, Italy

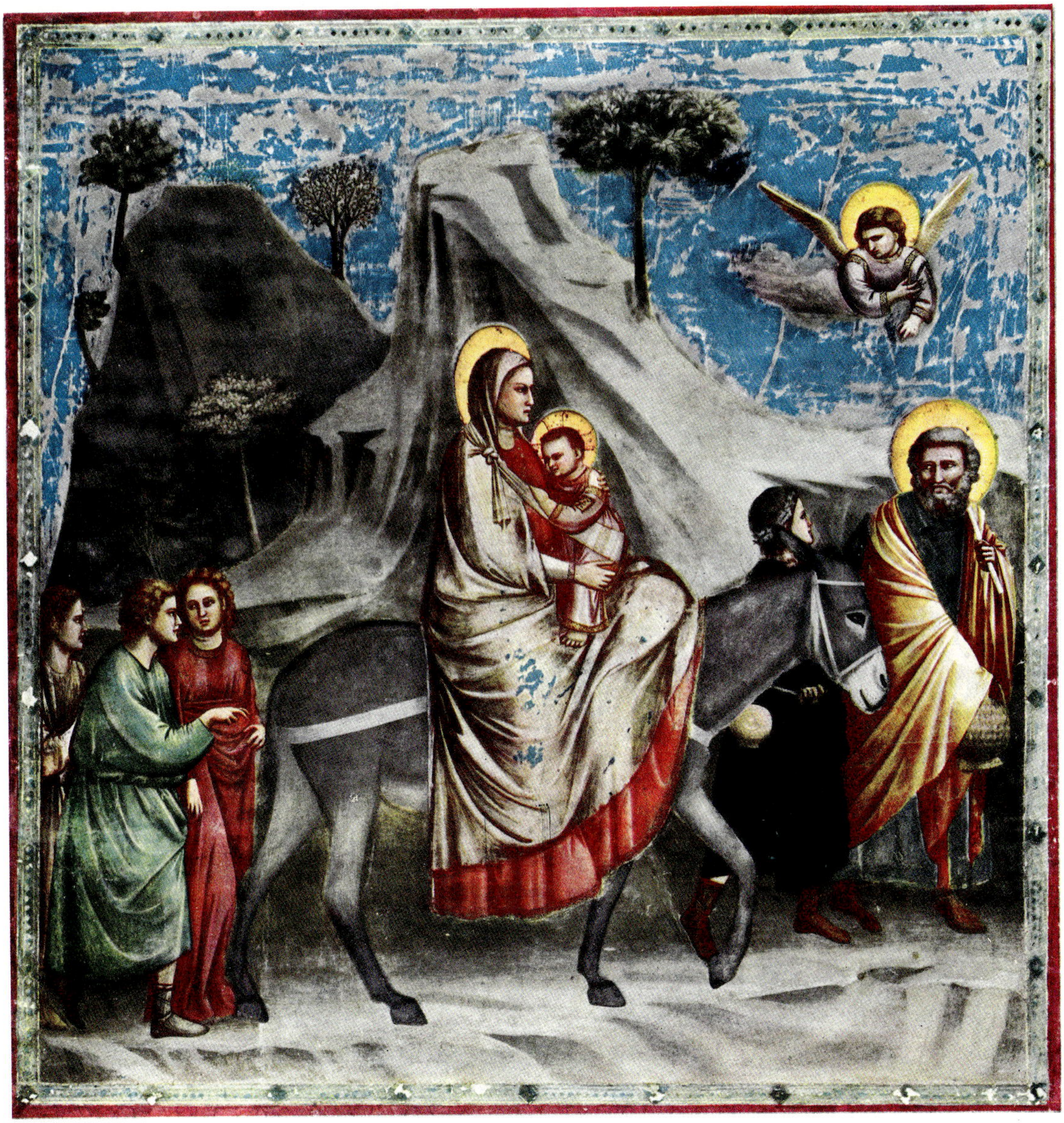

THE CHRISTMAS STORY sculptured 1298-1301
by Giovanni Pisano (about 1240-1320)

St. Andrea, Pistoia, Italy

Many Miraculous Events in One Sculptured Picture

THE Bible tells us that one day when the Virgin Mary was praying in Church, an Angel came to tell her that she was going to have a Baby Son.

The Baby, Jesus Christ, who was going to grow up to be the Savior of the world, was born in a stable in Bethlehem. A little donkey and an ox were there when the Holy Child was born.

Above, in Heaven, the Angels sang with joy. One of them announced to the nearby shepherds that Christ was born. The shepherds hastened to see the newborn Child.

Women came to the stable too, to help Mary take care of the Baby. They bathed Him and wrapped Him in swaddling clothes. It was a joyous day, the day the entire Christian world has celebrated ever since as Christmas.

This lovely story is all crowded into one sculptured picture by the medieval Italian sculptor, Giovanni Pisano. He carved it in white marble and it decorates one of the sides of a pulpit he had built for a Church in Pistoia.

Richly carved pulpits were the main sculptured decoration in Italian Churches of the Middle Ages. The sides of the pulpits were often crowded with sculptured stories.

In the upper left corner of this picture we see the beginning of our story: a smiling Angel announcing to Mary that she is about to become the Mother of Christ. Mary is deeply moved. She clutches her hand to her heart when the Holy Spirit descends upon her in the form of a dove.

The two triangular Gothic arches above her head tell us that this is happening in a Church, but the Church is not actually shown.

Neither is the stable shown in the part of the Christmas story that follows. Right next to the scene where the Angel announces the birth of Christ to Mary, we see Mary again. This time she is reclining on what should be a couch, though only a sign of it is shown in some folds of a sheet. But how sweet Mary's face is as she gently lifts the blanket that covers the newborn Jesus in His crib!

Next to the crib we see the donkey and the ox and, above, three Angels in adoration. A fourth Angel next to these, in the upper right corner, leads us to the third part of the story. This Angel looks and reaches down to one of the shepherds to tell him that Christ has been born. The leafy branches between them tell us that this is happening in a forest.

As the story continues, below the first shepherd we see another one. He has already heard the angelic message and we see him standing at the foot of Mary's couch looking at Mary and her Baby. His flock of sheep are next to him resting or grazing.

In front of Mary's couch we see the women who came to care for the Baby. One woman holds Him on her lap while she tests the water in the basin with her fingers. She wants to see whether the water that the other woman pours from a jug is right for the bath.

In the corner St. Joseph watches, deep in thought.

We must look carefully to make out all these scenes. Giovanni **Pisano** was a *medieval* sculptor; he did not feel that he had to tell the sacred story *as* it happened. He wanted only to remind us *that* it happened. He gives us only hints, wanting us to give all our attention to the holy persons. We have to know the story in advance to understand the picture.

But because Giovanni Pisano was an *Italian* sculptor, he made every gesture expressive. The woman who pours the water shows skill and care, and we can see that the other one knows exactly the right temperature for the bath.

The biggest and most important figure is the Virgin Mary facing the Angel. Her gestures and her face express more than can ever be told in words. It took an artist as great as Giovanni Pisano to give it shape, first in his own heart and soul and then in his beautiful marble sculpture.

Altar Paintings that Shine in Golden Glory

HERE, in the midst of light and shining gold, we see the Virgin Mary seated on a marble throne. She has been reading her prayer book when an Angel enters and kneels down before her.

The Angel wears a wreath of roses. In one hand he carries a rose branch. With the other he points up toward the Holy Spirit who descends from above in the shape of a dove. Golden words come from the mouth of the Angel. They are the words that announce to the Virgin that she is to become the Mother of Christ.

Drawing her mantle closer about her, the frail slender young woman turns away overwhelmed by the heavenly message.

The Virgin is gentle as a flower. The lilies next to her are a symbol of her purity. She is to become the Queen of Heaven. That is why the Angel kneels and is dressed as though he belonged in the court of a Queen. People are elegantly dressed in royal courts, and the Angel's garment is therefore brightened by a golden ribbon. His fluttering mantle points upward to show that he has just flown down from Heaven. His wings have graceful lines and a delicate jewel-like pattern. They are resplendent with many colors and touched with gold. Even his hands seem to take the form of an ornament.

The Virgin on the other side is much more simply dressed because she is still on earth. Over her dark red robe she wears a blue mantle that unfolds on the floor in lovely lines. The mantle is outlined by a golden border. The golden line of the border is now hidden among the folds, now visible. It surrounds the head of the Virgin like a delicate frame, then leads our eyes down to her hands.

Both Mary's face and the way she holds her hands tell us that she was reading her prayer-book when the Angel came, and that she has now cast down her eyes before the direct glance of the heavenly messenger. Roses and lilies bend gently toward her but she seems to be aware only of the Holy Spirit.

This picture was painted by Simone Martini in the town of Siena, in Italy. The courtly customs of aristocratic Siena are mirrored in the pictures of Sienese painters and Simone Martini was the finest and most famous among them.

The town of Siena is surrounded by gently sloping hills. It is protected from wind and weather. Aristocratic and courtly manners developed in those calm surroundings. The pictures that were painted in Siena are gentle and pleasing and graceful because of their delicate lines and fine colors. This aristocratic style of painting differs markedly from the strong clearly modeled shapes characteristic of democratic Florence.

THE ANNUNCIATION painted 1333
by Simone Martini (about 1285-1357)

Palazzo degli Uffizi, Florence, Italy

75

ST. GEORGE AND THE DRAGON (Relief) sculptured 1417
by Donatello (about 1386-1466)

Or' San Michele Florence, Italy

A Sculptured Story of St. George and the Dragon

AN OLD legend tells us that, in a kingdom near the sea, a horrible dragon threatened to poison the whole town with his breath unless the people fed him as he asked.

The dragon had a huge appetite. He demanded two sheep to eat every day. Finally the people ran out of sheep and all other animals too. Now they were forced to bring their own sons and daughters to feed the monster.

At last the only one left was the daughter of the King. Her father had her dressed in royal garments and sent to the dragon's cave. There the young Princess stood weeping when a young Knight came riding by on a horse.

The Princess told the Knight of the danger she was in and begged him to hurry away lest the dragon harm him too. But the Knight, who turned out to be no other than the heroic St. George, rode up to the dragon, pierced him with his lance, and saved the Princess and her people.

This story is carved in marble in a flattened-out kind of sculpture called *relief*. It was made by the Italian sculptor, Donatello, to decorate the base of his statue of St. George.

On the relief we see that the dragon has come out of the cave, his open mouth breathing poison. But we feel sure he is not going to harm St. George. He is strong and limber. His legs are tightly pressed to his horse. His mantle flutters behind him because he is galloping so swiftly. We see him thrusting his spear into the dragon's breast.

Donatello's horse, on which St. George is riding, does not look quite natural. To make horses look natural is one of the hardest things for an artist to do. (Donatello will do much better in his later years, as we shall see on p. 96).

But let us go back to our picture. The Princess stands in front of her father's palace nearby. She prays for St. George's victory. She looks something like the ancient caryatids we saw on page 28. They have the same sort of dress and hair-do, the same rounded oval cheeks and deep-set eyes.

The resemblance is here because this relief was carved in a period, called the Renaissance, when artists were inspired by the styles of ancient Greece and Rome. *Renaissance* is a French word meaning *rebirth*. We use this word for the time when the arts of the ancient Greeks and Romans were reborn—that is, when artists went back to imitating their works after the long centuries of the Middle Ages.

ST. GEORGE (Originally above Relief on opposite page)

The Statue of St. George

Above Donatello's relief of the dragon story stands his impressive statue of St. George. Standing firmly on his two feet, he is alive with energy. His brow is furrowed, his face alert for danger. Slender and erect, he is full of life.

His fine armor does not entirely hide his sinewy body, and we are aware of the muscles of his arms even though they are covered with rich decorations. His hands merely touch the narrow shield in front of him, but just by the way he holds his arms we can feel their power. We are sure this young hero would defeat any enemy.

When we compare Donatello's statue of St. George with the statue of St. Theodore by an unknown artist of the Middle Ages (p.58), we see how different these two sculptures are. St. Theodore does not stand firmly on his feet. He does not hold his head so high nor does he look alert. His face is calm under the soft locks of his hair. The halo behind his head suits him well: he is more of a saint while St. George is more of a fighter.

The statue of St. Theodore is an expression of the Middle Ages. St. George belongs to the time of the Renaissance when people, again, had a more down-to-earth view of the world.

National Museum, Florence, Italy

A Miracle is Painted as if it were Reality

THE Bible tells us the story of how Jesus went to Capernaum with his twelve Apostles. They wanted to enter the town through the city gates, but a toll had to be paid and neither Christ nor his Apostles had any money.

Christ told one of the Apostles, St. Peter, to go to the seashore where he would find a fish, and in the mouth of the fish he would find a coin to pay the toll.

St. Peter did as he was told. He went to the shore; he found the fish. And there in the fish's mouth was the coin. St. Peter gave it to the toll-taker, and Christ and his Apostles were then allowed to enter the town.

Masaccio, the first great painter of the Italian *Renaissance,* tells this story in the picture we see here. It is one picture but it has three parts.

In the central part of the painting we see the beginning of the story. In the exact center of the picture the toll-taker stands with his back to us, facing Christ. He extends his left hand toward Christ for the money while his right hand points to the gates of the city.

Christ, in turn, points to the seashore in a gesture that tells the toll-taker and St. Peter where the money will be found. St. Peter repeats this gesture as if repeating Christ's words.

In the left part of the picture we see St. Peter kneeling on the shore, taking the coin from the fish's mouth. This is the second part of the story.

The artist tells the third part on the right. Here, at the city gates, St. Peter hands the coin to the toll-taker.

The central part is the most important. Here all the people of the story are present: Christ surrounded by His Apostles and the toll-taker.

Christ's figure is a majestic one. At His right and left, the heads of two Apostles flank Him as an honor guard. The noble quiet figure of Christ becomes even more impressive in contrast to the toll-taker whose gestures concern only a practical thing: he asks for the money to admit the group.

Christ's gesture indicates a miracle. It is repeated by St. Peter but with less grandeur, because he is only the instrument used to perform Christ's miracle.

The other Apostles stand in the background, left and right, in well-balanced groups. Most of them are turned toward the city gates because that is where they are going.

Some of the heads, with the straight line from the forehead to the tip of the nose, resemble Greek portraits. All look earnest and dignified, showing us that they belong to Christ and to His world.

There is one exception: the man at the right end of the group. This man, different from the others, looks like someone from our own world. No one is quite sure who the painter meant him to be. Some scholars think he may be Masaccio, the painter himself.

Although a miracle was painted in this picture, the entire scene looks very real. This is partly because the artist made nearer figures bigger and those farther away smaller, as we see them in real life. The toll-taker is the biggest figure in this picture because he is nearest to us, and St. Peter at the distant seashore is the smallest.

The same is true of the parts of the building: The front pillar of the little porch is bigger than the one behind it. The wintry landscape, the bare hills, and the bare trees are all drawn according to this rule. We call this rule *perspective.*

THE TOLL MONEY painted about 1427 by Masaccio (1400-1428)

Masaccio was the first painter of the Italian Renaissance to use perspective, an important feature of Renaissance art. He rounded people and buildings and landscapes to make them look real.

It is the great gift of Masaccio that he could make us see the noble characters of the Bible in their real greatness.

Sta. Maria del Carmine, Florence, Italy

THE GHENT ALTAR PIECE
(closed) painting completed 1432
by Hubert van Eyck (about 1366-1426)
and Jan van Eyck (about 1390-1441)

This World-Famous Altar was Painted by Two Brothers

St. Bavon, Ghent, Belgium
Copyright A.C.L. Brussel

THERE are several famous paintings by Jan Van Eyck in churches and museums throughout the world. But all we know about Hubert is what Jan wrote on this Ghent altar-piece: that there never was a greater painter than his brother Hubert.

This altar-piece is indeed a thing of exquisite beauty.

In northern Europe altar-pieces were often built like cabinets with doors, called wings, that could be opened. The outsides of the wings usually show paintings in different shades of gray, with, perhaps, a few dim colors added.

Here we see the wings closed. In the upper part an Angel is announcing to the Virgin Mary that she is to become the Mother of Christ. In the lower part the couple who gave the altar-piece to the Church, the donors, are praying. They were real people and are therefore painted in natural colors. In contrast, the sacred figures are painted in shades of gray: John the Baptist with the lamb on his arm and John the Evangelist with a cup in his hand.

THE GHENT ALTAR PIECE (open)
THE MYSTIC LAMB

Copyright A.C.L. Brussel

Imposing as the outside of this altar is, its full splendor is shown only when it is opened. Here we see a picture of heaven in full rich colors and shimmering gold.

In the upper part God is enthroned between the Virgin Mary and St. John the Baptist. Next to them Angels sing and play their musical instruments. Adam and Eve stand at either side.

In the lower part we see the symbolic Lamb of the Bible on an altar surrounded by the heavenly choirs.

Part of these choirs can be seen right in the central panel. Behind the altar surrounded by Angels at the right and left, we see the choirs of holy martyrs assembling. In the foreground Apostles and Prophets surround the Fountain of Life. Next to them at the right stand the holy dignitaries of the Church, at their left the holy Kings and Princes.

On the two panels at the right we see the holy hermits making their pilgrimage to the sacred shrine. On the left the holy Knights approach on horseback.

This magnificent altar-piece marks the beginning of the Renaissance in the northern countries of Europe.

This Picture is a Legal Document

WHEN we look at this portrait of *The Arnolfini Couple,* we feel a warm radiance coming from it. This is partly because of the warm harmony of the complementary colors, red and green. But there is more to the radiance of this picture than mere colors. It has a solemn feeling that reminds us of Church.

Let's see what is really there. Certainly no Church. We see a simple bedroom with a bed in it, a chair, a little table before the window, a chandelier hanging from the ceiling, a mirror on the wall. At the foot of the bed stands a couple with a little dog between them. Their shoes are lying on the floor. His are next to him, hers in the back of the room.

The only solemn thing we can see in the picture is the raised right hand of the man. It is the ancient gesture of taking an oath, and we use it even today. We can almost hear the words "Raise your right hand and . . ."

The man's face shows earnest thought. His other hand holds the woman's hand and we feel that he wants to hold it forever. Her little face is as serious as his. It bends down as if agreeing with him.

The mirror between these two people looks like an official seal to this solemn joining of hands. The rosary hanging next to it reminds us of the string attached to an official seal.

The writing, with its curlicues around the mirror, looks like the fancy signature on a legal document. What does it say? It reads "Jan van Eyck (the painter) was here." And if we look closely into the mirror that shows the backs of the couple, we see the painter himself entering the room with another man. They are here as witnesses to the marriage ceremony of Giovanni Arnolfini and his bride, Jeanne de Cenami. The portrait of this couple is a picture of their marriage vow.

Looking a little higher at the chandelier, we see that there is just one candle burning in it. Why a candle at all, we wonder, when there is bright daylight all over the room? It is the marriage candle, an age-old custom for the wedding ceremony.

The little dog between the bride and groom represents faithfulness. The shoes lying on the floor remind us of what the Bible says: "Take off your shoes, for the ground on which you stand is hallowed ground."

It is because of all this that we feel solemn when we look at the portrait of *The Arnolfini Couple.*

Everything in this picture is painted true to nature. The different materials—the whitewash on the wall, the wooden floor, the metal chandelier, the heavy weave of drapery, the velvet in Mr. Arnolfini's cloak, the linen in the bride's headgear, the difference between the furs on his garment and on hers—all are painted as they look to the eye and feel to the touch.

The sunlight streaming through the open window bathes the entire scene in a kind of magic. It is the magic of Jan van Eyck, one of the greatest painters who ever lived.

THE ARNOLFINI COUPLE painted 1434
by Jan van Eyck (about 1390-1441)

Reproduced by courtesy of the Trustees,
National Gallery, London, England

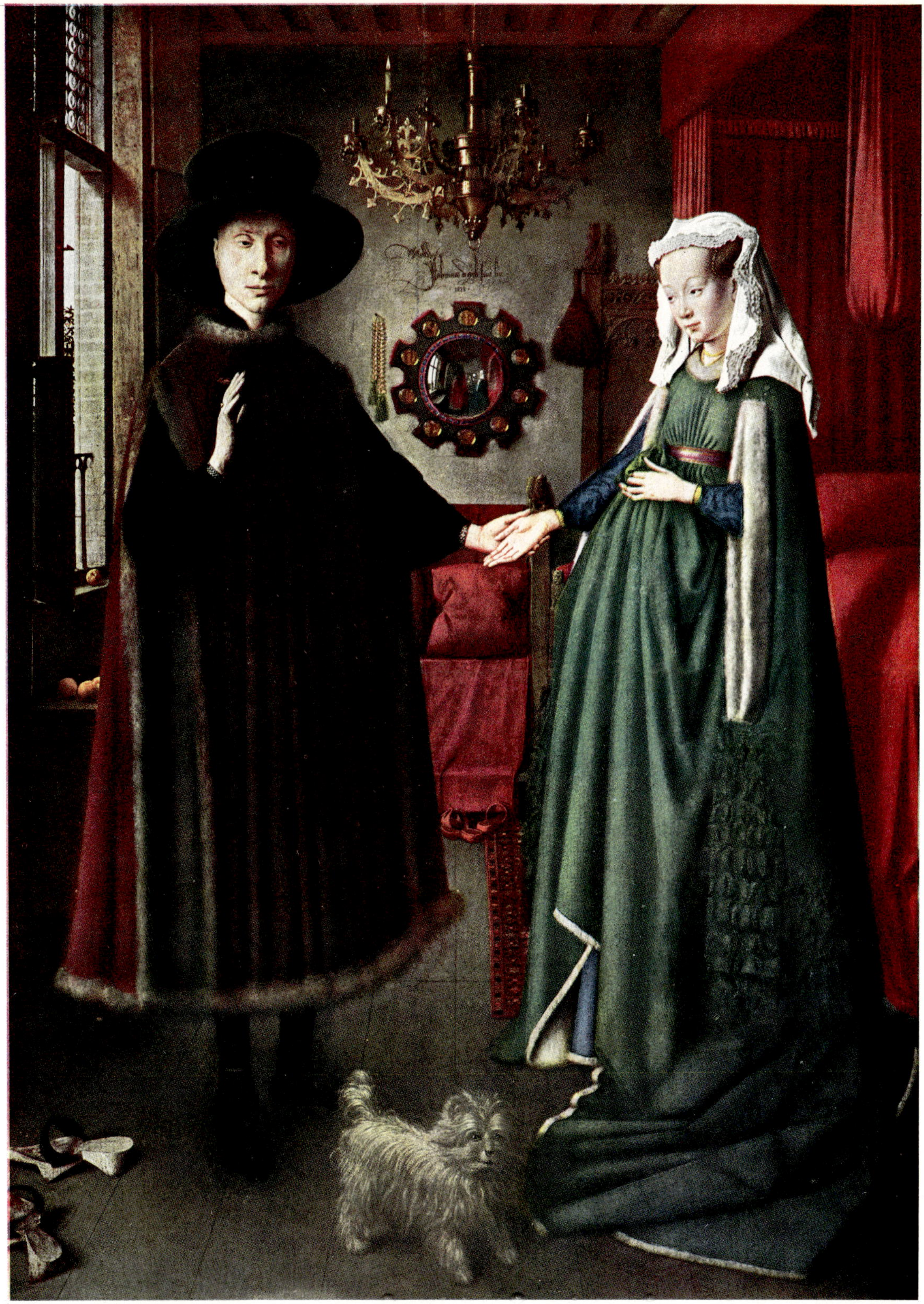

Why This Portrait is More Than a Simple Likeness

THE young lady in this picture is entirely wrapped in thought. Her head is slightly bent down, her eyes are downcast, her hands joined together in a rather strange way. Although we cannot see it, we think she must be kneeling in a pew because of the posture of her erect body and the way her hands and forearms rest. Her delicate features and her soft skin look transparent. The clear outlines of her head and neck seem to be more ornamental lines than an imitation of the lines in nature. Yet they are not unnatural.

The lady's veil looks as fresh as if it had just been taken from the box where it had been lying gently folded. We can see the slight creases in it. But again, the outline of her veil is harder than it would be in real life. It forms a lovely frame around her face, made more interesting by the pattern of the creases. The clear line of the necklace on the lady's bosom is mainly decorative, but it serves also to lead our eyes down to her hands.

These hands were apparently very important to the artist although he covered them up to the fingers in his portrait. What do they tell us about the lady they belong to? Actually, they look disturbingly unnatural. The fingers interweave in a criss-cross pattern, and they too look more like an ornament than like real flesh and blood. We have to look very carefully to find out which finger is which. But when, finally, we *have* found out with what deep feeling the fingers are pressed together, we understand more about the devotion of the young lady than if we had been less puzzled by these "unnatural" hands. The artist has achieved his aim.

He wanted to make us think about the too speckless perfection of every line, every detail. The portrait mirrors the purity of the lady's heart and her perfect devotion. Even though her hands are not clasped in prayer in the usual way, it is obvious, the painter shows us, that the young lady is kneeling in silent prayer.

Roger van der Weyden did not copy nature for its own sake. He emphasized something that was more important to him: the human soul. At the same period and in the same country Jan van Eyck tried to put all the truth of life into his pictures while Roger van der Weyden clung to the medieval ideal of spiritual beauty.

PORTRAIT OF A YOUNG LADY painted about 1460
by Roger van der Weyden (about 1400-1464)

National Gallery of Art, Washington, D. C.
Mellon Collection

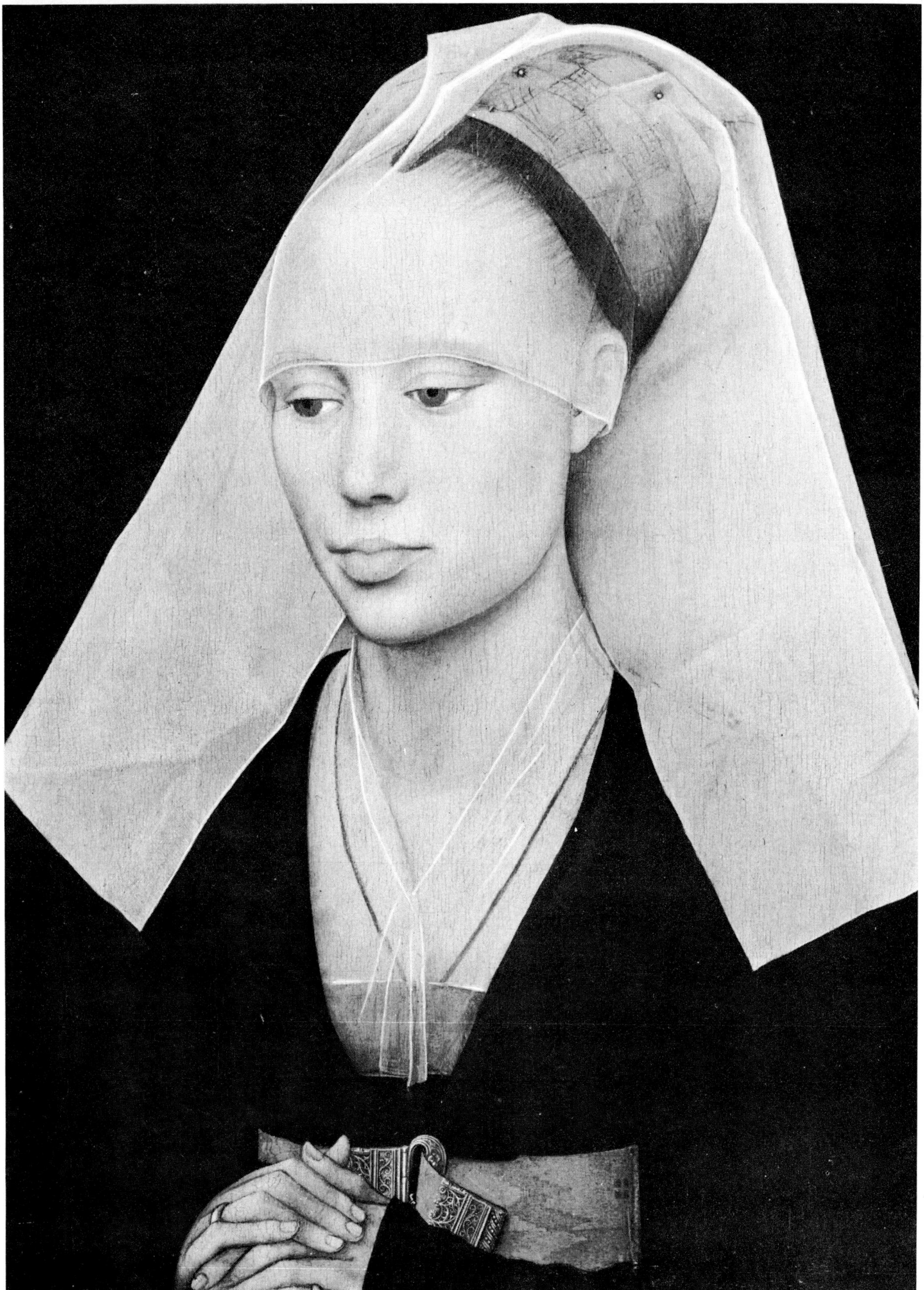

Detail from opposite page

This Artist Makes Us *Feel* a Miracle as Well as See It

A LEGEND tells us that after Christ had arisen from His grave, He went to see His Mother. That is the story told in this picture by the Flemish painter, Roger van der Weyden.

From the arched doorway we feel a cool breeze streaming toward us. This is not only because of the cool gray and blue colors. It is because we also feel the coolness of the sanctuary. Here the Virgin Mary knelt in prayer weeping for her Son who had died. Suddenly she felt a gentle presence that made her turn around. Now, with awe and wonder in her eyes, she sees a miracle: her Son who had died and was buried, has entered the place where she was praying. He has come from His tomb as we can see through the open door.

Through this door Christ has entered and approached His Mother. His footsteps hardly touch the ground. There is a hush about Him. With raised hands He asks for silence.

His plea is answered by the raised hands and the awed expression of His Mother. She was about to rise from her knees to meet her Son, but she stopped halfway. Her lips will keep silence while her eyes and outstretched hands will follow Him as He passes her. Then she will turn back toward her prayer-stool and her prayer-book. It has been half-closed for the moment only. We know she will reopen it. The artist has made us see what *has* happened as well as what is going to happen.

Another reason we see motion in this picture is that the artist has painted the figures in motion: Christ actually taking steps, Mary half-kneeling, her head and hands turning one way, the rest of her body in another.

The scene is far from being natural. It would be impossible to find in any Church an actual enclosure like the one fenced in by a narrow ledge where the Virgin had retired to pray. In our picture it symbolizes the Virgin's privacy.

The arched doorway looks like a Church door and would never be found in the *middle* of a Church. Here it frames the picture to show us how very sacred this scene is. Further scenes from the life of the Virgin, painted in white on the arch, look like the sculptures often seen on Church doors.

Again we see that Roger van der Weyden did not merely copy nature. He painted the cooler air of a spiritual world to make us feel that his story is a supernatural and miraculous one.

CHRIST APPEARS TO HIS MOTHER painted about 1445 by Roger van der Weyden (about 1400-1464)

Courtesy of the Metropolitan Museum of Art, New York, N. Y.

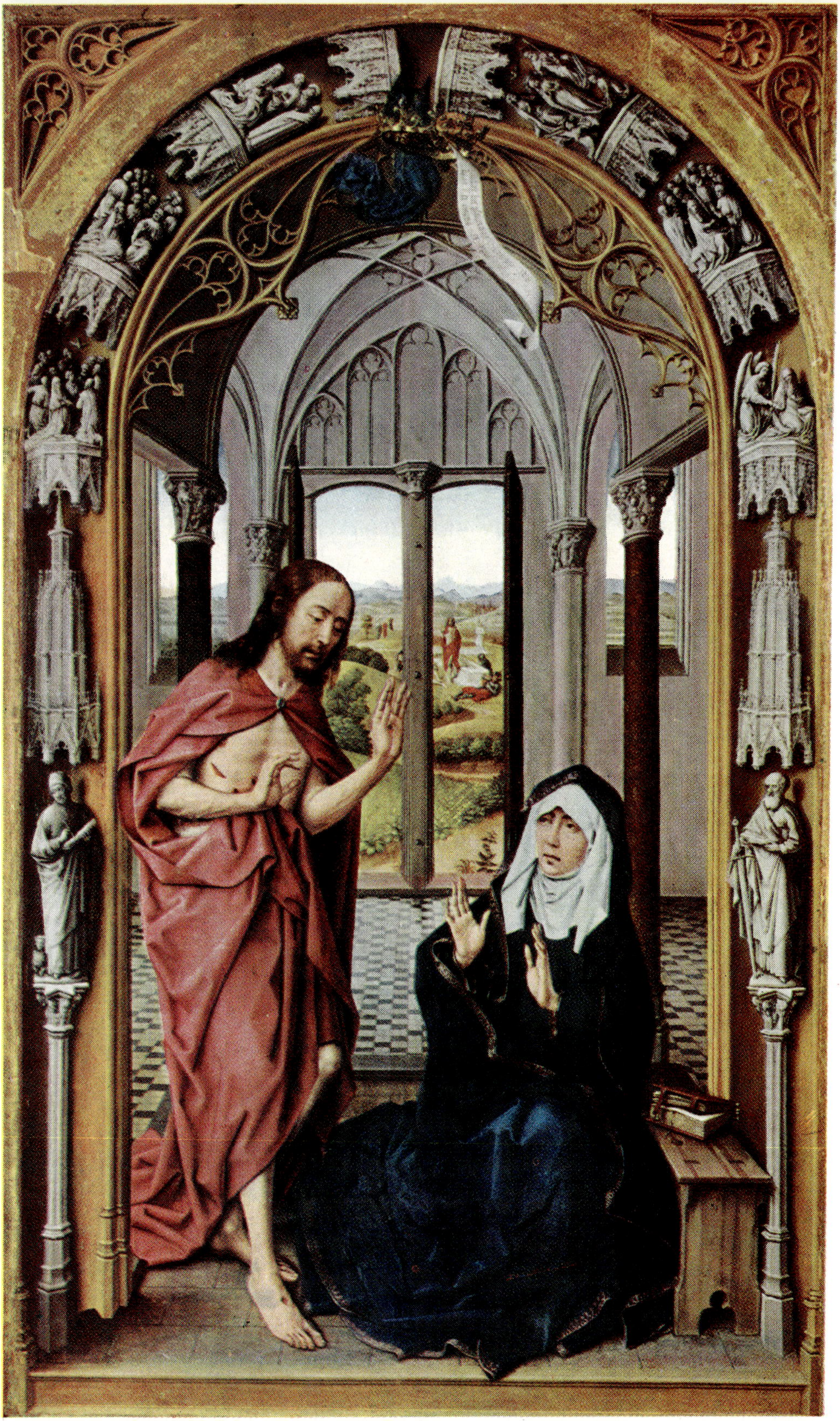

ROOM OF THE BRIDE AND GROOM painted 1468-1474
by Andrea Mantegna (1431-1508)

Gonzaga Palace, Mantua, Italy

The People in This Picture are Around Us

IN Italy the walls of a room were often completely covered with paintings that seemed to be extensions of the room itself. In the room we see here, the walls are painted to look like an open porch.

The people under the painted arches are members of the Gonzaga family, and they look as though they were actually in the room.

There is a story about this family that stirred the interest of all Italy.

It happened that Federigo Gonzaga, son of the governing Count Lodovico, did not then wish to marry the Princess his father had chosen for him. He fled the court of his angry father and went to live, under a false name and a disguise, in Naples. A few of his faithful friends joined him in his exile.

Federigo's mother, the Countess, who was worried about her son, sent messengers to find the fugitives. When they were found, the messengers reported to the Countess that the young men were living in great hardship. They had to work at hard labor, and they were not used to it.

The Countess was deeply moved by this news. On her knees she begged her husband to forgive their son Federigo.

Meanwhile the King of Naples had found out that the young fugitives in his land were noblemen in disguise. Because he felt sorry for Federigo, he wrote to Count Lodovico asking him to forgive his son.

In the pictures on the opposite page we see what happened when the letter was delivered to Count Lodovico.

The entire Gonzaga family is assembled on a terrace. Count Lodovico, at the left, sits on his throne discussing with his counselor the letter in his hand.

The Countess looks at him anxiously. She does not even notice her little granddaughter who is trying to cheer her up with an apple. The dwarf, on the other side of the Countess, knows that this is no time for jokes. All the members of the family are tensely waiting to hear what the Count is going to say.

Only the lively girl in the background seems to have other things on her mind, for she looks toward the stairs of the terrace. There we see Federigo. Returned from his exile, he

Detail of main wall

is about to climb the steps. But he is stopped by a courtier who asks him to wait until the Count has made his decision.

In real life the Count did forgive Federigo, who finally married the lovely Princess. They lived happily ever after, and everyone else was happy about it too. That is why this magnificent room was dedicated to the newlyweds, and why the greatest North Italian painter of that time, Andrea Mantegna, was asked to put the story into a painting.

Mantegna made people look natural and did not mind painting them as they were even if they were ugly. But in so doing he gave them importance and dignity too, for he knew how to add the quality of greatness to whatever he painted.

The room he painted here looks so real that we feel we can actually look through the ceiling and that the painted clouds are actually clouds in the sky. But from the railing above, Mantegna painted a number of cupids looking down at us to show that this story, after all, is being told in an imaginative painting.

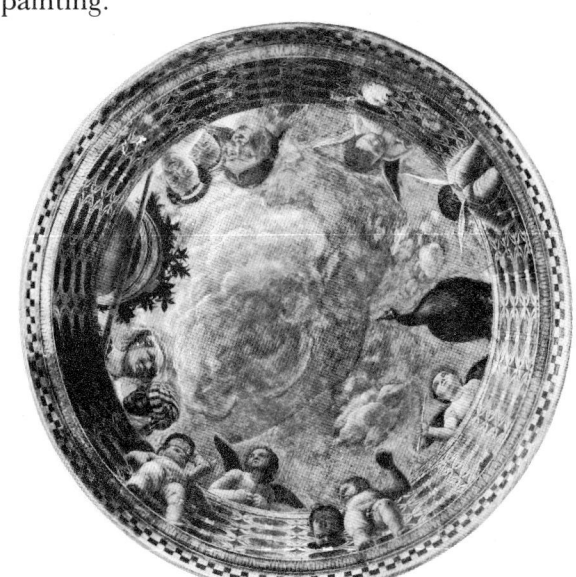

Detail of ceiling

THE BATTLE OF CONSTANTINE painted about 1465
by Piero della Francesca (about 1419-1492)

St. Francesco, Arezzo, Italy

A Battle Won without a Fight

IN THE early days of Christianity, and for centuries, the old Romans persecuted the Christians. But more and more people became Christians, and the pagan Roman Empire became weaker and weaker. Different leaders tried to get into power and they were forever fighting one another.

One of the greatest struggles was between Emperor Constantine and Emperor Maxentius. Each at the head of his army, they met not far from the city of Rome. The opposing camps made ready for battle. Legend tells us that on the night before the battle the pagan Emperor Constantine had a dream. An Angel appeared to him, holding a cross and speaking the words: "In this sign you shall win."

The next day Constantine's army **stood** under the sign of the cross and did indeed win the battle, while the opposing pagan Emperor went down to defeat and drowned in the Tiber River.

From then on Christians were not persecuted any more in the Roman Empire, and soon afterwards Christianity ruled in the Western World.

The story of the Holy Cross was painted on the walls of a chapel in Arezzo, Italy, by Piero della Francesca.

In this picture we see the scene of the battle of Constantine. Unfortunately, part of this painting was destroyed by water seeping in through a leakage in the roof. But even damaged as it is, it is most impressive.

On this bright winter morning we see clouds swimming in a clear-blue sky. The clouds are light gray with pink edges as they often are just after sunrise. A little winding river divides the plain where the two armies met. The river is of the bluest blue you ever saw. The mere color of the quiet little water suggests a sharp barrier between the two armies. To the left of it all is order and purpose; to the right, disorder and despair.

Constantine's army stands on the left bank of the river, under the Roman flag with the Roman eagle on it. The soldiers in their saddles are poised for battle, spears held aloft. They make a multitude of bright colors, strong and gay.

Detail in color

In his outstretched hand Constantine holds a little white cross out to the foe. The magic of the sacred sign has frightened the enemy soldiers who retreat in confusion.

One horseman has broken through the frozen river. We see his effort to reach the shore, but we already know how the story ends.

In our colored picture the right side of the painting is missing. But even the fragment shows us some of the brilliance that dazzles the eye of those who enter the chapel. All the walls are covered by paintings of Piero della Francesca with the story of the Holy Cross.

Men and horses in these paintings are rigid in their motions, because the paintings still belong to the early period of the Renaissance, but the colors are beautifully natural. We feel the air as only Piero della Francesca could make it felt. It is shining and clear as only Piero della Francesca could make it look.

Most striking of all is the victorious power of the little white cross, held out with so simple a gesture yet signifying so much.

Piero della Francesca's paintings are not only beautiful but also full of meaning. He was not only a great painter but also a great man.

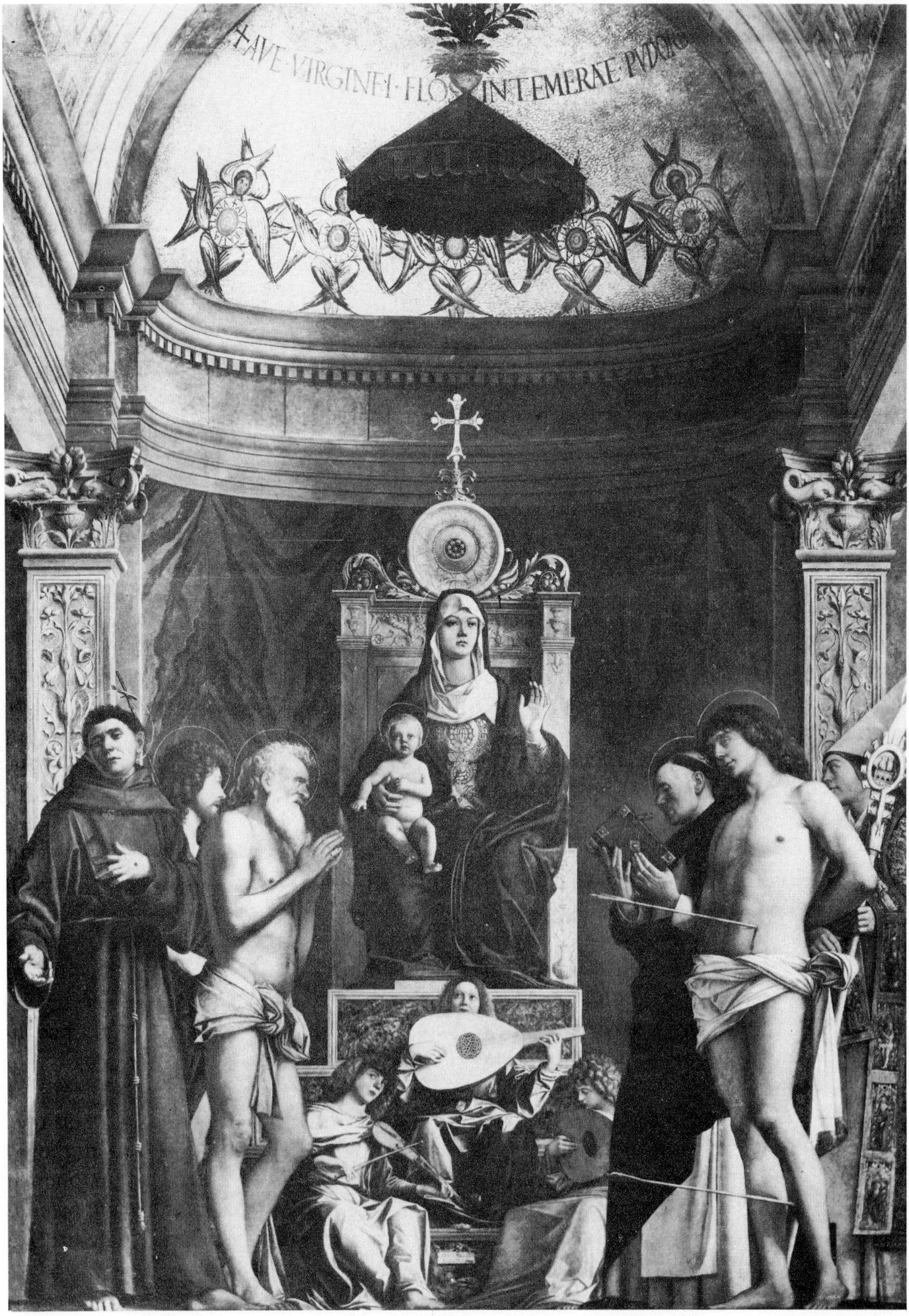
AVE·VIRGINEI·FLOS·INTEMERATE

We Look into Heaven—It is a Part of the Church

LEGEND tells us that after the Virgin Mary had died, Angels came to her grave and carried her up to Heaven.

In this picture, high above our eyes, we see her, the Madonna, Queen of Heaven, on her throne.

The throne is painted to look like white marble. It is decorated with the same sort of fine carvings as we find on the painted pilasters at the sides of the apse.

This picture is now in the Academy of Fine Arts in Venice. When it was still in the Church of St. Job, for which it was painted, it was flanked by pilasters of real marble that looked exactly the same as the painted ones.

This was done for a purpose. The real pilasters seemed to belong to the painting, but they were also part of the real chapel where the painting was placed above the altar. The picture looked as if it were a continuation of the chapel. The Queen of Heaven seemed to be in the same room with those who were in the chapel.

Her raised hand asks for quiet devotion. The Baby Jesus on her lap looks upward with a solemn expression, His hand is also slightly raised as if in adoration. Or is He listening to the prayers of the old Saint next to him? This Saint is St. Job. He is the only one who is directly connected with the Holy Child and His Mother as he raises his eyes and folded hands toward them. This is because this picture was painted for a church that was dedicated to St. Job.

The other Saint next to the throne is the scholarly St. Dominic, reading a book.

The arrows in the body of the Saint next to him show us that he is St. Sebastian because we know that he died of wounds caused by arrows.

In the background we can see the figures of St. John at the left and St. Augustine (the bishop) at the right, while St. Francis turns to us and invites us to join in worship, as heavenly music is played by the Angels on the steps of the throne.

We can almost feel the warm golden light that streams from the golden mosaic of the apse. It strikes the lute of the Angel in the center, and we can all but hear the celestial music.

Looking at this beautiful painting we feel that we are actually part of the heavenly gathering. This is the special magic of the artist Giovanni Bellini, the first great Renaissance painter of golden Venice. He was able to make his magnificent buildings and his heavenly figures look real; yet he painted them with such radiant beauty that as we look from our shadowy place in the chapel we can only wonder and worship.

THE MADONNA OF ST. JOB painted 1480
by Giovanni Bellini (about 1431-1516)

Academy, Venice, Italy

In Venice Even Portraits Have Radiant Colors

FOR many centuries the pictures artists painted were almost all of religious subjects. In early paintings even portraits of real persons were put into religious pictures, as we saw in the *Ghent Altar-piece* (p. 80) and in Masaccio's *Toll Money* (p. 78-79).

During the Middle Ages people did not think of having portraits made of themselves. But during the Renaissance, when people became more interested in the world around them, portrait painting became popular, particularly in Venice.

This picture, by Giovanni Bellini, is a portrait of a young Venetian gentleman. We see no special devotion in his face; he is just thoughtful. He wears a simple jacket, but the scarf over his bonnet is decorative, as was the fashion of the day. The bright red color of his jacket and his shining black scarf accent the pale features framed by his dark hair.

A similar color contrast gives interest to his gaze. The clearest white in the picture is the white of his eye, as the black of his eye is the darkest. This contrast is brought out even more by the little white dot in the black that highlights the young man's gaze.

The eye was most keenly observed by Bellini. He was the first of the Venetian painters to give so much human expression to his figures. The thoughtful mood of this young man is so catching that we find ourselves feeling dreamy and thoughtful just looking at him.

The young man's black scarf sets his figure apart from the clouded blue sky. The lively colors of his garment are particularly effective against this pale background, and the clouded sky is exactly the right setting for his moody features.

All the painters of Venice loved to paint the sky and the clouds. In Venice light changes from hour to hour, even from minute to minute. It can turn in a moment from radiant blue to pink and gold, from a shining brilliance to subdued dusky tones.

This is probably why light and color are more important than drawing in Venetian art, and why most Venetian artists became painters rather than sculptors.

In contrast to the city of Florence, Venice had very few sculptors. In Florence the light is clear, almost harsh. This sort of light makes all shapes look clear so that they can be readily reproduced in drawing or in sculpture. That is why Florentine art is so famous for good drawing and sculpture.

But Venice has given us another form of beauty: paintings of rich and mellow colors, soft in mood and delicately warm in feeling.

PORTRAIT OF A YOUNG MAN painted about 1480
by Giovanni Bellini (about 1431-1516)

National Gallery of Art, Washington, D. C.
Mellon Collection

GATTAMELATA sculptured about 1448 by Donatello (1386-1466)

First Monument of a General on Horseback

Padua, Italy

THE proud man we see here on his trotting horse is General Gattamelata. Gattamelata is a nickname: it is Italian for "mixed-color cat." You know, of course, that mixed-color cats are the best mouse-catchers. That is why this General got the nickname of Gattamelata. He was the shrewdest of Generals in outwitting the enemy.

In this monument General Gattamelata sits in his saddle fully armed. But he is perfectly relaxed, and easy with the reins. With his General's staff in his hand, he seems to be riding slowly along the lines, mustering his armies.

Gattamelata is square-headed and bulky and his horse is bulky and heavy too.

To make the four slender legs of a horse support such a heavy mass in the materials of sculpture is a most difficult task. Stone would be sure to break. It can be done only in hollow bronze.

To show a horse in motion, at least one leg has to be lifted off the ground. That is why Donatello, the sculptor of this monument, put a ball under one forefoot of this horse. He did not know how to make a horse balance on three legs, and so he did not dare to lift the foot without support. But still he wanted to make the horse look as if it were marching.

Donatello made both horse and rider look simple and impressive. Yet we can see, by the delicate workmanship on the ornaments in the General's armor, that he was also a master of fine detail. This was a skill he learned when he began his career as a jeweler. But being a great artist and also a great man, Donatello made this monument look really great and really monumental.

COLLEONI sculptured 1479-1488
by Andrea Verocchio (1435-1488)

Second Monument of a General on Horseback

Venice, Italy

IN THIS picture we see a monument of another warrior, General Colleoni. It was made in Venice but also by a Florentine sculptor, Andrea Verocchio. This monument was begun about thirty years after Donatello's monument of Gattamelata, and it took ten years to complete it.

Like Gattamelata, General Colleoni sits in his saddle fully armed, even to a helmet. But there is nothing relaxed about Colleoni. Although his hand seems barely to touch the reins, we feel that he is directing his horse with great energy by the pressure of his knees. The horse seems to be walking as if on springs. The slenderness of its legs seems to quicken its gait. The General grimly surveys his troops, almost standing in the stirrups, ready for action.

In spite of his heavier armor, General Colleoni rides a lighter animal than Gattamelata's. Here the horse is carefully groomed, mane and tail. The fine ornaments of the harness show that the sculptor wanted to give a decorative rather than a monumental effect.

Since this later artist, Verocchio, knew how to make horse and rider balance on only three of the horse's legs, he could lift one foreleg and leave it without support. That is another reason why we feel that this slender animal can move along at a quicker pace than Gattamelata's heavy battle-horse.

Both monuments are placed on high bases so that the outlines of horses and riders stand out imposingly against the sky. Both stand on Venetian ground, although they were made by Florentine sculptors. That was because Venice had no important sculptors, being the home of great painters, while Florence was the home of the most outstanding sculptors.

PALAZZO RUCELLAI built 1451
by Leon Battista Alberti (1404-1472)

Renaissance Palaces

In Florence
the Design is Sharp

Florence, Italy

THIS is the famous palace of the Rucellai family in Florence. They had their palace designed by the most modern architect of the time, Leon Battista Alberti.

The time was the Renaissance. To be modern at that time, strangely enough, an architect had to imitate the art of the ancient Greeks and Romans.

The architect of this palace did that by repeating the design of Greek and Roman styles on the front of the three floors of the house. Pilasters, as we saw them on the Colosseum (p. 44), seem to support the cross-beams. But they do not give real support. They are merely decoration. There is solid wall behind them.

The pilasters supporting the cross-beams are simplest on the first floors. They get fancier on the second and still fancier on the third. The stone blocks of the wall also get finer and smaller from floor to floor.

The windows are topped by Roman arches. The openings are flanked by half columns. These and a full column in the middle support the cross-beams of the windows.

Another Renaissance feature of the building is its symmetry. In any symmetrical design both halves of the design mirror one another.

This entire palace looks rather sharp as was usual in Florentine palaces at the time of the Renaissance. But the architect was able to make it look both noble and simple, fitting well into the narrow streets of Florence.

Men who looked like Giuliano Medici (p.100) lived in palaces like these.

PALAZZO VENDRAMIN-CALERGHI
built 1481
by Pietro Lombardo (1435-1515)

In Venice a Similar
Design Looks Softer

Venice, Italy

THIS is the Venetian palace where the great German composer Richard Wagner died. It was built by Pietro Lombardo, in a style similar to the Florentine palace of the Rucellai on the opposite page. The most striking difference between the two palaces is that the Florentine palace looks hard because of its sharp design while the Venetian palace looks softer and friendlier.

Here the architect used columns instead of pilasters. Columns are rounded, not hard and angular as pilasters are. Columns shed soft and melting shadows while the pilasters' shadows are sharp and straight.

Here the wall, where it can be seen, is smooth as if it were covered by a soft skin, while in Florence we see what seem to be the naked bones of which the palace is built: the stones themselves.

The symmetry of the Venetian palace is emphasized by the single door in the center. The palace also looks richer and more interesting because the simple rhythm of windows and columns is varied by ornamental wall spaces between the columns. The balcony on the second floor gives the same effect.

Last but not least, the Venetian palace stands right over water and not on a street. Instead of streets, Venice has canals where people get about in small boats called gondolas. Marble steps leading to the gondolas from the palace give even greater elegance to the building.

The young man in a red garment (p.95) lived in a palace like this one.

GIULIANO MEDICI sculptured about 1475
by Andrea Verocchio (1435-1488)

National Gallery of Art, Washington, D. C.
Mellon Collection

The Man of the Renaissance is Bold and Fearless

THIS sculptured bust is a portrait of Giuliano de Medici, a member of the most famous family in Florence. The Medicis were wealthy bankers and great patrons of the arts. Their palace was a meeting place of artists, poets, and philosophers. In and around Florence the Medicis had many fine homes decorated by the best sculptors and painters.

This bust shows Giuliano as a typical man of the Renaissance. His head is thrown back proudly; his neck is straight on his wide shoulders. He looks fresh and vigorous, ready for action.

Compared to the quiet earnestness of Gothic figures (p. 58-59) we find a challenge in Giuliano's stiff neck, squared shoulders, and unswerving eyes. His glance is not humbly lowered or lifted to God in prayer; he looks straight ahead.

Andrea Verocchio, who made this portrait, was the best sculptor of his time. He was a real artist of the Renaissance. He modeled Giuliano's face in large plain shapes with a few vigorous shadows. The proud face is surrounded by a frame of elaborate elegant curls full of changing lights and shadows, making the face itself look even more impressive.

Giuliano's ornate armor becomes wider toward the bottom, giving a secure base to the slender figure. A winged head on the armor reminds us of the Gorgon on the armor of Pallas Athena (p. 12). It is a good example of how Renaissance artists used ornaments of ancient Greece. But this is an unimportant detail. The important thing is that the artists now looked squarely at the world around them as the old Greeks and Romans did.

THE MADONNA OF THE LILIES
painted about 1480
by Sandro Botticelli
(1446-1510)

Staatliche Museen, Berlin, Germany

Our Lady is Sweet and Gentle

HERE we see the Madonna holding her Baby with slender hands as she listens to a concert of Angels around her. The choir is singing a song in her praise. Each Angel carries a white lily, a symbol of the Madonna's purity, and each holds the lily-stem straight up. That is, all but one. That one uses his stem to point to the song they are singing from the book. The Angels on the other side of the Madonna wait for their turn to chime in.

The Virgin is gentle and dreamy-eyed. Botticelli, the painter, made her look fragile and tender. People in the Medicis' sophisticated circle expected any beautiful lady to look like that whether she was the Christian Madonna or the pagan goddess of love, Venus (p.103).

Botticelli loved to paint flowers, as well as lovely ladies, because they too are fragile and tender. He liked their delicate shapes, their lovely designs, their beautiful colors.

When he painted his many pictures of the Madonna, he always painted her with her head bending like a flower on its stem. He made her skin transparent, and he drew her eyes and brow, as well as her nose and mouth, with clear lines, ever so lightly touched with color. We almost doubt whether he meant her to look like real flesh and blood, because he gave her such heavenly flower-like beauty.

Botticelli was a Florentine, and, as with other Florentine painters, his outlines are clear and firm. He managed to make them so whether he was drawing gossamer veils, fragile lilies, pagan goddesses, or exquisite Madonnas.

THE BIRTH OF VENUS painted about 1485
by Sandro Botticelli (1446-1510)

Uffizi Gallery, Palazzo degli Uffizi, Florence, Italy

Venus Rises from the Sea

HERE, in the faint light of an early spring morning, before sunrise, we see Venus, the goddess of love and beauty, just risen from the sea. This, according to an ancient Greek legend, is how Venus was born.

Under a gray-blue sky, above pale waters rippled by the breeze, Venus approaches the shore. She is standing on a sea-shell. The sea-shell is her boat, her golden hair her sail.

But the shell does not float toward the shore by itself. We see a man with a woman beside him helping it along. The man is the Spring Wind, Zephyr. He is blowing Venus's sea-shell boat gently toward the land. The woman is Flora, the bringer of sweet flowers. Pink roses spring from her hands. Filling the air with their fragrance they float and fly around Flora and Zephyr, toward the lovely Venus.

Meanwhile, from under the shade of the orange trees, a slender maiden, graceful as a dancing hour of spring, comes hurrying over the mossy ground. She holds up a royal garment of purple-pink brocade embroidered with golden roses and bordered by a golden hem. The garment is meant to cover the shoulders of Venus. The maiden's dress is embroidered with flowers too. She wears a wreath of rose twigs around her neck and a belt of rose branches around her waist. Roses are the flowers of Venus, goddess of love.

Botticelli painted this story about the birth of Venus for one of the country houses of the Medici family. Among the artists, poets, and scholars surrounding the Medicis were some refugees who had recently come to Italy from Greece. They brought with them all the wonderful lore of the ancient Greeks. And soon paintings of the gay pagan gods and goddesses of Greek mythology began to appear in Italy together with the Bible-story pictures that were so popular in the Middle Ages.

There was a springtime atmosphere about all this. First of all, it was the springtime of the Renaissance when it happened. And this rebirth of ancient art took place largely in the beautiful Italian town of Florence—the town whose very name means "city of flowers."

The great Florentine painter Botticelli was inspired by this revival of ancient art. His *Birth of Venus* tells a story inspired by Greek mythology while the figure of Venus is reminiscent of a Greek sculpture by Praxiteles.

But the face of Venus looks much like his sweet and dreamy and shy Madonnas (p.101). We can tell by the look in her eyes that the artist thought of her as a heavenly being.

HEAD OF VENUS (Detail)

BOTTICELLI drew this face with one definite outline. He made the brows, eyes, nose, and mouth with just a few sure strokes of the brush.

Venus's face meets her neck at a sharp angle, and the neck itself grows out of unnaturally sloping shoulders. These imperfections are here because when Botticelli painted this picture his skill at drawing the human body was not yet at its peak. Yet that may be the very reason we feel so tender toward the girl in the picture. A rosebud is not yet a fully developed flower, but many of us find it even lovelier than a rose in full bloom.

THE LAST SUPPER painted about 1495-1498
by Leonardo da Vinci (1453-1519)

Monastery of Sta. Maria delle Grazie,
Milan, Italy

The Greatest Painting of the Last Supper

ON THE EVE of the Passover celebration, Jesus and his twelve Apostles sat down to the Passover meal. They were thirteen at the table. It was to be their last supper together.

At the table, Jesus, suddenly troubled, announced to the Apostles that one of them would betray Him. Jesus did not say it would be Judas Iscariot, and the Apostles themselves did not know who it would be.

The great Italian artist, Leonardo da Vinci, painted the most famous of all pictures of this scene. He painted it directly on the dining-room wall of a monastery in Milan.

The twelve Apostles form four groups along the side of the table. Jesus sits in the center. Having made his announcement, He extends both hands in a sad gesture.

Most of the Apostles have sprung to their feet in excitement. Jesus' figure is calm. We see it clearly outlined against the window in the background wall. Through the window we see a quiet landscape. The blue sky surrounds Jesus' head like a glory.

In the group to the right of Jesus we see a dark figure. He leans far back as if shrinking away from Jesus. His elbow is on the table, a money-bag clutched in his hand. We know he is Judas Iscariot, the traitor.

The money-bag in Judas' hand is his symbol. It reminds us that he was the one who kept the money for Jesus and the Apostles, and also that it was thirty pieces of silver for which he betrayed Jesus.

But we would recognize Judas as the evil enemy by the way Leonardo painted him, even if he were not holding the money-bag.

Next to Judas' shadowy profile we see the silvery head and white hand of St. Peter who leans forward toward the youthful St. John. Peter's finger points toward Jesus. He whispers into John's ear, prompting him to ask Jesus who the traitor is. Peter's right hand, holding his knife, is on his hip. As if by chance, the knife is pointed toward the back of Judas.

St. John's head is bent toward Peter. Of all the Apostles, John is Jesus' favorite. John is quiet as Jesus is. He has already accepted the Master's words.

At the left of Jesus, next to him, sits James the Younger. Trying to understand the terrifying words he has heard, he throws his arms wide apart, crying out.

Over James' shoulder we see St. Thomas, doubting Thomas, his doubt expressed in a raised finger.

On the other side of James, St. Philip bends forward toward Jesus, bringing both hands close to his breast. He seems to be saying. "You know my heart and You know that I shall never betray You." His face trembles with love and devotion.

These six Apostles around Jesus are in the center of what is happening.

Bartholomew and the older James lean toward them, while next to them old Andrew does not rise to see, but tries to listen. His raised hands seem to ask for quiet.

The remaining three Apostles at the right point toward the middle of the table. They are discussing Jesus' prediction that one of them will betray Him.

We understand at sight all that is happening in this great painting. But we gain new insight into the characters and feelings of the Apostles every time we look at them.

Leonardo da Vinci had thought deeply about human character and feeling. Innumerable drawings by his hand show this. He studied different types of people with different expressions on their faces. We feel the deep insight as well as the artistic genius of this great man in all his paintings. Both have remained unsurpassed thoughout the ages.

The deep insight of this great man has remained unsurpassed throughout the ages. This is one of the reasons why Leonardo da Vinci's *Last Supper* is the greatest of the many great paintings artists have made of this story.

Another reason, just as important, is that this painter of rare genius makes us see what is happening more clearly than any other painter has been able to do before him or since.

Detail: St. Philip

The Most Famous Portrait in the World

TO THE people of Florence, indeed to all the Italian people, it was known that Leonardo da Vinci was a genius. He was the first painter who could make portraits of people lifelike and beautiful at the same time.

That is why a wealthy merchant, Giocondo, commissioned him to paint a portrait of his beautiful young wife, Mona Lisa, also called "La Gioconda."

The story goes that Leonardo da Vinci took four years to paint this portrait. When he finished it, he was unwilling to give it to Giocondo or to anybody else. He took the portrait of Mona Lisa with him when he left Italy for France at the invitation of the French King.

Leonardo da Vinci died in France. That is why the portrait of Mona Lisa has remained in France. It is a proud possession of the French people.

Why is the *Mona Lisa* so famous? People have talked for centuries about her mysterious smile. Her smile is indeed mysterious: it seems to change.

How did the artist achieve this effect? We have seen how an expression can change in sculpture, for instance in the face of the *Hermes* by Praxiteles (p.34). There the rounded surfaces reflect the light so subtly that the statue seems to smile or to have a serious expression depending on how the light changes.

In a painting the change of light cannot make so much difference as in sculpture. But in the face of the *Mona Lisa,* faint shadows seem to come and go, veiling the exact outlines of her eyes and of her mouth. We cannot see their expression clearly. That is what makes her so mysterious.

There is a story that Leonardo had musicians play while he was painting Mona Lisa, so that she would not tire of sitting quietly as a model. The expression of her eyes shows us that she is listening. And now, if we look at her beautiful hands and think of them in connection with her face, we feel the expression more intensely. The right hand rests very lightly on the left. The middle finger has no support at all. We feel that it is following the music with a light beat.

When we look at the landscape behind this life-like figure we are stunned to see how unreal it looks. Mountain peaks and water, roads, a bridge, all appear in a dream-like uncertainty, as if to prove that Mona Lisa's mind is in a dream world.

Mona Lisa's dreaming figure and the dream world around her were created by Leonardo da Vinci's genius. This explains why the portrait of the Mona Lisa has become the most haunting and most famous portrait in the world.

MONA LISA painted about 1500-1504
by Leonardo da Vinci (1453-1519)

The Louvre, Paris, France

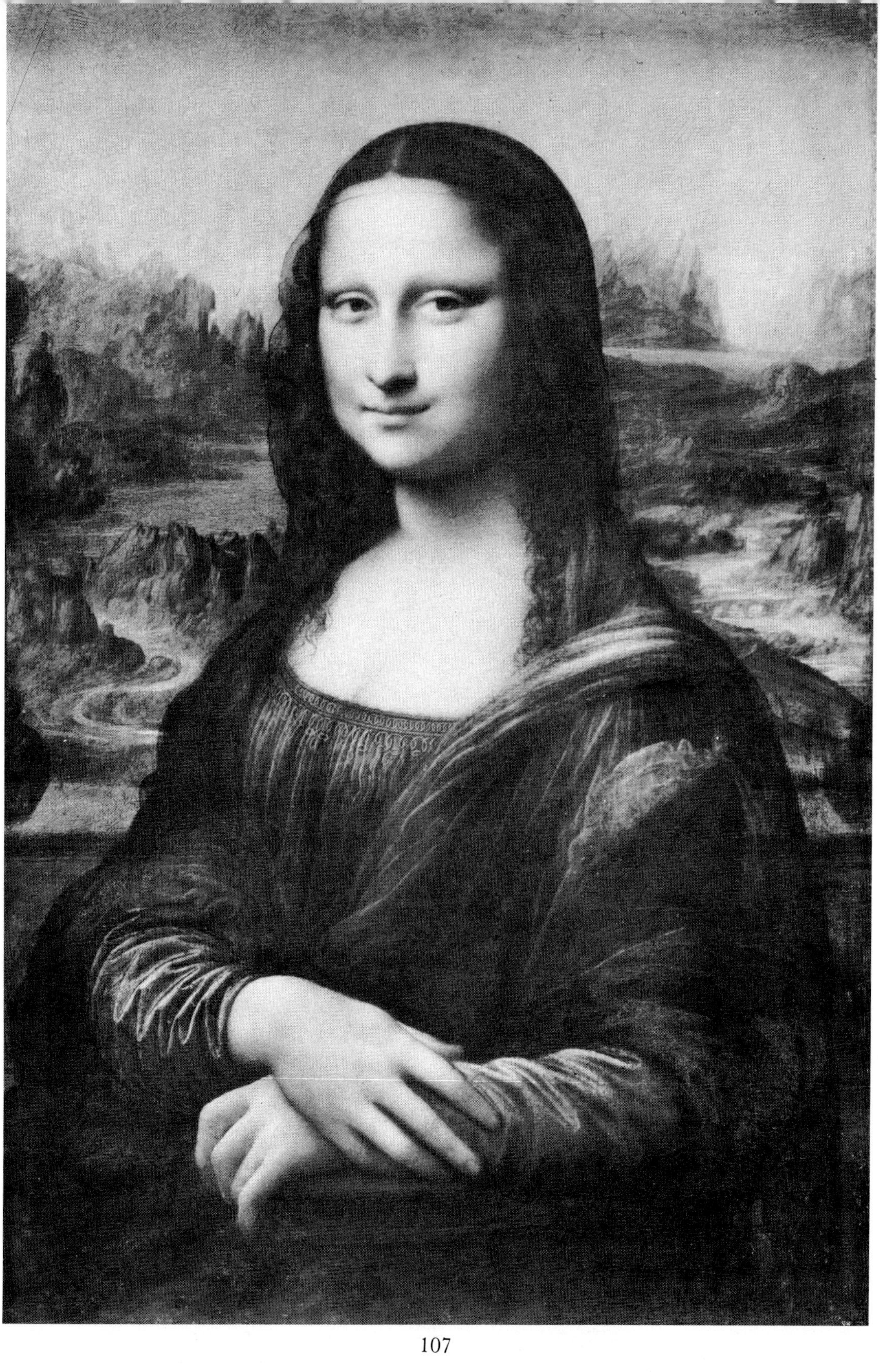

HEAD OF DAVID (Detail)

The Boy David Defeats the Giant Goliath

WE KNOW, from the Bible story of David and Goliath, that the young Israelite, David, was just a boy when he slew the Philistine giant Goliath, and that in so doing he freed his country.

The way it happened, you remember, was this: The Philistines declared war on Israel. The giant Goliath was the Philistine's most powerful fighter and enormously proud of his strength. Parading up and down in front of Israel's small army, he challenged any one who would meet him in single combat. The winner in this single combat would at the same time win the war for his country.

The young shepherd boy of Israel, David, offered to take up the challenge. The King of Israel agreed to let him try. He gave David his mightiest weapons and heaviest armor. But David, untrained as he was in war, knew his slender body could not sustain the weapons or the armor. He decided to meet the enemy with only a sling and a few stones.

With his first shot, David hit Goliath in the head and felled him. With only that simple weapon, plus his own faith and courage, the boy won a war and freed his country.

To honor the young Biblical hero, the liberty-loving people of Florence commissioned a young Florentine sculptor to make a statue of David. His name was Michelangelo Buonaroti, but because of his great fame he has become known as Michelangelo alone.

The Florentines gave him a huge marble block to work with. Unfortunately, however, another sculptor had tried to work on it before and had cut a big hole in it. The marble had remained unused for thirty years. But Michelangelo began work on it in spite of its defect. He was sure he could find some way of using the hole to good purpose.

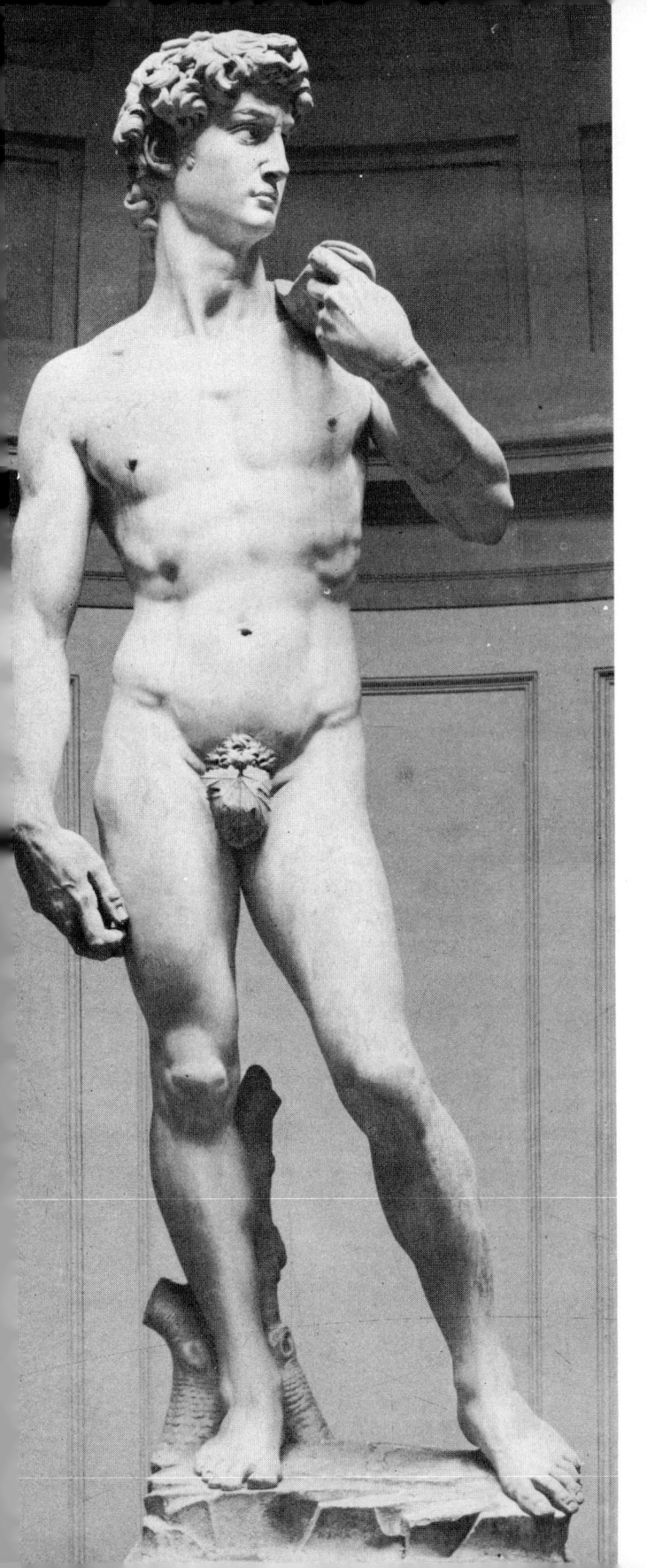

He chose for his statue the moment just before the fight when David was sizing up his enemy. He made his figure of David standing firmly on his right leg with his left leg well apart from it. The hole in the marble quite naturally became the space between.

David's head and neck are slightly withdrawn as he measures the distance between himself and his enemy. His face shows concentrated energy. With narrowed brows he ponders his chances. Holding a stone in his right hand, feeling and weighing its force, his left hand fingers the sling hanging over his shoulder. His glance seems to say, "Let the enemy come. I am ready."

A copy of Michelangelo's great statue of David still stands in front of the Town Hall in the city of Florence. It is eighteen feet high—the height of three six-footers one on top of the other. But the proportions of the figure are those of a young boy. The head, hands, and feet are large compared to the rest of the body, as a boy's are. David is slim but he looks hard as nails.

Michelangelo's work is often recognized by the muscular and forceful bodies in both his sculpture and his painting. Michelangelo was also an architect, and in this art too, he was always monumental and earnest. He was a master in all three arts.

Michelangelo was also a poet. His poems show us, by the beauty of their thought, how sublime and exalted his spirit was.

DAVID sculptured 1504
  by Michelangelo Buonaroti (1475-1564)

Academy, Florence, Italy

A Painted Story of St. George and the Dragon

WE ALREADY know the story of St. George and the dragon from the relief (p. 76) under the statue of St. George by the sculptor Donatello (p. 77). St. George was a most popular saint and his story has often been shown in sculpture and in paintings too.

The picture we see here was made by the painter Raphael. Raphael was one of the greatest painters of the Italian Renaissance. His fame is world-wide, although his painting career lasted only about fifteen years, because he died when he was very young. When he painted this picture of St. George he was not more than about twenty years old.

Raphael was a cheerful and agreeable young man as we can see by the way he painted the story of St. George and the dragon.

The scene of the painting is a fresh Spring meadow sprinkled with flowers under a light blue sky. The dragon, who is really not very dreadful in Raphael's painting, has come out of his cave under the softly rounded rocks topped by grass and a couple of tender young trees.

St. George wears an armor of steel, which is usually gray, but Raphael has painted it in a more friendly blue. St. George sits lightly in the saddle on his white horse. Although the horse is rearing, it does so good-humoredly. It looks gaily out of the picture at us, unconcerned about the fight. After all, the horse seems to feel, nothing really wrong could possibly happen on such a bright morning.

The trees and bushes of the friendly hills wear their first Spring foliage. The silvery edges of the leaves shimmer in the mild sunlight.

The lovely Princess in her red robe looks like a bright flower in the meadow. Her white veil flutters in the Spring breeze, as does the mantle of St. George and maybe even the tail of his white horse.

The Princess is on her knees praying—no doubt, that St. George will win the fight.

At a distance, the light towers of the imperilled city are shown against the pale blue horizon. We feel that the town will soon be liberated and people will again enjoy their lives, free from danger.

This picture shows us the hopeful outlook of a young and gifted painter. Like his St. George, Raphael himself gained an easy victory, in the field of painting. He was on his way to victory when he painted this picture. That is why it breathes the sunny health of a Spring day with everything about it friendly and light-hearted and gay.

ST. GEORGE AND THE DRAGON painted about 1505
by Raphael (1483-1520)

PHILOSOPHY painted 1508-1511
by Raphael (1483-1520)

The Vatican, Rome, Italy

A Gathering of Wise Men in Ancient Greece

SOON after Columbus discovered America, many new discoveries were also made in the world of art.

People were excited about the world around them. They wanted to see it both as it really was and as it appeared to their eyes. Artists were especially affected by this new curiosity. They began to make men and women, plants and animals, landscapes and buildings and everything in the landscapes and buildings as they really looked.

But the painter Raphael, who was only nine years old when America was discovered, went a step further: he painted the world to look real and beautiful too. His buildings are not only true likenesses but they are impressive as well. His men are not only life-like but also noble and important.

Raphael was already famous for his talent when he was still a very young man. That is why Pope Julius II invited him to come to Rome to decorate some of the rooms of the Vatican palace where the Popes live.

The first room to be decorated with paintings by Raphael was the room where the Pope signed legal documents, therefore called *The Room of Signature*. It became world-famous because of Raphael's paintings. The walls of this room are devoted to pictures telling stories of justice and wisdom.

One wall shows the wisdom of the ancient Greeks in a gathering of famous Greek philosophers. The philosophers have met in a big marble building and are being followed by a crowd of young men. That is why this painting is often called *The School of Athens*.

Lofty marble halls with high vaults are open against the sky. Numerous niches in the walls are adorned with sculptures. At the left we see a statue of Apollo, god of music and harmony, with a lyre in his hand. One of the aims of wisdom is to live in harmony. In the niche at the right stands the statue of Pallas Athena, goddess of knowledge and the arts.

Many scholars are gathered in the wide halls. They study and examine, they draw, they write. Two of them stand out under the central vault, clearly outlined against the blue sky. They are Plato and Aristotle, the most famous and venerated philosophers of ancient Greece. They express their different points of view as Aristotle points to the world before him and Plato points to heaven.

At Aristotle's side we see some scholars examining the globe and others studying geometry. The master measures something on a tablet with his compass while his pupils look on with lively interest.

At the side of Plato, his teacher Socrates is explaining problems to his pupils. Under these a group of wise men seem to be studying harmony.

In the detail below you see Plato and Aristotle.

Plato's lean features are painted with large sweeping lines. The deep-set eyes concentrate on deep thought and high ideals. Aristotle's firmly modeled face looks happier. It shows a more lively, more practical intelligence.

Both figures show great dignity and look very noble because the painter Raphael had real inner nobility and dignity himself. It is the greatness *in* the painter that makes him a great painter. It is also what makes him able to show us the beauty and greatness in the world.

PLATO AND ARISTOTLE (Detail)

The Loveliest Madonnas are Raphael's

IN THIS picture we see the Madonna sitting on a bench in a friendly landscape. The day is mild and clear: we can see the distant mountains as they melt into the light blue of the sky.

A few bushes to the right lead our eye up to a little Church on the hill. This reminds us that the young Mother and her Baby belong to the world of religion. Two light circles around the heads of Mother and Child are the only other signs of their sanctity. Raphael needed no signs of this kind to show what he meant. He painted the young Mother's sweet and dreamy face so gently that when we see it we can think only of the Madonna. In fact, when we say that a lovely girl looks like a Madonna, we have in mind the sort of face Raphael painted here.

Her wide eyes are not looking at anything particular, because they follow her thoughts. She is thinking so deeply that she seems not to notice that the Baby Jesus has put His little foot on her hand in her lap. With her other hand she supports the Child.

When we try to see the hands and the face of the Madonna together, we feel that while she seems to have forgotten the presence of the Child, she is thinking of Him and of what His future will be.

Compared to His Mother, little Jesus is painted to look bigger than a child of his age would naturally be. Raphael painted the Child that way to give Him importance in the picture. His expression is sweet but earnest. He looks down at us, because this picture was meant to be placed high, above an altar. The Child Jesus looks at us from His high place as if listening to our prayers and answering them.

Yet the little Jesus and His Mother are lovingly close as any human mother and her baby would be.

It is hard to believe that this simple young Madonna was modeled after a pagan Greek goddess. Look back at the sweet face of Praxiteles' Venus on page 34, and see how similar to it this Madonna's face is as Raphael painted it: the evenly rounded oval of the face with its gently modeled forehead, wide-set eyes, straight nose, and small mouth. This is because Raphael was an artist of the Renaissance who never stopped studying the art of the ancients.

But mark the differences: Raphael softened the beautiful face of Venus. He painted a finer and milder version of the ancient goddess and so gave new Christian meaning to an ancient pagan work of art.

Raphael gave new life to ancient beauty. In his paintings ancient art was reborn and developed to new perfection of a different kind. In Raphael the art of the Renaissance reached its peak.

THE SMALL COWPER MADONNA painted about 1508
by Raphael (1483-1520)

National Gallery of Art, Washington, D. C.
Widener Collection

SELF-PORTRAIT drawn 1484
by Albrecht Dürer (1471-1528)

A Great Master as a Boy

Owned by the Graphic Collection Albertina,
Vienna, Austria

ALBRECHT DÜRER was just a boy of about thirteen when he drew this portrait of himself from a mirror. In a mirror the right side looks like the left and vice versa. Dürer could not copy his *right* hand because he was drawing with it—and that is why he has no *left* hand in the drawing.

In his later years Dürer wrote that if you want to become a master you must begin drawing when you are very young and practise continually. Dürer himself practised like that and he became the greatest master of drawing in Germany.

The softness of his face and hair in this drawing shows us how keenly his eyes saw what was there. He was only a young boy, but even then he could make his portraits true to life. And he became better and better at it as time went on.

THE HARE painted 1502

This water color of a hare was made by Dürer when he was a mature and great master. Soft of body and pelt, fearful and alert, ready to jump, this hare looks and behaves like a real hare, and is endearing too.

Owned by the Graphic Collection Albertina,
Vienna, Austria

ST. EUSTACHE engraved about 1503
by Albrecht Dürer (1471-1528)

A Masterpiece of Engraving

Courtesy of the Metropolitan Museum of Art, New York, N. Y.

ST. EUSTACHE, you will remember from the stained glass window telling his story (p. 67), was converted to Christianity by the vision of a white deer with a crucifix between his antlers.

In this picture by the German master-craftsman, Albrecht Dürer, we see St. Eustache kneeling before his miraculous vision. He has dismounted, and his horse and dogs are patiently waiting while he holds up his hands in the ancient gesture of adoration.

We see his castle high up on the rocky hill where a gay hunting party had started out. Underneath there is a little river with a bridge, and there are buildings in the background. Many sorts of trees, young ones with light leafage and old ones all gnarled and bare, in many shapes and shades of gray, make the picture look lively and interesting. But in spite of so much detail, this picture makes us feel the religious stillness surrounding St. Eustache and his miraculous vision.

In the part of Europe Dürer came from, artists liked to show where things happened as well as how. They studied the landscape carefully and reproduced it faithfully in paintings or in engravings, as in this engraving by Dürer.

An engraving is made by carving a picture with a sharp implement on a copper plate. The grooves are filled in with printer's ink and the copper plate is then pressed onto paper. The imprint of the engraved lines reproduces the picture on the paper.

Many imprints can be made from one copper plate. That is why engravings are usually cheaper than paintings. But for an engraving by such a great master as Dürer museums will pay more than they will for a painting by a lesser artist.

ST. ANTHONY AND ST. PAUL
painted 1509-1511
by Mathias Grünewald
(dates unknown)

Museum Unterlinden, Colmar, France

Two Holy Men and the Animals that Helped Them

IN THE Middle Ages men who were especially religious often went into monasteries to become monks and devote their lives to learning and prayer.

But, according to the *Golden Legend,* the monk Anthony felt that this was not enough. He decided to go into the desert alone, to eat and drink only what he found there, and to dedicate his entire life to God.

The monk Anthony thought he was the first man ever to retire from the world in this way. But he dreamt one night that there was another hermit in the desert who was a better and holier man than himself.

When he awoke, Anthony thought there must actually be such a man; so he set out to search the woods for him. In his search he encountered a doe, and the doe led him to a hermit whose name was Paul.

Paul was a very old man who lived in the wilderness all alone. His only garment was a shirt of braided palm leaves, his only food was bread that a raven brought him.

When the monk Anthony came to him, the two men sat down and looked at each other with love and understanding. They got along so beautifully that they did not realize how fast the hours were passing. When meal-time came around, however, the raven arrived as usual. And lo, the bird had brought a double portion of bread, one for Paul and one for Anthony.

Finally Anthony returned to his hut. But alas, when he looked up, he saw an Angel carrying St. Paul's soul to heaven.

Anthony returned to the place where St. Paul had lived and found that he was indeed dead. He wanted to bury the holy man, but he had nothing to dig a grave with. As he was wondering what to do, two lions appeared. They dug the grave and returned to the forest. Anthony buried his friend. Then, discarding his monk's frock, he put on the humble garment of St. Paul, the first holy hermit.

In our picture we see the two holy men as they sit in the desert, and between them the doe that had guided Anthony to Paul. Above Anthony we see the raven bringing them the double portion of bread.

A lone palm tree with spiky leaves marks the hermit's quiet place. Dry moss covers the rocks and dead trees. A shallow brook keeps some sparse grasses alive.

In the distance mighty pale-tinted mountains melt into the sky. The air is calm and cool. The two holy men live only for the love of God. The rest of the world does not even exist for them. The miracle of the raven bringing their bread fills Anthony with wonder, but the older and holier Paul receives it with the thanks of one who has natural faith that God will give him his daily bread.

This picture is part of a monumental altar-piece now in Colmar, France. But originally it was painted for the St. Anthony monastery in Isenheim, Germany.

It was painted by a mysterious German Renaissance painter, Mathias Grünewald. We have no record of when he was born or when he died. But we know that he painted the pictures of this altar, and we can see that no one could more impressively have painted the quiet life of the hermits.

THE PROPHET JONAH (Detail) painted 1511
by Michelangelo Buonaroti (1475-1564)

The Most Magnificent Chapel in the World

ABOUT ten years before America was discovered by Christopher Columbus, another Italian, Pope Sixtus IV, ordered a series of magnificent frescoes to be made for the chapel he had had built in Rome—the Sistine Chapel.

The Pope asked some of the finest artists of Italy to paint the stories of Moses and of Christ on the chapel walls. Each one of these pictures was bigger than the whole wall of a good-sized room. Above these stories the same artists were to paint pictures of the Popes.

All these paintings, belonging to the period of the early Renaissance, made the Sistine Chapel the most richly decorated chapel of that time. But about twenty years later, when the Renaissance was at its height, the great artist Michelangelo added the most dazzling paintings to the ceiling of the chapel, making it even richer and more beautiful.

Michelangelo made the chapel look larger by painting architectural structures onto the vaulted ceiling. Into this painted setting of what looks like architecture, in the center, along the ceiling, he painted stories of the Creation, of Adam and Eve, and of Noah. At the sides he painted the majestic figures of prophets and sibyls. All these Michelangelo painted when he was a young man.

When he was old he added the story of the Last Judgment on the "narrow" wall above the altar. This wall is about 52 feet wide. Not really very narrow, you see, except comparatively. And it is 60 feet high—about six times the height of an ordinary room.

But it is not the colossal size of these paintings that makes Michelangelo's frescoes so remarkable. It is his tremendous greatness as an artist. His paintings in the Sistine Chapel are the most magnificent in the world.

THE SISTINE CHAPEL (Interior) built 1475-148▶
decorated by many artists (1481-1541)

The Vatican, Rome, Italy

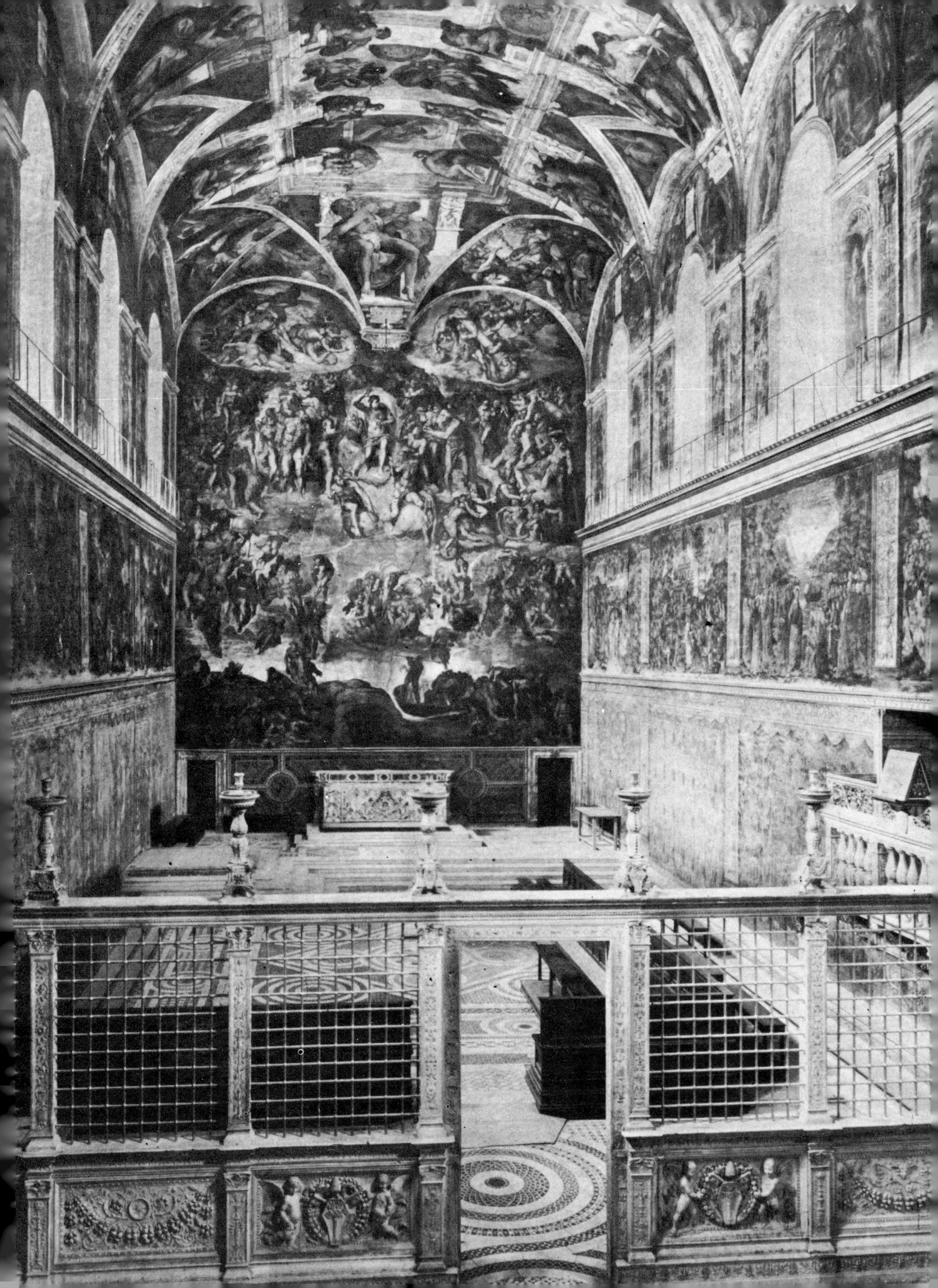

Two Heads and Two Hands Tell a Story

JUST like the house of the Medicis in Florence, the court of the Este Princes was a gathering place of scholars and poets in Ferrara. Like the Medicis, too, the Este Princes engaged the best artists to decorate their palace. Among these artists was the greatest of all the painters of Venice: Titian.

It was Titian who painted the picture on the opposite page for Prince Alfonso d'Este.

There you see the noble figure of Christ looking at a simple man who turns to Him, a golden coin in his outstretched hand. The tanned skin of his rather coarse face and hand shows us that he is a workingman. He is contrasted with Christ, who has an upright slender figure and pale and refined features. His hand seems to be almost transparent against the brown fist of the man. His face emerges with white radiance from the surrounding shadow. It is framed by his dark hair and beard. In his thoughtful expression we feel that he is answering the humble man's question about the money he holds in his hand, that he and all should pay what is due to everybody. This is what money is coined for.

The words of the Bible *"Render unto Caesar the things which are Caesar's, and unto God the things which are God's"* were inscribed on the money of Prince Alfonso d'Este, who had this picture set into the front of one of his cabinets.

This painting is not only meaningful and expressive but also beautiful because of the lovely coloring which was Titian's greatest glory.

Christ wears a red robe that falls into lively folds under His blue mantle. His figure not only takes up the biggest part of the picture, but has the rich color combination of red and blue in contrast with the simple white garment of the man who turns to Him with his question. It reminds us of another contrast, the contrast between the wealth of wisdom and the poverty of ignorance.

Mysterious shadows give depth to the picture. The lovely harmony of red and blue, with some yellow added for warmth, was often used by the painters of Venice. They often added white too, to make their pictures lighter.

The Venetian painters created unmatched beauty of color that remained unique for centuries in the world of art.

THE TRIBUTE MONEY painted about 1516
by Titian (1477-1576)

Dresden Gallery, Dresden, Germany

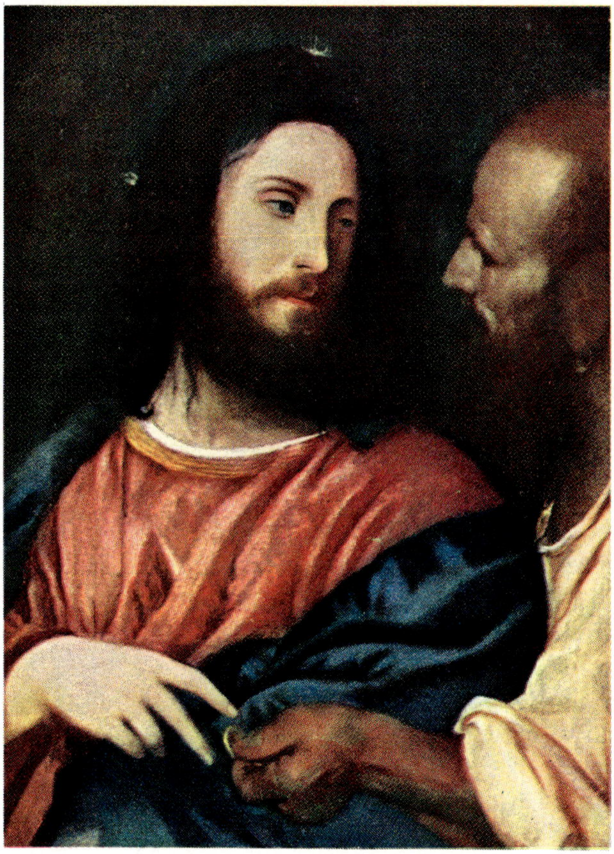

The Maiden and the Goddess of Love

THIS picture tells us the story of a beautiful maiden who did not want to marry, although a noble knight who loved her very much asked her to be his wife. It was only when Venus, the goddess of love, persuaded her to change her mind that she finally said yes to her suitor.

Let's try to read this story in the picture.

In the early evening light, when the colors of the sky are deepest and strongest, and the shadows below begin to soften the colors of the earth, we see a maiden seated at a fountain. She is clothed in festive garments of white and crimson satin and wears a wreath in her hair. She has the loveliness of a bride.

What is she thinking about? We can see in her eyes that her mind is on important matters. Perhaps she is thinking of her future husband and all that is in store for her.

At the other end of the fountain we see Venus, the goddess of beauty and love. We know she is Venus because she is even more beautiful than the maiden and she is unclothed. Painters almost always painted Venus that way so that the divine beauty of her body could be seen and appreciated. We see that she must have flown here because the red mantle about her shoulder is still fluttering.

Venus is bending toward the bride-to-be trying to persuade her to take the sacred vow of marriage. With her left hand Venus holds up a small bowl from which we see incense rising to the sky. The painter meant this as a sign of sacred love.

Between the figures of Venus and the maiden we see Venus' son, Cupid, the little god of love, reaching for roses in the water of the fountain. He is quite close to the bride-to-be because it is for her that he is gathering the roses. As you see, he has already put one rose on the rim of the fountain at her fingertips.

When we look at this picture closely, we find even more of the story. To the left, in the background, we see a castle. In all likelihood it is where the maiden lives. We can see that she is a lady of the nobility, richly dressed and bejewelled as she is. And it is a noble knight who is galloping toward the castle on his white horse. Surely he is the maiden's future bridegroom.

This part of the picture is full of shadows because it belongs to the earth. The lady is an earthly creature too. But Venus, the goddess, belongs to the higher sphere of the bright and radiant heavens. Around her the sky displays its color-magic, redoubled by reflection in the lake. A Church tower reaching into the sky points to heaven. The rest of the earth with its shepherds and sheep, prancing horses and dogs, is far below in the shadows.

Because of these contrasts, this picture is generally called *Earthly and Heavenly Love*. It was painted by Titian at the height of the Renaissance when artists made pictures look harmonious and beautiful and well-balanced. The beauty of ancient art, with its gods and goddesses of mythology, was reborn and given new warm life by the rich and mellow colors of Titian's masterly brush.

EARTHLY AND HEAVENLY LOVE painted about 1512 by Titian (1477-1576)

Galleria Borghese, Rome, Italy

The Boy Zeus Carried Away

IN GREEK mythology the twelve chief gods lived on Mount Olympus. The youthful goddess Hebe waited on them at their banquets and served them their food and drink of heavenly ambrosia and nectar. Zeus presided at their dinner table, and he wanted an especially handsome boy to pour his special nectar for him.

It so happened that the King of Troy had a beautiful little son, Ganymede. He was so very good-looking that Zeus thought it would be delightful to have him pour the nectar.

One sunny morning, therefore, Zeus decided to bring young Ganymede up to Mount Olympus. To do so he changed himself into an eagle and kidnaped the boy. The eagle was the biggest and strongest of the flying birds just as Zeus was the mightiest of the gods. As an eagle it was easy for Zeus to carry the young boy up to Mount Olympus, and from then on it was Ganymede who served the delicious nectar to the King of the gods.

In this picture we see the kidnaping as it takes place. Careful not to hurt the child, Zeus, in the form of the eagle, carries Ganymede toward heaven. With his claws the eagle holds the boy by his garment, and Ganymede, eager to fly up, holds fast to the thick feathers of the eagle's wings. But he also looks down at us a little sadly for he has had to leave his loved ones behind on earth. There we see his pet dog who looks up longingly at his young master soaring far above him into the blue sky. He had followed him up to the mountain peak, as we can see since the better part of the landscape is far below.

This is how the painter of this picture, Correggio, made us see how very far and high heaven is. Against the cool blue of the sky and the paler mountains in the distance, the youthful body of Ganymede is full of warmth and life. His flesh and skin look even more delicate against the withered tree-trunk in the foreground.

The Italian painter Correggio liked to paint lovely-looking people. They are always lovely whether they were painted for Churches or palaces, whether they were the figures of Christianity or of pagan mythology.

Correggio's men and women all have tender flesh and delicate skin. All his figures move gently and gracefully. Their bones are well covered with soft flesh, and we never see a bulging muscle. Correggio liked to paint young bodies of Angels or Cupids flying about and he painted them amazingly well. In his paintings we see them flying with ease as if it were the most natural thing for them to do. We can always recognize the rare paintings of Correggio by their lightness and grace, their sweet and smiling kind of beauty. Correggio was the finest artist of Parma, the lovely Italian town famous for its sweet-smelling Parma violets.

GANYMEDE painted about 1530 by Correggio (about 1489-1534)

Kunsthistorisches Museum, Vienna, Austria

They Learned to Know and to Love Nature

BETWEEN two lovely trees, behind the bushes in the foreground of this picture, we see a road winding along the border of a forest. The road leads toward the mountains in the distance. At the foot of the mountains we find a castle with towers overlooking the sea. Colorful clouds shimmer in a brilliant blue sky that becomes cloudlessly clear toward the horizon. Nowhere a human soul. The quiet beauty of nature speaks for itself alone.

This is perhaps the first pure landscape painting in European art. The painter, Albrecht Altdorfer, composed the picture without trying to tell a story or painting a person.

Altdorfer's interest in nature was part of people's awakened interest in the natural world that came at the time of the Renaissance. He was nearly the same age as Raphael, Michelangelo, and Titian, but they lived in sunny Italy and Altdorfer was a German, and that made a difference in his way of painting.

It was in northern Europe, of which Germany is a part, that landscape painting began, and for a good reason. There wind and weather are more variable than they are in Italy. That is why northern Europeans have always paid more attention to the land and the sky around them than do those who live in the south. They learned to know nature and to love it, and they wanted to see it in their pictures. Probably that is why it was a German artist who first considered painting a landscape for its own sake.

It is also why the Germans included landscapes with trees and plants and animals and houses in other pictures too, as in Dürer's engraving of St. Eustache (p.117) and in Grünewald's painting of St. Anthony and St. Paul (p.118-119).

Albrecht Altdorfer, who painted this pure landscape, was particularly fond of painting the charm of forests and mountains, and he has rarely been equalled in making the sky look exciting, colorful, and radiant.

LANDSCAPE painted about 1532
by Albrecht Altdorfer (about 1480-1538)

Old Pinakothek, Munich, Germany

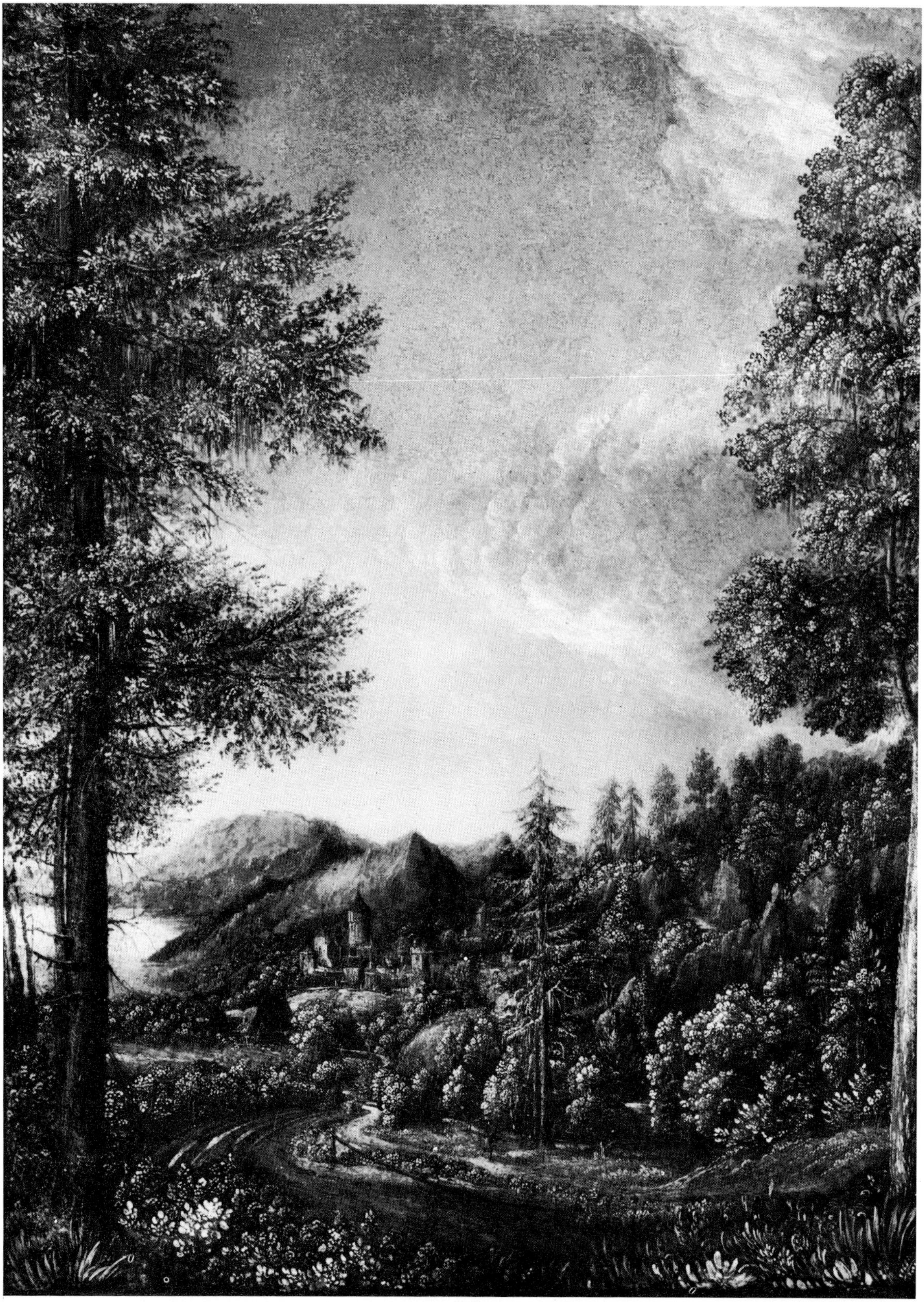

A Monument of Human Wrath

THE Bible tells us how Moses led the children of Israel from slavery in Egypt to freedom in their own country, the Promised Land. This took many years of wandering in the desert.

When the Israelites reached Mount Sinai, Moses went up to the top of the mountain. There God gave him two stone tablets on which was written the Divine Law that would assure his people of a good life. Moses brought the tablets down from Mount Sinai to his people.

On his way down he saw from a distance that his people were worshiping a golden calf, an idol.

Moses became very angry. He had led the Israelites out of slavery in Egypt so that they might learn to worship God. He thought they would understand that God is a Divine Being even though they could not see Him. But in just the short time while he was gone, they had returned to worshiping idols which they could see.

Feeling that all his efforts to lead the Israelites to a better life had failed, Moses smashed the tablets with the Divine Law on them.

Some time later Moses went to Mount Sinai for a second time, and he received two tablets with the Ten Commandments on them, the same Ten Commandments that are the basic Law even today for both Christians and Jews.

Michelangelo chose, when he made his world-famous statue, to show Moses in his moment of anger just before he smashed the tablets.

We see Moses wrestling with himself, the precious tablets under his right arm. He is half-sitting, perhaps about to rise in his mighty wrath. The position of his left arm shows him turning away from what he sees: his people worshiping the golden calf. But his other arm, holding the tablets, is firm and steady.

This is how Michelangelo makes us see Moses torn between two feelings: his firm wish to do as God commanded him and his rising anger against the people who have betrayed the good faith. We see both feelings struggling with tremendous force against each other in Moses' powerful mind and powerful body.

He is fingering his long beard, the Biblical sign of wise old age and dignity; but in his face there is righteous wrath.

The two prongs springing from Moses' head were meant, by the sculptor, to show the Lawgiver's divine wisdom. Painters used rays of golden lines for this purpose whenever they painted Moses.

In Michelangelo's statue Moses' forehead is furrowed over his brows. The muscles of his face are tense. His mouth is grim, and the set of his head shows him recoiling as, with burning eyes, he concentrates on the awful sight of the sinful people.

We know what is going to happen: Moses' wrath will win out. Forgetting his mission, he will rise and smash the Tablets of the Law.

All this Michelangelo makes us feel in his majestic statue of Moses in which he was able to show the lawgiver's superhuman greatness as only Michelangelo could. No wonder the people of Rome called him "Tremendous Michelangelo."

MOSES (Part of the burial monument of Pope Julius II) ordered 1508, finished 1543
by Michelangelo Buonaroti
(1475-1564)

St. Pietro in Vincoli, Rome, Italy

This Simply Painted Portrait is a Superb Likeness

A MAN of extraordinary talents, with the mouth-filling name of Hieronymus Holzschuher, was once a governor of the town of Nuremberg in Germany. He was only a little older than his friend Albrecht Dürer who painted this portrait of him.

In his late years Dürer was able to paint everything he saw exactly true to nature down to the last little hair. This is because Dürer was primarily an engraver and had spent many years practising the art of engraving, making many tiny fine lines with his sharp engraver's tool on a copper plate.

We see that skill in the way Dürer painted the fur collar of Holzschuher's coat—every hair separately drawn. Only an artist who was essentially an engraver would have painted details so painstakingly.

In painting Holzschuher's face, however, Dürer used his soft brush with freedom and sweep. He painted the man's features to look strongly modeled as if they had been done by a sculptor thinking in terms of pure shapes rather than of colors.

Dürer painted Holzschuher simply, without any objects in the background, to give the portrait itself more emphasis. The man's face, surrounded by his curly white hair and beard, is set right over his fur collar. That too makes the portrait look more like a sculptured bust than like a painting.

Only a few touches of color are added to the even complexion of the face, but those few are artfully applied and very effective. A strong healthy red accents the mouth, and nobody who ever saw them would forget the lively blue eyes of Hieronymus Holzschuher.

The clarity and vigor of Holzschuher's gaze shows us the clarity and vigor of his thoughts. We can see that he was a keen observer. The firm set of his mouth tells us that having once made a decision he will carry it out with firmness and energy.

In this painting, made in the artist's later years, Albrecht Dürer tells the strict truth and nothing but the truth. But he does it with the understanding of a friend and the imagination of a great artist. This portrait shows that the mature Dürer was able to select the most important shapes and colors and to organize them into one simple but superb likeness of his subject.

HIERONYMUS HOLZSCHUHER painted 1526
by Albrecht Dürer (1471-1528)

Kaiser Friedrich Museum, Berlin, Germany

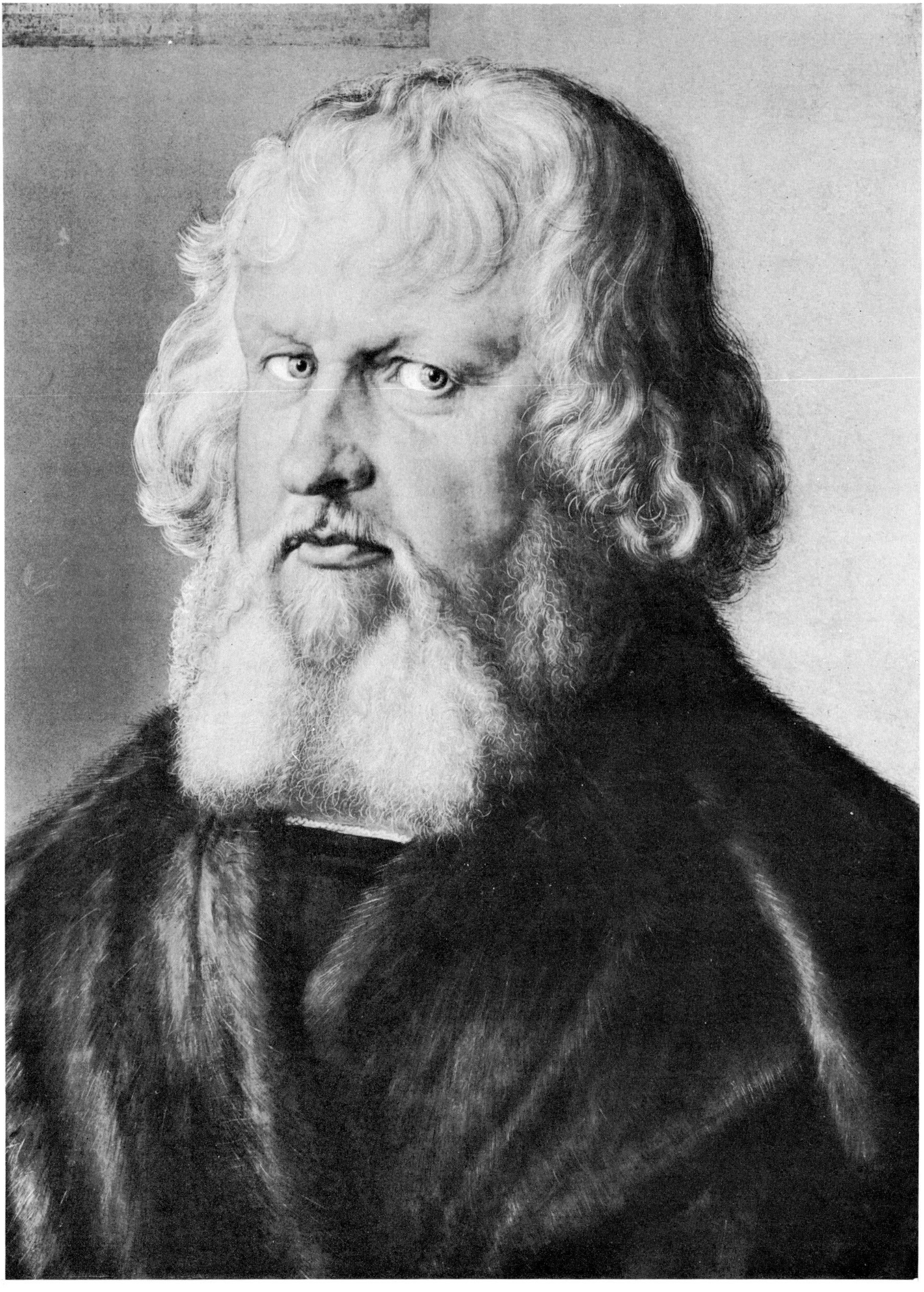

HENRY VIII, KING OF ENGLAND
Copy of a drawing by Holbein

Holbein Could Make an Infant Look Like a Prince

Possession of the State Graphic Collection, Munich, Germany

HENRY VIII of England was a powerful King, but he was most unhappy about one thing in his life: He was well in his middle years and he had no male heir to his throne. But finally the wish of his heart came true and a little son was born to his wife, the Queen.

The little boy was not two years old when the famous Hans Holbein painted his portrait and gave it to the King for a New Year's present.

The King, who was immensely pleased with the painting, gave the artist a golden goblet with a golden cover. Although the little Prince, who later became King Edward VI, was still an infant, the painter found a way to make him look like a real heir to the proud throne of England.

As you can see in the picture, the little Prince of Wales (the title of every first-born son of a King of England) is looking down toward us. This shows us that he is in a high position. The painter suggests that the child is sitting near a high window greeting his subjects below. His left hand rests on a velvet-covered window sill. He is holding a golden rattle, which is a baby's toy but here it reminds us of a scepter, the symbol of a ruler.

By the magic of Holbein's brush, the child's regal garments of scarlet and gold do not seem out of keeping with the sweet little face. In spite of the softness of the skin that we feel would be like silk to the touch, we do not wish to touch or kiss those round baby cheeks. The earnest expression of the little Prince who looks so squarely out of the picture holds us off. The way he greets us with his raised right hand may charm us, but we do not feel like hugging the lovable child. He is a little Prince and keeps us ordinary people at a distance.

The King must have admired Holbein for painting the child to look so much like a royal Prince. But the father had the additional satisfaction of recognizing his own features in his son's portrait as Holbein painted it.

King Henry's square face reveals energy and determination. His sharp eyes show that he was a shrewd man. His compressed mouth and pointed chin belong to a harsh if not ruthless character.

Holbein was able to make similar features appear in the infant's face. It is rather square too, but softened by baby flesh. The pointed chin isn't set. The small mouth recalls the father's small mouth but it is not compressed. Even the eyes in the baby's face look like the father's, but the baby's have softly curving lines and their expression is simple and earnest.

King Henry was probably too proud to care about his own looks, but it greatly flattered him to think he had a son who resembled him so much and looked so lovable at the same time. How Holbein accomplished this was the secret of his magic art.

PARVULE PATRISSA, PATRIÆ VIRTVTIS ET HÆRES
   ESTO, NIHIL MAIVS MAXIMVS ORBIS HABET.
GNATVM VIX POSSVNT COELVM ET NATVRA DEDISSE,
   HVIVS QVEM PATRIS, VICTVS HONORET HONOS.
ÆQVATO TANTVM, TANTI TV FACTA PARENTIS,
   VOTA HOMINVM, VIX QVO PROGREDIANTVR, HABENT
VINCITO, VICISTI. QVOT REGES PRISCVS ADORAT
   ORBIS, NEC TE QVI VINCERE POSSIT, ERIT.

Richard Morysin Car.

EDWARD, PRINCE OF WALES painted 1538
by Hans Holbein the Younger (1497-1543)

National Gallery of Art, Washington, D. C.
Mellon Collection

A Great Court Painter

HANS HOLBEIN, who painted the two Kings we see here, lived in Switzerland; but because he was such a famous painter, King Henry VIII called him to his court in England and gave him a yearly salary for the work he did there. In this way Holbein became what is known as a court painter.

Holbein is known chiefly for the portraits he painted of the Kings and Queens and other distinguished persons who lived at this period. It is, indeed, mainly from these portraits that we know what they looked like.

Holbein's portraits were usually just busts painted smaller than life size. Only rarely was he engaged to make a very large painting. But King Henry VIII did order him to paint one of monumental size for the wall over the mantel in a room of Whitehall Palace. The picture was to have the full figures of the King and Queen in the foreground and of the King's mother and father in the background.

This important painting was destroyed when a fire ravaged Whitehall Palace, but the so-called *cartoon* that Holbein made for it still exists and the picture we see here shows half of that cartoon.

A cartoon, in this sense, is a full-sized sketch for a mural painting, usually done in the fresco technique. That is, the painter works on fresh plaster on the wall before it dries. As the painter has to work very fast, a full-size cartoon is first traced on the wall.

Holbein finished this particular cartoon in oil paint, probably for the King's approval.

The King had good reason to like Holbein's cartoon. He looks impressive in it, standing in a military posture with his legs wide apart. His face is merely indicated here because it is likely that the painter made this cartoon before the King posed for it.

The artist painted the King's garments with every detail true to life: the jewels and the golden chains and the many finely embroidered ornaments. But his painting was in no way lost in details. Great simple lines of the body and ample folds of the cloak make this "cartoon" an imposing picture. The finished wall painting must have given an impression of royalty and power.

As it was the court painter's job to please the man he served, it became more and more important to make people look the way they would have liked to, rather than as they really did look. It has become proverbial to say of a portrait that flatters the subject too much, "It is as pretty as if a court painter had made it."

But Holbein could make people look true to life without hurting their feelings.

KINGS HENRY VII AND VIII
(Part of a "cartoon") painted 1537
by Hans Holbein the Younger (1497-1543)

Devonshire Collection, Chatsworth, England
Reproduced by permission of the Trustees of
the Chatsworth Settlement

A Spirited Leader of the Pope's Army

THIS is a portrait of Pier Luigi Farnese, a nephew of Pope Paul III. He was a brilliant General of the Papal Army and his victories won him the title of a Duke and the possession of two Italian dukedoms.

The General stands before us fully armed, his hand on his marshal's staff. A color-bearer at his side holds up the scarlet silk banner of the Papal Army: a glorious background for the General's proud head.

He is not wearing his helmet for he is not yet in the battle. He is planning it. His spirited thoughts are mirrored in his wide-open eyes peering out sharply from under the shadow of his dark brows. A dark beard and dark hair frame his sallow features. A big dark shadow outlines his cheekbone, making his narrow face look even narrower.

A magnificent black armor covers his lean erect figure. The well polished steel glitters with brilliant highlights. It is a symbol of impenetrable strength. It takes up the greater part of the picture.

Is it possible that the artist wanted to show, above all, the beauty of fine armor? No. The narrow face above the armor dominates the picture. It is like a flame lit up in the midst of darkness. But there are highlights on the armor that the painter uses to lead our eye from the man's intelligent shining forehead to his energetic hand. The outstretched finger seems to follow the General's thought. It also suggests a direction that will be followed by the entire Army.

In a line with the General's slender spirited hand the color-bearer's strong fist suggests that the common soldier is the one who carries out the leader's plans. Many strong fists will have to fight under the banner of this thoughtful energetic leader.

Leadership is superbly expressed in this portrait of Pier Luigi Farnese. Titian painted it when he was an old and experienced man of seventy. By his style of designing and painting, he made everyone he painted look like a very important person. When he painted someone of real importance, Titian would make him look positively regal in his portrait. No other painter was ever able to do this as Titian could.

That is why the Queen of France wanted Titian and no one else to paint a portrait of her husband, the King. She knew, however, that he could not paint it from life since the King would not go to Italy, where Titian lived, and Titian would not go to France. The Queen therefore had a life-like portrait of the King painted by a very good French painter. (The camera, of course, had not yet been invented; so there could not be a photograph). The Queen sent the painted portrait to Titian so that he would have before him the King's likeness. From this he was to paint the King's portrait as only he could do it.

Titian made many portraits of important people such as Princes and Kings. But for his art in painting Titian himself was greater than any of them.

PIER LUIGI FARNESE painted 1546
by Titian (1477-1576)

National Museum, Naples, Italy

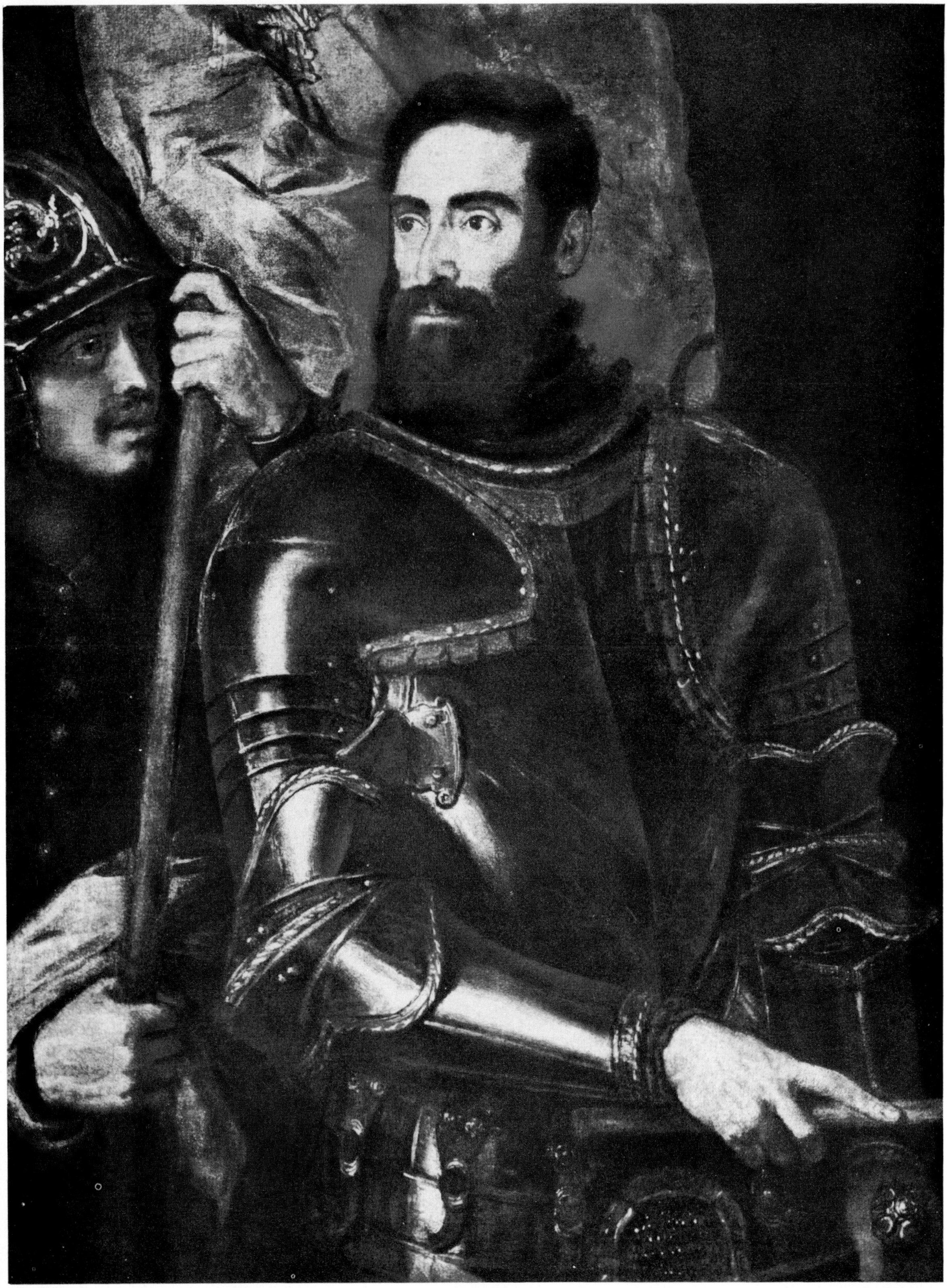

Detail of picture opposite

Venice Ruling with Justice and Peace

THE picture we see here is on the ceiling of a palace in Venice. It is painted much like the picture we saw in the room of the newlyweds in Mantua (p.89). But that picture was painted about a hundred years earlier, at the time of the early Renaissance, and at that time pictures looked simpler and not so pretty.

In the magnificent palaces of the later Renaissance, the ceilings of the rooms were richly decorated with gilded ornaments. Within the shimmering golden design, pictures were set in the ceiling and framed so that they looked like openings. Through these mock openings we can look up into what seems to be the actual sky, and at the beautiful things in it. We see these from an odd angle.

Here, for instance, pink marble stairs rising from the very high ceiling of a big hall lead up to a carved golden throne on top of the globe. Under the shimmering draperies adorning this throne sits a beautiful woman. She wears a silken damask robe. Her mantle is lined with ermine—a sign that she is a ruler. The golden staff she holds in her hand is a scepter, another sign of royalty. When we look closer, we can see that she wears a crown on her head. Who is she?

On the stairs at her feet rests a winged lion, the symbol of St. Mark, the protector of Venice. The lovely lady represents Venice, the proud and beautiful city that at that time ruled the sea.

She is being approached by two other beautiful women. One holds a scale and a sword, symbolizing Justice. The other holds branches of an olive tree, symbolizing Peace.

The picture represents St. Mark's city, Venice, ruling on high with Justice and Peace.

Within the golden ceiling pictures like this one have a stupendous effect. The blue sky and white clouds alone would add shining brilliance to the wide marble hall and its gilded ceiling. The bright gay colors, the lovely women, the shimmering silks add radiance to the already sumptuous golden richness.

The painter of this picture was Paolo Veronese. He decorated many public and private palaces in and near Venice with his colorful paintings. His figures are stately without being grave. His pictures, rich as they look, are never overloaded.

When we look at Veronese's paintings we feel the golden sunny warmth of a late summer day, colorful with flowers in full bloom, fragrant with the perfume of ripening fruit.

VENICE RULING painted about 1575-1577
by Paolo Veronese (1528-1588)

Ducal Palace, Venice, Italy

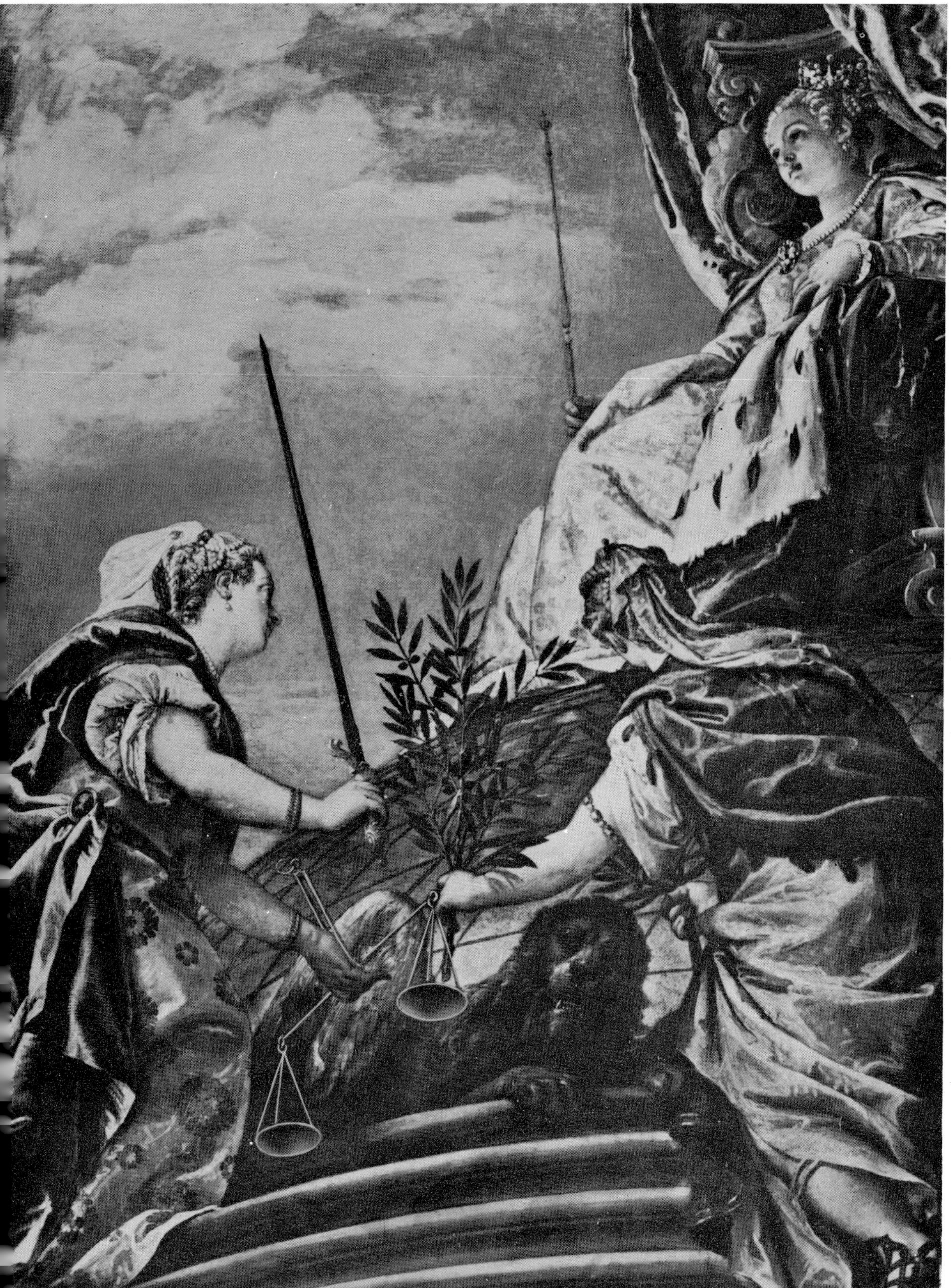

The Glutton's Paradise

THERE is a magic land, so the story goes, where everything is meant to be eaten. The roofs of the houses are shingled with pies, and even the dog's house is made of a big piece of bread. This, the scene of our picture, is the Land of Cockayne.

There the table is always full of food. Here the farmer need neither sow nor reap. Fat and lazy he lies under the table, his flail beside him.

The soldier does not fight. He does not need his spear or his iron glove. Stuffed with food he sleeps under the magic table.

The scholar rests with his papers under his head; he has put his book away for books are not needed in this lazy land. His eye is open only so that he can watch the wine as it flows into his open mouth from the overturned bottle on the table.

In this magic Land of Cockayne no one need so much as reach for the food. A boiled egg walks around, obligingly open, with a spoon in it. A chicken puts itself well-roasted onto a platter. The pig is roasted too and runs around with a carving knife neatly stuck into its crisp skin. The dessert is a hare made of gingerbread. Look at him frisking about the lawn.

How do you get into this land of plenty? First you must reach the sea of milk and you must then eat your way all through the mountain of rice—and there you are.

Peter Brueghel, the painter of this picture, was born in what is now Belgium. He was not so much interested in painting people true to life, but his characters look down-to-earth just the same. They look awkward and rather funny.

Brueghel went around among the peasants and studied the way they looked and acted. He painted them from different angles, looking at them from above so that they appear in different and odd positions. He did not look for beauty in people, but he loved beautiful landscapes. Even the little bit of sky and milky sea, the distant shore, and the hillside in the foreground of this picture are beautifully done. They show how closely he watched the subtle colors and shapes of nature.

Landscape painting was developed later in the countries of northern Europe. There, because of the cold, the human body had to be covered by heavy clothes, and therefore artists were less able to see its beauty.

Peter Brueghel saw people's follies and he loved to paint them doing ridiculous things. It was in nature that he saw eternal beauty.

THE LAND OF COCKAINE painted 1567
by Pieter Brueghel (about 1525-1569)

Alte Pinakothek, Munich, Germany

A Dramatic Painting of St. George and the Dragon

WE ALL know the story of St. George and how he defeated the dragon that endangered a whole city. We have seen other pictures of it in this book. The first is Donatello's relief (the sculpture on p.76), the second Raphael's painting (p.111). The sculpture was made during the early Renaissance, the painting at its peak. The picture we see here, by Tintoretto, was painted about half a century later, and is therefore very different from the other two.

At that late stage of the Renaissance simple beauty and harmony did not satisfy people any more. They wanted a change in art, a new angle. And because the people were unhappy at this time, they wanted excitement and danger in their pictures.

That is why Tintoretto painted the old story of St. George in such a new, dark, and dramatic way.

We seem to be drawn into the hilly landscape of the picture. We think we must be standing on a hilltop close by. From there we look down, at an odd new angle, and see what happens right next to us.

It is long before sunrise. The sky is leaden gray with clouds, and there is just a strip of faded light over the murky-colored sea. The city walls in the background melt into the dusky gray-green of the trees. In the foreground a bare old tree-trunk, and another cut-down stump in the middle of the picture, make the scene look barren and bleak.

With terror in her eyes the young Princess of the story runs toward us. Strangely enough, she seems to be rushing right out of the picture, away from the dreadful fight. Behind her lies a colorless dead body, one of the dragon's victims.

Directly above this body we see St. George on his horse. The horse is painted in the same gray-green color as the corpse. The front is almost lost in the dark where the fearful dragon emerges from the sea. That creature's wide-open mouth is full of vicious-looking teeth glittering in the shadow.

St. George charges at him on his galloping horse. His figure is dark. He thrusts his lowered spear into the monster's eye.

And yet, we are fearful of how the battle may end. In this desperate conflict only heaven can help.

But lo, as we look up into the sky we see a heavenly vision within many circles of light. It promises help and victory for St. George.

We know how the story is going to end: St. George will defeat the dragon and save the Princess and the unhappy town.

But the great Venetian painter Tintoretto showed us more of the sinister perils and threat of death than of the happy ending. Instead of painting in a pleasant and harmonious style as earlier artists did, Tintoretto painted thrilling discords. And yet his paintings have a harmony of their own, because a great artist always finds a harmonious solution to the problems of an inharmonious world.

ST. GEORGE AND THE DRAGON painted about 1555
by Jacopo Tintoretto (1518-1584)

Reproduced by courtesy of the Trustees,
of the National Gallery, London, England

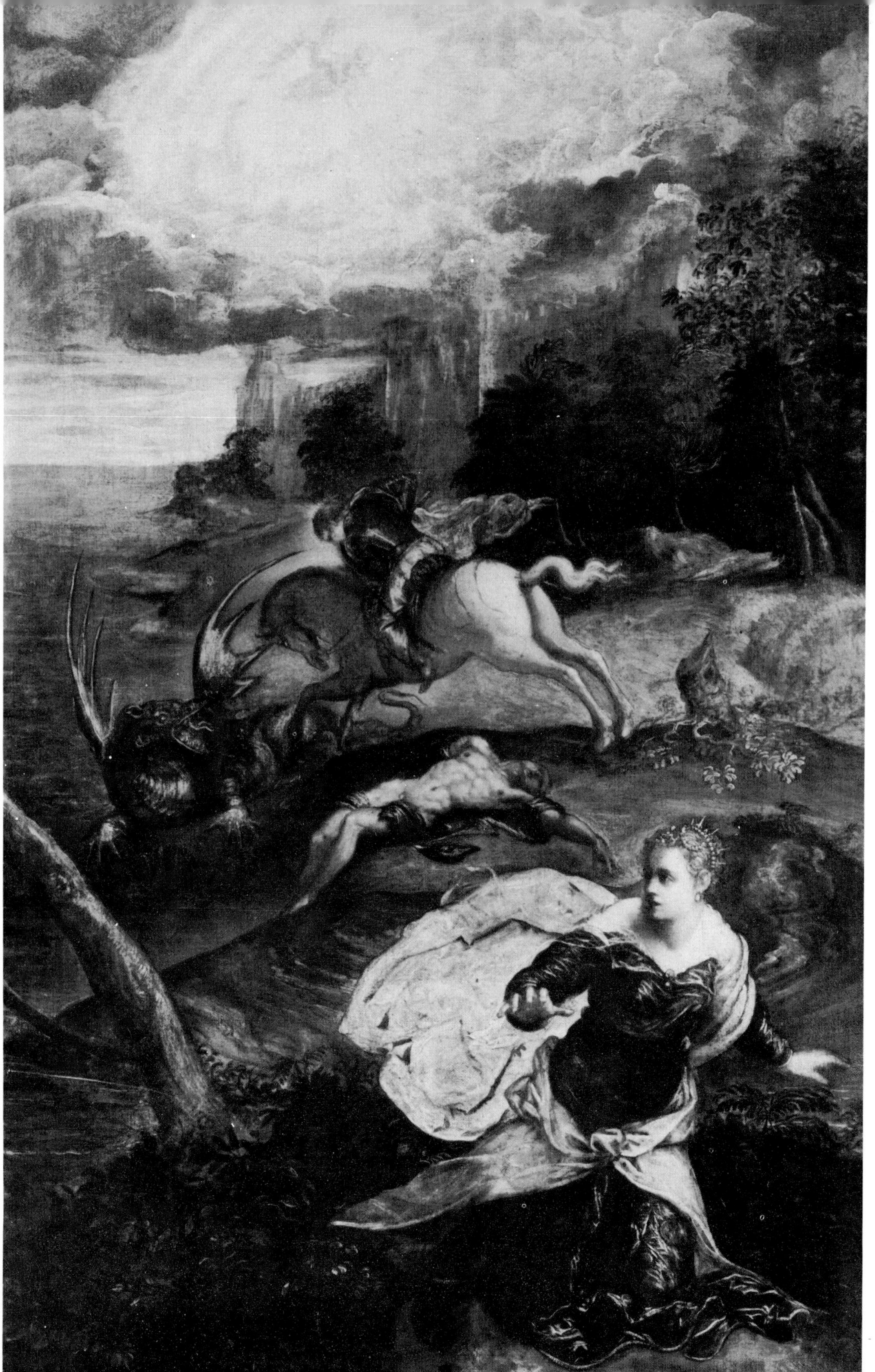

St. Martin Shares His Cloak with a Beggar

WHEN St. Martin was still a very young boy, he was made a knight so that he could serve in the Emperor's army in place of his father who was old and ill.

Martin was stationed in the town of Amiens, when one morning he went riding outside the city. As he was riding his white horse among the hills, a beggar approached him.

The beggar was so very poor that he didn't even have clothes, and that day no one had given him anything at all.

St. Martin's heart was full of pity. Having nothing else to give, he cut his cloak in two and gave one half to the beggar.

On the following night Christ, surrounded by Angels, appeared to St. Martin wearing half of the knight's cloak, the half he had given to the beggar the day before. In giving to the beggar, St. Martin was giving to Christ Himself.

In the picture we see St. Martin cutting his cloak in half with his sword. His figure is surrounded by the sky, and the distant city is in the valley far below. This is how the painter lifted St. Martin out of the ordinary world. Only the hoofs of his horse touch the ground.

The young man's face is full of pity as he bends his head toward the humble and naked beggar at his side.

Strangely broken clouds flash in an unusual way around the group. The shapes of the men and of the horse seem strange too. The beggar's legs don't look natural either. The proportions of the figures are drawn out. Everything in the picture is strange: real and unreal and at the same time miraculous, like a dream.

This dream-like miraculous quality is characteristic of El Greco's paintings.

El Greco's real name was Jacopo Theotocopuli, a Greek name because he was born in Greece. He went to Spain in later years and the Spaniards called him El Greco, meaning "the Greek."

El Greco was a very religious man. He painted mostly stories of the Bible or of miraculous legends. He wanted to show that his subjects did not belong to our commonplace world, that these were not ordinary people he painted but sacred characters.

This is why El Greco did not paint people with ordinary proportions or ordinary shapes. He felt that religious feelings alone were important. Thus he became a great painter of miraculous events and of better people in a better world.

ST. MARTIN painted about 1598
by El Greco (about 1548-1614)

National Gallery of Art, Washington, D. C.
Widener Collection

VICTORY sculptured about 1519
by Michelangelo Buonaroti (1475-1564)

Palazzo Vecchio, Florence, Italy

Figures of Two Young Men:

This One Shows the Flight of the Spirit

MANY years after Michelangelo had completed his beautiful statue of David, he made another statue of another victorious young man. This one is usually called *Victory*.

In this picture of the statue, we see the victor after the fight is over. He is standing next to the older man he has vanquished. His one knee is still on the neck of the enemy he has subdued, but his eyes look into the distance. He does not want to oppress his enemy; he would have considered that ignoble. He wants to rise higher and to further victories.

Michelangelo made us understand this thought partly by the scene itself but to an even greater extent by the way he formed the young man's figure. His slender body is perfectly developed. But more important are the expression of his face and the way his body is turned. These things show spiritual rather than physical strength.

With this thought in mind, let us go one step farther and ask what Michelangelo meant. Surely he meant to tell us that youth should not be satisfied with overcoming old obstacles but must seek and conquer a new world.

It was natural for Michelangelo to make a human body look perfectly beautiful and to balance it perfectly in motion. But in his later years particularly, Michelangelo wanted to express, above all, human thought and human feeling, and he did it superbly.

MERCURY sculptured about 1568
by Giovanni da Bologna (1529-1608)

This One Shows a Flying Body

National Gallery of Art, Washington, D. C.   Mellon Collection

EVER since the Renaissance, painters and sculptors have come to Italy from all over Europe to study art, especially to learn the Italians' secret of making human figures look beautiful.

A French sculptor named Jean de Boulogne was one of the many who traveled to Florence, Michelangelo's native city, to study. He became so thoroughly Italian that he came to be known as Giovanni da Bologna which is the Italian way of saying his name.

In this figure of *Mercury* the sculptor wanted to make a perfectly beautiful male body. Nor was he satisfied with making just a beautiful man. He wanted to show him in motion. Not just in any motion either, but flying.

To make a figure look as if it were flying, an artist has to balance it with perfect precision. And that is exactly what Giovanni da Bologna did in this statue. He balanced the figure so well, indeed, that it is resting on the toes of one foot. The statue is an almost lifesize heavy bronze figure. But it is supported by only a narrow piece of bronze that was made to signify a rising gust of wind.

This *Mercury* points upward to suggest that he is rising. We know that he is Mercury, the swift messenger of the ancient gods, by the wings attached to his helmet and to his heels, and by his winged stick with two serpents coiled about it.

Striking as the figure is, it does not make us wonder whether there is any deep meaning to it. But we are bound to admire the sculptor for inventing unusual motion in art and giving it a beautiful shape.

DAVID sculptured 1624
by Gian Lorenzo Bernini (1598-1680)

This David Hurls the Stone with Fury

THIS marble *David* by Bernini is very different from the one that Michelangelo made about a hundred years earlier (p.108-109). Michelangelo's David stands poised for action, and this one is in full swing hurling the stone.

David has discarded the armor the King had given him. We see him stepping over it with a big stride. Not caring in the least about it, he leaves it behind. He thinks of nothing but the job he has to do. His lips are drawn in between his teeth, as he gathers all his thoughts and all his strength. When he hurls the stone from his stiffly stretched sling, he wants to succeed in defeating his enemy.

His eyes are darkened under his fiercely wrinkled brow. His hair is disheveled. Altogether he is an uncouth youngster, but strong and muscular.

Palazzo Borghese, Rome, Italy

It is reported that Bernini portrayed himself in his *David*. But why did he make himself so unattractive?

Because that was precisely young Bernini's aim. He wanted, above all, to be truthful. He felt he should observe and render life as it was, full of motion and emotion, pretty or not.

His wish was to get away from the formal kind of beauty that artists before him had created. Maybe he was hinting at that wish when he let David leave the beautiful armor behind. He showed David's motion and his emotion even though they were not pretty—and in so doing he started a new style in sculpture that lasted for centuries.

SCIPIONE BORGHESE sculptured 1633
by Gian Lorenzo Bernini

A Marble Portrait that Seems to Breathe

Palazzo Borghese, Rome, Italy

BERNINI made this *David* for his patron, Cardinal Scipio Borghese.
Cardinal Borghese was one of the fabulously wealthy Princes of the Church. He lived in a sumptuous marble palace that he had had built in one of the most beautiful parks in Rome. He had the palace richly decorated by some of the most brilliant artists in Italy.

The greatest sculptor of the time, Gian Lorenzo Bernini, made several statues to add to the splendor of this magnificent palace. Bernini also carved this famous portrait of Cardinal Borghese who sponsored the young artist. You can see it in the Borghese Palace even today.

Bernini made this bust when he had fully mastered his art. The bones, the flesh, the skin all seem to live. We can tell, even from the white marble, that the Cardinal had ruddy cheeks and very red lips. We can tell that his robe was made of heavy silk and his collar of finest linen.

The Cardinal looks so alive that he seems to breathe and move. He is full of lively energy. Look at the jaunty angle of his hat! We can tell from this portrait that the Cardinal enjoyed his life. He must have loved food and wine, and he looks active too—but we can plainly see that he was as ready to think as he was to act. His head sits straight on his shoulders with the natural freedom of a man who stands his ground in life.

Bernini was able to make people look important and grand and still true to life.

ST. MATTHEW painted about 1592
by Michelangelo Caravaggio (1576-1609)

Two New Ways of Painting:

Real Life

(Picture destroyed in World War II)

THE Italian painter Caravaggio was a rough and tough revolutionary character. Many weird stories are told about his life and art. Here is a story about one of his paintings that was destroyed by bombs in World War II.

It was a picture of St. Matthew, painted toward the end of the 16th century, for one of the altars in a Roman Church.

At this time young Roman painters painted in a new manner, for people had become tired of the unusual angles and unusual long figures painted in the time of their fathers (p.140-147). Now people wanted more natural-looking pictures.

But Caravaggio's painting of St. Matthew turned out to be more "natural" than they bargained for. The priests refused to accept it and Caravaggio had to make another St. Matthew, one dignified enough to stand on an altar. The first painting—the one we see here—was bought by a Roman art collector who admired Caravaggio's art and did not mind his daring views of Biblical persons.

St. Matthew was a humble toll-taker before he became Christ's Apostle. Caravaggio wanted to show him as a lowly human creature writing his gospel by divine inspiration. An Angel is guiding his hand.

We see St. Matthew, his big heavy knees crossed, sitting awkwardly on a chair. His clumsy feet are coarse, his dusty bare sole seems to reach out of the picture toward us. His hand looks as if it were untrained to write, and he follows with wondering eyes the lines that, under the Angel's guidance, his pen leaves on the shining white pages of the book.

These pages are the lightest and most brilliant part of the painting, because Caravaggio wanted to show that writing the gospel was St. Matthew's most important mission.

The Angel's wings are the second whitest in the picture, to show that the Angel is a heavenly creature, although, except for his wings, he looks like any youth. His floating garment is only slightly different from St. Matthew's naturally-falling clothes.

Part of the scene is in darkness, as if it were in a cellar with the light coming through a small window. With strong contrasts of light and shadow Caravaggio models amazingly real-looking shapes, strong and simple.

Caravaggio's art was a revolution in painting.

Many painters followed his style, particularly in the northern countries of Europe. Caravaggio became a model for many great artists after him.

Ideal Beauty

BELOW we see Apollo, the Sun-god, setting out on his daily round. He drives his chariot, drawn by four dappled horses, high up in the clouds. The chariot is surrounded by lovely maidens called Horae, representing the hours. The first one points toward the earth below showing the way. In the form of a Cupid the Morning Star holds a torch to light the sky.

Aurora, beautiful Dawn, flying ahead, heralds the rising sun. Surrounded by dark but colorful clouds, she is both earnest and serene as she brings her flowers to the new day. Her figure is majestic yet light. The morning breeze makes her garments fly. We feel the freshness of morning on a hopeful sunny day.

Guido Reni, the painter of the Aurora, made his figures look real and beautiful at the same time. The noble and friendly loveliness of his style set an example for many great Italian painters who came after him.

AURORA (DAWN) painted 1613 by Guido Reni (1575-1642)   Palazzo Rospigliosi, Rome, Italy

This Painting Looks Better in a Mirror

ACCORDING to an ancient Greek tale, Adonis was a most handsome youth. He was an orphan, brought up by the nymphs of the woods. As he lived in the woods, it was natural for him to become a huntsman.

Because of his great courage and beauty he became a favorite of Venus, the goddess of beauty. Venus, gentle and womanly as she was, often went on hunts with Adonis because she was so devoted to him. But Venus was afraid of the perils that the reckless youth might encounter.

One day, when Adonis made ready to chase a ferocious boar, Venus had a premonition of evil. She insistently begged her friend to stay away from the hunt on this day. But in vain. Adonis left with his hounds and went on the trail of the boar. When he encountered the wild beast he was mortally wounded by its tusk and he bled to death.

Great was the sorrow of Venus! And all the women of Greece mourned the fabulous huntsman. For centuries Greek women celebrated an annual festival in his honor, strewing flowers on his grave.

This story was often painted in the Baroque period because at that time artists liked to show dramatic action and violent feelings in their works.

This picture was made by the greatest Baroque painter, the Flemish Peter Paul Rubens. It shows the moment when Venus tries to hold Adonis back as he is about to leave. Her little son, Cupid, puts his arms and a foot around Adonis' leg to keep him from going. But ahead of Adonis his two dogs are waiting, eager for the hunt. We know that their master will follow them.

We can read these things in the picture, though the motions seem awkward and left-handed, and Adonis does not seem really to be going forward.

But if we look at this painting in a mirror, everything is as it should be. Venus' right arm clasps Adonis' shoulder. The right arm of little Cupid holds Adonis' leg. Adonis carries his spear in his right hand. And we feel that he is really moving forward. The picture does not look awkward any more; and it is full of motion.

But why did the great Rubens paint this picture to look better in a mirror—that is, reversed? He did it because it was a model for a tapestry—that is, a woven picture—and a model for tapestry *has* to be reversed. This is why:

The weaver works on the wrong side of his tapestry in threads of many different colors. When he is finished with one or another color in a certain place, he leaves the threads hanging and cuts them off at a length of about two inches. This keeps the threads from slipping out. But all these hanging threads on the wrong side of the tapestry hide the design and make the picture look terribly untidy.

The right side of the tapestry, however, remains clear and clean. But as weavers always work on the wrong side of a tapestry, the model for their weaving has to be made in reverse so that the weaver can follow the design.

Rubens painted many models for tapestries. His skill was so great that he could plan the final effect to perfection. Many of his "left-handed" model paintings are treasured in the great museums of the world.

VENUS AND ADONIS painted about 1635 by Pieter Paul Rubens (1580-1640)

Courtesy of the Metropolitan Museum of Art

THE HAPPY VOYAGE OF CARDINAL INFANT FERDINAND painted 1635
by Pieter Paul Rubens (1580-1640)

By permission of the Fogg Art Museum,
Harvard University, Cambridge, Mass.

Rubens Made Fabulous Creatures Look Alive

WHEN the new governor of Flanders, Prince Ferdinand (whose title was Cardinal-Infant) entered the city of Antwerp, the wealthy Flemish people gave him a dazzling reception. They had entrusted the decoration of their city to Rubens, their greatest painter. He planned the triumphal arches and other magnificent architectural pieces which were to be covered with paintings and sculptures for this one day's festivity. He had an entire staff of artists to do the actual building, painting, and sculpture from his sketches. He himself lent a hand whenever he had time. The subjects of his pictures were figured out by the poet Gevartius. This learned man made the voyage of the governor into a miraculous event with all the gods of ancient Greece and Rome participating.

For instance, in our picture, a small sketch by Rubens' own hand, we see Neptune, the mighty god of the sea, quieting the stormy waves of the ocean for smooth sailing. Followed by water nymphs, Neptune rides on his sea-shell chariot. In his right hand he holds the trident, the sign of his power; with the left he commands the fiercely-blowing wind-gods to stop and keep their peace. We see three of the wind-gods riding wildly in the dark cloudy sky. But Neptune is sailing before the fleet. His vessel is drawn by four sea-horses. They look like fiery horses, but their forelegs have fins instead of hoofs, and they end in fish-tails. In the scuffle among the agitated waves, one of them gets on top of the other and puts his finned leg around the neck of his neighbor. They look so alive that we almost hear their wild neighing. In front of the horses, Triton, half-man half-fish, his cheeks puffed with wind, blows his shell horn. He is the herald announcing the approach of Neptune and of the new governor, Prince Ferdinand.

Of course this pictured story is entirely fanciful. But so great was the art of Rubens that he could make creatures that never existed look as alive as they do in these horses.

HORSES (Detail)

LORD JOHN
AND
LORD BERNARD STUART
painted about 1638
by Anthony van Dyck (1599-1641)

Courtesy of Lady Edwina Mountbatten of Burma
(Family possession since 1903)
Broadlands, Hampshire, England

Pride Goeth Before a Fall

AT THE time when the Pilgrims landed at Plymouth Rock, the Flemish painter of this picture, Anthony van Dyck, came to the court of Charles I of England, one of the Kings of the Stuart family. It was a time when trouble was brewing under the Stuarts. Besides religious persecution the people of England suffered many other grievances too. The overbearing behavior of the nobles who ruled England had become unendurable.

When the Stuart King's favorite noble, the Duke of Buckingham, visited France, he wore a silken garment covered with strings of pearls. The pearls were only loosely attached, and as the Duke moved through the crowd the pearls fell off one by one. The poor people in the streets stooped eagerly to pick them up. For them each pearl meant a fortune. If the Duke had wanted to be charitable he certainly chose a most humiliating way of practising charity. There was no end to the display of wealth and pride on the part of the royal court, and finally it led to a revolution.

This double portrait of Lords John and Bernard Stuart, Princes of royal blood, was painted shortly before the revolution in England. They hold their heads high. Their features are proud and haughty. The painter has placed them on a staircase so that the younger one seems to be looking far over our heads and the older one looks down, not so much *at* us as *on* us. High as he is standing, he seems to be stepping up even higher.

Both Princes wear elaborately tailored garments of shining silk, lace and embroidery. Their attitudes are leisurely. The younger's hand, hanging down aimlessly, fingers the folds of his cloak. The older seems to be lifting the hem of his cloak in an idle gesture.

All this was painted with wonderful mastery by the brush of the artist, Anthony van Dyck. He gives us the feel of the different materials, the softness of skin and hair. We know the Princes in all their aristocratic splendor.

English history tells us that both Princes were killed in the revolutionary war that brought the tyranny of the Stuarts to an end. But it is van Dyck's wonderfully painted portrait that shows us what they looked like.

Van Dyck had the particular gift of being able to express elegance and superior standing in his pictures. He painted the portraits of a great many historic persons all over Europe. It is because of his portraits that we know the looks of many historical characters we read about in books.

The portraits van Dyck painted also served other painters who later made pictures of historical characters of this time. (See Copley's *Charles I*, p. 196.)

Above all, van Dyck's beautiful portraits were models of style for painters, particularly in England, where portrait painting became more and more popular through the centuries.

THE NURSING OF BACCHUS
painted about 1630-1635
by Nicholas Poussin (1594-1665)

Reproduced by courtesy of the Trustees, of the National Gallery, London, England

The Strange Supper of the Baby Bacchus

BACCHUS, the god of wine, was brought up in the forest where, under majestic trees, the forest's fabulous inhabitants amuse themselves.

Here we see the baby Bacchus getting his evening meal. It is after sunset when the horizon is still glowing in brilliant red and orange hues over the distant dark blue mountains. Here, under some old trees with vines climbing around their trunks, a nymph looks on as two men are feeding the child. He drinks eagerly from the dish.

What is he drinking? Goat's milk, we might think, for a she-goat is standing nearby. But no. A little sprite points to a man squeezing a bunch of grapes into the child's cup. We can see that he is a sprite by his wings and that he is a wine-sprite by his wreath of vine leaves.

If we look closer, we can see that the person we first thought was a man has a hoofed hairy leg. He is a satyr. Satyrs were invented by the ancients with many more imaginary people of their mythology.

Ancient mythology has been a source of inspiration to artists since the Renaissance.

The artist who painted this picture lived at the time of Baroque art. His name was Nicholas Poussin and he was a Frenchman. But, as many other northern artists did, he came to Italy to study the wealth of art that was to be found there. Poussin stayed in Italy for the rest of his life. It was there that he painted quietly poetic scenes uniting the beauty of nature with the beauty of people. He became one of the greatest figures in the history of French art.

THE HERDSMAN
painted about 1655-1666
by Claude Lorrain
(1600-1682)

National Gallery of Art,
Washington, D. C.
Samuel H. Kress Collection

The Quiet Beauty of Nature

IN this picture the last rays of the setting sun leave the landscape indistinct. One light spot in the foreground attracts our attention, and we can make out two grazing sheep and a goat. A little farther back, at the right, there are more, but we can hardly see them in the shadows. We can see, a little more clearly, some cows also grazing. Their outlines are dark against the light gray river behind them.

Here the landscape is almost lost in the sun-mist. Majestic mountain ranges rise from the mist on one side of the river. On the other side hilly plains melt into a pallid sky.

Some graceful big trees in the foreground frame this quiet dreamlike scene of nature at its loveliest. Only when we look carefully and search the shadows of the trees do we discover the figure of the shepherd reclining against moss-covered rocks. He is as still, as entirely motionless as an ancient statue. There is greatness in his simple outline. His profile recalls the noble profiles of ancient Greece. He is completely relaxed. The passing hours do not exist for him. He seems as timeless as the landscape seems endless.

Our hearts are filled with awe by the magic art of this painter, Claude Lorrain.

He was another one of the French artists who went to Italy to paint, as did his friend Nicholas Poussin. But while Poussin liked to fill the quiet landscape in his pictures with ancient stories of men and gods, Claude Lorrain painted his landscapes with the figures of men subdued. His inspiration was the beauty of the landscape around Rome, the Eternal City. In painting the gentle play of its lights and shadows and the softened glow of its sunsets, Claude Lorrain was putting on canvas the poetic glorification of nature.

Street Arabs in Spain

IS IT really possible that such ragged, poor-looking children as those in this picture can be having as rich a feast as they seem to be? In front of them they have a basket full of fruits and vegetables and a satchel filled with raisin-bread and pastry. Since poor children don't usually have so many good things to eat, it must be that someone, wanting them to enjoy themselves, gave them all this delicious food.

They certainly are having a fine time. Full of fun, the first boy is about to drop a piece of pastry into his mouth. The little dog, who is one of the party too, watches the skill of the little fellow dropping the big piece of cake into his wide open mouth.

In Spain, even today, they often drink wine like this, holding the flask over their heads and letting the wine trickle into their mouths. In this way many people can drink from the bottle without bothering with drinking glasses. The gesture was usual in one way, but it is funny that the little boy should eat pastry like that. He does it precisely because it is fun. His companion looks on with a grin. But maybe the watchful little dog is not so much concerned with his young master's performance. He might be looking for the next move: a delicious bite for himself.

These children are so light-hearted and fun-loving and gay that we feel like smiling when we look at them.

In America it would be hard to believe that such ragged and tattered children could feel so happy. In fact we cannot quite imagine that such children exist. But in Spain, centuries ago when this picture was painted, children like this were a common sight.

The painter of this picture was the Spaniard, Esteban Murillo. He was born just a couple of years before our Pilgrim Fathers landed and a few years after Caravaggio (p. 152-153) died. Caravaggio's natural way of painting everything, down to the dust on people's feet, was followed by many other artists.

The Spanish painter, Murillo, followed the trend started by Caravaggio when he painted unimportant subjects like this. Not only the children are painted true to life, but also the appetizing crusty bread and the colorful luscious fruit which looks so mouth-watering that we feel like having a bite ourselves. This is the sort of painting that looks particularly charming on the wall of a dining-room.

THE PASTRY-EATERS painted about 1660
by Esteban Murillo (1617-1682)

Alte Pinakothek, Munich, Germany

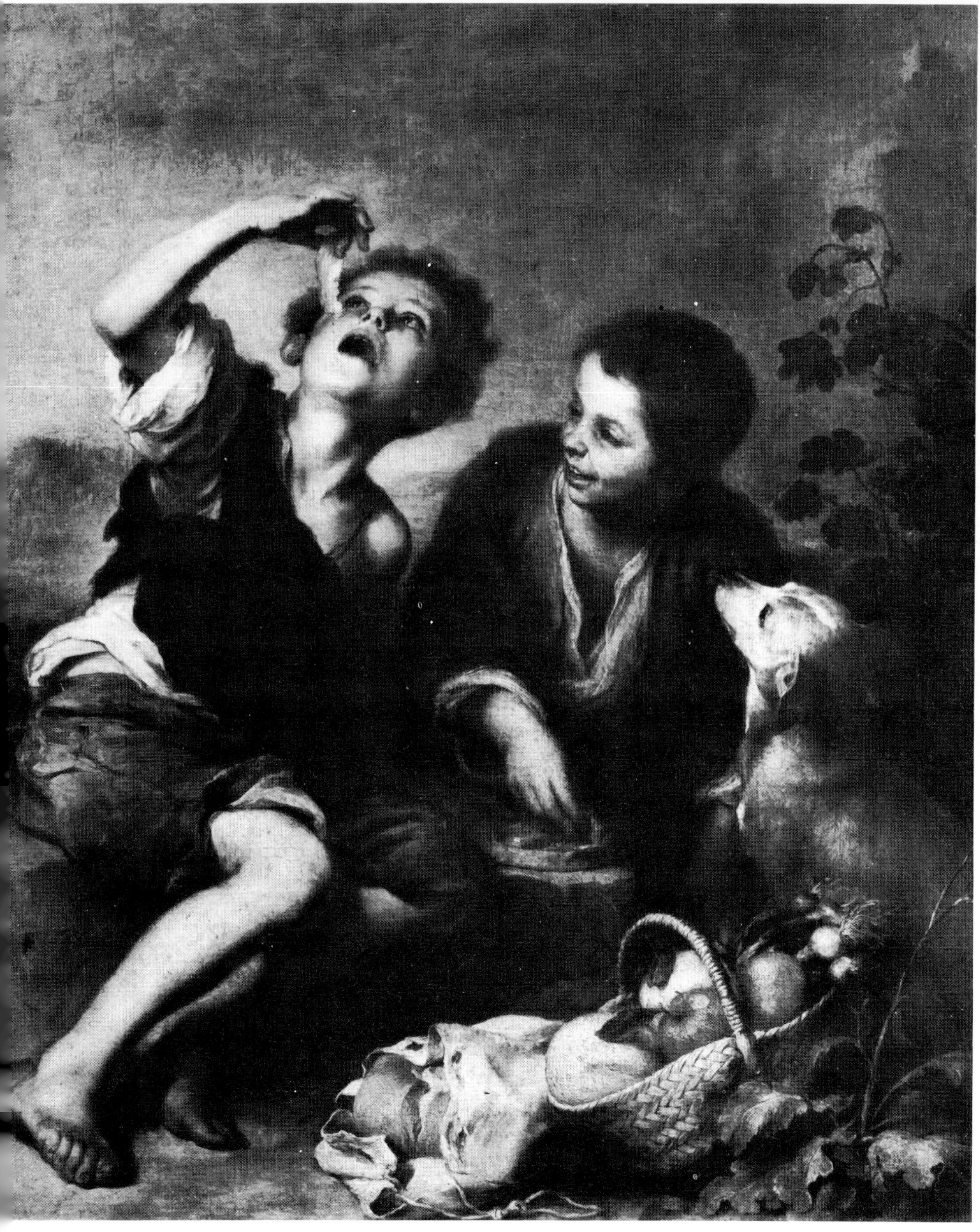

Detail of picture opposite

This Prince is a Poor Little Rich Boy

THE ONLY son and heir of King Philip IV of Spain died when he was still a child. But toward the end of the King's life the Queen bore him another son. They called him Philip Prosper.

Philip Prosper was a sickly baby. But because he was the only successor to the proud throne of Spain, his father had his portrait painted when he was only two years old.

The portrait was to be painted by the King's court painter, Diego Velazquez. Velazquez was an artist of rare genius. He was able to make a beautiful and moving painting even of a mere portrait.

Velazquez gave dignity and deep meaning to the portrait of little Prince Philip Prosper, without taking anything away from his child-like expression.

In the painting Philip Prosper stands in the kind of skirted frock that children of his age wore at that time. He looks very small and pale in the wide dark room richly hung with heavy silk draperies.

We cannot see the full height or width of the room, but the painter makes us feel how very wide and high it is in contrast to the small child. The room opens into another room in the background and we feel that there are many more large rooms around the tiny Prince. The rich deep red draperies and furniture add to the magnificence of the infant's surroundings.

Philip Prosper's garment blends well with this red room. It is painted in a lighter shade of red, made to look even lighter by a white apron, a collar, and ruffled white cuffs. Silver bells hanging from his belt give a soft silvery hue to the little Prince's garments. Softest and tenderest of all is the silver-blond of the little boy's silky hair.

He stands there child-like yet upright and straight as becomes a Prince—and very lonely. He rests his hand on the back of an armchair of deep red velvet trimmed with gold. It is on the chair that we find the child's only companion, his little dog. Soft and almost sad, the pet with his big black eyes seems to be telling part of the child's story. Our eyes keep wandering from the child to his pet and back to the child.

Our hearts are filled with tenderness toward the lonely little boy in his regal surroundings emerging from the shadows with his earnest baby face and figure. We are deeply stirred by this picture of a real child who is such a lonely little Prince.

Velazquez painted this portrait when he was an old man. By then, after the experience of a long life, he had the wisdom of old age. That is why there is so much tenderness and understanding in this stirring picture.

PRINCE PHILIP PROSPER painted about 1659
by Diego Velazquez (1599-1660)
Kunsthistorisches Museum, Vienna, Austria

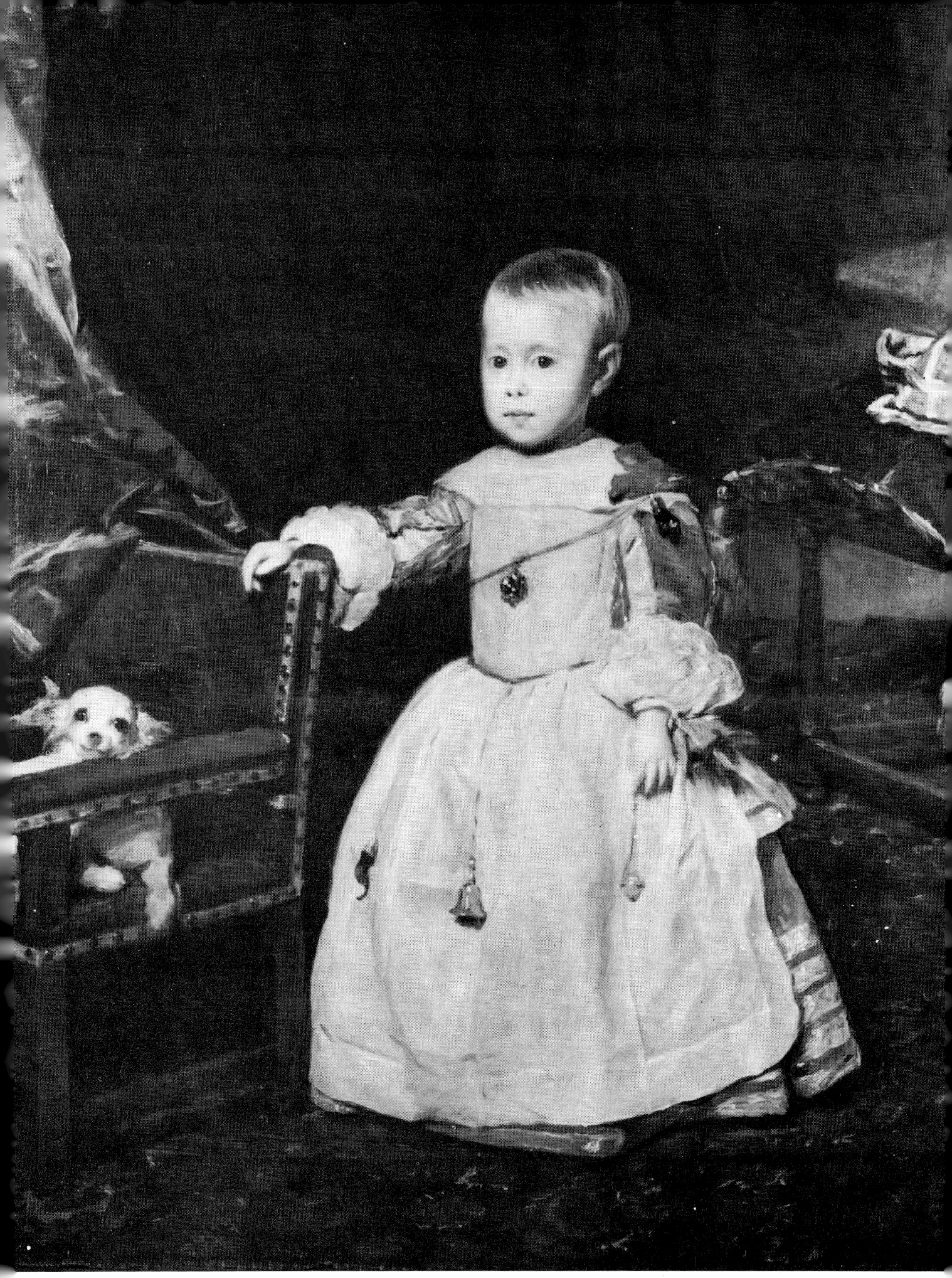

The Story of Breda's Surrender

THE CLOUDS hang low in the sky. Only a few rays of the sun can penetrate them to shed light on the scene below. There is something fearful in the air. We can almost hear the explosion in the distance where we see fiery smoke rising toward the sky.

The dark iron lances at the right look menacing as if they were bars of a prison window. At the left, in the foreground, a group of sad and silent men stand waiting. One of them raises a finger for silence. He is listening to the words spoken by the two men in the center and checking to make sure he hears them correctly.

One of the two has stepped forward from the men's own ranks. His richer garments show us that he is their leader. He has dismounted from his horse. Bowing slightly he offers the key of the city to the man in black armor.

This man, obviously the leader of the opposing army, has dismounted too. He has stepped out from under the forest of lances of the Spanish army. He is the victorious General Spinola, who after a long siege, had forced the brave Dutch defenders of the town of Breda to surrender.

With a gesture of benevolence General Spinola puts his hand on the shoulder of his defeated enemy, the Dutch Prince of Nassau. The victor has a look of kindness in his face as he bends toward the humbled man before him.

It is a gripping picture painted by Diego Velazquez, the greatest of Spanish artists. He was the court painter of King Philip IV of Spain, and it was for the King's summer residence that he made this great picture. It was meant to express the strength of the Spanish army, but also Spanish generosity toward an enemy after surrender.

The painter's heart seems to have been with the humbled Dutch. He makes us feel the pain in the simple faces of the defeated men. Yet Velazquez was, after all, a Spaniard. That is why, when he painted his own portrait in this picture, he put himself on the Spanish side. We see him there, in a wide hat, at the extreme right of the picture, under the Spanish flag.

Probably he put himself into this picture because he was so proud of it. And he had good reason to be, for no one has ever seen a greater picture commemorating an historical event than this magnificent *Surrender of Breda* by Velazquez.

THE LANCES painted 1635
by Diego Velazquez (1599-1660)

The Prado, Madrid, Spain

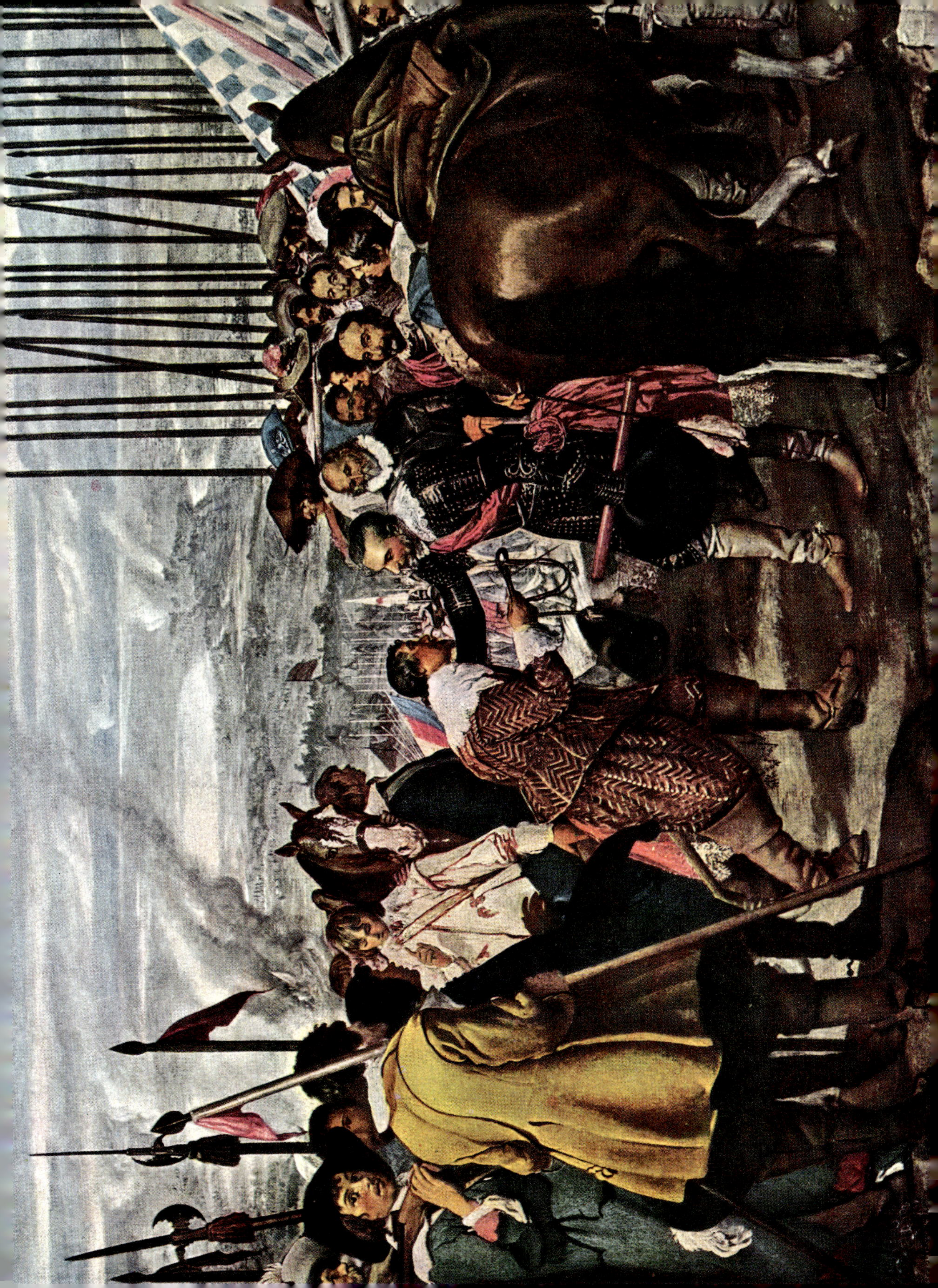

LAUGHING CHILD
painted about 1623-1625
by Frans Hals (1581-1666)

Courtesy Mr. Hans Cohn, Hollywood, California

The Smiling People of Holland

AS SOON as Holland gained her freedom in her revolutionary war, democracy was established and the arts began to flourish. The Dutch were happy with their newly won liberty and their little country.

One of their greatest painters, Frans Hals, liked to paint happy smiles on the faces of the Dutch people.

Look at the happy laughter of the little girl here!

See the smiling contentment of this young couple as the two of them sit in the comfortable shadow of a tree! They found this quiet spot where they could take their ease on a mossy slope, away from the people promenading near the fine country house in the park ornate with sculpture and a fountain.

Our two people seem very happy to be alone together. The man looks completely contented. And why shouldn't he be? The loveliest girl is sittting next to him and she rests her hand on his shoulder in natural affection. The mischievous smile on her face is so catching that just looking at her makes us smile too.

The sky is bright, and the big white clouds make it even more lively, just as the stylish starched ruffle around the girl's neck makes the freshness of her pink cheeks and her laughing eyes look livelier.

PORTRAIT OF A COUPLE painted about 1621
by Frans Hals (1581-1666)

Courtesy of the Rijks Museum,
Amsterdam, Holland

A branch of evergreen ivy on the ground joins the two figures together. It seems to be a wedding picture. It was painted two centuries after another wedding picture, Jan van Eyck's painting of the Arnolfini couple. (p.83).

The Arnolfini couple looked solemn and earnest compared to the smiling couple here. There man and wife joined their hands ceremoniously; here the two people simply sit together. But the way they sit tells us most eloquently: "We belong together."

Van Eyck's painting is full of sunshine and rich colors. Hals put his people into the shadow and he uses only dark colors, but his painting has inner warmth because of the warm expression on the people's faces.

Instead of putting in every detail with a very fine brush as van Eyck did, Hals painted with easy wide brush-strokes. He put light touches of paint in just the right places. With only a few strokes Hals makes us feel the difference between the girl's taffeta frock and the heavier silk of the man's suit, the transparent linen and dainty lace of the collars and cuffs.

Frans Hals' easy-going mastery of the brush reflects his easy-going view of the world. But the deeply penetrating eye of this great master enabled him to capture a smile that comes from deep within the heart.

TITUS READING painted about 1657
by Rembrandt van Rijn (1606-1669)

Kunsthistorisches Museum, Vienna, Austria

Rembrandt's Beloved Son Reading

REMBRANDT van Rijn was the greatest of all Dutch painters. His genius made him both successful and popular when he was very young. He married early and loved his wife Saskia very much. But she died after a few years of marriage leaving only a small son named Titus to her husband.

Titus was his father's pride and joy and became a real blessing to the artist. For Rembrandt was not a practical man. He wanted to paint in his own way whether his pictures pleased the public or not. Finally Rembrandt became very poor.

When Titus grew up he took care of his father's affairs. Throughout his short life the son stood at his father's side.

The picture of Titus we see here is one Rembrandt painted of the boy reading.

Titus' features show intense interest in his book. It must be a very good book indeed; the pages look as if they had been turned often; they open in many places. But Titus' dreaming eyes, his withdrawn lips, the way his hands hold the book—all these tell us better than the book itself that there must be a treasure in the much used pages.

Titus' figure is only dimly lighted. It melts into the background. But the way it is painted tells us many things.

The posture of the boy alone would show us that he is living the story he is reading. The highlights on his brow, his nose, his mouth, his hands all show that he is holding his breath. His dreamy eyes and, indeed, the expression of his whole face speak of a quiet hour of enjoyment that we can share by the grace of Rembrandt's great art.

Rembrandt's pictures highlight the essential things only. He thought that the rest of the world might as well be dimmed out since it is not important.

IN THE etching below, *The Three Trees,* Rembrandt makes his trees dark and sets them against a bright and luminous sky. Here a storm has swept away the clouds, but the rest of the sky is covered with darkness. A quick rain blows across one corner of the picture. Underneath, on the ground, a fisherman holds his rod in the quiet water. His wife, crouching on the ground next to him, watches for his catch.

Farther in the background we see cows grazing and men walking about. On the horizon, we see the wings of a windmill. All this is only faintly drawn. On the hill a passing haywagon is followed by a man, and sitting on the hilltop we see a lonely man drawing a picture.

The people are as small as midgets compared with the turmoil of the sky and the three trees that stand out mighty and unmoved. We feel that they have been standing there year after year, steadfast against wind and weather. They have become the heroes of Rembrandt's etching.

THE THREE TREES etched 1643
by Rembrandt

Courtesy of the Chicago Institute of Art

How Jacob Blessed His Grandsons

THE story of this picture comes to us out of the Old Testament.

The patriarch Jacob, you may remember, lived to be a very old man. At the age of a hundred and seventy-four he became ill and had to take to his bed.

Jacob's son, Joseph, knowing that his father was about to die, brought his wife and his two little sons to the old man's house. He wanted the boys to be blessed by their dying grandfather as Jacob himself had been blessed by his father, Isaac, before he died.

Manasseh and Ephraim were the boys' names. According to custom, Manasseh, the first-born, should have been the first to be blessed. But Jacob extended his right hand to give his first blessing to Ephraim, the second-born.

Joseph thought his father had made a mistake because of his failing eyesight. But no. Jacob told Joseph that both children would be blessed and would prosper but that the greater blessing would be given to the younger boy. Ephraim's descendants, he said, would become a greater nation than Manasseh's.

This is the story the great artist, Rembrandt, painted in this picture.

In the shadows of the darkened sickroom we see Jacob, the patriarch, on his bed. He lifts himself from his pillows, looking frail and very old. But in the expression of his face we can see that his powers of thought and feeling have not suffered from the years. There is all the wisdom of his miraculous old age written in his features. With a solemn and loving gesture he extends his arm toward Ephraim. Joseph tries to direct his father's hand to the first-born, Manasseh, but it is Ephraim's head that the old man touches first.

Ephraim looks like a little angel. His hands are crossed over his heart as he bends his head with humble gratitude and devotion. Next to him Manasseh awaits his turn with misty eyes.

In the background we see Joseph's wife, the children's mother. Her figure is almost lost in the darkness. To the patriarch's blessing she seems to be adding a silent blessing of her own. There is a devout stillness about this moment.

Rembrandt, the painter of the picture, makes us feel deeply about this solemn event. Close and sacred family bonds and the timeless significance of the Holy Bible speak in this picture, as only Rembrandt was able to make them speak.

Rembrandt read and studied the Bible all his life long. He drew and etched and painted the Biblical scenes as he re-lived the sacred stories in his own heart. In his pictures the Good Book comes closer to us by many hundreds of years.

Because he refused to serve the rich and mighty, Rembrandt was free to make his pictures as he wanted to. A simple man in the way he lived, Rembrandt's greatness was his all-embracing heart and his ceaseless effort to paint what he so deeply felt.

JACOB'S BLESSING painted about 1657
by Rembrandt van Rijn (1606-1669)

Phot. Staatliche Kunstsammlungen
Kassel, Germany

THE STUDIO OF THE PAINTER (Uncut picture)

Inspiration in the Artist's Studio

IN THIS picture we get a look into the painter's studio. A curtain has been drawn aside and we can watch the painter silently at work. He is sitting before his easel looking at his model who stands in the streaming sunlight.

The light comes from a window that we cannot see because it is hidden behind the curtain. In front of the curtain there is a dark red chair in the shadow. In the light we see a table with silks and velvets on it, a plaster mask, some books—things that belong in a painter's studio. On the wall hangs a map. A big gilded chandelier gives the scene a festive mood.

The model, a lovely girl draped in shimmering blue silk, stands with downcast eyes as if lost in a dream. She is not only the artist's actual model but also his inspiration. As such she leads the artist into a realm of beauty.

Everything about the girl has a meaning. The light gold book she holds against her heart is the symbol of poetry. The slender trumpet in her hand stands for music and is also an old symbol of fame.

The girl's head is crowned with a wreath of laurel. This symbol of an artist's reward inspires the painter to hope he may one day be so crowned. We see him just as he is painting the wreath on his canvas. The map on the wall shows the lands where the painter hopes his name will be known. He believes that the trumpet of his fame will resound over land and sea and in the cities of the world.

When the young Dutch artist, Vermeer van Delft, painted this picture, he purposely painted the figure of the artist—himself—from the back. In so doing he expressed the thought that a painter's features were not important. It was only his inspiration and his work that mattered. He was sure he would win his laurels because he knew he could capture his beautiful vision on his canvas.

He shows all this here by drawing aside a curtain and leading us into a place of golden light and poetic dreams.

This is just what Vermeer van Delft achieved in his career as a painter. He gave us a lighter, brighter, more colorful view of the world than the painters who came before him had done. He drew a curtain from the darkish world of the older Dutch painters.

Instead of the warm harmonies of red and green that the older painters had preferred, he painted in cooler combinations like blue and yellow and opened the eyes of his countrymen to the charm of light colors. He showed us the subtle differences in whites and grays. He made us see the beauty of the pattern of a map a little blurred against a wall of white, of the plain wall itself in the changing lights and shadows.

Above all, he bathed the world in sunshine and made it look gentle and gay.

THE STUDIO OF THE PAINTER painted about 1660
by Jan Vermeer van Delft (1632-1675)

Kunsthistorisches Museum, Vienna, Austria

A Gay Family Feast—with Some Tears

IN HOLLAND the Feast of St. Nicholas, who is our Santa Claus, is celebrated with much gayety on December 5. This is the day when children put their shoes at the fireplace to be filled with sweets if the children have been good or with a bunch of bare twigs if they have been naughty.

In our picture the Dutch painter Jan Steen takes us right into his home on the Eve of the Feast of St. Nicholas.

We can see that it is evening, for the room is only dimly lit by the setting sun. The reddish glow highlights the white linen collars and hoods that surround merry faces and —oh yes—one that is not merry at all. The brightest white collar belongs to one little boy who is crying as his older sister shows him his shoe with twigs in it.

But we are pretty sure that everything is going to turn out right, for the crying boy's younger brother smiles good-naturedly while he pokes his forefinger at the crying one. And if we look carefully, we can see Grandma in the dark background secretly beckoning to him to come with her into the other room. Surely she has some goodies there for her sad little grandson. For everybody must be happy on this day.

They are all smiling: the little girl carrying her load of presents, the Mother holding out her arms to the child, and the Father sitting contentedly in the middle of the crowd. There must be considerable noise of laughter and song and shouting, just as there would be on any such occasion. There is no end to the festivities in this room. The eldest brother, with the baby of the family on his arm, is beckoning to someone we cannot see.

We feel the warmth of real life here. The painter has made this scene as true to life as if we were looking at it in a mirror.

Dutch painters often painted like that. Most of them made pictures of simple people, fun-loving and gay, for the simple fun-loving people who liked such pictures.

Jan Steen painted mostly scenes of his own family, and an easy-going happy family it was. He did not care to paint anything but good fun and warm gayety as he saw it around him, and that he did—with admirable skill.

THE EVE OF ST. NICHOLAS painted about 1665
by Jan Steen (1626-1679)

Courtesy of the Rijks Museum,
Amsterdam, Holland

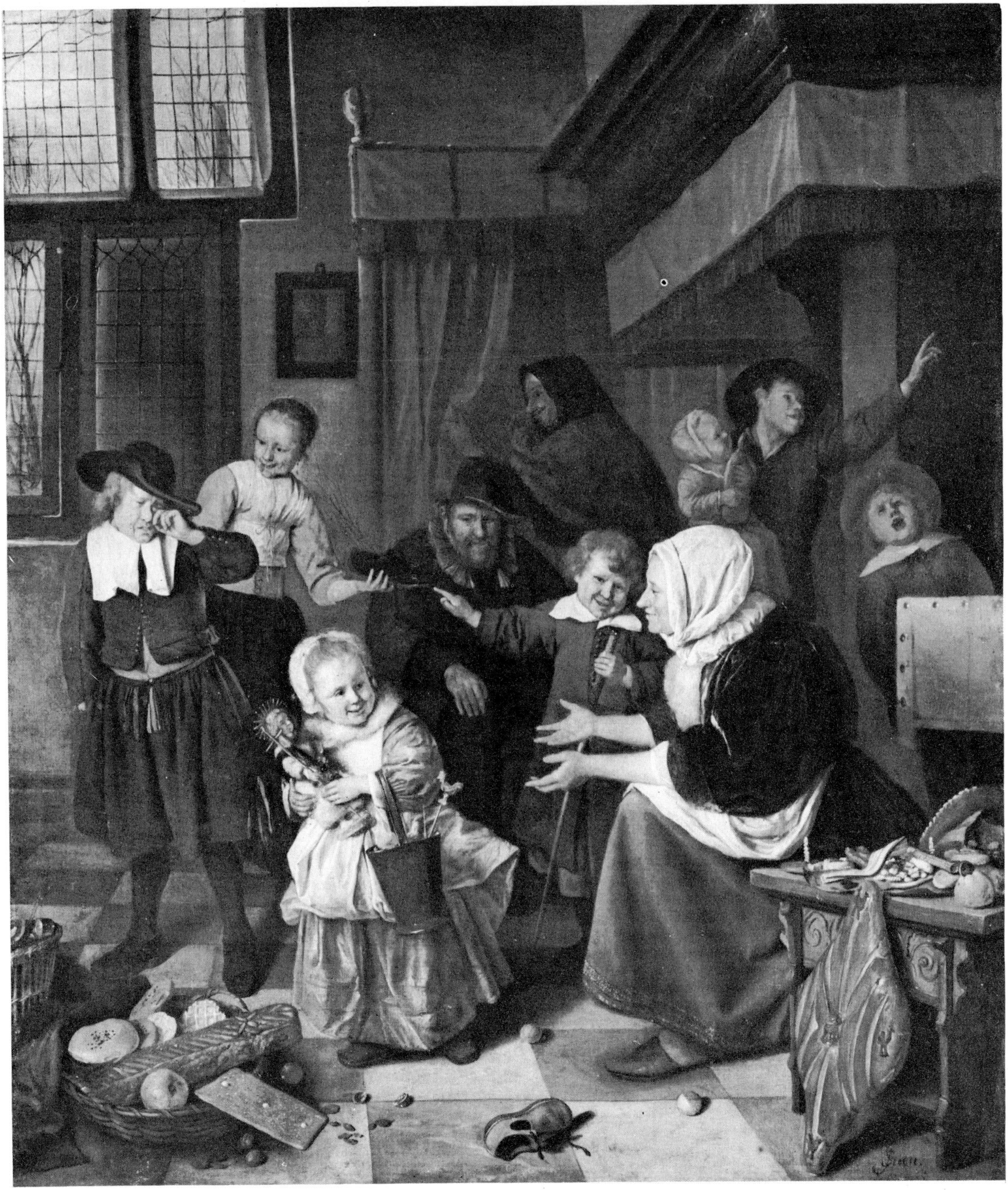

WATERING CATTLE painted about 1660 by Aelbert Cuyp (1620-1691)

Courtesy of the Museum of Fine Arts, Budapest, Hungary

The Dutch Loved to Paint the Sky and the Sea

THE Dutch master, Aelbert Cuyp, the painter of this picture, loved and made us love the quiet slow-moving life along the shore of the North Sea near Holland. In most of his paintings he took delight in showing us the quiet water of an inlet under a sky both high and wide, covered with clouds.

In this picture he shows us quietness by painting a group of cows standing contentedly in shallow water, looking with their big soft cow eyes at the soft and quiet inlet.

It is a lazy day. The landscape is dipped in soft warm golden sunshine. Nothing seems to move. The distant small sailboats lie still in the water. These things we see in the lower part of the picture.

Above, against the clear light blue sky, we see clouds in subtle gold and pink and gray. The wandering clouds make us feel the peaceful and eternal change of shapes in the infinite expanse of the sky.

Our glance wanders back to the foreground with the masterfully painted cows, their gold and brown colors blending so well into the moist heavy air. They seem to express the good-natured life we find so pleasant in little Holland. There the restful plains, the still waters of the lazy streams, and an ever-cloudy sky are in constant harmony.

Better than anyone else Aelbert Cuyp could paint a peaceful mood, the tender shine of that moist heavy air. He was an unassuming artist who glorified what seems most commonplace in life. Never flashy, his paintings are born of loving smiles and bring about loving smiles in the beholder.

THE BIG FOREST painted about 1655 by Jacob Ruisdael (1628-1682)   Kunsthistorisches Museum, Vienna, Austria

They Loved to Paint Their Forests Too

THE Dutch people loved the view of their wide open sea, but also their sparse forests. A much rarer sight to them, forests were not painted as often as the sea. A forest seemed solemn and important to them. That is why their paintings of forests are usually very large. This picture, for instance, is almost six feet long.

We see a group of trees along a roadside, with another group in the distance. Between the trees and above them we see the cloudy Dutch sky, and behind the tree-trunks we guess rather than see a plain in the mild sunlight. But there is a thicket at the left, and a shallow brook crossing the road in the foreground. The big shadow gives us the feeling of still more trees—majestic ones—close by.

But the tired wanderer by the roadside was not seeking shade. He is sitting in the sun and not taking advantage of the shade of the most magnificent big trees behind him.

The painter put him right next to the majestic tree to show the contrast between mere man and the overwhelming greatness of nature.

Jacob Ruisdael, the painter of this picture, was a grave and earnest man. He made us feel his own earnest view of nature, his own solemn admiration of the great forests that outlive us humans by many centuries.

VERSAILLES PALACE built 1655-1682
by Louis Le Vau (1612-1670) and J. Hardouin Mansart (1646-1708)

Versailles, France

The Sun King's Palace

THIS picture shows but a small part of Versailles Palace, because the entire Palace is so big that it couldn't be photographed except from the air. In an aerial photograph, however, we couldn't see the front of the Palace as we would see it if we were there.

Versailles Palace is rich and noble-looking. It is not overloaded with ornaments. The order of the Greek columns makes the decoration dignified, and they serve as "breakfronts" in the long extension of this immense building.

It was the aim of the architects who built it not to make the Palace *look* colossal although it had to *be* colossal to house the enormous court of Louis XIV. All the noblemen and noblewomen wanted to have a part in the luxurious life of gay and splendid festivities arranged by the royal household.

The Palace of Versailles has a main front with receding wings next to it. This is so that it would have more space without looking showy. Besides, long stretches of uniform windows would become monotonous.

The breakfronts are of plain wall to make a solid base, with either one or three windows on the first floor. The second, the finest floor, has the columns added. The top floor is much lower and serves as a base for sculptured ornaments that crown the building.

Versailles Palace was a fitting residence for the King of France, Louis XIV, who became known as the Sun-King.

LOUIS XIV sculptured 1665
by Gian Lorenzo Bernini (1598-1680)

A Great Sculptor Meets a Great King

Versailles Palace, Versailles, France

KING LOUIS XIV of France, whose portrait-bust we see here, seems to be a superior person and one who knows it. The bust was sculptured in white marble by the Italian Gian Lorenzo Bernini. The artist was almost seventy years old when he was called to France. There he made this bust of the King which has remained a cherished possession of the French nation.

In the bust King Louis looks as if he had flown in from somewhere in outer space because of the cloud-like sweep of his wind-blown garment.

But above the drapery the King looks real enough. His metal armor gives power and weight to his figure; his elaborate lace collar gives him distinction. Surrounded by breezy locks, his face with its lifted chin looks proud. The King's keen eyes and open glance tell us that his pride is not due merely to his station, but to his superior power of thought and to his energy.

A more daring, dashing portrait can't be found anywhere in the world. This is partly because by the time he had reached this age, the sculptor Bernini had the mastery to make this bust an exciting one. The wind-blown silken drapery, the metal armor, the lace collar and the curly hair—the fine detail in all these are combined in one beautiful composition.

But more important is the artist's way of giving expression to the King's character.

When the Italian sculptor Bernini met the French King Louis XIV, it was a meeting of two great and dazzling personalities. The result was an extraordinary work of art.

COMPANY IN THE PARK painted about 1717
by Antoine Watteau (1684-1721)

The Louvre, Paris, France

Life is Playful—Life is Graceful

HERE we see a picnic in a park with men and women and children sitting around or taking walks on velvety meadows under giant trees. Rosy pink clouds drift in the sky. The sky is reflected in the smooth mirror of a lake.

A little girl stands day-dreaming on the shore of the lake. She has forgotten her little dog, so he decides to play with some other children on the grass. Even the grown-ups are playing games. It is like fairyland.

Everything in this picture seems a little unreal. The tall trees are not oaks or pines or elms or spruces or maples. They just look like trees in general without looking like any trees we know. They are light and lovely, painted in pale green with silvery tones.

The people are slender and graceful and pretty; too much so to be real. They wear garments just like the children's, of shimmering silk in soft pastel shades. They make a most delicate and lovely picture.

Antoine Watteau, the painter, was not interested in real life. He painted a kind of fairyland, full of grace and charm, that his fancy alone could dream up.

Most of his pictures are small in size: not more than two or three feet wide or long. They give us just the right sort of decoration for a wall over a love-seat or an old-fashioned small piano in a small and intimate room.

THE ALLEGORY OF PAINTING painted 1765
by Francois Boucher
(1703-1770)

National Gallery of Art, Washington, D. C.
Samuel H. Kress Collection

Life among the Clouds

WHO is the pretty girl in this picture? And where is she? The drapery of her silken garment melts into the clouds. Is she perhaps a goddess? No, for goddesses are always sublimely beautiful and this girl is just pretty.

But let us find out about her. She holds a crayon in her hand, and behind her we see a painter's palette with a number of brushes and some rolled-up drawing paper.

We see her drawing the outlines of a little winged child. She looks at the model posing for the picture. He holds a burning torch and there is a quiver full of arrows at his side. These are the symbols of Cupid. They tell us that the little winged child is Cupid, the god of love.

Maybe the canvas, crayon, palette, brushes, and drawing paper are also symbols and tell us the meaning of the girl?

Her tools are the tools of painting and she *is* painting. Finally, a little sprite holds up a wreath of laurel to her. Laurel has always been an artist's reward. The girl must represent the art of painting.

We have had to describe this picture carefully and translate the symbols into words. We call this an allegory, and that is why this picture is called *The Allegory of Painting*.

It was painted by the great French artist Francois Boucher, who often painted allegories. Most of his pictures are full of pretty girls and Cupids and sprites in soft light shades of pink and blue and green and gray.

They are just the right sort of decoration for a gay and elegant room where people like to chat and dance.

COUNT SINZENDORF painted about 1717
by Hyacinth Rigaud (1659-1743)

Too Much Pomp and Glitter

Kunsthistorisches Museum, Vienna, Austria

SHINING and glittering rich silks and velvets fill this picture which is a portrait of the eighteenth century Austrian Ambassador to Paris, Count Sinzendorf. The draperies of his garment look as if they were being stirred by the wind to make them look more impressive. Among all the pomp we can hardly see the man's figure. His proud fat face is framed by the ample locks of his wig, according to the fashion of the time—and they were very convenient for hiding a balding head too.

The Count holds his hand on his hip with his little finger crooked in a silly gesture of "elegance." His other hand seems to be resting, but does not really rest, on some object made of velvet. Nothing is genuine about this man. He is all *pose* and empty gestures.

This picture, showing the useless display of wealth and pride, was admirably painted by the French master, Hyacinth Rigaud. But there is too much glitter of material and too little natural character in it. Noblemen in France at that time indulged in luxury as the English had done the century before. (p. 158). A change to greater simplicity came before the century was over.

STAIRCASE OF WÜRZBURG PALACE
built 1744-1753
by Balthasar Neumann (1687-1753)
Ceiling painted about 1753
by Giovanni Baptista Tiepolo (1696-1770)

The Splendor of Gracious Living

Wurzburg, Germany

IN THIS picture we see the famous staircase of Würzburg Palace in Germany. The great German architect Balthazar Neumann built it of gilded white stucco and marble. Ornate with marble sculptures, the staircase has dazzling width and height.

But space even more dazzling was added above the staircase by the great Italian painter, Giovanni Baptista Tiepolo, who painted a make-believe world on the ceiling which covered the real building.

On a single fresco painted above the 100-foot long and 60-foot wide staircase, Tiepolo showed Mount Olympus with all the gods and heroes of Greek mythology. Allegorical figures (p. 183) representing the arts and sciences were added to the brilliant gathering.

At the sides Tiepolo painted allegories of the continents with many figures of men and beasts and buildings, all under a light blue sky.

White clouds shining in the sunshine make the background of this immense fresco particularly bright and gay. It is a Venetian sky, for Tiepolo was a Venetian painter. He added rich deep colors to give the painting a look of reality. This had been the style of Venetian painting since Giovanni Bellini (p. 95), Titian (p. 124), and Veronese (p. 140).

But Tiepolo's paintings surpass them all in size, splendor, and gayety. No painter since Giovanni Baptista Tiepolo has painted pictures of such beauty on such a grand scale.

How a Noblewoman Avenged a Soldier's Brutality

AN ANCIENT Greek story tells us how Timoclea, a Greek noblewoman, was insulted in time of war by a brutal enemy soldier. It happened when the town in which Timoclea had been living was invaded by Thracian troops. Her house was ransacked and it was the commander of the enemy troops who insulted her.

Timoclea avenged the offense by killing the brutal soldier. For that deed she was brought before a tribunal to be judged. But she was acquitted because her bearing showed her to be a noblewoman— sufficient reason, at that time, for those who judged her.

This is very different from the Biblical stories and Christian legends that told of good deeds performed by heroic or saintly characters, of love and faith, or of courageous fights for a good cause. Those were the stories that decorated churches or were put up on altars for the benefit of all, high and low.

The story of Timoclea, however, decorated a palace—the palace of a Venetian nobleman. It was painted at a time when, to the high and mighty, wealth and rich living were more important than religious devotion. The story of Timoclea was meant to please and flatter such people.

The picture shows us Timoclea sitting on a rich brocaded pillow under a white marble arch of her palace porch. She is clad in shimmering silk garments of enchantingly beautiful light colors. Behind her stands a lady-in-waiting also wearing sumptuous silks.

Timoclea holds on to the pillow beneath her with one hand while she raises the other in horror because a brutal soldier next to her has lifted his fist to strike her.

The soldier's brown muscular arm and hand are contrasted with hers so soft and white and gentle in motion. His garments of deep rich red and blue add strength of color to his strong bulky figure, and they blend superbly with the color of his weather-beaten face.

Strangely enough, the colors and the modeling make the soldier look attractive rather than repulsive as we would expect. But at that period painters were more concerned with achieving a pleasing effect than with revealing character.

Remember the fanciful pictures by the French painters Watteau and Boucher (p.182-183) of the same period? The figures they painted look pretty and playful, especially in contrast to the noble and dashing characters in this picture by the Italian artist Giovanni Baptista Tiepolo. Tiepolo's colors are the radiant and forceful Venetian colors rather than the soft and subdued hues the French painters used.

Giovanni Baptista Tiepolo himself was very quick with his brush. It is said that he once painted the story of the Last Supper in a single day. How unlike the earlier painters, who often devoted many years to painting a single picture! Leonardo da Vinci, you remember, took several years to paint his *Last Supper* (p.105).

But in Tiepolo's time decoration was pompous and brilliant and done with technical skill rather than with deep devotion to fulfilling an artistic task.

In the revolutionary times that followed the time of glittering pomp, art again became simpler and studiously truthful, as we shall see (p.196-202).

TIMOCLEA AND THE THRACIAN COMMANDER painted about 1753
by Giovanni Baptista Tiepolo

National Gallery of Art, Washington, D. C.
Samuel H. Kress Collection

Fashions may Change but not Little Boys

IN HIS smart coat a little boy with carefully groomed hair stands in front of his mother to say goodby before going to school. But why are his eyes downcast? And why the guilty look on his face?

Why? Because of the disorder on the floor. All his toys are lying around: his shuttlecock, his feather ball, and some cards he has used to build houses with. The toys all seem to be pointing at him. But he has his books under his arm ready to leave for school. Will he close the table drawer before he dashes out through the open door? And will he stop to pick up his toys?

His mother seems to be scolding him for his untidiness. She has too many other things to do as we can see by the open mending-basket at her side. She has just brushed the little boy's hat to make him look spick and span. Now she is telling him gently what she thinks.

He listens, yes, but is he sorry? No. His eyes may be downcast because he knows he is wrong, but they are also on the hat he wants to grab. Look at his feet: they all but say "Let's get going."

This story is told here by the French painter Jean Simeon Chardin. He was inspired by Dutch art (p. 176-179). He looked at the little happenings in the world around him as the Dutch painters did. But Chardin was a Frenchman and therefore his paintings have a clearer, stricter order than those of the casual Dutch painters.

Everything in this painting is arranged to make the story clear.

Chardin, unlike the Dutch, did not care to make materials look as though we could feel them. We can't tell what fabrics the clothes are made of or the upholstery either. We do not feel the warmth of sunlight. Chardin's colors haven't the full rich or brilliantly clear tones of the Dutch painters.

Chardin's colors have subtler tones of pale colors on a grayish background. His colors are similar to those of other French painters such as Watteau (p. 182) or Boucher (p. 183). But Chardin's colors, for all their gentle charm, have also a quality that is quite down to earth.

This French master tells his story subtly. The first thing we notice in this picture is that the little boy is ready to leave for school. We have to look closely to see the mischief and find out that the painter had his tongue in his cheek from the beginning.

GOODBY BEFORE SCHOOL painted 1739
by Jean Simeon Chardin (1699-1779)

National Gallery, Ottawa, Canada

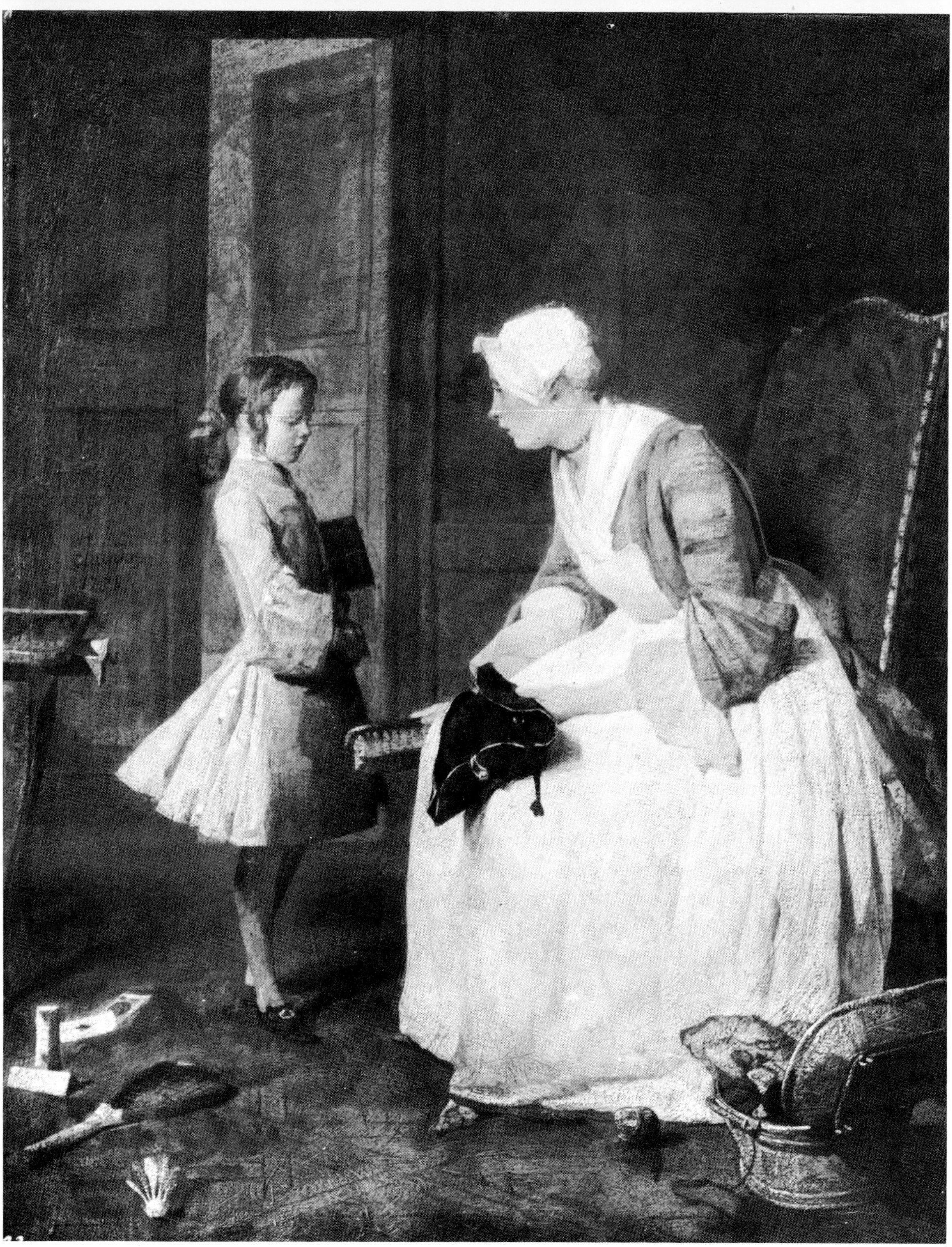

A Group Portrait of Children—and Some Fun

THIS is certainly a lively gathering of children. Something must be going on. But what? Let's see. A baby is sitting in a little old-fashioned go-cart. Baby is attracted by a couple of cherries her older sister is holding. The little one reaches eagerly for the cherries, but Big Sister isn't paying attention. Her mind is on something else. Her eyes seem to wander as if she were listening and we can see what she is listening to: On the other side of the room her little brother, sitting in a high-backed chair, is turning the handle of the music box on his knees. His eyes are on the bird-cage where a little bird is trying to outsing the music.

Another sister is dancing to the tune, holding her apron in one hand and her pretty flowered dress in the other. Here she goes: with the tip of her pointed shoe lightly touching the floor, her foot moves to the rhythm.

Big Sister would like to dance too. She has already picked up her apron, but she has put it over her arm because she has to mind the baby. Only half her mind is on the music as she holds on to baby's hand. The cherries, obviously meant for baby, seem to be following the rhythm of the dance.

But besides baby, there is someone else in the room who is disappointed: the cat. The cat has jumped up to the back of the little boy's chair to watch the singing bird. The cat's paw is ready to grab the bird, but the little singer is well protected in its golden cage, and the cat is just as far from reaching it as the baby is from reaching the delicious cherries.

The English painter, William Hogarth, made his portrait, *The Graham Children,* into this delightful story. It is safe to say that the children are wearing their prettiest dresses. They are made of silk but they are not meant to be swanky. A rich silken drapery hangs from the ceiling, but we feel that it was not added for pomp. It is there to round out the color composition of the picture, for the color of the drapery repeats the color of baby's dress in a warmer hue. It is gayety above all that the painter aimed at in this picture.

Gayety, in fact, was what Hogarth cared for most in all his work. He was an excellent observer of human nature, and he kept his eye on the funny side. Therefore, when he painted *The Graham Children,* he painted the children true to their natures and in a lively manner with gay colors. He did it in a mischievous way, to make the beholder smile.

THE GRAHAM CHILDREN
painted 1742
by William Hogarth
(1697-1764)

National Gallery, London, England

A Small Boy in the Costume of a Big King

A MERRY little boy smiles gaily at us. Why is he smiling? Why is he standing in such a funny way with his legs wide apart? He is dressed up in a most unusual costume. He does not look his usual self—that we can see. Even his pet dog has to sniff him to make sure that he is his master. The other dog indignantly turns his back on him because of his disguise.

The little boy is Master Crewe dressed up like King Henry VIII of England. We know the King from the portrait made of him about two hundred years earlier, by his court painter, Hans Holbein (p.137).

Henry VIII was a mighty and self-willed person—ruthless, in fact. Hans Holbein had painted him in a challenging pose and he looks like a man of great daring.

Master Crewe has to smile at the thought that he is impersonating such a terrible tyrant. But another reason may be that the nose of his little dog is tickling him.

Except for this sweet childish smile, Master Crewe copies the King to a t. Gloves and dagger in hand, as the King has, he wears the same hat over his soft hair, the same dress with the same chains, even the same Order of the Garter under his left knee. Only the fur-trimmed coat around his shoulder is made of soft shining velvet instead of the rigid silk embroidered cloak of King Henry VIII.

Sir Joshua Reynolds, the painter of this picture, made that change because he preferred a softer, more mellow style of painting. This English painter liked to melt figures into a dark-toned background as Velasquez in Spain (p.166) and Rembrandt in Holland (p.170-173), for instance, had done before him.

In this picture of Master Crewe as Henry VIII, Reynolds gave his portrait special interest by giving the child a disguise. He liked to paint children in pictures with an extra story added. He did this, perhaps, because portrait painting was not regarded as a particularly high form of art. In the field of painting the artist was praised for composing the story in a picture and for the way he told it, just as much as for the life-like quality of its painting. During Reynolds' time there was little other than portrait painting in his native England. The English are very much interested in people, but they seem to have felt that stories can be told better in words than in pictures. This has always been done by their great poets and writers. The painting of historic events in England has never equalled the superb literature which is England's glory.

MASTER CREWE AS HENRY VIII painted 1770
by Sir Joshua Reynolds (1723-1792)

By permission The Marchioness of Crewe, owner, London, England

This Picture Won an Argument

THE Blue Boy by Thomas Gainsborough is one of the most famous paintings in the world. It has an interesting story.

While Sir Joshua Reynolds was enjoying official glory as president of the Royal Academy, his most important rival in portrait painting was Thomas Gainsborough. He taught himself because he did not believe painting could be taught in a school. While the Royal Academy argued the case, Gainsborough fought back with pictures. Let's see how he did it.

For instance, at the Academy they taught that blue, being a cold color, should never dominate a painting because it would not be effective. It should be used, they said, only in the background or in small quantities. Gainsborough painted the portrait of a boy called Master Buttel to show how wrong he considered that idea.

The public, enraptured by the dominating blue of the picture, called it *The Blue Boy*.

Looking at this painting we are at once struck with the beauty of the shimmering blue silk. The color seems to sing: in higher and lower tones. Every color-note is different from the others, as singing voices are, yet they all blend together in one harmony. The painter is the orchestra leader, but instead of a baton he holds a brush which moves around in various ways: in smoother rhythms here, in livelier motion there, now with full force, then with restraint quietly and smoothly. He makes us almost feel his own delight in the painting.

Gainsborough used a simple background: a hillside under an evening sky covered with clouds. The colors have faded into darkish browns and grays. The boy's blue silk suit radiates against these dull hues. It is highlighted by the white lace collar and cuffs and the white slits of the jacket. The white feather of the hat and the white stockings with their shadows guide our eyes down to the shadowy ground.

Gainsborough won another artistic argument against Sir Joshua Reynolds with this same picture. Reynolds thought that he had to add some story to his portraits. (Remember Master Crewe on p.190?) Gainsborough thought this unnecessary. He painted Master Buttel simply as the boy looked when he stopped for a chat on his evening walk. It is exactly this natural simplicity that we find so appealing. The intelligent face of the boy is very much alive. His features are fine and sensitive. Whoever looks into his attentive eyes will always remember him as a person, not only for his blue garment.

At the Exhibition of the Royal Academy of 1770 Gainsborough's *Blue Boy* was the hit of the show.

THE BLUE BOY painted 1770
by Thomas Gainsborough (1727-1788)

Huntington Library, San Marino, Calif.

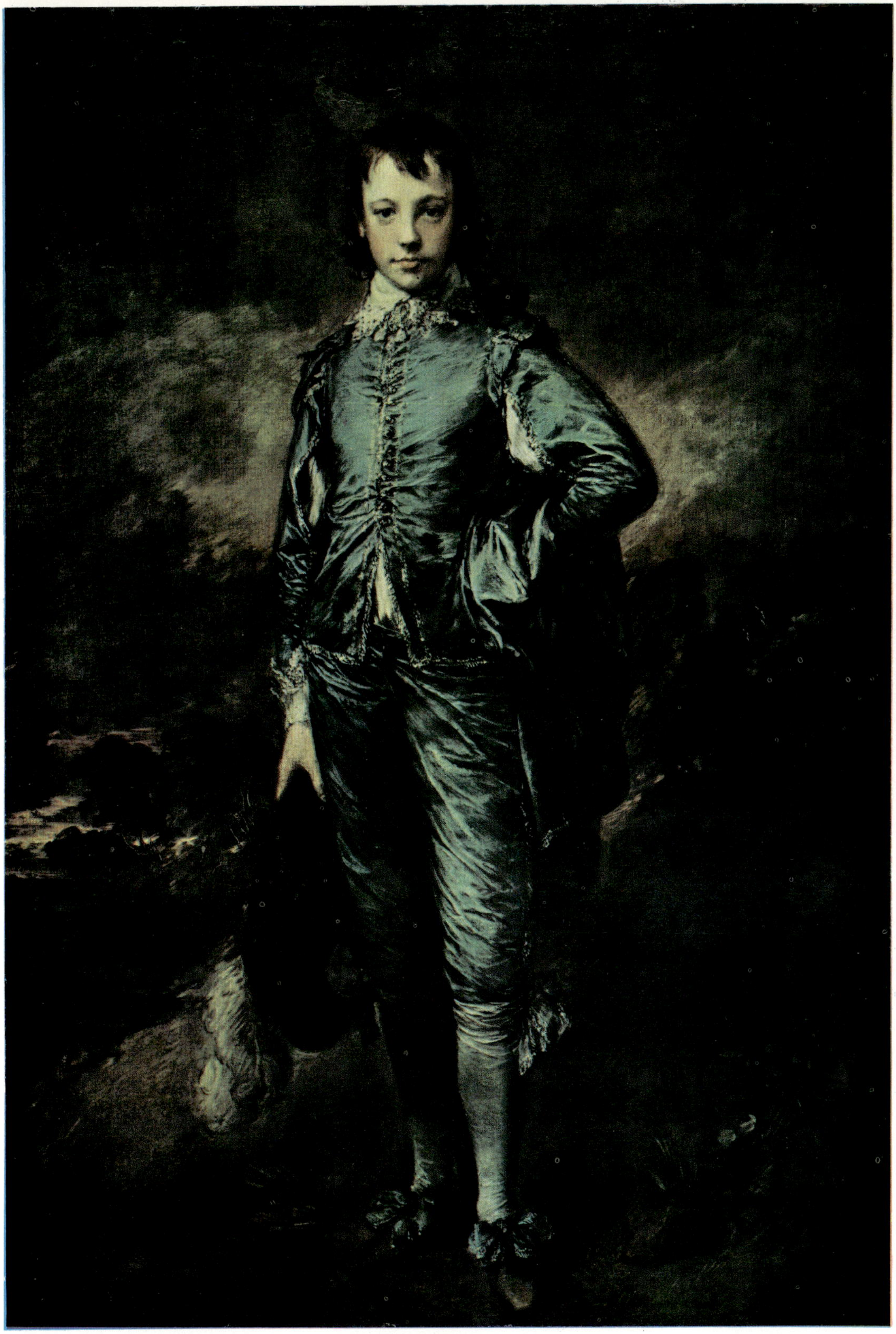

CHARLES I painted 1785
by John Singleton Copley (1737-1815)

Courtesy of the Trustees of the Boston Public Library, Boston, Mass.

The First Documentary Was Painted by an American

IT WAS two years after the American and four years before the French Revolution when the American painter, John Singleton Copley, exhibited this big historical picture at the Royal Academy in London.

Copley, who was living in England, wanted to show how revolutionary the times were. He therefore painted an historical event that recalled the English Revolution.

This is the story Copley painted: The Stuart King, Charles I of England, appeared before Parliament with armed soldiers. He wanted to punish five particular Parliament members who had often opposed his orders. But these five had been hidden from the King by the other members. This led to the break between the King and his Parliament and in time to the English Revolution.

Copley's picture was something entirely new in historical painting. It was the first time a painter had actually *studied* the historical records of an event which had happened over a century before. He was not satisfied with stories about it. He examined old portraits of the people who were present at the event. We know of at least five such portraits painted by Van Dyck (see his *Stuart Princes*, p.158-159) that Copley used as models.

The painter has chosen the moment after the King, standing on the Speaker's platform, ordered the Speaker of the House to surrender the five impeached members of Parliament. But the Speaker, although respectfully half-kneeling before the King, points to the assembly and tells the King that he cannot obey because he is a servant of Parliament and therefore only its spokesman.

These happenings were recorded by the clerk of Parliament. We see him writing in his book at the right end of the picture.

Revolution was in the air. This was a very exciting picture because it reminded people that nations would no longer suffer indignities but would fight injustice and tyranny. It was particularly forceful because Copley had shown the event as it actually happened. He told the truth, the whole truth, and nothing but the truth.

BENJAMIN FRANKLIN sculptured 1778
by Antoine Houdon (1741-1828)

Courtesy of the Metropolitan Museum of Art, New York, N. Y.

THE French sculptor Houdon made this marble bust of Benjamin Franklin when he went to France as minister from the young America in 1778. It shows Franklin's keen mind as well as his sense of humor. Above all, it shows his simple dignity, for the bust itself is simple and dignified.

Note the difference between the simple style of this bust—so appropriate for the time of revolutions, both American and French—and Bernini's dazzling bust of Louis XIV, King of France (p.181).

MADAME RÉCAMIER painted 1800
by Jacques Louis David (1748-1825)

The Louvre, Paris, France

Keeper of the Sacred Flame

IN PARIS, at the time of the French Revolution, there lived a beautiful young woman. She was gentle and intelligent. She did not take part in partisan politics. But her house became a meeting place of leading men and women in the world of art and literature. Her name was Madame Récamier.

Jacques Louis David, the great French painter of the Revolution, made this world-famous portrait of Madame Récamier. He painted her clothed in flowing white garments made in the ancient Greek style that was again the fashion of the day.

We see Madame Récamier resting on a Greek sofa. Behind her back burns a Greek oil-lamp on top of an antique lamp-stand. The room is bare.

Her face is gentle and earnest. Her neck is slim and straight. She is relaxed but there is wakeful poise in her resting figure and there is nothing limp or lazy about her. Her lightly closed hand shows her active energy. She resembles the spirited Caryatids (p.28), and she reminds us of the ancient priestesses who had to guard the sacred flame. The antique setting was enough background to make her look like a monument.

David's portraits of the important people of the French Revolution are often painted monuments to what they stood for.

NAPOLEON CROSSING THE ALPS
painted 1800 or 1801
by Jacques Louis David
(1748-1825)

A Painted Monument to Napoleon

Belvedere Museum, Vienna, Austria

THIS other picture by David is another expressive monument on canvas. It is the portrait of the victorious General of the French Revolution, the leader of the French Republic, Napoleon Bonaparte.

He sits firmly in the saddle of his rearing horse. Looking out of the picture, he seems to be saying, "Look upward! Although the road is new and full of danger, you must follow it if your goal is high." The red mantle slung around his shoulder is blown upward by the wind like a flag.

His earnest calm face holds the promise that his path is well planned. His shining forehead, his straight nose and firmly set mouth are steady while everything else in the picture is in motion. Napoleon's face shows his outstanding mind and energy. We know he will master powerful forces as surely as he is mastering his fiery-eyed powerful horse.

The names of Hannibal, Charlemagne, and Bonaparte are hewn in the rock at his feet. The former two had braved the same dangerous heights in olden times. But the name Bonaparte stands out in the clearest lettering because for David his was the noblest task: to defeat the enemies of France and of freedom.

THE PEACEABLE KINGDOM painted about 1830
by Edward Hicks (1780-1849)

An American Ideal:

Peace on Earth

Courtesy of the Brooklyn Museum, Brooklyn, N.Y.

THE Pennsylvania Quaker, Edward Hicks, who painted this picture, did not have the skill to make either his human or his animal figures quite life-like (in contrast to the picture on the opposite page). That was because Hicks did not learn to paint in an art academy. He taught himself to paint just so that he could express his ideas in pictures. His ideas and ideals were more important to him than pleasing the eye with beautiful painting.

Hicks painted *The Peaceable Kingdom*—the scene we see above—many more times. He chose this particular scene because as a Quaker he believed in peace, and as an American he believed that America was destined to make the world a better place. In this composition he linked an American historical event with a Bible story.

In the first part of the picture, in the background at the left, we see a quiet river winding among friendly hills. On the ground under a tree with golden leaves, stands the Quaker leader William Penn, for whom the state of Pennsylvania was named (see Vol. 9, p. 42).

Penn has just made peace with the Indians. Then in the foreground we see Isaiah's Biblical words coming true: "The wolf shall dwell with the lamb, and the leopard shall lie down with the kid; and the calf and the young lion and the fatling together: and a little child shall lead them. And the cow and the bear shall feed; their young ones shall lie down together; and the lion shall eat straw like the ox."

Everything is here. The somewhat bewildered lion and leopard sit quietly among the domestic animals and the little children. Even the straw is there drawn with lovely curving lines.

Hicks' clumsy way of expressing his ideas makes us smile, but our smile comes from the heart because the fine heart of the artist has touched ours.

STAIRCASE GROUP painted about 1795
by Charles Wilson Peale (1741-1827)

The Picture George Washington Bowed to

IT IS said that when George Washington saw this picture exhibited in a doorframe with steps jutting out into the room, he bowed to it, thinking he was bowing to the actual sons of his friend, Charles Wilson Peale, who painted the picture.

The boys are painted in the pose of Van Dyck's Stuart Princes (p.158). The younger boy stands higher in the background, the older is stepping up the stairs. Both turn their faces toward us as the Princes do. Even the turn in the wall is in the same place. But now look at the differences!

Courtesy of the Philadelphia Museum of Art

Instead of two proud cold Princes we see two eager warm-hearted boys. The younger looks at us invitingly and beckons. The older has the tools of his profession in hand: a palette and brushes. He is really climbing the stairs, not only putting up his foot. He too looks at us in a friendly way.

Instead of the rich fancy garments of the Princes, the Peale boys wear simple and sensible clothes. The staircase is lit by friendly sunshine so that everything can be clearly seen, while in Van Dyck's painting the glittering figures melt into the dark.

Peale, the American revolutionary, painted the beauty of clean-cut shapes, not that of bewitching colors and materials. Instead of pride and empty pretense, Peale expressed natural friendliness and simple truth.

Why This Scene Appealed to the Painter

THE English painter, John Constable, was the same age as Turner, whose dramatic *Téméraire* we shall see on page 207. Constable too had a new way of looking at nature, but his was entirely different from Turner's.

While Turner traveled a great deal, Constable hardly moved from the small stretch of English landscape on the banks of the Stour River that was his home.

Along the Stour the weeping willow trees have narrow leaves that are green on top and silvery below. The slightest wind ripples the light leaves, and anybody can understand that the mellow green color of the willows is actually composed of two colors, a clear strong green and silver gray.

This is perhaps the cause of John Constable's particular way of painting this lovely landscape. Unlike the painters before him, he painted with small strokes of the brush in different shades. The effect was a richer color and warmer life in his pictures.

Constable loved the placid world around him so much that he did not look for more exciting subjects than the small events of everyday life. But he gave width and breathing space to his pictures. The one we see here, his famous *Hay-Wain,* is a six-footer. But we must look at the painting inch by inch to appreciate the love and care and insight of Constable's artistry.

The title of the painting does not hint at a story. It is a very general landscape painting. The painter gave it three different titles: Each one of the three titles tells us something about what Constable meant to paint. The first, *House on the Stour,* tells us that he was interested in any house at any part of the Stour River.

The second, *Landscape: Noon,* tells us something more revealing, because it was a new thing to paint a landscape at a particular hour, except, of course, a sunrise or sunset which are *events* that can be seen. But Constable always observed the landscape and the sky in the light of a special time without showing the position of the sun. Here he chose noon. Noon-time can be detected in a picture only by thorough observation.

That was probably why Constable chose the third title, *The Hay-Wain.* That title immediately distinguishes this picture from other views of a house on a bank of the Stour. It was the sensible thing to do.

When we look at the picture the hay-wain in it does not seem particularly important. It fits most naturally into the landscape. The clouded sky, the shallow river, the sleepy cottage, the loaded hay-wain drawn by rustic horses—these all belong together. They all have something heavy and solid about them. The only lively spot in the picture is the little dog who greets the returning hay-wain with merry barking and a wagging tail.

The picture's solid heaviness tells us that the painter was a solid and reliable person who worked with untiring devotion. It also tells of his deep love for nature at its simplest. He felt that painting what he saw as he alone saw it made these simple subjects worthy of being painted.

Constable's method of painting won the admiration of the young French painters of his time. His idea of painting landscapes as they look in the particular light of a particular time of day was developed by the great painters of the next hundred years.

THE HAY-WAIN painted 1821
by John Constable (1776-1837)

National Gallery, London, England

DON MANUEL OSORIO DE ZUNIGA painted 1784
by Francisco de Goya (1746-1828)
(See Frontispiece)

This Little Boy is Master of His Pets

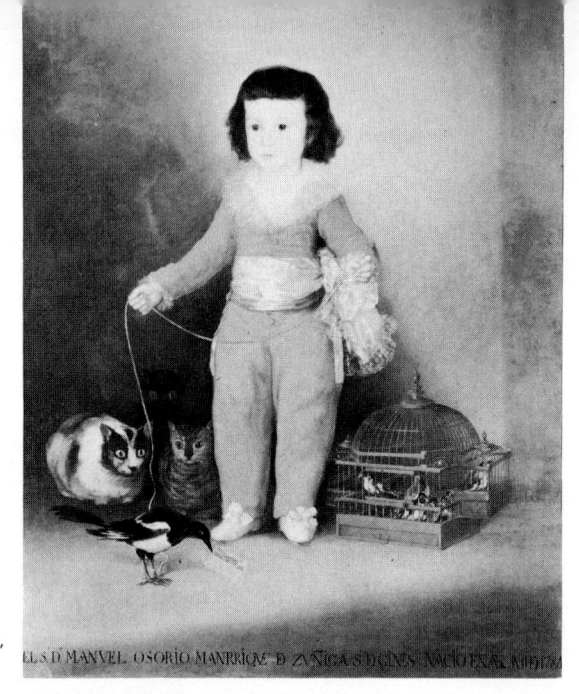

Courtesy of the Metropolitan Museum of Art,
New York, N. Y.,

AT THE bottom of this picture you can read a very long name that belongs to this very small boy, not more than four years old: Signor Don Manuel Osorio Manrique de Zuniga, Señor de Gines.

But in spite of the nobility of his name, the little boy is not shown in a rich setting. We see him standing simply against a plain gray wall, surrounded only by his pets.

At his left there is a cage full of small birds. At his right a magpie carries in his beak a card reading, "Francisco Goya." It is the name of the Spanish artist who painted the picture.

Attached to the magpie's leg is a cord held, at the other end, by the little boy. He seems to feel it is up to him to protect the magpie from the three cats lurking in the background. The cats, with their burning eyes, look vicious and frightening. We all know that cats like to eat birds. The painter shows us those in the cage well protected, but he has left the magpie entirely in the care of his little master.

The painter's idea might have been this: Don Manuel is just a little boy now; but, as his name indicates, when he grows up he will be the master of many people. Then it will be up to him to care for their safety and happiness as he cares for the safety of his pets now.

The big black eyes of the little boy make us feel that his mind is active and thoughtful. He already knows that there are lovely song-birds in the world but that there are scary dangers too.

Goya's particular gift was to make people look very much alive. Here he gave a lively red color to the little boy's suit and highlighted it with the shimmering white satin sash, the white shoes, and the filmy white collar. The child's dark eyes within his delicate little face look even bigger and more alive because they are framed by his dark hair.

Goya made the expression in the faces he painted so lively and interesting that they make us stop and wonder about them. We feel that there are stories in all of Goya's portraits, and we will be marveling about them all for a long time.

The Bullfight is a Spanish Pastime

THE AMERICAN MARIANO CEBALLOS RIDING THE BULL made 1825 (lithograph)
by Francisco de Goya (1746-1828)

IN SPAIN a skilled bullfighter is called a *toreador*. An oustanding toreador must have the courage of a hero to face a wild and powerful bull.

A famous American bullfighter named Mariano Ceballos, who lived over a hundred years ago, astounded the world with his extraordinary skill and courage. The painter Goya was at that time a very old man, but he was still interested in bullfights.

Goya was a great painter, and he also made etchings as Rembrandt did (p.171). When he was almost eighty Goya learned the newly discovered art of lithography. In lithography the artist draws his picture on a stone tablet with a special chalk; then many prints of the picture are made on paper.

Goya's art reached a high peak after a long life of constant painting and drawing. By making his pictures in an entirely new way, he proved himself a very modern artist.

Before that artists made pictures of what they knew to be there rather than of what they actually saw. They gave details even in the far background. Goya did not show us actual people in the background. But we feel they are there just the same.

In Goya's picture showing the bullfight of Mariano Ceballos, we are aware of masses of excited spectators behind a wall protecting them. There are also people right in the arena forming a circle around the amazing bullfighter from America. We see him sitting in a saddle on one bull and brandishing a short spear at the other.

The bull under him kicks up his hind legs perilously. The picadors wave their cloths. We cannot see their faces, but the artist has made us feel their quick and excited action. The toreador is the main figure in this picture, so he is shown with more detail. All the violent motion seems to center in him. In contrast, the bull facing him is motionless. This makes the scene humorous, but it is tense and scary too.

This mixture of fear and fun is what makes Goya's art unique.

The Fighting *Téméraire* is Tugged to Its Last Berth

THE setting sun has dyed the clouds blood-red within the golden glory of the sky. The blood-red and the gold are reflected in the water. We feel that tragedy is in the air. The sea itself is still. Over where the sky is still blue and white with clouds, the sea shimmers in blue and silver.

Here we see the old proud ship, the *Téméraire*. Of great renown and valor, she had part in England's most glorious sea battle, fighting next to Admiral Nelson's flagship when he defeated the French fleet. Though fatally wounded, Nelson kept his command to the end. The order of the day was "England expects every man to do his duty." The sea power of France was broken at Trafalgar in 1805.

The high-masted *Téméraire* survived, but she finally became obsolete when the more practical steamboat was invented. The *Téméraire* had to be sunk.

The English landscape painter, William Turner, painted a colorful dramatic picture of this event.

He made the richly carved body of the ship gleam golden and silvery. In the darkened surface of the water her image is mirrored down to the lower edge of the picture, as if foretelling that here the ship will be sunk. Next to the noble *Téméraire* an ugly little tugboat sends a spurt of vicious flames and soot from her black chimney toward the towering masts.

The painter makes us feel that with the sinking of the *Téméraire* much of the valiant glory of olden times will be buried. It will be succeeded by a more practical if less beautiful future. The dark tugboat, the black buoy, the shadowy city in the background all serve to heighten the silvery beauty of the pale ship.

The spectacular sunset seems to suggest that the sinking of the *Téméraire* is like the sinking of a shining bright golden day.

William Turner started an entirely new way of landscape painting in telling dramatic stories about the colorfully shining sea and the sky. But his paintings, particularly those of his later years, have more brilliance and color than loving new observation. For our present-day taste his yellow golden pictures of water and air are like too many repetitions of a once thrilling hit song. But it would be unjust to forget Turner's early devotion to painting turbulent water and raging fire and smoke and steam, and he painted them as no one before him had ever done.

THE FIGHTING TÉMÉRAIRE painted 1838
by William Turner (1775-1851)

National Gallery, London, England

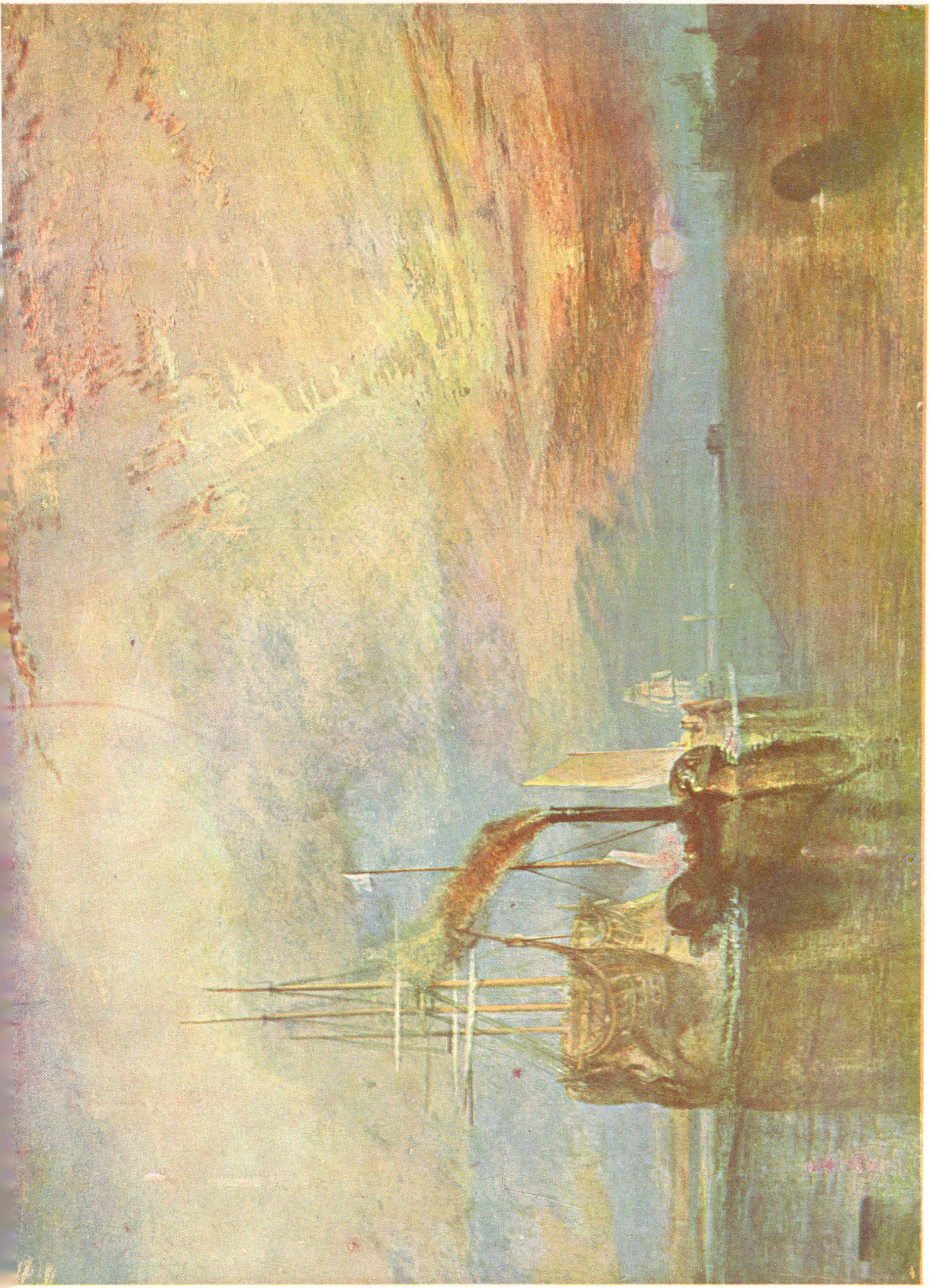

Hunts and Dangers of Africa

WHEN, over a hundred years ago, the French government became engaged in a war in Africa, African life became the center of interest in France.

The inhabitants of North Africa were Arabs, and they were unlike Europeans in many ways. They wore interesting strange-looking clothes: no trousers, no jackets, no hats or caps. Long pieces of cloth were wound around their heads to shield them from the burning sun. Colorful mantles flew around their shoulders as they galloped through the desert on their lively horses.

The wild beasts of the desert were a constant threat to their lives. The lonely rider hunting for his daily food was often attacked by the powerful king of beasts, the lion. The Arabs' most reliable friends were their horses. They were swift-footed and as courageous as their masters. Arabian horses are known to be the finest even today.

The French painter Eugene Delacroix was excited by this kind of danger. In his fancy he took part in adventurous Arabian life. In his thoughts he saw the wild beasts in all their fury—and he put them down on paper with his pencil for his famous etchings. He painted many action-packed pictures of the desert and its inhabitants.

In this picture an Arab riding on his white horse along the desert cliffs is suddenly attacked by a lion. The hungry lion has sprung out of the dark rocks and at the Arab's horse. The wild beast has slid under the horse, turned, and grabbed it between his powerful paws, biting its leg.

The Arab rider has swiftly drawn his sword and, kneeling on his horse, he leans forward to plunge the sword into the lion's neck. His horse will be freed and in another second the Arab will dismount to finish the fight.

Arabs are most skillful on horseback. They can change their position, dismount and remount, even when galloping swiftly as the wind.

Delacroix excelled in painting all this fury and motion. He makes us feel every bit of the fight. The sudden light on the horse is like lightning. We can see its pain in the way its noble head is turned and twisted on its muscular neck. The Arab's flying mantle makes us feel how rapid and forceful the fight is. The mighty bulk of the lion shows a formidable enemy. The somber landscape, the sudden changes of dark and light, give us the feeling of a thunderstorm.

The great French artist Delacroix was a master in painting unusual and exciting subjects. His wild beasts look wonderfully scary in his etchings, and we feel the same excitement in the colors he used with such fine artistry in his paintings.

THE LION HUNT painted about 1850
by Eugene Delacroix (1799-1863)

The Art Institute of Chicago

Daumier was primarily a lithographer. He made his cartoons plead for justice and liberty. This one warns the Constitution not to cut Liberty too short.

Daumier Made His Pictures Fight for Human Rights

Courtesy Harry B. Gutman, New York, N. Y.

ALL day long the washerwoman has been doing her laundry-work down at the riverbank. Now she is on her way home with her little girl.

The child is very small. Only with effort can she climb the high stairs. But she raises her foot bravely knowing that her mother's helping hand will be there when she needs it. But only when she needs it. The little girl wants to try climbing all by herself and her mother wants her to be as independent as she can.

With a gentle gesture the heavy woman bends down to the little one holding her hand, guiding, watching, helping. We see all of a mother's love and care outlined in the dark figure drawn against the light background of the river and the houses on the river-bank. The sky has darkened. It is that late hour of the day after sunset when pale waters and white houses still reflect the dimming light.

The washerwoman's figure is dark because it is so late. She had worked as long as there was enough light to see clearly what she was doing.

But there was also another reason that the French artist Honoré Daumier made this picture look so dark. He did not want to show any particular town or river or any particular washerwoman. Any river or any town would do, because he felt that his story about a poor hard-working woman and her child would be as true in one place as in another.

A general pale scenery is a perfect background for Daumier's figures. It makes them look more important, glowing as they are with deep warm colors. The straight outlines and plain surfaces of the staircase accent the forceful modeling of the human figures.

No details are needed in these two figures. Together they look like a monument to a mother's love and care. Daumier felt that only a big unified form would do justice to such a big all-important subject.

Mothers helping their children have often been painted, and more often than not such pictures make us smile at the helplessness of the little ones. But Daumier did not want us to smile. Nor did he want to make us cry about the hardships of poor people's lives. He wanted us to feel respect for the fine human feeling he expressed in a working mother and her child. He wanted to show us that poor people have fine qualities like anybody else.

THE WASHERWOMAN
painted about 1861
by Honoré Daumier
(1808-1879)

Metropolitan Museum of Art, New York, N. Y.

REMEMBRANCE OF MORTEFONTAINE painted 1864
by Camille Corot (1796-1875)

The Louvre, Paris, France

Corot Made People Part of the Landscape

IN AN exhibition of paintings someone said to Corot: "Mr. Corot, you have painted fairies in this forest, but fairies do not exist."

"*I* can see them," replied Corot. Landscapes were fairyland to him.

He painted his *Remembrance of Mortefontaine,* the picture we see above, when he was an accomplished artist. He had made so many sketches outdoors that he knew just how any landscape looked at any hour and in any light. He knew exactly what sort of tree grew in what sort of place. He knew what a young tree looked like and an old one. He could also fit people most naturally into any landscape whether it was a forest or the shore of a lake.

The surrounding greenery is reflected in the calm surface of the lake. A slender young girl reaches up for some fresh branches from a tree. Her baby sister reaches up too, but she is too small to pick branches. She is a little dumpling of a child barely able to walk. The other sister, old enough to know that she cannot reach so high, contents herself with picking the flowers on the ground.

All three figures seem to be as necessary a part of the picture as the age-old tree that spreads its majestic branches over the scene. In the silvery light the leaves seem to breathe the cool morning air. And suddenly, by the magic art of Corot, we breathe it too. Our heart is touched as his was, by his memory of Mortefontaine.

THE GLEANERS painted 1857
by Jean François Millet (1815-1875)

The Louvre, Paris, France

People Came First with Millet

ANOTHER great French landscape painter of the same time, Millet, has been praised for the "Biblical" quality of his pictures. When we look at a painting by Millet we can see that, like Corot, he too could paint the landscape so truly that we can all but breathe it. But Millet, above all, was interested in landscapes with people in them—simple working people.

The Biblical words: "In the sweat of thy face shalt thou eat bread" come to mind when we look at the picture above. When we see these three women gleaners, we feel that for thousands of years women have been working like this at harvest-time when the fields are bare and the crops heaped into stacks as we see them in the background here.

The rhythmic motion of bending, reaching, picking and gathering the stalks seems to go on eternally under the hot white sun. We respect these people who sweat untiringly at their work so that they may earn their daily bread.

A hundred years have passed since Millet painted his loving and beautiful pictures of people who work in the fields. Since then machines have been invented to do the hardest part of the work for us. But Millet's paintings have never gone out of date because men's efforts to do their work well have never ceased.

THE WAVE painted 1870
by Gustave Courbet (1819-1877)

The Louvre, Paris, France

This French Artist Painted the Overwhelming Power of the Sea

THE French painter Gustave Courbet called the seascape we see here *The Wave*. It is a very large picture because the painter wanted to impress us with the grandeur of the ocean. He wanted to paint the sea alone.

When we look at this painting we feel as if it were right before us, as if seen from a large picture-window in a house on the shore. The wave looks as if it were life-size. It approaches. The boats in the corner look like toys in a giant's hand.

The wave gathers its power from both sides. It mounts and immediately turns over into white foam, then runs up the rocky slope in a splash. From there it will be sucked back again, and the next wave will have risen and gathered and turned over. For the sea sends its mighty messengers to the shore one after the other—when in the mood. It is in the mood right now. The sky is covered with clouds and shows little of its placid blue. Underneath, the blue-green sea shows its irresistible force in a way that we feel to be entirely real.

Courbet called himself a realist. Whatever he painted seems real to us. There was sweeping force in the man and there is sweeping force in his pictures too.

BREEZING UP painted 1875
by Winslow Homer (1836-1910)

National Gallery of Art, Washington, D. C.
Gift of the W. L. and May T. Mellon Foundation

This American Painter Gave the Sea a Human Touch

HERE we are at sea. The day is fine. There is sunshine but not too much of it, for the sky is crowded with light clouds. The breeze is just right. It blows strongly enough into the sail of the *Gloucester* to bring it in, in time, to the distant village we can barely see on the horizon.

The waves are lively. They turn the boat to one side. Some of the surf washes over the top. You can almost smell the salty spray.

The old sailor handles the ropes expertly. The three youngsters seem to be enjoying the trip, each in his own way. The first is stretched out luxuriously in the bow next to the mast. The smallest of the boys loves sailing too, but he is a little timid as he clutches the edge of the boat that he is sitting on. It may be his first trip. The third fellow sits at the helm. He is the one who directs the boat as he handles the rudder. He is watchfully eyeing their destination.

A fishing boat with four sails enlivens the sea, and we can see one more white sail on the horizon.

Winslow Homer, the American painter, was an ardent lover of the sea as Courbet was. But while Courbet never tired of painting the rolling waves of the sea itself, Homer liked to enliven his pictures with people. His sea is a part of the human life that this American painter liked so much to observe.

A Painted Tribute to a Gentle Old Mother

THIS picture shows a much older lady than we think of as our mother. She looks more like our great grandmother, or grandmother if she happens to be very old. But Whistler was almost old enough to be a grandfather when he painted this picture of his mother. Besides, the lady looks as she does because she lived at a time that was quieter and more restful than ours. When Whistler painted this picture, America's covered wagons had just been replaced by railroads.

Whistler's painting is a goodbye to a less colorful and less lively period, which, however, had a placid charm of its own. It is the same sort of charm as the memory of some quiet rainy day when you were curled up indoors with your favorite book, even though you usually prefer to play outdoors and have fun.

There is a steady order in the painting. The wide light wall with the straight curtain, the straight baseboard and the straight picture on it, the chair and footrest straight along the wall—these all show that in this old lady's home everything is straightened out. There is a quiet rhythm in the plain lines.

Against this angular background the old lady's figure has a softly curving line. In the entire flat-looking picture the only rounded shape is her face and even that is not firmly modeled. The clean-cut clarity of her profile has mellowed with age. It droops like a faded flower.

Whistler named this picture *Arrangement in Gray and Black,* with good reason. It gives the painter's feelings about his mother rather than just her portrait. The subtle grading of grays creates a placid mood. The Japanese silk curtain has a faint but varied pattern. The painter put his signature on the curtain, in the shape of a butterfly. Butterflies are often used for a decoration in Japanese art and Whistler admired Japanese art as both the curtain and the butterfly show.

The picture on the wall also has its own significance. It is the brightest white spot in the painting, framed by the darkest black. Just so the old lady's white hands with the frilly white handkerchief are contrasted with her black dress. Her head in the white bonnet does not show these sharp contrasts. This part of the picture, the most important, is handled in a softer way. The colors of the face, the bonnet, the hair are subtly shaded one against the other. The sheer white linen, the lacy edges of the bonnet show a number of different shades and materials.

Within the arrangement of simple shapes and shades in the picture, this face looks soft and kind. Whistler's painting is very much like a musical arrangement, a song to be sung to his mother, to whom he was completely devoted.

ARRANGEMENT IN GRAY AND BLACK painted 1871
by James McNeill Whistler (1834-1903)

The Louvre, Paris, France

CHILD WITH SWORD painted about 1867
by Edouard Manet (1832-1883)

Manet had a new approach to portrait-painting. He liked to show people not posing for their portraits but as if caught by chance when they were doing something casual. This boy, for instance, just happens to be carrying a sword obviously not his own because it is so much too big for him.

Manet's Special Way of Painting What He Saw

Courtesy of the Metropolitan Museum of Art, New York, N. Y.

THE French painter Edouard Manet had studied the old masters with great care, and he soon became a master of his art himself. But only the young revolutionary painters appreciated his work. The older artists often rejected it.

They had two reasons. One was his way of painting. He did not paint well-rounded figures with many shadows as they thought he should. He chose to get the effects he wanted with a flat way of painting. To capture what he wanted he drew his outlines and selected his colors with unerring skill.

The other reason some of the older artists rejected him was that he did not care to paint anything for the sake of the story in it. He wanted to paint for art's sake. That is, he wanted to make his pictures interesting by *the way he painted them,* not by what he painted. He made a point of choosing some casual moment to catch in his pictures, as we can see in this one called *In the Boat.*

Unlike painters before him, Manet did not paint the entire sea up to the distant horizon with the sky above it, nor did he paint the entire boat as was the custom (p.214-215). He looked at the boat from a close range and painted only a fraction of the sail and just a small part of the boat with the water next to it. He painted only what he could see with a quick look. The sailor in the boat is facing us, but we do not see his features with all the single shapes of eyes, nose, and mouth. Manet purposely painted like that because he knew that when we look in the direction of the sunlight we don't see shapes very clearly. And Manet painted what he saw.

IN THE BOAT painted 1874
by Edouard Manet (1832-1883)

Courtesy of the Metropolitan Museum of Art,
New York, N. Y.

    The big life-size figure of the sailor dominates this picture, even though it is painted with so few details. The outlines of his body almost alone give the impression of a strong and massive figure.

    The young woman's profile is not painted with much detail either. Her face is in shadow too, and it is formed with only a few touches of color. But her striped dress, spreading out in different shades of blue, is most painstakingly painted for all its casual look. By contrast the blue of her dress brings out the shining beauty of the water painted in a subtly different shade of blue. This water seems to be the real source of light streaming toward us from the radiantly shining picture. The striking colors and composition of the painting would make it outshine any picture that might be hanging near it on a wall.

    Manet painted this picture when he was a mature artist and had joined the Impressionist painters. Manet was a little older than most of the Impressionists. He did not follow their manner of dissolving sunshine into many colors, but he achieved the effect of bright outdoors just the same.

    The young painters looked up to Manet as their master, and a great master of painting he was.

**RACE HORSES painted about 1878
by Edgar Degas**

Degas loved to paint the trained bodies of race horses. Here we see them with their colorful jockeys warming up before the races on the green meadow.

Degas Loved to Paint Motion

Courtesy: Museum of Fine Arts, Boston, Mass.

HAVE you ever seen a snapshot of someone you know snapped when he or she had no idea the picture was being taken? A picture like that is so much more fun to look at than a posed photograph, for in a casual snap the subject may be caught making a face or raising a foot in mid-air or something like that.

In the field of painting, the French artist Edgar Degas relished nothing more than drawing people when they did not know they were being watched.

He particularly enjoyed painting them in motion, and more than anything else he liked to paint ballet dancers. He liked them especially because they do not move any which way, but are trained to move with rhythm and grace. Ballet dancers interested him not only when they were dancing on the stage but even more at odd moments off stage: in training, at rehearsals, or in the wings waiting for their cues.

In our picture we see four dancers standing in the wings among canvas walls with bushes painted on them. One of the dancers makes it quite clear that the bushes are only flat theater props, for she leans against them with the flat of her hand as she could never do if they were real bushes.

Degas loved this sort of little joke. He surprises us by showing us something behind the scenes that the public in the theater is not supposed to see. He shows us this painted world for what it really is. By the little trick of showing one of the dancers against the make-believe bush we realize that the fields, the haystacks, and the sky full of clouds are all stage props too.

Degas shows us the dancers for what they really are, too, not for what they seem to be on the stage where they perform with studied precision.

Here, behind the scenes, we see that they are human and can be tired, for one of them leans wearily against a support. Degas shows us that ballet dancers have to do the routine things of life just as other girls do. The three dancers in front are fixing the shoulder straps of their ballet dresses.

FOUR DANCERS painted about 1899
by Edgar Degas (1839-1917)

National Gallery of Art, Washington, D. C.
Chester Dale Collection

All three slender figures bend slightly backward and reach over their shoulders with the same grace and ease. But each of the three moves differently, each has a different turn of the head. They are not performing now; they are just being themselves. But their trained bodies are always graceful.

The different position of their arms makes an interesting pattern in smooth plain flesh color, contrasting with their many-hued dresses. The brilliant limelight of the stage is toned down here in the shadow of the wings. It makes for softly glittering color harmonies of yellow, orange, brown, green, and violet, with a rosy shimmer over the entire scene.

In this picture we see natural motion as only Degas was able to observe it with his keen eye. And we see subtle and beautiful color harmonies as only his exquisite taste could compose them. Degas leads us into the colorful and rhythmic dreamland of classical ballet even behind the scene.

America's French Sweetheart

THE painter of this picture, Auguste Renoir, was one of a group of young French artists who decided to paint a fresher, more direct view of what they saw than their elders had done. They called themselves *Impressionists* because they painted their impressions of nature where they found it—outdoors—and they did not paint the pictures over in their studios. The best landscape painter of the group was Monet (p.226-227) and their best figure painter was Renoir.

Like Monet, Renoir did not look for important or exciting subject matter to paint. He thought, for instance, that he would like to paint a little girl just as she looked when she stopped on her way to water her flowers in the garden. Painting her just as she was, Renoir felt, would make a truer portrait than anything he could paint in a studio. The older masters had always painted their pictures in the usual studio light amid studio surroundings and therefore they lacked the freshness and directness of Renoir's portraits.

In this picture we see how well Renoir succeeded. The little blonde girl, blue-eyed, with fresh round cheeks and a red mouth, stands right in the middle of the picture in her high-buttoned blue shoes. Long ago when this picture was painted, when our great-grandmothers were little girls, shoes like that were the fashion. The little girl's dress is also in the fashion of the time, and so are the frilly white pantalets that show a bit below her skirt.

These things are not painted with much detail. But Renoir painted this picture with painstaking care. For instance, he was careful to keep us from noticing at once that the little girl is standing in the exact center of the painting. If he had made that plainly evident, the picture would have looked measured out and we should miss much of its easy-going freshness. But Renoir skillfully divided the garden's greenery by a curved foot-path. The foot-path is graveled in a pinkish tan that blends with the little girl's legs.

To accent her figure the blue of her garment is pure blue. But in order not to make the color too harsh an accent, the painter made the neighboring rose-bush more bluish than green. Among the blue-green leaves the roses themselves are the same color as the child's complexion. The paler roses are heightened by a few that are a real rose-red just as the little girl's complexion is heightened by her rose-red mouth. Her eyes are two bright blue spots in her rosy face. The ribbon in her hair is of the same red as the geraniums we see next to the little girl's head—the geraniums that grow in the flower-bed in the background.

The green grass surrounds the child's head and hands like a frame. The hands look at first as if they were mere patches, but then we notice that these patches are carefully shaped. We can see the secure grip of the chubby fingers on the watering can and around the flowers.

We could go on and find many more details to prove how much care Renoir took when he put his colors on the canvas. He observed his subject and planned his picture painstakingly.

But the pains were all his. We who look at his painting get only pleasure from it. We enjoy its easy freshness, the light touch of the painter's brush. So directly does this picture touch our hearts that it has come to be known as America's French Sweetheart.

GIRL WITH WATERING CAN painted 1874
by Auguste Renoir (1840-1919)

National Gallery of Art, Washington, D. C.
Chester Dale Collection

THE CITIZENS OF CALAIS sculptured 1884-1888 (Plaster cast)
by Auguste Rodin (1840-1912)

Calais, France

A Revolution in Sculpture

THIS sculpture tells the story of how six French citizens saved their town, Calais, from the wrath of an English King.

It was during the famous Hundred Years War in the Middle Ages that the English besieged the city of Calais. The King of France had abandoned the town. The English King Edward demanded unconditional surrender. But there was one condition under which he was willing to spare the inhabitants. Six of the noblest citizens had to leave the city barefooted, with ropes around their necks, the key to the town and to the castle in their hands. "I will do with them as I please," were the King's words.

First the wealthiest citizen got up. "I am ready to die for my country," he said.

Then five other men of the city rose, one by one, to sacrifice themselves. They undressed, keeping on only their shirts. They hung ropes around their necks and took the key to the town and to the castle. Thus they went over to the enemy's camp.

They had already been handed over to the executioner when the prayers and tears of the Queen softened the King's heart. He agreed to pardon them.

More than five hundred years after these citizens of Calais had saved their town, a monument to the memory of their heroic deed was planned. Auguste Rodin, the foremost sculptor of France, was commissioned to make it.

Rodin wanted the monument of the six men to stand in the market-place of the city, on a base just slightly above the pavement. He did not want it put on a pedestal. He felt that the heroes of the past ought to stand among the people of the present, to remind them of the six who had been ready to suffer and to die so that the rest might live in peace.

The six men stand in a group, but each one faces his future in a different way.

The first tries hard to understand the inhuman malice of the King's request.

The second, the oldest of the six, has made his decision: although his shoulders are bent and his face is sad, he is resigned to losing his life.

The third, who carries the key, stands upright. His arms are stiffened by his rigid decision. He is bitter. But if he has to surrender the key and himself he will do so courageously.

The fourth, a tender youth whom we see in the background, raises his upturned hands in resignation. He has no questions, no regrets, and he is without bitterness. If he can save so many by sacrificing his own life, he is willing to die. He turns to two other desperate figures as if to comfort them in their despair. (These two are hidden in this photograph).

Rodin's was a new, a previously unheard-of way of representing heroes in a sculptured monument. Heroes were not supposed to show pain or human weakness. They were supposed to make any sacrifice gladly. Rodin made a point of showing that a hero can make a great sacrifice even if he feels pain and suffering. He wanted his monument to show truth instead of a pose.

His way of modeling was also new and revolutionary. He did not smooth the shapes of faces and figures or draperies as sculptors before him had done. He used deep shadows more as painters do. This gives his sculptures an unfinished look, fitting well into a period of art when casual looks were popular.

These were revolutionary ideas. Rodin's unusual sculpture was not accepted by the city of Calais until years after it had been finished by the artist; and, contrary to his wishes, it was put up, according to the old custom, on a pedestal.

But today we have fully accepted Rodin's thought. Now there are copies of this sculpture, *The Citizens of Calais,* in great museums all over the world. They stand, without a pedestal, as originally planned by this great artist who expressed strong feelings in strong expressive gestures.

ROCK OF ETRETAS painted 1890
by Claude Monet (1840-1926)

The Triumph of Sunshine

Courtesy of the Metropolitan Museum of Art,
New York, N. Y.

THE French painter Claude Monet painted this picture about a hundred years after the American Revolution. Monet also started a revolution, but his was in the art of landscape painting.

He went outdoors and stayed there to paint his pictures. This was in contrast to the older painters who may have made sketches outdoors but painted their darkish pictures indoors.

Monet was not much interested in any particular scenery. In this picture, for instance, he selected a bare rock jutting out into the sea. The rock itself is grayish-yellow, but its many tiny cavities and ridges break the sunshine into as many rainbows. A rainbow is sunshine broken into colors. Monet watched these colors very carefully and put them on his canvas—and there was sunshine.

Then he went on and looked at the sea. The water was even more brilliant than the rock because water itself is shiny, full of tiny waves breaking and mirroring the sunshine. Monet observed the sea very carefully, and when he put his colors on, the sea sparkled even brighter than the rock. Finally he painted the air and he made that even lighter and brighter than the sea.

When his painting was finished it was so brimful of sunshine that it would brighten the dullest room.

Monet never stopped studying the play of sunshine. But when he was older he preferred the softer sunshine and milder light of early or late hours of the day.

PALAZZO MULA painted 1908
by Claude Monet (1840-1926)

National Gallery of Art, Washington, D. C.
Chester Dale Collection

Light and Beauty

THE deep subdued tones of this picture show us the water and the air even more shining if less brilliant than the preceding picture. Here we breathe the humid air of Venice. Although the painter did not show us the sky, he was able to make us feel the air above the water in front of the old Palazzo Mula. The palace front shimmers softly in a purple hue.

The water here is even more water-like and limpid than in Monet's earlier pictures. Although not as brilliant and vigorous as those he made in his youth, Monet's paintings had become even stronger in a soft and mellow way.

When Monet painted this red and blue picture of a Venetian palace and the water in front of it, he exclaimed, "All this unusual light! It is so beautiful! I can almost forget how old I am."

This unusual light and the red and blue colors have always been important features of Venetian painting and they were often and superbly painted by the old Venetian masters. The charm of this unique atmosphere captivated the aged Monet, and he captured the magic beauty of Venetian light as he alone, the old master of sunshine and light, could do it.

A New Way of Painting Mothers and Children

WHEN the great American painter, Mary Cassatt, painted this picture, bathrooms were not as common as they are today. There were wash-stands, each with a basin and a jug, in people's bedrooms. Morning and night Mother came to wash her little ones. First she washed the face, then the body, and then the basin was put down on the floor for the feet.

In this picture Mother is about to finish the job. The little girl has been washed and dried. She is sitting in Mother's lap only partly wrapped in the bath towel. Mother is going to make sure that the little girl's feet are just as clean as the rest of her. The little girl watches carefully. She feels almost big enough to do the job for herself.

This may not seem like a very interesting subject for a painting, and when the picture was painted it was even less interesting because there was nothing unusual about bathing like that.

But Mary Cassatt wanted to paint just that kind of intimate familiar scene. Like her teacher Degas (p.220-221), she wanted to make pictures of people doing ordinary things at moments when they thought no one was looking at them.

One more reason why Mary Cassatt liked to paint pictures of people unaware that they were being observed is that it was the kind of thing Japanese artists did, and Japanese art was very fashionable just then.

Another interesting feature of Mary Cassatt's painting is the unusual angle from which she looked at her subjects. Before Japanese prints had become the rage, painters looked at whatever they were painting from the eye-level of a grown person and from a considerable distance. Mary Cassatt, like the Japanese, has us looking *down* at this scene and from quite close range. This is why the floor seems to slant and also why we see the heads rather than the faces of mother and child. It is a very hard thing to draw people correctly at such an odd angle. Mary Cassatt did it amazingly well.

She also organized her picture with great artistic wisdom. Mother's striped dress is a fine background to the little girl's soft body and so are the soft folds of the bath towel. The two dark heads together make us feel how close mother and her child are. Mother holds her little girl around the waist, and because she is still a child, the little girl holds on to her mother's knee. But she is big enough to be helpful by holding up her leg with her other hand while mother does the actual washing.

And now let us look at the faces of mother and child and notice what Mary Cassatt has told us about them in their expressions. The mother's face seems to be saying, "Look, my child, and see how I am washing you." And the child, watching attentively, seems to be saying, "Yes, Mother dear, I am learning."

Mary Cassatt was a loving and keen observer of mothers and children. She painted them with warm feeling because she had a woman's heart. In this she was unlike her teacher, Degas, who was interested only in the beauty of motion and color. Also, Mary Cassatt was an American. Like other American painters she felt that human feelings were just as important in painting as good drawing and interesting patterns.

THE BATH painted about 1892
by Mary Cassatt (1845-1926)

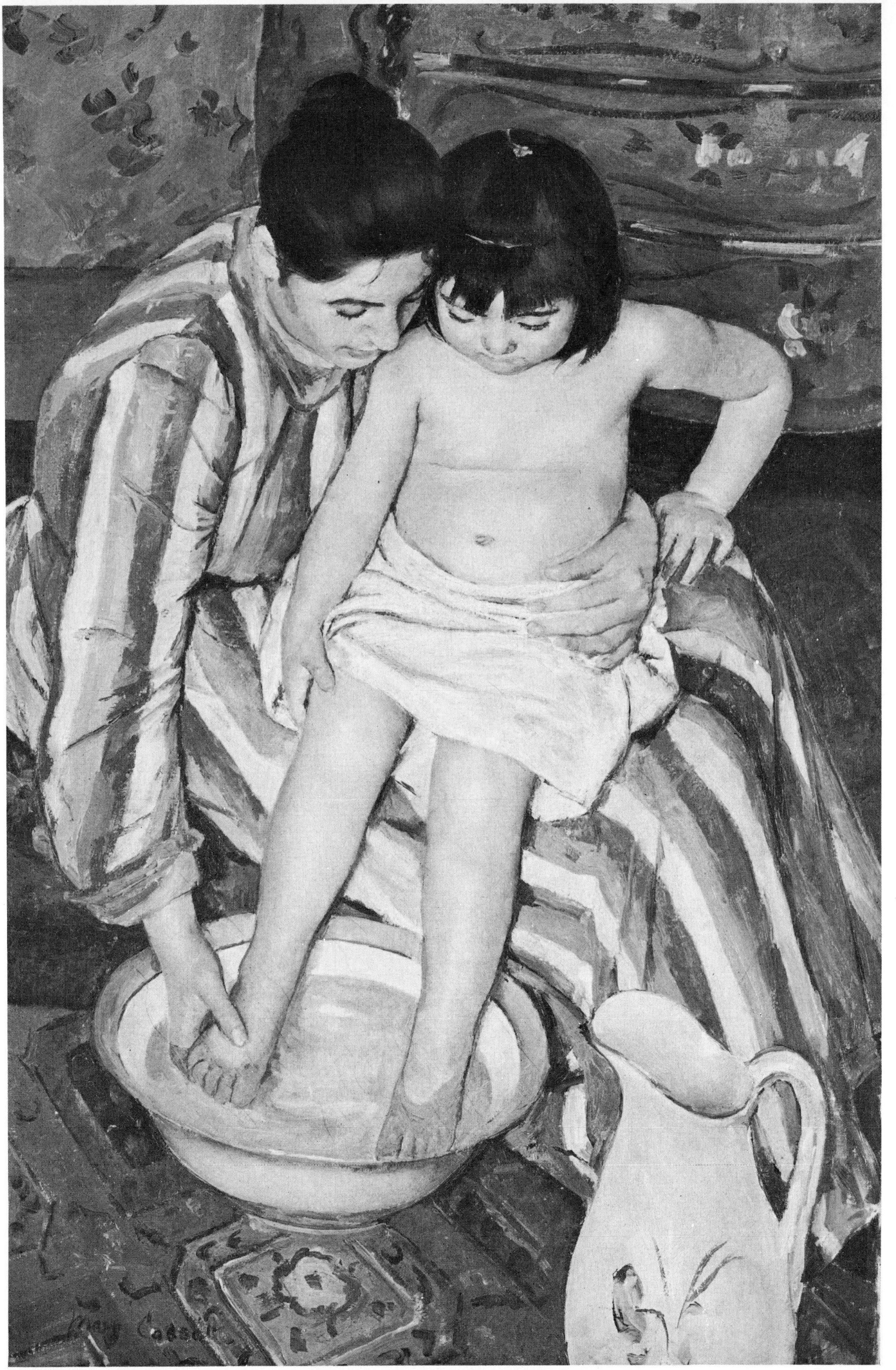
Mary Cassatt

MOUNT STE. VICTOIRE painted about 1885
by Paul Cézanne (1839-1906)

Courtesy of the Metropolitan Museum of Art,
New York, N. Y.

Cézanne Made Us See Greatness in Order

ONE of the greatest of modern landscape painters, perhaps the very greatest, was the French artist Paul Cézanne. He took part in the exhibitions of the Impressionists. They revolutionized art by showing light pictures that they had painted outdoors in sunshine. This was a daring new approach to painting.

By the time the Impressionists had reached their middle years, each of them had developed his own way of painting. Cézanne became more and more interested in organizing his pictures clearly as we can tell by looking at the painting we see here.

It is one of Cézanne's favorite views: Mount St. Victoire rising above the valley near his home in southern France. We see it from the edge of a hill among fir-trees.

Cézanne organized his painting with energetic lines. Right in the middle, a big fir-tree divides the picture from top to bottom. The tree is not strictly vertical because that would make the picture look rigid. It leans a little to the right as if it were swaying. The viaduct that divides the picture from left to right is not strictly horizontal either. It is softened by curving ever so slightly downward in the same direction as the mountain slopes.

To make the picture look straight and firm Cézanne balanced these lines with a group of other fir trees. They are roughly a straight group, with one trunk leaning in the opposite direction from the one in the middle. This way a wedge is cut into the left half of the picture where the highest peak of Mount St. Victoire rises over the little village in clear outline. It is toward this peak that the main road leads us—the road that begins in the middle of the right side of the painting.

Cézanne chose his few light colors with loving care. He used them all in the front of the picture—the part that frames the bottom of the view. Starting with the grayish pink of the rocky hill he continues with different shades of green in the pines. It is here that he gives us the strongest and richest color-effect in his delicate painting. He follows with orange and gray on the house-top and finally he gathers all the blue of the sky in the little pond.

From among the rich green firs Mount St. Victoire arises in lovely pale pink and blue colors. There is more of the friendly pink where the mountain is bare and more cool blue where it is covered by forests that look blue in the distance.

Cézanne used different shades of green and orange to show the clean-cut patches of corn and vegetable fields among other fields left plain around the light cubes of houses. The majestic and serene pink-blue blocks of Mount St. Victoire crown the wide valley at the top of the picture. A misty blue sky envelopes the view with tenderness.

Whenever Cézanne painted any small part of the great world he put it in strict order. Then he added the charm of soft light colors and the world he painted so severely became lovable and serene.

THE BLACK CLOCK painted 1869-1870
by Paul Cézanne (1839-1906)

During Cézanne's younger years he often used more somber shades, as we can see in his early painting, *The Black Clock*. Here he exaggerated the dark shadows of the creases in the tablecloth to give the effect of rhythm and order. But the pink shell on the table hints of his later love for delicate charming colors.

Permission of Mr. Edward G. Robinson,
Hollywood, Calif.

This Picture Shows That Art is in The Artist's Mind, Not Only in His Hand

WHEN the great French painter Auguste Renoir was over sixty, a baby son was born to him. The baby was named Claude, but he was called Coco by his family. Soon he was known as Coco to the entire world, because every year the famous artist painted a new portrait of his little son.

By the time he painted this picture the old master was suffering severely from rheumatism. He was no longer able to hold his brush in his fingers. It had to be tied to his hand by a bandage. The artist was able to vary the pressure of the brush with his hand and to direct it with his arm.

Renoir gave a soft pearly pink effect to the picture we see here, showing his little son painting at an easel. Coco's blond hair, his light complexion, and his light gray smock all melt into harmonious pink shades.

Coco seems to be quite a small boy although he is sitting at a real easel, the kind grown-up painters use. But, after all, we would expect a painter's son to start out like a professional. If we look carefully, we can follow a rounded line leading from the child's forehead through his shoulder and elbow, hand and brush, to his canvas. In this rounded line Renoir wanted to show us how thoughtful Coco was when he was painting, how he put on canvas only what he had first figured out in his mind.

Renoir even makes us see that Coco is actually painting a still-life of the flower-vase on the table. We understand this by the way Renoir arranged his picture. The flower-vase seems to be the starting point of the rounded line from Coco's forehead to his brush and canvas. This tells us that the flower-vase will go onto the canvas, first through the little painter's mind and then his brush. Thus Renoir shows us in a painting what he so often said in words: that the artist works first with his mind and then with his hands.

He proved this even more clearly in his own latest works. Toward the end of his life he was completely crippled, hand and foot. But he still made sculptures even though he had to do it through the hands of a friend. By giving directions to the actual sculptor Renoir remained the artist who really created the figures.

These sculptures are known and valued throughout the world as Renoir's masterpieces. In them we can easily recognize the style of Renoir's latest years. No other artist could have conceived the rhythm of these richly curving lines, this quality of flesh that seems so full of life. Nobody else had this wonderful way of showing how the parts of the body work together.

In spite of his handicaps Renoir remained a happy man to the end, because he never stopped creating new works of art that gave him joy and satisfaction as long as he lived.

CLAUDE AT THE EASEL painted 1906
by Auguste Renoir (1840-1919)

By permission of Mrs. Josiah Titzell, Georgetown, Conn.

We Can See the Artist's Pain in His Tortured Pictures

THE Dutch-born Vincent van Gogh was a very unhappy man. From his childhood on he looked at the gloomy side of life. He knew this and tried to overcome his unhappiness by leaving his native Holland, where the sky was so often clouded, to seek for brighter days in sunny France.

His first stop was Paris, the artistic center in his day. His great talent and diligence soon made him a master of the brush in the manner of the then modern Impressionist painters. But van Gogh was still unhappy. He longed for days that were always sunny with skies forever brilliantly blue. He wanted to paint even lighter and brighter pictures than the Impressionists did. He left Paris and settled finally in the south of France where he hoped to find the happiness he had sought for so long.

Van Gogh's dream of happiness didn't come true, as we know from the many letters he wrote and the many pictures he painted.

He did paint the southern light and the brilliant colors around him. He did give full value to the beauty of the trees and meadows and of the distant mountains. He made us feel the air above the valleys and the breeze chasing the light clouds in the sky. But he always added something else too—something showing that his soul was sick.

The restless outlines of the trees and mountains reflect the painter's own restlessness. The curly nervous brush-strokes come out of his own nervousness.

Look at the outlines of the cypresses. They twist and wind as if they were in pain. The quiet of the sky itself seems to be disturbed by those brush-strokes. Even the grass on the sunny hilltop seems to wind and move in curves.

There is tense drama in this simple picture. If you look at it from a distance and with narrowed eyes, as painters look at pictures, you will see the sunny light grass and sky and mountains rather than van Gogh's slashing curved lines of paint. But bathed in sunshine though the cypresses are, you feel that there is something sinister in them just the same.

Whatever van Gogh painted had the mark of his sick soul. He was a master at painting colors in their brilliant beauty and he could paint the sunny brightness of the southern sky to perfection too. But in the pictures we can always see the streak of darkness that came from the painter's heart. There are always those nervous brush-strokes of his. They are van Gogh's personal handwriting that reveal his inner agitation. He was a great painter, one who as he touches us with beauty also touches us with pain.

CYPRESSES painted 1889
by Vincent Van Gogh (1853-1890)

Courtesy of the Metropolitan Museum of Art,
New York, N. Y.

The Magic Ring of the Nibelungs

WHEN Richard Wagner's *Ring of the Nibelungs* was performed at the Metropolitan Opera House in New York, the great American painter, Albert Pinkham Ryder, was so greatly impressed by the magical music drama that he went home and started to paint a picture about it. He worked at it all night and all the next day and did not sleep or eat until he finished it.

The story of Wagner's opera is based on an old Germanic saga. It tells us that in the Rhine River in Germany there was once a treasure of shining gold, guarded by three beautiful Rhine maidens. They swam around the treasure, singing, laughing, and playing, for they knew that only someone willing to live without love could ever take the treasure away. If there were such a one he could seize the magic treasure of the Rhine.

One day there came to the Rhine a wicked and ugly dwarf called Alberich the Nibelung. He was so greedy for power and wealth that he cursed love and ruled it out of his life so that he could capture the golden treasure. When he got it, he had a ring made of some of the gold, a ring of magic power.

But the gods of the Germanic saga wanted the treasure for themselves, and they tricked Alberich into surrendering all the gold, the magic ring included. In revenge, Alberich, the Nibelung, put a curse upon the ring so that it would bring death to its owner. The treasure and the ring soon came into the possession of the giant Fafnir, who had changed into a dragon to guard it. But the dragon was slain by the fearless hero, Siegfried.

Siegfried did not care about the treasure, but, following the advice of a little bird in the forest, he took the ring with him. The accursed ring finally proved Siegfried's undoing. One last chance, however, was given to him.

One day, as Siegfried was riding along the banks of the Rhine, he heard the Rhine maidens singing. He stopped to talk to them. The maidens asked Siegfried to give them the ring. But he refused. Then the Rhine maidens told Siegfried that he would die before the day was over if he did not return the ring to the waters where it belonged.

But Siegfried, the fearless one, paid them no heed. He rode along—to be killed that very evening.

The music-drama closes with Siegfried's funeral. According to the old Germanic rite, his body was burned on a funeral pyre. The Rhine flowed up over the flames, and so the fateful ring of the Nibelungs was restored to the waters of the river.

The artist, Ryder, chose to paint the ominous scene when Siegfried was being warned by the Rhine maidens.

The painting has a magic quality. The lonely horseman, Siegfried, having heard their song in the dark, has stopped his horse among the trees to look for the Rhine maidens in the shining water. Their figures seem to be foretelling an uncertain and dangerous future.

Mysteriously changing lights and shadows make us feel the scary mood of the dark forest. One big tree fills the better part of the picture. It suggests that even a hero is small when compared with the forces of nature.

In the picture these forces seem to unite. The majestic dark branches of the tree become part of the sky. The sky itself is dark against the lightness of the moon, half hidden behind

SIEGFRIED AND THE RHINE MAIDENS painted about 1891
by Albert Pinkham Ryder (1847-1917)

National Gallery of Art, Washington, D. C.
Mellon Collection

wildly wandering clouds. But the lightest and most important part of the picture is the shining water of the Rhine. This is because the entire story is based on the treasure of the Rhine and the magic ring made of its gold.

   The rhythmical change of light and dark, the melodiously changing shapes and lines are in the mood of the song. It is a song for the eye that Ryder painted while he was under the spell of Wagner's dramatic music.

   Unlike many other modern artists, Ryder has a story to tell and paints more of his natural impressions than they do. But still his main goal is the aim of modern art—to give music to the eye.

Gauguin Sought Happiness in a Primitive World

THE French painter Paul Gauguin was tired of civilization and crowded cities. He went in search of a fairyland in which he might find happiness. He found it in the distant isles of the Pacific Ocean. There, among the uneducated primitive islanders, his dreams came true.

They couldn't read or write. They went around with practically no clothes on, and they had almost no furniture in their simple houses. They ate the fruit that grew wild on their island, and they hunted or fished for other food.

Paul Gauguin loved this primitive life. He painted many pictures in these Pacific islands. We see one of them here.

In the foreground we see a blue river. It flows between sloping hills of pink stone under an emerald lawn. The river disappears in the blue mountains on the horizon. The sky that we can see through tree-branches has a strange greenish hue. We know that somewhere the sky must be very red for we see its reflection in orange-colored splashes on the blue water. A white horse is standing there drinking to quench his thirst. A magnificent white flower grows on the shore nearby. Next to it two young birds open their beaks to sing their song.

In the background a naked yellow-brown rider directs his horse to the water for his evening drink. Another naked brown man on his orange-colored horse returned from the watering place riding toward the blue mountains over the velvety green grass.

We can feel the warm humid air that follows hot days. Everything, the people, the horses, and even the tree and water are leisurely and still. Everything looks lovely in a dreamy unreal manner.

This was Paul Gauguin's aim. Unlike the Impressionists Gauguin did not want to paint from nature. He thought that art was a matter of the artist's feeling rather than of what he saw with his eyes alone. He didn't try to catch new beauty out of nature's wealth. He wanted to pour the wealth of his own feelings into beautiful and harmonious pictures.

He didn't think it was important to use colors as he saw them. Instead, he said, whatever color can be **seen** should be used in its purest shade to get a bright and brilliant painting.

He didn't think, either, that it was necessary to use shadows to make figures look well-rounded to make us feel that we might touch them all around.

But, as artists often do, he did not always paint according to what he said. In that too he followed his feelings rather than his thoughts.

Gauguin's feelings were strong and he was able to express them in pictures so that the pictures, in turn, make us feel what he felt.

Gauguin created beautiful rhythmic patterns and harmonious order in all his works. They all have a strange sort of quiet like a lovely but somewhat **sad** song.

THE WHITE HORSE painted 1898
by Paul Gaugin (1848-1903)

The Louvre, Paris, France

THE ADAMS MEMORIAL
sculptured 1887
by Augustus St. Gaudens
(1848-1907)

Detail

"The Greatest Man-Made Thing in America"

THE statue we see on the opposite page was called by one of England's great authors, John Galsworthy, "the greatest man-made thing in America."

It is the figure of a mysterious woman. It forms the center of the Adams Memorial in Rock Creek Cemetery, Washington, D.C.

The Adams Memorial was erected to the memory of the wife of Henry Adams, who was one of America's most distinguished scholars.

Adams had dark cypresses and holly planted around the monument, and with the passing of time they grew so thick that the monument is hidden from the casual passerby. Henry Adams wanted it to be seen only by those who really cared.

The monument is built of polished dark red granite. A red granite screen had hidden the central figure even before the shrubbery had grown around it. The bronze has become green with age and has gained new beauty as it contrasts with the red granite block behind it. A bench invites the visitor to stop and look quietly.

There is a hush about the figure of this mysterious woman. She is seated on a rock, deep in thought within her ample cloak. When we look at her from one point we feel the majesty of death. From another point we feel quiet sadness. From still another our feeling is one of love and pity for the lonely woman.

The majestic monument that makes us feel and think so deeply brings us close to the great man who erected it. It is the work of the American sculptor Augustus St. Gaudens. But surely Henry Adams had his say too, for he was an extraordinary man.

He was the grandson of the great American President John Quincy Adams, and great-grandson of President John Adams. Henry Adams' father was our Ambassador to England during the Civil War.

Henry Adams himself was not only a historian of merit but also a poet—and a lover of the fine arts. He was the friend of several artists, among them Augustus St. Gaudens, the sculptor of this figure. It is certain that Henry Adams told his friend what his ideas for his wife's monument were. We do not know how great his share really was, but the result is a stirring work of art of outstanding nobility and grandeur.

Rock Creek Cemetery, Washington, D. C.

A Sunday Afternoon of Long Ago

THE contribution to painting made by the young French painter, Georges Seurat, was a revolution in favor of order and scientific laws. He painted this life-size picture after the Impressionists had formed their group. Seurat had studied their aims and their method of painting, and he started out on his own from there. He was what is known as a Post-Impressionist because he came *after* the Impressionists.

First he developed a scientific method of painting color. The Impressionists had painted a color as they saw it: dissolved by light into many colors (p.222-228). But Seurat *figured out* a color chart whereby he could put dots of different colors on his canvas. When you look at a picture painted in this way, the color dots blend to give you just the right impression.

In drawing his pictures Seurat also used the scientific method of perspective. He looked at his subject from a distance and at some height, and he drew the people farther away from him smaller than those nearer according to the laws of perspective.

Seurat made very clean-cut outlines, in contrast to the Impressionists who said that in nature clean-cut outlines dissolve in light. Seurat's method makes his people look stiff, but his views are neater than the Impressionists.

Impressionists preferred to catch people as they happened to look at a given moment. But Seurat looked for the expression of lasting character.

Now let us look carefully at his painting because Seurat himself observed most carefully. He made three hundred studies for *The Grand Jatte*. That is how he was able to give us so perfect an impression of a sunny afternoon in Spring. The shadows are already long, but in the sunshine the sky and water are still radiantly blue and the grass is shining green. The ladies' parasols are still open to protect them from the sun.

We see men and women and children enjoying themselves on the promenade along the water. The man wearing casual clothes looks thoughtful in contrast to his fashionably dressed neighbor. We notice how quietly the lady behind the two is doing her needlework and how coolly the stylish young lady, sitting stiffly under her raised parasol, examines the sailboats on the water. The simple young girl next to her bends lovingly over the little bouquet of flowers she has gathered.

We can guess what sort of people the men and women are. We can even tell which dog belongs to whom. And the little monkey couldn't belong to anybody but to the extravagantly fashionable woman with her big bustle.

Seurat exaggerated. His painting looks stiff because he did so much figuring. But we enjoy Seurat's well-calculated peaceful views because of his great love of nature and people, of order and beauty. He was able to show us that we can all enjoy a beautiful sunshiny afternoon even though we are different in other ways.

Seurat's painting points toward the future when clarity and order were to become the most important aim of art.

LA GRANDE JATTE painted 1884-1886
by Georges Seurat (1859-1891)
The Chicago Institute of Art

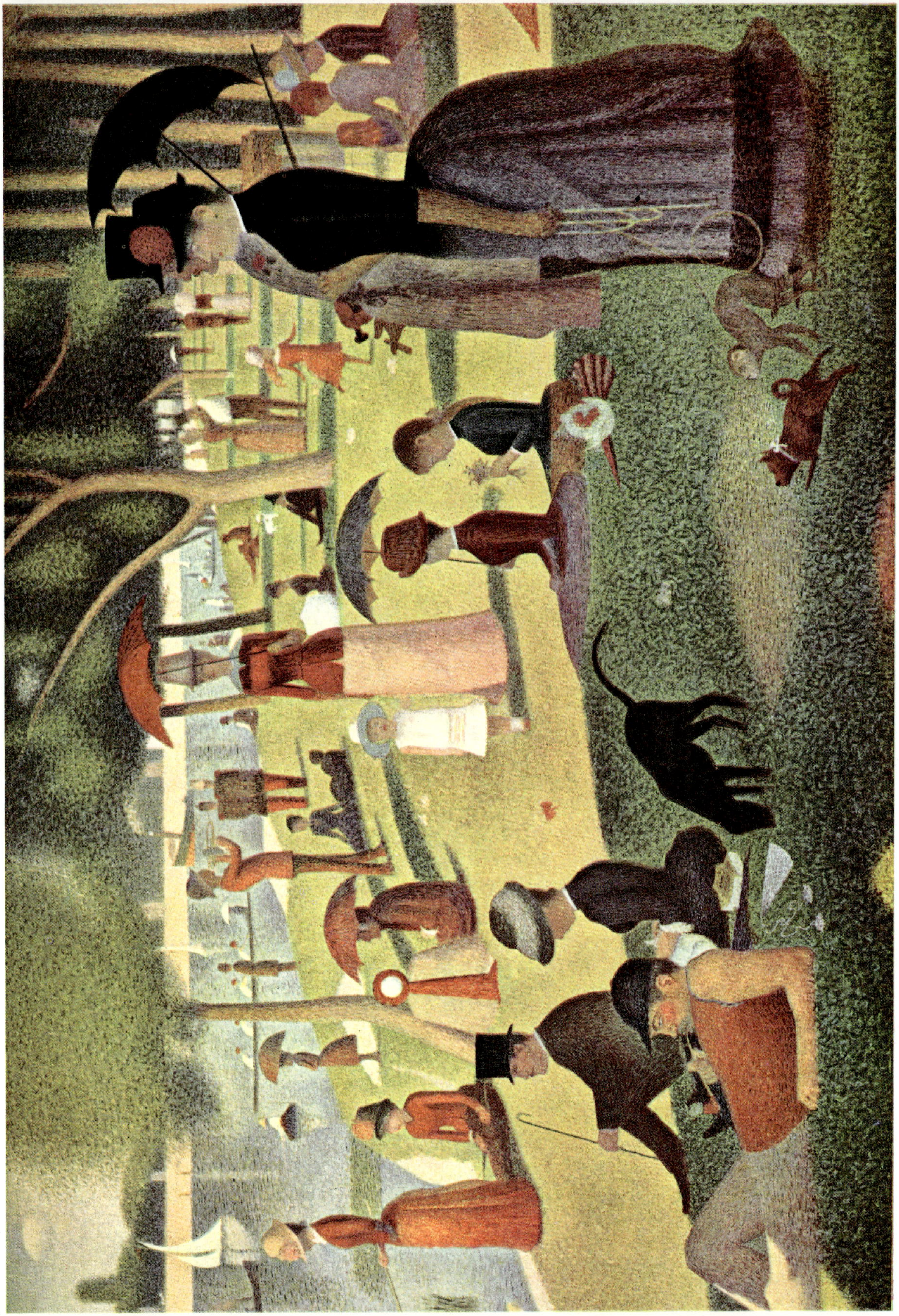

HOMAGE TO CÉZANNE sculptured 1912 by Aristide Maillol (1861-1944)　　　　Tuileries Gardens, Paris, France

This Sculptor Carved a Woman's Figure in Marble

AFTER the death of the greatest French painter of his time, Paul Cézanne, the great French sculptor Aristide Maillol was asked to make a monument to his memory. It was meant to be a tribute to the painter, and that is what Maillol called his sculpture: *Homage to Cézanne.*

As we can see in our picture, the sculptor formed this monument in the shape of a reclining woman holding a bunch of laurel in her extended hand. It is carved of white marble.

As a base for the figure, the artist used an angular marble block suggesting a couch. At the upper end a smaller block is added to suggest a pillow.

There is nobility and earnestness in everything about her figure. Although she is shaped in completely natural forms, we can see at once that the artist did not want to make her an entirely real woman. There is no unimportant detail anywhere on her. The sculptor did not attempt to make her flesh look soft as a woman's flesh really is. The stone against which she is leaning makes no imprint on the solid clear line of her body. She is meant to represent an *idea:* the spirit or the genius of art.

The clear rhythmic order and simple arrangement of the parts of the woman's body remind us of Cézanne's own art (p.230-231). The reason for this is that these two artists had a great deal in common. Rhythmic solid order and simplicity of arrangement characterize the works of both.

Maillol's work also recalls the solid simple figures of the Greeks. His love for the beauty of the human form is felt in all his works, and his sculptures glorify that beauty.

Maillol's sculptures always express ideas.

244

PICADOR sculptured 1926
by Pablo Gargallo (1881-1934)

This Sculptor Made a Face of Iron Sheets

Courtesy of the Museum of Modern Art, New York, N. Y. Gift of A. Conger Goodyear

THE picador plays a very important part in bullfights, next in importance to the toreador (p.204-205). The picador is the one who sticks a long sharp dagger into the bull's neck to infuriate him to the utmost frenzy. He must be daring in his approach and alert enough to get away before the bull can strike back.

In the picture above we can see the picador's fearless determination to act and his tense concentration.

We feel that we can see his entire figure, bent forward, on his toes, eager to attack and yet ready to withdraw in a flash.

But when we examine what we actually see, there are only a few iron sheets welded together and wrought in a few simple shapes, stuck up on an iron bar.

The Spanish sculptor Pablo Gargallo was such a great master of sculpture that without giving actual shape to marble or bronze he could give a figure a wealth of expression. He knew the play of light and shadow on shapes so perfectly that he could create the impression of an entire person by cutting sheets of iron to the right shape. In this sculpture we can see the picador's jaw is set. We see his eye piercing because the artist knew exactly where to cut and how wide to make the two small squares that stand for the eyes. He knew how to give the right outline to the nose and mouth made of flat metal to make us see that the picador is holding his breath in the very moment of action.

The flat round hat with the cockade, the sideburns, the lock on the ear—all these things make it clear that the man is a Spanish bullfighter. But they serve also to round out the statue to an impressive form giving importance to a piece of modern sculpture.

Though his means were so different from Rodin's, Gargallo thought, as Rodin did too, that the play of light and shadow makes the picture in the eye of whoever is looking at the artist's creation. The ever-changing light gives an exciting life to Gargallo's *Picador*.

This Jungle was Made Up in the Artist's Mind

UNDER a blue-green sky lush green leaves and sumptuous flowers crowd the view. The thicket looks full of exotic plants in endless variety. They all look unfamiliar and strange to us. Two animal faces almost entirely hidden under the trees add a scary touch to the fantastic scenery. But is it really so strange and fantastic?

No. When we look closely and notice what is really there, the plants we see in the forest are all familiar.

There are a few blades of grass in front, then three tufts of snake-plants, the kind we so often see on window-sills. The grand pale blooming stem is the hyacinth in springtime. Behind a few palm leaves there are three lotus flowers that look rather like tulips, and behind a rubber plant of the kind also to be found in many homes, we see some leafy branches with lilac leaves. Two shapes like pineapple tops and some more painted leaves of the same kind complete the *Equatorial Jungle*.

All are simply drawn and painted in a primitive style.

But the French painter Henri Rousseau was well able to give the charm of a fabulous jungle to the painting. How did he do it?

He enlarged the well-known shapes of simple plants and he painted them in uniform colors or just two shades of green. He varied plants and colors as we never see them in nature around us. They seem to come from a dream. The lights and shadows fall according to the artist's whim—and according to his unfailing sense of rhythm. The animals, that look like monkeys and birds, have unusual shapes. They too belong to dreamland. We find them unexpectedly among the shadows, and the whole effect makes us feel the mystery of a moonlit night.

This picture was painted in France where people know much less about jungles than Americans do. Europe is separated from primeval forests by an ocean while many of us live not far from them. But even to us the painting suggests unheard-of animal and plant life under hot equatorial skies.

Henri Rousseau was a toll-taker by profession. He taught himself the art of painting, but his pictures became popular among artists and critics. They appreciated his fine sense of color and rhythm and mystery. He has the gift of leading us into beautiful lands with that feeling of scariness we enjoy so much in fairy tales.

EQUATORIAL JUNGLE painted 1909
by Henri Rousseau (1844-1910)

National Gallery of Art, Washington, D. C.
Chester Dale Collection

An American Tale of Patriotism

THE historical story of Paul Revere and his midnight ride has long ago found its way into our hearts.

It *sounds* like an ancient legend of unselfish service of one for all. It *is* a legend of American alertness and readiness for action. But it did not actually become a legend until the American poet, Henry Wadsworth Longfellow, put it into his famous poem.

The American painter, Grant Wood, therefore painted *The Midnight Ride of Paul Revere* as if to illustrate a story-book legend well known to us all.

In this picture he shows us the darkness of the night and the brightness of the moonlight. With firm outlines he draws the simple village church with its high steeple that can be seen far over the land. It is from such a church tower that the signal came for Paul Revere to mount his horse. And there, right next to the church, we see him galloping through the village, having awakened the sleeping people as he rode. With a twinkle in his eye the painter shows the village people in their nightgowns as if they had come straight out of their beds on to the street.

The houses he paints look like toy houses, and the landscape looks like a toy landscape. But the long white road rising over the hills and broken by valleys goes on into the distance beyond where we can see it. It is the artist's way of showing us how boundless was the achievement of the lonely rider.

The few small dots we see at the beginning of the road are meant to be people spurred to action by "the hurry of hoofs in a village street."

As Longfellow told us,

"You know the rest. In the books you have read
How the British regulars fired and fled . . ."

And that is why the painter knew he had no need to tell us the whole story from beginning to end. He did not paint the dramatic moment of the story's beginning nor did he tell us the exciting results. He made, instead, a well-rounded composition that sums up the mood of the whole story.

He gave his picture a poetic rhythm. His clean-cut shapes bring the rhythm alive as meter brings the rhythm alive in verse.

Grant Wood was a modern artist. Only a modern painter would have dared to simplify shapes as he did. He spent several years studying modern art in Paris. But he lived and died in Iowa, in the very heart of America, and his art reflected his native land.

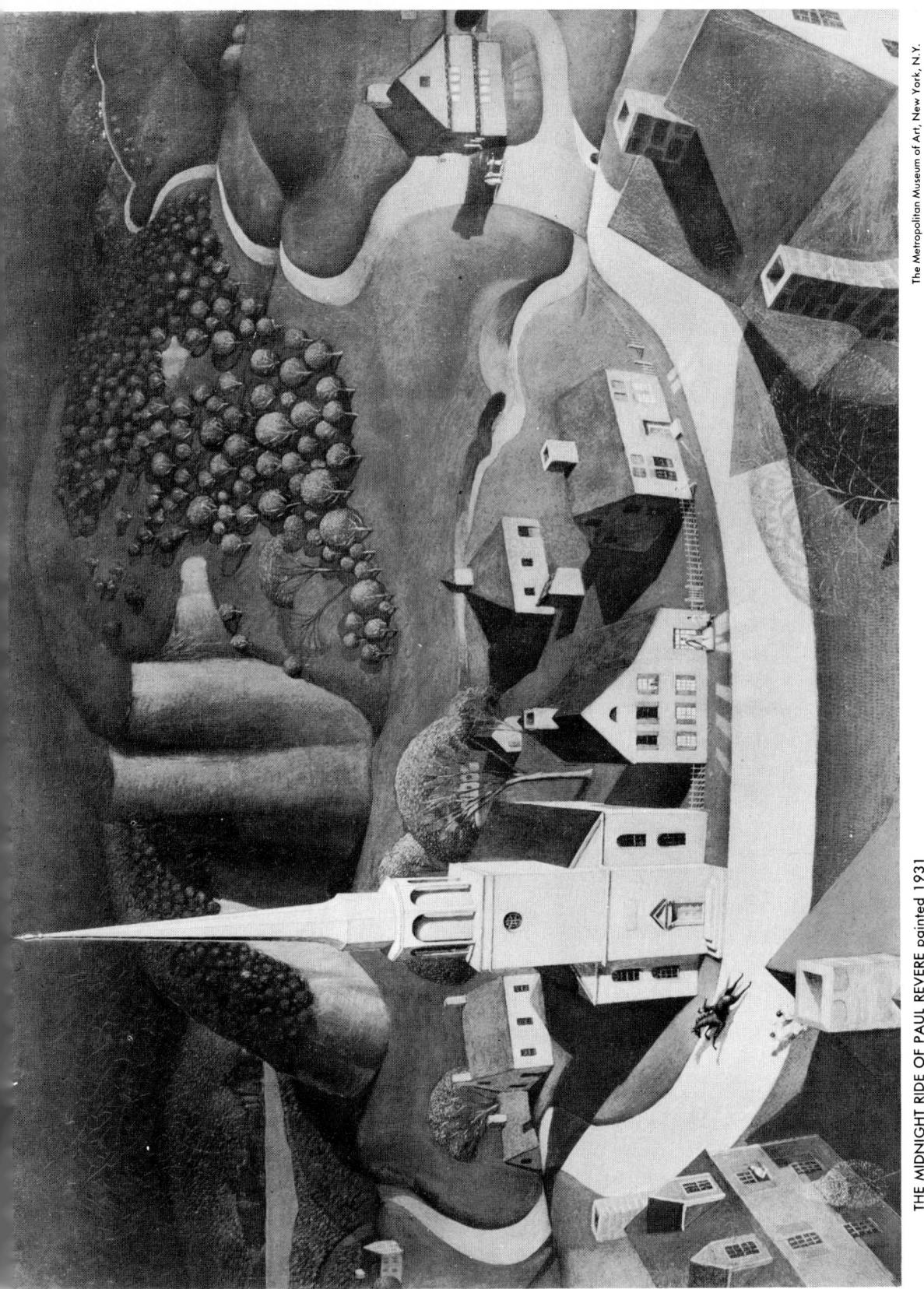

THE MIDNIGHT RIDE OF PAUL REVERE painted 1931
by Grant Wood (1892-1942)

The Metropolitan Museum of Art, New York, N.Y.

One of the "Wild Beasts"

AT FIRST glance, *Goldfish and Sculpture,* by the modern French painter, Henri Matisse, seems rather primitive: just a few objects standing together, it is not even clear where. There are only a few colors: blue, green, red, and tan, and just a few shades of each.

But how delightfully gay the picture is! It would cheer up any room—that is, if we are willing to accept the fact that Matisse has no interest in copying objects or in making them look "real."

When we look at the cheerful color-spots in this picture and recognize the swimming goldfish, the pretty flowers in the vase, and the lively motion of the sculptured figure, we feel like smiling. All the colors are set off by clean-cut clear outlines. A blue background makes us think of a clear sunny day.

A few straight lines divide the blue. Other lines separate it from the tan, red, and green in the background. These three colors too are separated by straight lines, making them look like a back wall. Because of the way the lines are drawn in the blue parts of the picture, they look like the sides and ground of clean-cut space. Into this space the painter has put various objects. The shelf and mirror on the right suggest that this part of the picture is another wall.

But why did Matisse paint this picture in such a primitive way? We can see why if we compare his *Variation on a Still Life by De Heem,* with De Heem's original (p.7).

De Heem's painting looks almost like a photograph. The velvet tablecloth is definitely velvet, the linen is linen. The shiny silver objects are silver. The sparkling glass nothing but glass. The fruits look so fresh and fragrant we can almost taste them.

Matisse's version of the Still Life looks as if he had tried to copy De Heem's painting but failed. But this is not so. We know that Matisse could have made the picture life-like because when he was a young man he did so to perfection.

What, then, was Matisse trying to do in his very different version of De Heem's picture?

First, Matisse arranged the objects in clearer order. He straightened out the crease in the linen cloth with a wide black line. He put a similar black line on the drapery in the background. This gives us a clear feeling of the width of the table.

Second, Matisse tried to create clearer order by drawing outlines with heavy definite strokes. He left out details and painted objects merely as shapes. In this way Matisse made a picture of rhythmically ordered shapes and colors out of the scene De Heem had so faithfully copied.

Matisse headed a group of young revolutionary artists who tried new ways of simplified painting. But people did not understand their work. And because they did not understand, they ridiculed the painters by calling them wild beasts or, in French, *Fauves.*

In time, however, people began to understand and appreciate the *Fauves.* Matisse came to be admired as one of the great painters of our time.

GOLDFISH AND SCULPTURE painted 1911
by Henri Matisse (1862-1954)

251

Courtesy of Museum of Modern Art,
New York, N. Y.
Gift of Mr. John Hay Whitney

The United Nations
"Neither Shall They Learn War Any More"

FOR THOUSANDS of years wars between nations have been growing more deadly. But now at last, people have come to realize that nations must solve their problems peacefully in spite of their differences. To try to work out such solutions, they formed an organization called the United Nations.

It is appropriate that the home of the United Nations Organization was built in New York City where people of so many different nationalities live and work together—and where, in the harbor, the Statue of Liberty holds her torch high, lighting the way for all who come to America's shores.

The United Nations Building stands high too, trying to shed its light around the world. Here every member's language is made understandable to all and every member's point of view is presented to all the others.

The home of the United Nations really consists of three buildings. In the General Assembly building the delegates of the nations gather for their discussions. Most of the work involved is done in the towering Secretariat building. We can see these two buildings in the picture here. The five-story Conference building is not in this picture.

All these buildings were erected by the modern method of steel construction—a practical and solid way of building. A framework of upright steel columns and horizontal steel girders is set up first. Sheets of concrete separate one story from another. The frames at the sides are filled with hollow bricks and other light material, with a decorative covering.

In the United Nations building the outer walls are covered with slabs of white Vermont marble which has the peculiar quality of becoming marbled—that is, clouded with light gray streaks—after a few months' exposure to sun and air. Thus a design of natural beauty adorns the walls.

The narrow side walls of the 650-foot tall Secretariat building are entirely covered with marble in contrast to the wide north and south façades which gleam with sheets of glittering glass windows framed by aluminum bands.

On the walls of the General Assembly building windows alternate with the solid marble or are used decoratively to break the wall's surface. One side and the top of this building bend in a slight curve to make the structure look more graceful. A shallow dome in the middle of the roof covers the assembly hall which seats 750 delegates and 1300 spectators.

Fifteen nations sent their best architects to form an International Board of Design to plan the United Nations buildings. They agreed to use their fifty-third plan.

Wallace K. Harrison was the director of planning. Harrison's aim was to make the building look stately and dignified. Le Courbusier, the great modern architect of France, wanted the design to express harmony. Architect Niemeyer, the glass expert of Brazil, felt that the modern look of solid glass would best represent the true spirit of our age. Dr. Liang of China thought of glass, because it is clear and practical, as symbolic of civilization. The building is bathed in sunshine and light. Space and greenery surround it.

UNITED NATIONS BUILDING
built 1950-1952
by architects of various nations

Courtesy of the
United Nations Organization

Rich and poor contributed to the building. A full square mile of enormously valuable ground was donated for the site by John D. Rockefeller Jr. But the sparkling fountain in front was paid for with the pennies and nickels of America's school children.

As a symbol of man's striving for peace, these words of the prophet Isaiah are carved in stone to greet the visitor:

> "They shall beat their swords into plowshares and their spears into pruning hooks. Nation shall not lift up sword against nation, neither shall they learn war any more."

To Love and to Cherish

A CLEAR blue sky smiles through the window, but the two young people standing before it are in an earnest mood. The young man has put his arm around the girl's shoulder. In his gesture and in the expression of his face we can read the promise of the marriage ceremony: "To have and to hold, to love and to cherish." His face also asks a question, and we can read the answer in the girl's expression. It says "I do." And her dreamy eyes tell us that it will be "for better or for worse until death us do part."

He holds out his hand to her and she puts her hand into his, to seal their promises to each other.

He is firm and forceful in his gay red clothes. She is soft and feminine in her garments of gentler white and yellow. Her veil is like a bridal veil. But it is not white; it is a soft mossy green. Picasso made it green because he wanted it to symbolize life, and green is the color of life in nature. It is the color of fields and forests when they come to life under a spring or summer sky of tender blue. It is this kind of blue sky that frames the girl in the green veil.

The green of her veil and the red of the young man's garment form a color harmony in this painting by the great Spanish artist Pablo Picasso. You may remember that there was this same harmony of red and green in the marriage picture of the Arnolfini couple by Jan van Eyck painted five hundred years earlier (p.83).

Though the two pictures tell a similar story of a promise of love, they are amazingly different. In van Eyck's picture we see every detail as precisely as we would in a photograph. Picasso does not show us details, not even the shape of the room or the materials in the garments. The young couple's hands and arms are drawn with outlines alone, and only a few lines and mere touches of color form the faces.

But the gestures of the coarsely drawn arms and hands are full of gentle expression. In the lightly painted features we can sense the young man's question and the young woman's answer. We feel close to these young people.

In Picasso's painting there are no details to be examined for meaning as there are in Jan van Eyck's picture. We must understand Picasso's painting with our hearts.

No sunlight streams through this windows as it does in the Arnolfini's room. Yet Picasso put a tender light around his young couple. The purple-pink drapery is suggested rather than portrayed. But the lovely soft color completes the picture with a gay sweet note.

The young couple's Grecian profiles remind us of ancient Greek art. So do the simple outlines of their figures and their marble-smooth colorless faces.

Picasso used that style as a sort of quotation, as we do when we reach for the words of a poet to express something important. Picasso's artistic "quotations" plus his mastery of simple lines made it possible for him to tell us important things.

His genius was already recognized when he was in his teens. His endless study and experimentation made him the greatest master of our time.

THE LOVERS painted 1923
by Pablo Picasso (1881-   )

National Gallery of Art, Washington, D. C.
Chester Dale Collection

A Seal with Neither Head nor Tail

HERE is the sleek body of a seal with all his funny awkwardness! He has the odd balance we see only in seals. Here he is poised for action: as though deciding whether to plunge into the water or snap up a fish in the air. Yet this seal is made of marble, and he has neither head nor tail, no flippers, no beady eyes, no proud mustaches.

How then did the sculptor, Brancusi, make us recognize his statue as a seal? He did it partly by careful observation of the *shapes* of seals. That is how he was able to make the curving outline of the seal's body remarkably true to life, so charged with the energy we see in real seals.

But the artist also observed the *nature* of the seal. A live seal swims quickly through the water like a fish. But with his short flippers he looks more like an alligator. Like an alligator, a seal can live both in the water and on the shore. But never will an alligator try to straighten out and reach upward without support as a seal does.

As a seal tries to raise himself higher and higher, he reminds us of a young bird trying to fly. The seal's body, so powerful yet so helpless, makes us smile.

Brancusi's sculptured seal of white marble makes us smile too. But the artist has also made us see beauty in the bold effort of the animal reaching out for something he would like to achieve.

There is something beautiful in the clean-cut form and in the white marble surface. It is beauty of a kind Brancusi alone has been able to bring out. Just look at the plain surface of the round stone where the seal is perched. Then notice the exquisite softness of the seal's body. What a contrast!

Never before have we seen balance in sculpture as we do in this white marble seal reaching out into space. Brancusi created a new kind of balance and a new kind of line. In this line the eye of the artist captured grace and rhythm for us, and his artist-hands shaped them to our delight.

This is what every great artist does: He captures new beauty for us, each one in a new and individual way. He makes us see and dream. Every great artist gives us a picture or a sculpture created out of the wealth of his imagination. But he must work, too, with hands skilled by never-ending practice. That is what enables him to put his inner picture into shape. The story of art is the story of great men forever striving to harmonize truth and beauty.

THE WHITE SEAL sculptured about 1936
by Constantine Brancusi (1876-1957)

Courtesy of the Solomon R. Guggenheim Museum

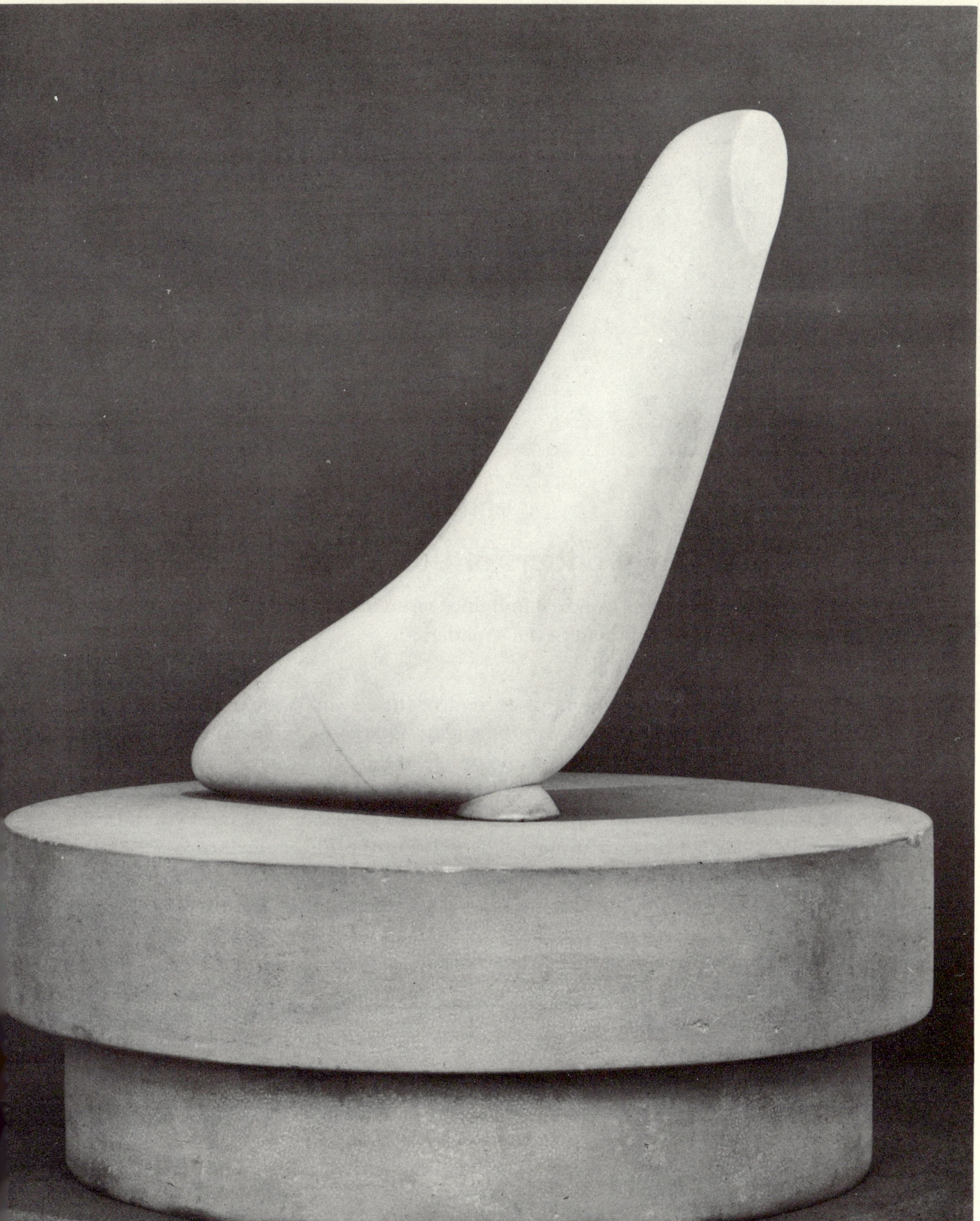

PYRAMIDS OF GIZEH built about 5000 B.C. by unknown builders

The Seven Wonders of the Ancient World

PEOPLE have always prized wonders, and since seven has long been considered a magic number, the ancient world had Seven Wonders:

1. The Pyramids of Egypt

The Pyramids in Egypt are the most ancient of the Seven Wonders. They are huge burial monuments to the rulers of Egypt, the mighty Pharaohs. Some have been standing for five thousand years, almost as long as the people of the earth can retrace their history.

Even today people raise small mounds over the graves of their loved ones, but a Pharaoh's grave had to have a monument as high as a mountain. The tallest of the Pyramids, the *Cheops Pyramid,* so called because it marks the grave of the Pharaoh Cheops, is 481 feet high. It covers thirteen acres of ground.

But the Pyramids were not built for the sake of greatness alone. They were planned to last. That was their practical purpose. But they were also meant to look impressive. That is why they were built in their particularly impressive shape.

The shape of the Pyramids was designed by an artist. They are indeed works of art. But the names of the artists who built them are not known. We have records only of the Pharaohs whose monuments they are. We do not know, even today, how they were built—only that the work was done by thousands of slaves.

Some Pyramids were richly decorated on the inside by sculptured reliefs; and the burial chamber of the Pharaoh contained art objects of all sorts and sizes and colors.

The Pyramids—alone of the Seven Wonders—are still standing. The other six have been destroyed.

2. The Lighthouse of Pharos

This lighthouse was also built in ancient Egypt. On top of it there was a fire which was kept burning night and day, and its light was intensified by the many mirrors arranged to reflect it. The light of the fire—a colossal beacon—could be seen forty miles away.

We are not sure whether the Lighthouse of Pharos was originally a work of art, but we do know that all the rest of the Wonders *were*.

3. The Hanging Gardens of Babylon

These famous Hanging Gardens were in Babylon, a part of the world we know today as the Middle East. The Gardens belonged to the powerful Queen Semiramis. They grew on soil supported by tall arches far above the ground and a miraculous view it was.

All the rest of the Wonders (4, 5, 6, and 7) were works of *Greek* art.

4. The Zeus Statue of Olympia

The gold and ivory statue of Zeus, King of the gods was enshrined in the Temple of Olympia, Greece. Seated on a magnificent throne adorned by colorful precious stones, Zeus held in one hand a statue of Nike and in the other his royal scepter with an eagle on top.

This famous statue was sculptured by Phidias (p.12-13). It was so impressive that a poet, describing it, said that if this sculptured Zeus nodded his head, Mount Olympus itself would tremble.

But the greatest praise was given by another poet who said that whoever was troubled in his heart became happy again at the sight of this Zeus, Phidias's greatest work.

5. The Temple of Diana in Ephesos

This Temple was so magnificent that an evil man thought he could immortalize his name by burning it down. But it is the temple, not the man, that is forever enshrined in our minds—one of the Seven Wonders of the world.

6. The Colossus of Rhodes

This was an enormous bronze statue of the Greek god Apollo (p.36; p.153). The statue was so truly colossal that ships could pass between its legs.

7. The Mausoleum of Halicarnassos

This, like the Pyramids, was also a burial monument. It was erected by the widow of King Mausolos to his memory. The matchless beauty of this monument gained world-wide fame, and even today we speak of a tomb as a mausoleum.

• • • • • •

The Seven Wonders of the ancient world were known in only one part of the earth. But beyond that, in distant India and the Far East, artists have been creating miraculously beautiful things ever since those ancient times.

Great Art of the Orient

TAJ MAHAL built about 1630 by order of the Emperor Shah Jahan

Courtesy of the Indian Delegation to the U.N.

THE TAJ MAHAL AT AGRA Mohammedan Architecture

Long after all the Wonders of the Ancient World, except the Pyramids, had been destroyed, another burial monument also became famous. It is sometimes called one of the Seven Wonders of the modern World. It was built at Agra near Delphi in India, and was named Taj Mahal.

The Taj Mahal, a Mohammedan temple, was erected by Shah Jahan, Emperor of India, to mark the grave of his beloved wife.

The walls of the Taj Mahal are white marble, but they look like lace because they are so finely carved. Standing in the midst of a beautiful garden, this graceful temple is mirrored in the water of a white marble basin set into emerald greenery.

Even today travelers from distant countries visit this beautiful monument to an enduring love.

VISHNU TEMPLE IN INDIA built about 15th century
by unknown architect

A HINDU TEMPLE GATE
Hindu Architecture

Courtesy of the Metropolitan
Museum of Art, N. Y.

This magnificent gate is an example of the greatness of Hindu religious architecture. In India entire islands are turned into temples covered with sculptures of the gods.

BUDDHA Indian stone relief, sculptured eighth century
by unknown sculptor

BUDDHA
Indian Buddhist Sculpture

Courtesy of the Metropolitan
Museum of Art, N. Y.

The East Indian Prince Gautama Buddha was the founder of a religion, Buddhism, named for him. He found many followers in India, China, and Japan. This statue shows him in deep thought. That is because Buddha was a philosopher and Buddhism is a philosophical religion.

CRAG WITH MISTY VALLEY BELOW Ming painting in Sung style by unknown painter

CRAG WITH MISTY VALLEY BELOW

Chinese Landscape

Courtesy of the Fogg Art Museum
Harvard University, Cambridge, Mass.

Landscape painting is the greatest achievement of Chinese art. The Chinese loved "the haze, mist, and haunting spirit of the mountains," as one of their great painters put it. As this picture shows, the Chinese do not think of man as the most important thing in the world. In their paintings people are very small compared to the majesty of the landscape.

THE WAVE printed about 1838 by Hokusai (1760-1849)

THE BIG WAVE

Japanese Woodcut

Courtesy of the Metropolitan Museum of Art, N. Y.

Colored woodcuts have been most popular in Japanese art. One of the most famous is *The Big Wave* by Hokusai. You can see the white peak of Mt. Fujiyama in the curve of the wave. And, if you look carefully, you will find three partly hidden boats among the frothy mountainous waves.

Stories of Artists Who Changed the Trend of Art

How Did Art Begin?

A GREEK legend tells us this story about the beginning of sculpture: There was a young couple engaged to be married. But there was a war going on and the young man had to join the army. The evening before he left, the two were sitting at a table where a little oil lamp shed its light. As they sat quietly, the girl noticed how clearly her lover's shadow was cast on the wall. She quickly made an outline of it and, after he left, she filled in the outline with clay and moulded it to his likeness.

That is how the poetic mind of the Greeks imagined the beginning of art. But we know that pictures existed for many thousands of years before Greek civilization. The ancient cavemen had drawn animals on the walls of their caves. It is believed that once when a caveman was very hungry he imagined that the bumps in the walls of his caves were shaped like the animals he used for food. These he outlined with colored earth. That was, probably, the very beginning of art.

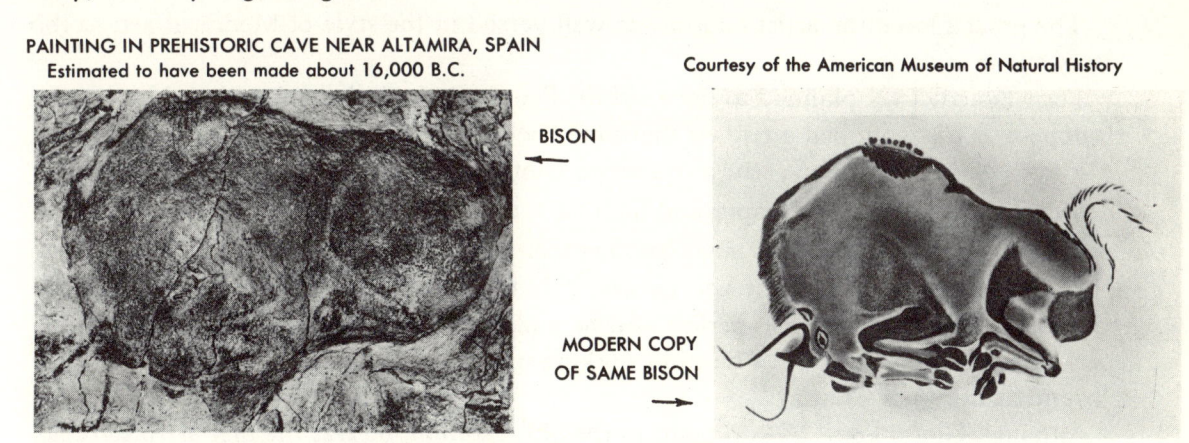

PAINTING IN PREHISTORIC CAVE NEAR ALTAMIRA, SPAIN
Estimated to have been made about 16,000 B.C.

Courtesy of the American Museum of Natural History

← BISON

MODERN COPY OF SAME BISON →

The Story of a Competition of Two Greek Painters

Many thousands of years passed between the cavemen and even the most primitive beginnings of Greek art (p.14-15). These early works were not real likenesses. But later, as another story tells us, the Greeks succeeded in making likenesses look wonderfully real.

The story goes that two of their great painters, Parrhasius and Zeuxis, each made a picture to compete with the other's. Zeuxis painted a still-life showing a basket of fruit. It was Spring and the window was open. Some birds flew in and started to pick at the painted fruit. Zeuxis, feeling sure he had won the contest, said to Parrhasius: "You see how real my painting looks? Now let me see what you have done."

He went to the easel and tried to draw the curtain aside. But that was when he lost out. The curtain was merely painted! Zeuxis had deceived only dumb birds, but Parrhasius had fooled even the keen eye of a painter.

Greek artists did indeed create life-like figures (p.34-35). But their first aim was to create harmonious rhythms and spirited beauty.

LION drawn in the 13th century
by Villard de Honnecourt

This Lion was Drawn from Life in the Middle Ages

When, in the thirteenth century, the French architect Villard de Honnecourt drew a picture of this lion in his note-book, he wrote that it was drawn from life. But to us the lion does not look natural at all. This is because in the Middle Ages artists stylized everything they drew according to specific rules. Drawings were all made to look flat.

A Story of Giotto and the Pope

The great Florentine artist Giotto was well versed in the style of Medieval art, as this story shows.

Pope Benedict IX planned to have old St. Peter's Cathedral decorated and he wanted it done by a distinguished artist. At that time Giotto was the world's most famous painter. But to make sure, the Pope sent a courier to Giotto for a sample of his art. Giotto simply drew a circle on a piece of paper and handed it to the Pope's envoy. The messenger, expecting some brilliant picture, was disappointed.

But Giotto said, "The Pope will be well able to judge." And he was right. The Pope saw that Giotto's circle was as perfect as if he had drawn it with a compass. It showed the perfect mastery of the artist's hand in making a clean-cut shape. In Italy they still say "round as the O of Giotto."

Although Giotto knew how to paint in the old tradition, he was the first artist to break with the style of imitating lifeless flat patterns as painters then used to do. Giotto was the first artist since the ancients to give his painted figures well-rounded shapes, making us feel that they could be touched on all sides. All his figures stand or move in space.

According to Italian art history, the Renaissance started with Giotto.

New Things are Often Laughed at

But it was another hundred years until Renaissance art became popular. The first aim of Renaissance artists was to make their figures look realistic. They didn't mind making them ugly if that made them look natural. That is why the modern young sculptor Donatello (We saw his St. George on p.77) lost out in a competition with an older artist.

The subject of the competition was the figure of Christ on the cross. Donatello made Christ look like any real man, not caring for the ancient pattern of idealized beauty. But the Florentine people were not yet ready to accept this new approach. To ridicule Donatello they said "He crucified a peasant." But as time went on they learned to accept real-looking figures and to admire Donatello's art.

From a painting by Masaccio

How the Rules of Perspective were Shown to the Florentines

One sunny morning of the year 1419 the great Florentine architect Filippo Brunelleschi went out into the market-place in Florence with a cunning gadget in his hands. It was a deep frame with a glass in it instead of a picture. But anyone who looked through the framed glass at the market-place could see only a part of it, as if it were a picture.

Brunelleschi then drew on the glass what could be seen through the framed glass. In his drawing all the parallel lines came together at one point—at eye-level. Consequently, the farther a subject was from the eye, the smaller it appeared in the drawing. This is the law of perspective, and it was readily accepted by the Florentine artists.

The great Florentine Masaccio was the first to use this law in his paintings (p.78-79).

ANNUNCIATION painted about 1438 by Fra Giovanni da Fiesole (1387-1455)

Here New Rules and Old Traditions Work Together

Monastery of St. Marco, Florence, Italy

Some artists, even those who immediately accepted the realism of perspective, refused to be realistic to the extent of making their figures look ugly.

Giovanni da Fiesole was one of these. His love of heavenly beauty was so great that he came to be known as the Angelic Brother: Fra Angelico. Fra Angelico spent most of his life in a Florentine monastery whose walls are still decorated with his paintings.

This *Annunciation* shows how Fra Angelico combined the new with the old. He designed a white porch next to a garden according to the realistic rules of perspective. But the young Virgin with her arms crossed on her breast is idealistically lovely in her humble simplicity. The Angel bringing the heavenly message also looks gentle and sweet in the old tradition.

The Rebirth of Ancient Art

Early Renaissance artists also studied and imitated ancient art.

Donatello had already studied sculpture of the ancients. Later Botticelli modeled his *Venus* from an ancient *Venus* (p.102). He did not yet know how to make the parts of the body hang together. It took one of the greatest geniuses of all time, Leonardo da Vinci, to bring to art the important study of anatomy.

Genius of the Florentine Renaissance: Leonardo da Vinci

Leonardo da Vinci was also a Florentine artist, but he worked for a long time in Milan. When he asked the Prince of Milan for a job, he wrote that he could do the work of an engineer. He could build tricky bridges and weapons of war. He was as good an architect as any. As a sculptor he could make anything a sculptor could, including monuments of riders on horseback. He also would be a match for any painter. Leonardo proved that he could live up to all his promises. Everything he made was both true to life and at the same time radiant with exquisite beauty.

How to Paint Ideally Beautiful Pictures: Raphael

At the time of the Renaissance artists often *discussed* the problem of making their pictures beautiful. Some thought they could do it by picking beautiful models. Others meant to select the beautiful part of many models and to combine them. But Raphael said, "I paint the idea I have in my mind." That was what gave his paintings the beauty of an ideal.

The Most Gigantic Figure in Art: Michelangelo

Younger than Leonardo, older than Raphael, Michelangelo outlived both by about forty years. People have never stopped marveling at Michelangelo's greatness. But he had to work hard too. When he painted the ceiling of the Sistine Chapel, he had to do the work lying on his back on a high scaffold—and it took him years to finish it.

His first great sponsor, Pope Julius II, often quarreled with him. The Pope would give him one thing to do and then, before he had time to finish, order him to do another. Once, feeling too burdened, Michelangelo ran away from Rome. It was several months before he sought the Pope's pardon. A Bishop tried to excuse Michelangelo by telling the Pope that artists are quite ignorant about everything except their art. But the Pope reprimanded the Bishop sternly: It is you who are ignorant to reproach him.

The Greatest Church in the World

Michelangelo's last great achievement was the rebuilding of St. Peter's Cathedral.

This was late in the Renaissance. Now artists who had humbly studied and copied the great masterpieces of the ancients aspired to outdo them. That is why, in rebuilding St. Peter's, Michelangelo gave it the size and proportions of the Colosseum and added a cupola to match the magnificent vaulting of the Pantheon (p.44-45).

We can still see Michelangelo's architectural masterpiece in Rome—but only from the rear. The long nave, later added to the front, hides part of the cupola; but from a distance it can be seen rising like a majestic mountain as Rome melts into the surrounding hills.

ST. PETER'S CATHEDRAL IN ROME.
This part of the Cathedral, built in 1558-1606, was designed by Michelangelo (1475-1564)

Art Mirrors the Thought of Its Time.

When Michelangelo built St. Peter's, the times were full of turmoil. Protestants had separated from the Catholic Church. Art, like a mirror, reflected the unrest and excitement of the times. Now artists wanted to make their works thrilling and impressive, not just natural and beautiful. (p.136-149). Artists expressed strange ideas about what a figure should look like. Those who were interested in things of the spirit made figures look like flames, writhing, hardly touching the ground and tapering toward the top. Remember Greco's *St. Martin* (p. 147)? Or Michelangelo's *Victory* (p.148)? Other artists, more interested in the body, made figures in interesting motion. They were not interested in expressing ideas. A good example for that approach is Giovanni da Bologna's *Mercury* (p.149).

For surprising effects, painters often showed unusual views from odd angles.

This period, following the high Renaissance, is known as the *Manneristic* period because of these mannerisms of the painters.

Pictures that Fought for Artistic Ideas

After *Mannerism* artists again took a more natural view in the period we call *Baroque*.

Caravaggio was one of the most ardent revolutionaries against *Mannerism*. But his teacher was a Mannerist painter. To ridicule him and his teachings, Caravaggio painted a giant looking down at one of the teacher's paintings and putting out his tongue at it.

Caravaggio in turn was ridiculed in a painting which showed him as a hairy wild creature sitting before his easel, an ape at his knee. This picture meant that an artist should not ape nature, but, being a human, should express noble and fine ideas.

There was one thing that both Mannerist and Baroque artists had in common: love of motion. Motion gave excitement to Manneristic art and sweep and grandeur to Baroque art. Remember the *Aurora* by Reni (p.153)? Or Bernini's *David* (p.150) and his *Louis XIV* (p.181)? Or Rubens' *Neptune* (p.156)? These fanciful works of art gave churches and palaces a dazzling richness everywhere—except in little democratic Holland. There people liked to look at the world as it was. There they valued an artist for his love of simple quiet things and his human understanding (p.168-179).

Except in Holland, rich decorative art was popular from the time of the French King Louis XIV on. It remained so until a new democratic trend brought about a period of revolutions and simpler art everywhere.

A Scientific Discovery About the Magic of Light

We have seen before (p.78-79) how much the scientific discovery of the rules of perspective influenced the trend of art.

The great English scientist, Sir Isaac Newton, had made a discovery about light that had a tremendous effect on future painting. Looking, one day, at a prism, he noticed that a ray of sunlight, going through it, dissolved into a rainbow. But it was not until a century ago that painters began to study Newton's discovery about light and to use it in applying color to their canvases. Since then, up to our own day, the use of light and color has been the chief concern of most painters (p.202-255).

Different Ways of Studying Nature

One morning the painter Corot (p.212) went up to a hill near Rome in the company of three other French painters. They had all come to study art in the Eternal City. That day they all wanted to paint the same view of Rome from the same spot at the same time. The weather was fine and the four young men started to paint. When they had all finished their work they compared their pictures to see which was best. But it was hard to tell because each picture looked entirely different from all the others. One showed the majesty of Rome, another the sunny light that enveloped the Eternal City. The third artist had painted the colorful gayety of the southern view. Corot himself had concentrated on the clean-cut shapes of the square houses and the cupola of St. Peter's rising above them.

Pictures are as different as the people who paint them. But there is also another basic difference, depending on the artist's way of looking at nature, as the following story will show.

One day two French painters, Daumier and Daubigny, decided to paint some ducks. They made a date to go to the country together. The day was sunny and the two painters, reaching the little lake where the ducks were swimming, sat down on the grassy shore.

Daubigny took out his sketch-book and pencil and started drawing the ducks. Daumier didn't budge; he just sat and looked. His friend finally asked, "Aren't you going to do any work at all?" But Daumier replied, "I make my sketches in my mind!" And, as a result, the ducks Daumier drew at home were much more truly ducks and more alive than those Daubigny had copied from life. It is the great mind that creates great art.

The Artist's Road to Immortality

An ancient legend tells us this tale about the great Chinese landscape painter Wu Taotse.

He spent his life painting the beloved rivers and trees and mountains of his country as they appeared to his artistic imagination. One day, when he was a very old man, he finished a painting of a magnificent mountain reaching the sky. As he put on the last brush stroke, an opening appeared in the painted mountain. The painter entered into it and was never seen again on earth. It is thus *through his work* that an artist enters into the eternal realm of the immortals.

The Story of Music

By Ruth Goode

ILLUSTRATED BY

Rafaello Busoni

Table of Contents for The Story of Music

	PAGE
What Music Is	271
The Difference Between Music and Noise	277
How Did Music Begin?	282
Music in Ancient Times	288
Wonderful Musical Discoveries in Ancient Greece	291
How Music Was Preserved During the Dark Ages	298
How to Read Music	302
Songs the People Sang Long Ago	307
Great Music Begins	312
The Beginning of Harmony	317
Music Becomes Entertainment	319
Johann Sebastian Bach—The Greatest of a Musical Family	321
Mr. Handel of London Town	327
How a Simple Melody Becomes a Great Symphony	330
"Papa" Haydn and the Symphony	335
Marvelous Mozart	338
Beethoven, the Unhappy Genius	340
The Exciting World of Romantic Music	344
Franz Schubert's Lovely Songs and Symphonies	346
Mendelssohn, the Boy Who Wrote Fairyland Music	348
Schumann Wrote Music of Childhood	350
Brahms, the Third of the Three Great B's	353
Music of Far Lands and People	355
Richard Wagner and the Opera Revolution	366
Romantic Operas of France and Italy	369
Musical Poets and Painters of Europe	371
English and American Composers of the Twentieth Century	377
Meet the Musical Instruments of Today	379
How the Instruments are Generally Placed in a Symphony Orchestra	380a–380c
The Musical Instruments by Sections	380d–380h
Listening to the Music of Our Time	387
Recommended Records	389
Musical Terms	391

What Music Is

MUSIC is all around us, every day of our lives. It is so familiar that we take it for granted and hardly think of it as music.

We hum as we walk along, and sing a tune when we are happy. People whistle at their work. Hardly any of us can help tapping our feet in time to the band as the parade goes by. Mothers sing lullabies to their babies, and children sing nursery rhymes when they are a little older. We have all been hearing and making music almost since we were born.

Television and radio programs sing and play to us. Often we hear music without realizing it, as when we are watching a motion picture or a television play. Even when we do not really listen to it, the music is part of the play or the movie and may even be specially written for it. Music can make an exciting story more exciting, a sad one sadder, a happy one gayer.

We play games and dance to music. We sing and we play instruments in school and at home, and we hear and sing music in church. We have music for Christmas and other holidays. Without music, life would be so strange that we can hardly imagine it.

The world around us is full of musical sounds. In the country, birds and brooks, rain and wind make a kind of music. So do the waves at the seashore. In the city, bus tires hum on the street, airplane motors whirr overhead, and railroad trains click on the rails. In factories we hear machinery hum and throb.

Of course a good deal of what we hear around us is not music but just noise. Both noise and music are made up of sounds. But there is a difference. Sounds by themselves are not music. How does a musical composer make music out of sounds? Perhaps we can find out.

What We Hear in Music

Composers make music out of many of the sounds we hear around us. They use bird songs and water and wind and many more of nature's sounds for their songs and symphonies and compositions for various instruments. Would you ever think that a bee buzzing around was making music? A famous composer thought so, and he made the bee's buzzing into a composition for the violin called *The Flight of the Bumblebee*. The composer's name was Rimski-Korsakov.

Many composers have been inspired by the sounds of nature. Antonio Vivaldi, who lived in Italy nearly three hundred years ago, wrote a composition for orchestra called *The Four Seasons*. In it we can hear nature's sounds for each of the different seasons. We can hear the cuckoo and the rush of a sudden shower in the music devoted to spring. There are the humming insects and the ripple of a cool stream, the song of birds, and the whisper of a summer breeze in the summer music. In the autumn section we hear the joyful sounds of harvest and hunting; and in the winter part there is a gay skating party, with the sounds of skaters falling down and of the ice breaking.

All these sounds are made by instruments in the orchestra, of course. But they are close enough to the real sounds for us to recognize them. Yet the music does more than just imitate real sounds. It also gives us the *feeling* of the seasons. There are no actual sounds for freshness or laziness or crispness; but the music itself makes us *remember* these moods of the seasons. While the music plays sounds like the icy rain of winter beating on the windows and the friendly crackling of a fire on the hearth, it also reminds us of the quiet pleasure of being snug indoors while the winter gale howls outside.

Thunderstorms are a favorite inspiration with many composers. One of the greatest composers, Ludwig van Beethoven, wrote nine great symphonies, and in the *Sixth Symphony* there is a famous thunderstorm. This symphony is also called the *Pastoral Symphony* because it is music about the country and the life of farmers and shepherds. Besides the sound of the thunderstorms he used the songs of birds and other happy country sounds, as well as tunes the country people sang and danced to in Austria where he lived when he was writing this symphony.

But Beethoven, and other composers who made music of nature's sounds, did not just repeat the sounds they heard around them in the country. They used these sounds in their music to *tell us something*. Beethoven's music tells us about the peacefulness and beauty of the country, about the gaiety of the country people, about the excitement of a sudden storm, and about the people's happiness when the storm is over.

Music also tells us *the composer's own feelings*. Beethoven's symphony expresses his own happiness about being in the country and among the country people. We may never have seen Beethoven's country, and we know that the people he wrote about lived long before our time. They spoke a different language, and in many ways their lives were different from ours. Yet as we listen to Beethoven's music, we can understand his feelings about the country and its people. We also have *feelings of our own* that his melodies call up in us. Music can speak to us from many lands and across many years.

How the Composer Uses a Melody

How does the composer tell us all this in his music? He does it with the melodies that he makes out of sounds he hears around him or sounds he hears in his own imagination, and with the ways in which he directs these melodies to be played by the different instruments. He does it with different combinations of sounds, and with different rhythms. He does it by having the melody played fast or slow, loud or soft, in big rich sounds that seem to fill the room, or in thin sounds that seem to come from far away. He has as many ways of making his melodies sound as the painter has of making objects and scenes look on his canvas.

One of the greatest pleasures in listening to music comes when we learn to follow the melody as it grows from a simple tune to a great song or symphony. For example, after the storm in Beethoven's great symphony about the country, we hear the cheerful call of the shepherd, happy that the storm is over. The call is just three bright little notes. In the sudden stillness after the storm, we hear these three notes from the clarinets in the orchestra, playing all alone, like a single shepherd calling from a hillside. The call comes twice, slowly, and then several times more, quickly and gaily. Then the French horns in the orchestra take up the call in a different voice, like someone answering from another hillside. Then the violins catch the three notes and add to them, and they become a melody.

Now the whole orchestra joins in, and the simple little melody becomes a great song of thanksgiving and happiness that runs through the whole last part of the symphony. We do not need any words to this song to tell us that it is happy. The big full sound of all the instruments playing together, the big rhythm and swing of the melody, growing and swelling, all express happiness. The little melody is no longer just a shepherd's song but a song of happiness for everyone, and it makes us happy too as we listen.

This is how a great composer like Beethoven, beginning with just three little notes, can tell us not only about the happiness of the country people but about his own love of the country and his joy in it, too. And this is how we can share his feelings in our own imagination, even though we are not standing on a green hillside but only sitting in a room, listening to music.

It is true that we must really listen to the music to enjoy it. We know that when someone speaks to us and we are not listening, whatever that person may be saying is just sound without meaning. In the same way, music that we do not listen to is just sound without meaning. But when we listen, we hear what the composer is telling us in his music. The more we listen to great music, the more we can hear and the more we understand how the composer used the sounds and rhythms of the world around and of his own imagination, wove them together, and made them into music that expresses his feelings and ideas.

By listening, we soon learn to follow a melody, like the shepherd's song of Beethoven's symphony, all through a great piece of music. Often we hear first one melody, then another and still another. We follow the melodies as they grow and change. We hear them mingle with each other, and separate again. We hear them sometimes played by one instrument, then by another, or by groups of instruments together. With each change the melody may sound different, and we enjoy meeting it again in a new form, and with new feelings. Listening to music in this way is like listening to a story.

HOW THREE LITTLE NOTES GROW INTO A GREAT MELODY

Beethoven's "Sixth Symphony," the "Pastoral Symphony" is about life in the country, with the sounds of birds, brooks, and songs and dances of the country people. A thunderstorm comes up, and we hear the roll of thunder, the crackle of lightning, the rush of wind. Then the storm dies away, and in the stillness we hear a shepherd piping from a hillside to show that the storm is over.

Here is the call, just three little notes:

Even if you cannot read music, you can see the pattern of these three notes repeated in the bars of music below. When you hear the symphony played, this is how you will hear the call:

First the clarinets, all alone while the orchestra is still, play it

Slowly once . . . again . . . and then quickly and gaily, four times more. Now the French horns answer in a different voice

Once . . . again . . . and, like the clarinets, four times more.

And now the violins catch the three notes, add to them, and they grow into a melody. Here is the beginning of it as the violins play it:

See how the three-note call comes again and again in the melody.

Once the violins have played it, the whole orchestra joins in, and the melody grows and swells into a great song of thanksgiving and happiness to the end of the symphony. This melody is the theme of the last movement of Beethoven's "Pastoral symphony."

The Noises of Our Modern World in Music

Besides the sounds of nature, composers of today have made a great deal of music out of such sounds as machinery humming and rattling, sirens howling through traffic, and the many other noises that are part of our world. In their music modern composers tell us how they feel about this busy, complicated world of engines and machines in big, crowded cities.

In a composition called *An American in Paris,* by the American composer, George Gershwin, we hear the sound of feet walking briskly along the pavements, the noise of many people and of automobiles hurrying through the busy streets, and the sound that taxicab horns make in Paris. Gershwin wove the sound of taxicab horns and of walking feet together into a melody that expresses the excitement, and also the homesickness, of being in a big foreign city, far from home. (Some taxicab horns from Paris are actually used as instruments in the orchestra for this musical work.)

Locomotives, Trains and Taxis in Music

A modern composer in France, Arthur Honegger, wrote a whole piece of music about a train locomotive. He named it *Pacific 231,* the number of the train. When you listen to this composition played by the orchestra, you hear the great locomotive puffing steam, the slow thumping of its pistons, the creak and rattle of the cars. You hear it getting started, beginning to roll. You feel the power of the great engine, the excitement as it gathers speed. When it races at last along the rails and across the counry, you feel the space and distance of the miles it travels. Honegger's music makes you feel the same wonder and admiration that the composer himself felt for the powerful, big locomotive.

But the composer has given you these feelings, not just by repeating the noises a train makes. He has expressed them in the melodies he made out of the sounds and rhythms that trains brought to his mind. He shaped the train's sounds and his ideas about them into a fine musical composition, in order to share his feelings about trains with all of us.

Another composer wrote some famous music about a train, too. This was the South American composer, Heitor Villa-Lobos. But while the French composer Honegger chose a huge locomotive that pulls trains across many miles at high speed, Villa-Lobos wrote about a little train that chugs up and down the mountains of his country of Brazil, carrying the berry-pickers who pick the coffee berries growing on the sides of those high mountains. In *The Little Train of the Caipira,* we can hear the little train go puffing and bumping over the mountain, stopping to pick up a group of workers, starting again—*chuh chuh chuh*—up the steep track. We can hear snatches of the songs the berry-pickers sing, and we seem to hear them laughing and talking as the little train huffs and chuffs along through the clear thin mountain air. It is a gay little train, and the music that Villa-Lobos wrote for it makes us feel its gaiety and the merry spirits of the people who ride on it over the mountain.

TAXI HORNS AND A HOMESICK AMERICAN IN PARIS

The American composer George Gershwin made a trip to Paris, and then wrote music to tell how he felt about that great city. When you hear the orchestra play "AN AMERICAN IN PARIS" listen for the music that describes a walk along a Paris street with its lively sights and sounds, like this:

From **AN AMERICAN IN PARIS** *by* GEORGE GERSHWIN

Here is the walking music—brisk and jaunty—but at the end a little downward glide into a blue note—Homesick?

Walking again, but more slowly—here are the taxi horns—the taxi horns are the jaunty ones now—Real taxi horns are used as instruments in the orchestra for this.

And now from the violins, a small sigh—Yes, homesick! Later comes a really blue melody!

Copyright 1930 New World Music Corp., New York. Used by permission.

The Difference Between Music and Noise

NOW WE may be able to say what the difference is between music and noise, or just sounds.

Music has meaning. It tells us something that cannot be told in words. Of course certain noises tell us things too. The noise of a lawnmower means that someone not far away is mowing his lawn. The sharp rat-tat-tat of the riveter tells us that a building is being built. Sounds like this give us *information*. But when a composer puts these noises into his music, we hear something more than just sounds we can recognize. As we listen, we also hear the composer's *ideas and feelings* about these sounds. He has written this music so that we can share these feelings with him.

Music has melody. When you are singing or playing, one musical note leads you to another musical note, and that one to another, until you have several notes that follow each other. That string of notes is a melody. We saw how Beethoven made the melody of the shepherds' song out of three notes. In the same way, the first melody in a piece of music may lead to another melody, or to the same melody played by a different instrument, or faster or slower, louder or softer, perhaps with new notes added to it. Now, a mere sound does not do that. A sound may be repeated again and again, and even be mixed with other sounds, but it does not *lead* anywhere and it does not make a melody.

Music has rhythm. There are many kinds of rhythm. We hear the three rhythmic steps in a waltz: TUM ti ti, TUM ti ti. Or the four beats in a march: ONE two three four, ONE two three four. A noise need not have any rhythm. The riveting machine chatters —rat-tat-tat-tat-tat—until the rivet is in place. After a long while or a short while, it stops. There is no regular beat to it at all. After lunch, maybe, or whenever the workman is ready, the noise begins again on the next rivet. It is jerky and irregular. We cannot count on any steady rhythm as we can in music. Of course we do hear a kind of rhythm in some of the sounds around us. Waves on a beach make a regular *slap-wash, slap-wash*. A train on the track goes CLICKety CLICKety. The feet of the people marching in the parade sound LEFT right, LEFT right. When we hear such regular rhythms in the real sounds of the world, we call them *musical* rhythms. But most noises and ordinary sounds do not have rhythm. Music has.

There is still another difference between noise and music, and this one is explained by science. All sound is caused by a vibration. If you stretch a string very tightly, and then strike it, you may see it quiver rapidly, or you may feel it tickle your finger. It is vibrating. If it is a strong enough string and you can stretch it very tightly indeed, you may hear it twang.

When you sing or speak, your vocal cords vibrate. The violin bow makes the strings of the violin vibrate. The drumstick hitting the drum makes the skin across it vibrate. When you blow into a trumpet, the tiny opening through which the air is forced makes the stream of air vibrate. In some instruments, like the clarinet, there is a small reed in the mouthpiece and this, too, vibrates with the air when you blow. When you strike a key on the piano, the strings of that key vibrate inside the piano.

All sounds, however quiet or noisy, are caused by vibration. But a musical sound or tone has *regular* vibrations, while other sounds and noises have *irregular* vibrations.

So now we know what music is. Music is a composition of sounds that have regular vibrations, put together so that they have rhythm, melody, and meaning. In making music out of sounds, the composer plans them the way an architect plans a building so that the finished work will be both strong and beautiful. He shapes his sounds together the way a sculptor shapes a statue. He fits them to each other the way a cabinetmaker fits the parts of a fine table. The composer arranges his sounds in a kind of order, the way a storyteller arranges his story, so that one part leads to the next and there will be a beginning, a middle, and an end.

When the composer has done all these things to make sounds into a finished piece of music, we call it a composition.

Many Kinds of Music

There are many kinds of music. There is music written for one voice to sing or for many voices to sing together. Some music is written to be played on one instrument, some for several or many instruments. As we go on in this story of music, we will see that music has to be written differently for different instruments and voices, and for all the different combinations of them. We will see how a composer finds his ideas for a musical composition, and decides whether he will write a small piece, like a song or a piano solo, or a big piece for a choir or chorus of voices or for a whole orchestra. Or he may write a *duet,* for two instruments like a flute and clarinet; or a *trio,* for three, perhaps a piano, violin, and 'cello; a *quartet,* for two violins, a viola, and a 'cello; or a piece for any number and any combination of instruments that he chooses. He may write a *concerto,* for an orchestra with a solo instrument like a piano or a violin to carry the leading part. Or he may write an *opera,* which is a play with the actors singing and the orchestra playing the story in music. Or a *ballet,* in which the story is told by dancers dancing to the music of the orchestra.

In all these different forms of music, the composer chooses the sounds he thinks will best express his idea. He does not depend only on sounds we can recognize out of the real world. Sometimes he uses melodies we already know, folk tunes and even nursery rhymes.

Of course you know the tune of *Twinkle, Twinkle, Little Star.* Here it is:

Twin - kle twin - kle lit - tle star, How I won - der what you are.

Children sing different words to this same tune in different countries. Erno Dohnanyi, who grew up in a part of Europe called Bohemia, certainly knew it in his childhood. When he grew up and became a composer, he wrote the tune, in a number of different ways, in an amusing composition called *Variations on a Nursery Tune.* Another composer who lived two hundred and fifty years ago, J. C. Bach, used the tune in one of his compositions, and so did the great composer Mozart.

Many composers enjoy taking a simple tune and then writing all kinds of different music around it. It gives them a chance to use all their skill in creating different moods, with different rhythms, different harmonies, and different groups of instruments, all out of the same little tune. We enjoy listening to a composition like this, too, because we know the tune and can follow it through all its changes. A composition like this is called *Variations on a theme. Theme* is another word for tune or melody. It is a word we meet often in reading or talking about music. *Variations,* of course, means changes or different ways of using the original tune or theme.

If you like to listen to jazz, you have noticed that jazz musicians play something like variations on a theme when they take a familiar song and then play all around it. They have a wonderful time inventing new turns and rhythms on the tune. The great composers had the same pleasure, and it is a pleasure we can enjoy as listeners too. This is called *improvising.*

Stories in Music

Composers often tell a story in their music. In *Billy the Kid,* Aaron Copland, one of the most important modern American composers, tells the story of the famous boy outlaw of the West. In his music we hear many of the sounds of a little Western town of the old days. We hear the rhythm of horses' hoofs, the gay dance of some of the people, and the noise of a gun fight in the street, in which Billy's mother is accidentally killed. After this tragedy Billy begins his wild career. The music tells us of his desperate adventures, his capture and escape, and finally the wide loneliness of the prairie at night where Billy hides, and where he is caught at last by the sheriff's men.

Sometimes a composer makes a musical picture of a place. Another American composer, Ferde Grofé, makes a picture in his *Grand Canyon Suite* of a wonder of nature that many of us go to see, the Grand Canyon of the Colorado River. A *suite* is a group of musical compositions, usually with some connecting idea. Ferde Grofé's suite about the Grand Canyon has five parts: *Sunrise, The Painted Desert, On the Trail, Sunset,* and *Cloudburst.* As we can see by the titles, each of these parts of the suite paints a different musical picture of the Grand Canyon.

In the part called *On the Trail,* we hear the donkey's hoofs in a rhythm that turns into a melody. This lazy, jogging little melody runs into another melody that seems to grow out of it. The two melodies go on through the composition together, played by different groups of instruments, just as if we were actually riding along the trail, the rhythm of our donkey's footsteps would clip-clop along as an accompaniment to our feelings and experiences on a visit to the Grand Canyon.

Music That Needs No Words

Some of the greatest music of all, music that makes us feel most deeply, is just beautiful music without a story or a picture. It is music made out of melodies the composer had dreamed and put together with all his skill, to tell us thoughts so profoundly beautiful that neither words nor pictures can express them—thoughts of which only music can speak.

Just as there are many kinds of music, so there are many ways of listening to it. As we go on in this story of music, we will learn more about the different kinds of music, and how to enjoy them all. We will learn more especially about the music that does not tell a story or paint a picture, the music that has its own special meaning for us just as music.

The more we know about music and the more we listen, the more we can enjoy listening to music in all the different ways there are. Music began very very long ago. Yet even the oldest music is new to us the first time we hear it. Let us see what we can discover on a musical journey back through the centuries.

HOW IT FEELS TO RIDE A DONKEY THROUGH THE GRAND CANYON

Composers often make musical pictures of a scene. The American composer Ferde Grofé, in his "Grand Canyon Suite" for symphony orchestra, describes in music the Grand Canyon of the Colorado River. He pictures the Grand Canyon at sunrise, at sunset, and in a cloudburst, the Painted Desert, and a ride along the trail. The music tells us what we would see and hear on our ride, and how it would feel.

How does a composer tell us all this, without words, without the colors and shapes of a painting, with only notes played by an orchestra? One way is through melodies he creates out of actual sounds. On a ride through the Grand Canyon, we would be sure to hear the sound of our donkey's hoofs. This is how Ferde Grofé describes our ride, beginning with the sound of the donkey's hoofs:

From THE GRAND CANYON SUITE: ON THE TRAIL *by* FERDE GROFÉ

Here is the donkey's jogging-along rhythm—

Here it has grown into a tune, and the tune goes on from here, the notes changing here and there but the rhythms staying the same—

And here is the new melody that seems to grow out of the jogging tune—a big, easy, agreeable melody that might be like the big sky and wide spaces we see as we are riding on the trail, or like our thoughts and feelings about the sky and the space and the mountains.

Copyright 1932 Robbins Music Corporation. Used by special permission of copyright proprietor.

How Did Music Begin?

TODAY we can hear a hundred musicians playing together in an orchestra. We can hear men and women singing and playing in operas and concerts. We can turn on the television, radio, or phonograph, and hear music of all kinds.

There are thousands of music schools and music teachers. Libraries have rooms full of printed music, music on records, and books about music. We have a great variety of musical instruments. Some of our instruments are so complicated that it takes years of study and practice to play them well. (We are lucky that it takes only a little practice, sometimes none at all, to enjoy listening to them!)

There is a great deal of music for us to hear in the world today. How did it ever begin?

Some Clues to the Beginnings of Music

One of the most interesting and curious facts about music is that we do not really know exactly how it began. But there are many clues, and scholars and scientists have studied these clues to figure out how people first began to sing and play music.

Did people in long-ago times make the rhythms of music before they made musical sounds? Did they begin by tapping and stamping their feet and clapping their hands? Or did they first sing out signals to each other in the forest? Did they imitate the sounds they heard in nature, the bird songs and animal noises? Or did they shout out to express pleasure or excitement or anger or some other feelings, and did these cries turn to words and then their words to chants, and so to songs?

Finding answers to these questions is something like a detective story. Some of the clues have been discovered by the scientists called *anthropologists*. These scientists travel to far-away places in the world today and study the simple primitive tribes who live there. The anthropologists have discovered that some of these tribes do imitate the songs of birds in making their music.

Anthropologists have found another clue to how people began to make songs. They have heard some primitive peoples of today making up songs in the same way as people probably did long ago. For instance, in the Indian Ocean, there is a group of islands called the Andaman Islands. If you were taking a trip around the world, and you happened to stop at the Andaman Islands, you might find on the shore an island man making a boat. He is singing as he works on his boat. He sings the same small tune over and over, changing it until he is satisfied.

The words he sings are not very important. If you were making that boat, you might be thinking, "My friend Johnny wants me to get this boat finished, so I have to work fast." And you might think of saying or singing the words in a little tune. And that is exactly what the island man is doing.

This is the way the people of the Andaman Islands, and other primitive people too, make their songs. Not long ago some European scientists made recordings of the songs little children make up while they are playing, and the scientists compared the children's songs with some songs they, or other scientists, had recorded among primitive tribes. They found the children's songs remarkably like those of the primitive men and women. This discovery is one of the important clues to how songs first were made, long ago when there was no civilization and all the people on earth were simple and primitive like the boatmaker on the Andaman Islands.

FAR TO THE NORTH, NEAR THE ARCTIC CIRCLE, THERE IS A KIND OF WILD DUCK WHOSE CALL IS A LITTLE TUNE OF SIX NOTES, LIKE THIS:

TRIBES THAT LIVE ON THE PENINSULA OF KAMCHATKA, IN THE NORTHERN PART OF ASIA, HAVE MANY TUNES THAT THEY HAVE MADE OUT OF THIS WILD DUCK'S CALL.

Digging for Clues in Ancient Ruins

For most of the clues to how music and musical instruments began, it would not be enough to take a trip around the world. You would have to take a trip backward in time through many centuries. You would also have to travel to many lands in your journey through the centuries. Music became important in different countries at different times, in the same way as did the other arts such as painting and sculpture, dancing, poetry, and drama.

We have been talking about the anthropologists who study the primitive people living today. The *archeologists,* another kind of scientist, search through the ruins of ancient lands to learn about people in the past. They dig for the old buried cities where people lived many thousands of years ago. They find tools, sculpture, bits of vases, and parts of walls and buildings. They find jewelry and clay tablets with strange writing on them, some of which they have learned to read. In the pictures carved and painted on the ancient walls and vases, people are shown dressed in the kind of clothes they wore then, and many are playing on instruments, singing and dancing, clapping their hands and tapping their feet. Among the instruments shown in these pictures, we can recognize some like our drums and cymbals, our harps and other stringed instruments, our trumpets and flutes.

Some very old, very simple musical instruments have been found by the scientists who study these things. In France some caves were discovered where men lived in the days before they knew how to build houses. In those days people took shelter wherever they found it, and a cave was a very good shelter. In the caves in France there are paintings of animals on the walls, made by these men of long ago. Perhaps you have seen pictures of some of these paintings of prehistoric buffaloes, with high arched backs and very slender legs. In France, too, a whistle was found, made out of an animal bone with a hole drilled in it. Even though this whistle is several thousand years old, when it is blown it still sounds a shrill musical note. Some caveman of long ago made this whistle, probably to signal to his dogs or to other cavemen in the forest. Later on, huntsmen used hunting horns in the same way. The caveman's bone whistle is one of our clues to how men came to make some musical instruments. This whistle, made for signalling, is an ancient ancestor of our wind instruments today.

In the days when people believed in gods and goddesses, they told stories of how the gods invented music and musical instruments. The Greeks had a legend of how Hermes, the messenger of the gods, was walking along the beach one day, and tripped over a tortoise shell. As he kicked it, it made lovely musical sounds. He found that the sinews of the animal had remained stretched across the opening of the empty shell, and when he plucked them, they sounded. From this, the Greeks said, Hermes invented the lyre, and from the lyre came the harp and all the stringed instruments.

There are many such charming stories, but they are just stories the people made up to explain things they did not understand. There is a better explanation of how stringed instruments began. The explanation was discovered among the Zulus, a brave people in South Africa who once were very warlike. The Zulus are scornful of the bow and arrow, which they consider a cowardly weapon. But they do use a bow as a musical instrument!

The Zulu musical bow is like an ordinary bow with which to shoot an arrow, except for two things: On the string there is a ring which is moved up and down to make the string sound different notes; and attached to the handle is a hollow gourd which acts as a sounding box to make the sound louder

This is a good clue to how men got the idea of a stringed instrument. From the twang of a bow-string they found out that a tightly stretched string made a musical note when it was plucked. They heard how a big bow made a deeper note than a little bow, and from this they figured out that strings of different lengths made different notes. Some ancestor of the Zulus in South Africa invented the movable ring to lengthen or shorten the string on a bow for the purpose of making it sound different notes. Some other inventor of ancient days tried stringing a bow with strings of different lengths, for the same purpose. We know that it happened this way, because in Egypt, inside the Pyramids, there are pictures painted on the walls showing ancient Egyptian musicians playing on harps that still look like bows with many strings.

From pictures like these in the Pyramids and other ancient buildings, we know what kinds of instruments the people played in long-ago times. But we can only guess how their music sounded because pictures cannot sing and play for us, and of course they did not have records and record-players! They did not even have a system of notes for writing their music down, as we do today. Our system of writing music began only a thousand years ago, as we will see later in this story.

Still, from clues like the musical bow and the bone whistle, we can discover a good deal about the instruments the ancients had and the kind of music they made on them. In our imaginary journey back through the centuries, let us see how some other musical instruments began.

Sticks, Shells, and Grasses

It is hard to imagine the world so long ago, when people did not live in towns or villages but wandered through the forests or across the deserts, hunting for their food. They found shelter in caves or made rough homes hastily out of whatever they could: stones or the branches of trees or the hide of an animal they had killed. At first they could not think about making music, or shaping pots out of clay, or weaving cloth, or any of the other arts. They had too much to do just to protect themselves from winter cold, storms, and wild animals, and to provide themselves with food. Even today, there are tribes in the deep jungles of South America who live too worried a life with all these natural dangers to have time or thought for any of the arts.

Yet we have clues that people began making music and inventing musical instruments even before they had invented many of the tools that are so familiar to us today. In New Guinea, an island near Australia, the natives still do not know how to use a wheel—not even on a cart or wheelbarrow. They still lift and carry the heaviest burdens instead of rolling or wheeling them. But they sing and dance to music, and they have several simple musical instruments of their own invention. As soon as men began to live together in families or tribes, as soon as they began to hunt together and plant crops for food, they began to sing and make rhythms with simple instruments.

Let us imagine a boy of those days, no older than yourself, walking down the forest path, feeling happy. Perhaps he picked up a stick and struck a hollow log as any boy might do. THUMP! the sound rolled through the forest, a fine big sound, big enough to be heard in the next village. Perhaps the boy had helped his father stretch an animal skin over the hollow frame of a canoe, and when he hit that stretched skin it made a sound, too. So one day he stretched a skin over the log, and he had a drum.

Or a little girl of long ago may have been walking along the beach, helping her mother find shellfish for the family's food. Perhaps she picked up two hollow shells and struck them together, and she had a pair of clappers. Or she strung small shells on a stick and shook them, and she had a rattle.

Drums, clappers, and rattles made like this are found among the most primitive tribes. They are the oldest musical instruments. They are called *percussion instruments,* from a word that means *to strike*. In the Metropolitan Museum of Art in New York City there is a pair of beautiful ancient Egyptian clappers made of ivory and shaped like a pair of hands. Egyptian and other ancient priests had a kind of rattle, called a *systrum,* which they shook in time to their chanting, not only to help the music but also because they believed its sound would keep evil spirits from coming into the temple.

That little girl of long ago, walking along the beach, might have been looking for conches. These are big, nourishing shellfish which people in many parts of the world like to eat even today. If the narrow end of a conch is knocked out and blown into, the fish can be blown out. Imagine that little girl's surprise, when she blew the fish out and, still blowing, heard a pretty sound come out of the shell!

Conch shells were the first trumpets, before men learned to use metals like copper and bronze. Greek statues of Triton, a sea god who was supposed to be half man and half fish, show him blowing on a conch shell trumpet.

Later the Romans, a warlike people who conquered most of Europe and even parts of Asia and Africa, made great use of the trumpet with its stirring sound. A victorious General would march in triumph through the streets of Rome, with trumpeters marching and blowing ahead of him. Arches of triumph were built across the streets of the city to honor really great victories, and many of these are still standing. There are always figures blowing trumpets on these arches.

Let us imagine a boy of long ago walking along a river bank, listening to the wind blowing softly over the hollow river grasses, the reeds. Perhaps he breaks a reed off and blows through it; it makes a lovely sound. If he were to cut a few holes in it at different distances down its length, he would have the beginnings of a flute. If he cut a few hollow reeds of different lengths he could make different tones with them. Tied together, a group of reeds or tubes of different lengths make an old instrument called the syrinx, or *Pan-pipes,* named after the forest god Pan who is often pictured blowing on a set of pipes made of a bundle of reeds. The Pan-pipes are the great-grandfather of the organ we hear in church, which is also made of pipes of different lengths and thicknesses, although very much bigger.

Almost every child has sometime held a blade of grass between his thumbs and blown on it to make a whistling sound. Someone long ago discovered this interesting effect, and put a straw or a strip of reed inside a hollow tube, to make a different sound from a flute. If he used one piece of reed inside the tube, he was inventing the clarinet. If he used two pieces, he was making the ancestor of an oboe or a bassoon. The ancient Egyptian musicians played clarinets, which have one reed inside them, and oboes, which have two reeds.

So now we have followed the clues, like detectives, and discovered how people long ago invented drums, rattles, and clappers, flutes and trumpets and reed instruments, and stringed instruments, too. These are the instruments of just such an orchestra as we see carved and painted on the walls of cities where people lived thousands of years ago.

Music in Ancient Times

IN THE days of long ago, music was thought to have magical powers. People believed that a medicine man or physician had to chant the right song to make the patient well. They thought certain songs had to be sung to give the men of the tribe courage for war or for hunting, and certain other ones to make the crops grow. Even today, tribes of American Indians sing certain songs when they need rain.

This belief in the great power of music has come down through the ages. In the Bible story, David, the shepherd lad, was brought to the palace so that his wonderful singing and harp-playing might cure King Saul of a sickness.

Later, people tried to explain the soothing effect of music by saying that certain vibrations in the sound made by the musical instrument had a healing effect on a sick person's nerves. Nowadays, even though doctors know that vibrations have nothing to do with the good effect, music is played in hospitals and sometimes in dentists' offices. Music helps people to bear discomfort and pain.

The ancient tribes knew that music helps to make physical labor seem easier. The Egyptians had a story about how a famous flute-player had built one of their great cities, just by playing his flute. Perhaps this was their way of saying that work is better done when the workers have music, and we know this is true. Probably there were musicians playing for the thousands of slaves who labored to build the Pyramids. In our songbooks today we have many work songs and sea chanties from the days when men sang together to keep time at their work. In modern offices and factories, pleasant music is played through loudspeakers because it has been found that this keeps people from becoming tired at their work.

Other peoples of the past had other beliefs about the great powers of music. The Chinese have a beautiful story about a famous music master named Wen, who as a young man went to a faraway city to study the zither. But after three years he still could not learn to play a melody on the instrument. His teacher told him he might as well go back to his own village, since he was not learning anything by staying. But Wen said he could not play until he felt the music in his heart. He went away for a while, and came back and begged his teacher to test him. His teacher consented to listen, and Wen began to play. When he struck the first string, spring came, a cool wind blew, and the trees bore fruit. When he struck the second string, the leaves broke into autumn colors. When he struck the third string, snow fell and the lakes and rivers froze. When he struck the fourth string, the sun burned hot and thawed the ice. Finally he played the last string and the other four together, with such harmony that "lovely winds murmured, clouds of good luck came up, sweet dew fell, the springs welled up powerfully." Wen felt the music now, truly, in his heart.

So goes the ancient Chinese story. But when they told this story of how music had power to change the seasons of the year, the Chinese did not think of it as magic. They believed that everything in the world worked together in harmony, and that the secret of this harmony was to be found in music. Whenever a new Emperor of China was crowned, he sent his chief musician through the land to regulate the music and see that people were playing in tune. For, as the Chinese wise men said, the previous Emperor would not have fallen if the music had been right!

Probably this was the way that ancient peoples tried to explain the great power that music has to make people feel calm and serene, or happy and gay, or thoughtful and even sad. Soldiers march better when they have a band playing stirring music, and in the old days no army went out to battle without its trumpeters and drummers to urge the warriors on. A King who was troubled with his problems would call his musicians to sing and play for him. Every occasion and every ceremony had its music in ancient times.

Music in the Bible

The Bible tells us how important music was in olden times. When Moses led the ancient Hebrews safely across the Red Sea in their escape from Egypt, his sister Miriam took a little drum called a timbrel and led the women in dancing and singing their gratitude to the Lord. That was the beginning of a kind of singing that we still do in religious services today, in which the leader sings a verse and the choir or the congregation sing the next verse in answer. This is called *antiphonal* singing, meaning voices "against" or answering each other. It is also the way the minister and the congregation read the Psalms aloud during the service. Some of the great church music of long ago was composed that way, and some music that is written for instruments without singers is composed that way, too.

The Bible tells us that King David was a great musician and poet, who wrote both the music and the words of the Psalms in the Bible. His son, the great and wise King Solomon, was also a famous musician and poet. The Bible tells us that when King Solomon built the Temple in Jerusalem, he ordered two hundred thousand trumpets and forty thousand other instruments for the Temple musicians to play.

What Ancient Music Was About

It is interesting to discover on our musical journey that the people of long ago sang and made music about the same things as we do now. They made music in praise of the gods they believed in, and songs of prayer for help and protection. They had story songs to tell of the adventures of their gods and goddesses and heroes. One of the songs of a very ancient people, called the Sumerians, tells the story of a great flood, like the flood in the Bible for which Noah built the ark.

They had work songs. An ancient Egyptian work song, called the *Oxen Song,* was translated by scholars from Egyptian picture writing, and here it is:

>Thresh for yourselves, Oxen!
>Thresh for yourselves!
>Straw for your fodder,
>Corn for your masters.
>Give yourselves no rest!

Even older than this song is a song of the Sumerians in which a pick-ax and a plow have an argument, each boasting about how useful and valuable it is to man.

The ancient peoples had songs of wisdom. Here is one from Egypt, which is as sensible now as it was then. It tells us how foolish it is to lie awake at night, worrying:

>Lay thee not down at night fearing the morrow;
>When day dawns, what is the morrow like?
>Man knoweth not how the morrow may be.

They had wedding songs and songs that celebrated other important events too. They had love songs. An Egyptian song of love is this one, which tells in beautiful words how the lover has not seen his beloved since "seven days from yesterday" and he has become sick. The magicians and master-physicians cannot cure him. The words go on:

>Better for me is my beloved than any remedies.
>When I see her, then I am well;
>When she opens her eye, my limbs are young again;
>When she speaks, I am strong.
>And when I embrace her, she banishes evil,
>And it passes from me for seven days.

Love-sickness must be a very old sickness indeed, because this poem about it is three thousand years old!

For many many centuries, music and words were closely tied together. The musicians were poets as well, and wrote both the words and music of their songs. They were carefully taught, and people held them in great respect. The arts of singing and playing music were kept secret by the teachers and handed on only to their particular pupils. A very old clay tablet, containing the words of a song in several of the languages of that time, says that this information is only for those who are in the secret.

Perhaps this was the ancient people's way of saying that music was a difficult art to perform, even then, and that to become a good musician one had to study and practice just as musicians do today. Perhaps it was also their way of saying that music was very powerful in its effect on people, and that only those who knew how to use it properly should be allowed to play and sing.

Wonderful Musical Discoveries in Ancient Greece

BESIDES the Bible people—that is, the ancient Hebrews and the early Christians—the people we know most about in long-ago times are the Greeks and the Romans. The Greeks, especially, gave us the beginnings of many of the subjects we study today, such as mathematics, astronomy, and medicine. We still study the writings of their philosophers and their political thinkers. We still admire their beautiful statues, and some of our finest buildings are designed in the style of the temples they built to their gods and goddesses.

The Greeks lived in a warm sunny land, nearly surrounded by the clear blue waters of the Mediterranean Sea. They loved health and cleanliness, and especially they loved beauty wherever they could find it or make it. They believed that anything beautiful—a statue or a building or a poem—was beautiful not by chance or accident but because it had order and harmony. They believed that the whole universe was founded on a kind of order and harmony, and that art and science and the way people lived could all be made orderly and harmonious too.

Naturally music was an important part of their beautiful way of living. Their scientists studied the science of sound, which is called *acoustics*. Their poets were musicians, and their great dramas, which are still performed on the stage nowadays, were spoken to music.

They considered music important to government, too. If a government was to be good, they thought, it had to have true rhythm and right harmony. In this, we see, they had something of the same idea as the ancient Chinese.

Their boys and girls were taught music along with reading and writing and mathematics. Greek boys and girls were allowed to learn and listen to only certain kinds of music, the kinds that would help them to be good children and later good citizens.

You have probably heard about the Olympic Games. They are held once every four years, each time in a different country, and each country sends its best athletes to compete in them. The idea of these games comes from the Greeks of three thousands years ago. They held Olympic Games for their athletes every four years in honor of their gods and goddesses. The games were named Olympic Games after Olympus, a mountain in Greece where the gods and goddesses were thought to live. Part of the competition was devoted to music. The poet-musicians competed in singing their poems in honor of the gods. There were also contests of music without words, played on a reed instrument called the *aulos*.

We would expect the Greeks to make rules to bring order into music as they did with everything else. And so they did. They saw how closely music was tied to mathematics. Their great mathematician, Pythagoras, made this discovery in an experiment with stringed instruments. He is the one who discovered the mathematical reason for the *octave*.

The Wonderful Discovery of the Octave

Let's just stop and see what we mean by this important musical word, *octave*. If you can sing the scale — DO, RE, MI, FA, SOL, LA, TI, DO — you know that it has eight notes, and that high DO sounds the same as low DO. Try now to go from low DO to high DO without singing the notes in between. Usually, even if we can sing only a little, we find it easier to go from DO to DO than from DO to any other note in the scale. The eight notes from DO to DO are called an *octave,* from the Latin word for *eight*.

Long before the Greeks, people must have been singing naturally in octaves. Whenever a group of people sang together, the low voices and the high voices singing the same melody, the singers had to find notes that went naturally and pleasingly together and followed the melody correctly. The notes that are an octave apart are the easiest to sing together.

The Greek mathematician Pythagoras discovered that there was a mathematical reason for this, when he made an experiment with strings. If you have a violin or guitar or ukelele string, you can make this experiment too. His string was probably stretched and fastened on a musical instrument. But you can do as well by stretching your string between the legs of a chair, close to the floor but not touching it.

Now Pythagoras already knew that strings of different lengths make different sounds. He also knew that the *shorter* the string is, the *higher* the note it sounds. People knew this long before the time of Pythagoras, and had strings of different lengths on their instruments to make different notes.

What Pythagoras was trying to find out was *exactly how much* higher or lower the note would be according to the length of the string. When we talk about how high or low a note is, we call it the *pitch* of the note. So what Pythagoras wanted to know was how much the *pitch* of the note was changed by changing the length of the string.

In his experiment, Pythagoras first struck a note on his string. Then he put his finger on the string and held it down exactly in the middle, and struck a note on one of the two *halves* of the string. The note sounded by half the string was *exactly an octave higher* than the note sounded by the whole string.

So now he knew: when a string is divided in half, the pitch is raised an octave higher.

Why was this? Do you remember that in our explanation of sound, we said that all sound is caused by vibrations? When you strike a string, it quivers rapidly, or vibrates, and it is the vibrating of the string that makes the sound. The shorter the string is, the faster it vibrates, and the faster the vibrations, the higher the note. A string *half* as long makes vibrations *twice* as fast, and this sounds a note *exactly an octave higher*.

This was a marvelous discovery. It told us why we tend to sing in octaves, why notes an octave apart sound the same to us, and why our musical scale seems to fit so naturally into an octave. Pythagoras showed that the octave is a *natural* part of sound.

(The pitch of a string is also affected by the thickness of the string, and by how tightly the string is stretched. A thicker string or a looser one sounds a lower note than a thinner string or a tighter one. To tune a stringed instrument, we tighten or loosen the string, and a string tuned to a low note is usually thicker than a string meant to play high notes.)

The next question Pythagoras wanted to answer was whether other notes had a natural relationship, too. He tried putting his finger on a spot two-thirds of the string's length. He found that this sounded just a *fifth* higher. (On our scale, this is from DO to SOL, five notes.) Then he held the string at three-quarters of its length, and it sounded a note a *fourth* higher (from SOL to DO, four notes). So he decided that the octave, the fifth, and the fourth were all connected to each other as natural parts of any sound.

We have a word for how these particular notes are connected in a musical sound. They are *overtones*. Every note has its overtones, sister notes that sound softly with the note that is played. The string actually vibrates not only as a whole, but also in certain regular parts: by halves, by thirds, by quarters, and so on in smaller and smaller sections. If you strike a note on a piano and listen very closely, you can hear the overtones. You can hear them even more clearly on big church bells.

Here is an experiment you can try on the piano, in order to hear the overtones. Press down a key, so slowly that it does not sound, and hold it down. You can use any key, but to make this explanation easier to follow, let's say you press down middle C. Now hold down that middle C, and *strike* the C an octave lower. You should hear the middle C you are holding down, even though you have not struck it.

Now hold down the *fifth* note above, the G above middle C. Strike the low C again. You should hear the G, the fifth.

Now hold down the key a *fourth* above that G. This will be the next C above middle C, two octaves above the low C you are striking. Strike the low C. You should hear the high C, the overtone of the fourth.

You may be able to get one more overtone. That is the *third* note above the one you have just heard, E above high C, and it is the overtone of the third. There are more overtones, going on up the scale, but they are fainter each time and they do not match the piano's notes exactly because of the way we tune our pianos today so we cannot really hear them. A violinist can play them; they are called the *harmonics* on a violin. Sometimes a composer wants the violin to sound the high, silvery note of an overtone instead of the full sound of the whole string. The violinist does this by touching the string to make it vibrate in parts.

A flutist can play the high notes on his flute only by blowing hard enough to sound the overtones, because the finger holes of his flute cover only one octave. In the old days when trumpets did not yet have valves, the only way a trumpeter could play a scale was by blowing hard enough to sound the overtones. And that must have been hard blowing!

The overtones seem to provide the natural combinations of *notes that people can sing when they sing together.* These combinations became the basis of *harmony,* which came later in the story of music, as we shall see. The octave, the fifth, and the fourth were the first combinations of notes that went together in music. Later the third became popular too, and it is the most familiar harmony we know today for singing songs and ballads. Of course harmony in music went on to become much more varied than just the use of overtones, but that is a later part of our story.

HERE IS AN EXAMPLE OF FAMILIAR HARMONY IN THIRDS:

Way down up - on the Swan - ee riv - er, Far, far a - way

AS YOU SEE, THE HARMONY IS ALL IN THIRDS EXCEPT FOR THE WORD "SWANEE." "SWAN" IS HARMONIZED WITH A FOURTH, AND "EE" WITH A SIXTH —THAT IS, SIX NOTES APART.

What Is a Scale?

When you sing DO RE MI FA SOL LA TI DO, or play the eight white keys on the piano from C to the next higher C, you are singing or playing our modern *major scale*.

A scale is any series of notes arranged like the steps of a staircase, from low to high or high to low. Our major scale is the series of eight notes beginning DO RE MI. Other peoples, for example the Chinese, the Hindus, and the Arabs, use very different scales from ours. The scales the ancient peoples used were more like those of the Oriental peoples today than like ours.

The difference between one scale and another is in the *intervals*. An *interval* is the difference in pitch between one note and the next, and it is measured in *tones*. This sounds harder to understand than it really is. When you sing DO-RE, or play C-D on the piano, that is a whole tone. Try now to sing a note between DO and RE: DO DI RE. Or play the black note between C and D on the piano: C, C sharp, D. That in-between note is a half-step, or a *semi-tone*. The black keys on the piano sound the semi-tones between the white keys. When we go a half-step or semi-tone *up* from a note, we call it a *sharp*. When we go a half-step *down,* we call it a *flat*. In our modern scale, a sharp and a flat may be the same note. The black key between C and D is called either C sharp or D flat, depending on the music we are playing.

Our Western scales today, both major and minor, are made up of whole tones and semitones, whole steps and half-steps, and the semi-tones come in certain definite places in the scale. In the major scale, the interval from DO to RE is a whole tone, and from RE to MI it is a whole tone. But from MI to FA it is a semi-tone. (You will notice there is no black note between these two tones, E and F, on the piano.) And again between the seventh an eighth notes of the octave, TI and DO, the interval is a semi-tone. (Again, there is no black note between these two tones, B and C, on the piano.)

You can try this out with your own voice, listening hard to the whole steps and the half-steps, the whole tones and the semi-tones, as you sing DO RE MI FA SOL LA TI DO. You can sound out the difference on the piano with its white and black piano keys. On the piano, the major scale in the octave beginning with C as DO is the only one that uses only white piano keys. This is called the *key* of C, and it means that in this key the scale begins with C.

To play a major scale in any other *key*—that is, beginning with any other note—you have to play a black piano key at certain places to make the whole tone or the semi-tone come where it belongs in the scale.

Would you like to see how this works? Let's play the scale in the key of D—that is, beginning with D. Now DO comes on the note D, and RE is on E. DO and RE are a whole tone apart, and so are the notes D and E. But when we come to MI, we cannot use the note F because that is only a semi-tone from E. So we raise the F to F sharp, the black piano key. Now we have only a semi-tone to the next note G, but that is all right, because from MI to FA we need only a semi-tone. And we can play the white piano keys A and B for SOL and LA. The next white piano key C, is only a semi-tone, so we must strike the black one, C sharp, for TI. Then we have a semi-tone, C sharp to D, and that's fine, because we need only a semi-tone from TI to DO. And now we have played the major scale in the key of D, which means beginning with the note D, and we have seen that the key of D has two sharps, F sharp and C sharp.

One reason why Oriental music sounds strange to us is that they use not only semi-tones but quarter-tones and even smaller intervals in their scales. The Greeks used quarter-tones. The Arabs today use one-third tones. They also use different harmonies from ours, and their rhythms are different. We will learn more about harmony and rhythm later on in this story.

The Greeks Had Music for Every Mood

The Greeks did not have a system of scales like ours. They had a musical system known as *modes*. The word *mode* suggests mood, and the Greeks did express different moods in music with their different modes, because each mode had its proper use. The Dorian Mode, for instance, was used for warlike music. It will give you an idea of what this sounded like if you play the notes from E to E on the piano, playing only the *white* keys. You will see the half-steps come in different places from the half-steps in our major scale. You can sing it if you will begin the scale not with DO but with MI. Every Greek mode had its semi-tones in certain specified places, and this made each one different from the others.

Another mode, the Greeks said, was for soft or sad music. This is the one Greek mode that corresponds to our major scale, the familiar DO RE MI FA, and it seems odd to us that they should have thought it sad. But the Greeks wrote all their modes from the highest note downward, and perhaps if you sing DO TI LA SOL softly, it may sound sorrowful.

They had a third mode for religious music, and a fourth one for "breaking horses and the reception of guests" and also "for pleasure, love, and good cheer." That seems to have been such a useful mode, we are rather surprised to read in the scholarly books that the Greeks considered it old-fashioned and discarded it!

The astronomer Ptolemy, who lived in the Greek city of Alexandria about 150 years after the birth of Christ, wrote down the Greek theory of music, and scholars continued to write about it for centuries after.

But we do not really know how ancient Greek music sounded. There are only a few bits of it left to us, written down in their own way for voices and instrument, and we can never be sure we are playing and singing it the way the Greeks did. Their music was sung by one singer or a chorus, sometimes accompanied by their reed instrument, the *aulos*, or by a stringed instrument called the *kithara*. They had large choruses, but they did not have large orchestras like the Egyptians or the Hebrews, and they were scornful of the Egyptian harp with many strings. We think it odd that they were satisfied with the rather weak tones of their aulos and kithara and did not seem to want stronger-sounding instruments. The great rich sounds of a symphony orchestra or a chorus of many voices singing in harmony, such as we are accustomed to, were kinds of music the Greeks could not even imagine.

Yet since this gifted, artistic people of long ago left us such wonderful statues and buildings, poetry and plays, we wish there were some way for us to know their music.

The Warrior Romans Enjoyed War-like Music

Unlike the Greeks, the ancient Romans were warriors and governors rather than artists or philosophers. They sent their armies from their great city of Rome, in Italy, all over the world they knew, even as far north as the islands of Britain. They built roads and water systems, many of which we can still see when we travel abroad today, two thousand years later. They had names we still use for many cities and provinces, although time has changed the way we spell and pronounce them. The modern English city of Chester was a place called *Castra,* which meant a miltary camp. Through the centuries, Castra has gradually changed to Chester. And their Londinium is today's London. They left their language, called Latin, in many countries so that it is part of our modern languages today.

But the Romans did not contribute much to art or literature or music. Instead they borrowed from the Greeks. Although they conquered the Greeks and made many of them slaves, they actually spread the civilization of that golden land of art and beauty. Their sculptors imitated the statues of the Greeks, and their poets and playwrights followed Greek examples. Their music, too, was based on Greek music, although the warrior Romans liked the bold brassy sound of trumpets and developed this kind of instrument, which we call the *brasses* in the orchestra today.

The Early Christians Had to Sing in Hiding

Meanwhile, during the time when the Romans were the masters of the world, something happened that was to be of tremendous importance to all the peoples of the future, and incidentally to music, too. Jesus Christ was born, and He lived, during this time, in the Roman province called Judea in Palestine. The first followers of Jesus were persecuted by the Romans. Every so often, as we know, a group of them were thrown to the lions in the Colosseum, the great open-air sport stadium in Rome, for the amusement of the people. The religious services of the Christians were forbidden, and they secretly met and chanted their hymns and prayers in the ancient cellars and passageways, called the Catacombs, under the city of Rome.

In time a Roman Emperor, Constantine, became Christian, and the Romans spread Christianity over the whole Empire. With the religion of Christianity the Romans spread the music of the early Christian Church service.

Then another great event took place. A horde of barbarian tribes, called the Teutonic tribes, swept across Europe from the east, destroying cities the Romans had built and even a good part of the city of Rome itself. The struggles of these newcomers to find homes and establish nations for themselves kept Europe in a state of war for at least a hundred years. Meanwhile schools and libraries were burned or fell into ruin. As the Roman Empire crumbled, all the art and learning the Romans had preserved from Greek and even older civilizations was practically lost to the Western world for centuries to come. These centuries, from about 500 A.D. to about 1000 A.D., are called the Dark Ages. Interesting changes came about in music during the Dark Ages, as we shall see.

How Music Was Preserved During the Dark Ages

THE LAST Roman Emperor surrendered to the barbarians in the year 476 A.D. For a long time afterward, the rival leaders of the barbarians went on fighting among themselves. All over Europe these were troubled times. There were few cities, traveling was hard and dangerous, and most people lived their whole lives in the villages where they were born. They hardly ever saw anyone or heard any news from outside their own village. The land that they lived on belonged to a leader who was usually called by a noble title, such as Count or Baron. The people worked for the nobleman, farmed his land, and fought on his side when he needed them. In return he gave them his protection. Each nobleman had his own little army of soldiers who lived in his castle with him and his family. This was the way people lived for nearly a thousand years.

There were hardly any schools, and most people did not know how to read and write. Through these years, the scholars and learned people were priests and monks.

The musicians, too, were mostly priests and monks or people trained by them. Music was part of religion, as it had always been, and so the study of music was carried on in the churches through these centuries.

The church music scholars were hard at work even before the end of the Roman Empire. About the year 384 A.D., St. Ambrose, the Bishop of the Italian city of Milan, collected the hymns and chants that were being used in church services. He also wrote down four modes like those of the Greeks, and explained how they were to be used in church music.

The interesting thing about the work of St. Ambrose and the other church scholars is that this is the way the music of ancient times was preserved and brought down through the centuries to modern times. The music that St. Ambrose collected was already very old. Some of it was certainly sung by the early Christians in the Catacombs. Some of it went back to the Greeks. Some of it may have been the same music that was sung in King Solomon's Temple. And some of the music may have come from the time when Moses's sister Miriam led the women in singing and dancing after the ancient Hebrews had crossed the Red Sea in their escape from Egypt. We know that that kind of singing —a leader and a chorus or two choruses answering each other—was the way the Psalms were sung all through the great days of the Temple in Jerusalem, and it is still the way parts of both the Christian and the Jewish services are sung today.

About two hundred and fifty years after St. Ambrose, Pope Gregory revised the church music again and added four more modes like the modes of the Greeks. The form of church music that he wrote down is still called *Gregorian Chant*. Another name for it is *plain song*.

Gregorian Chant is solemn and grand, but it sounds rather bare to our ears. By Pope Gregory's time, the thousands of trumpets in King Solomon's Temple music had long been forgotten. The organ had not yet been invented, and singing in church was not accompanied by any instrument. Also, although the great churches and cathedrals had many singers in their choirs, they all sang the same notes, the high voices singing an octave above the low ones. There were no *chords,* or groups of notes sounding together in *harmony,* such as we are accustomed to in our music today.

The church musicians gradually set about filling out the sound of their music. Instead of octaves, they wrote parts for the different voices at different *intervals.* They had the low voices and the medium low voices sing a fifth and a fourth *below* the principal voices, and then they added another part a fourth *above* the principal voices. Today we call the very low voices the *basses,* and the medium low voices the *baritones.* We call the highest voices the *sopranos.* At that time no women or girls but only men and boys sang in the church choirs, so the high or soprano part was sung by the boys.

The melody sung by the principal voices was always sung out clear and strong. This was called the *tenor* voice, from a Latin word meaning *to hold,* because this was the voice that *held* the melody. The other voices were considered merely decoration. Other decorations, such as turns and runs and connecting notes, were added later.

Here is a little bit of Gregorian Chant in four parts, from the tenth century:

Singing music in parts like this, in intervals of fifths and fourths, was called *organum*. Later, when the organ itself began to be used in the churches, the music for it followed the same lines. The great organ thundered out the melody, leading the singers.

How Music Came to Be Written Down

Through the centuries of the Dark Ages, in narrow damp chilly monastery rooms called cells, monks sat by daylight and flickering oil light, writing and writing. They wrote on wax tablets with a pointed tool called a *stylus*. For more permanent copies they wrote on dried sheepskin, called parchment, with quill pens. They drew beautiful letters with flourishes, and decorated them with tiny pictures of saints and angels, birds and animals and flowers, beautifully colored in blue and red and gold. They copied the Bible and the stories of saints and martyrs, the teachings of the great churchmen and the prayers of the church service. And they copied music.

For by this time, with churches everywhere in Europe and so many men and boys singing in the church choirs, some way had to be found to write down the music if they were to sing it correctly. So a method of *notation*, or music writing, was being developed.

When you open a music book today, you find the notes written on five lines. There are also many other signs on the lines besides just the notes. Each sign means something to the person singing or playing the music. It took nearly a thousand years to develop this written language of music. We needed this musical language for the many kinds of beautiful and interesting music we have today. Our opera singers and choruses, and especially the many musicians playing different instruments in an orchestra, could never sing and play together if they did not have music to read. Written music tells a performer what notes to play and it also tells how the composer meant the music to sound.

Nearly a thousand years ago, in one of the Benedictine monasteries in Italy, the monk Guido D'Arezzo sat and worked over this written language of music. He added another line, and still another, to the *staff*, as we call the group of horizontal lines. Gregorian

Chant is written on a staff of four lines in the old manuscripts. But Guido added a fifth line, and his five-line staff is what we use today.

Each line and each space between the lines represented a note of the scale. For a long time, as far back as the Greeks, the notes had been called by the letters of the alphabet. So the staff had to have a *clef* sign (*clef* is the French word for *key*) to say which notes (or letters) the staff held. The first clef sign was an F, which the monks wrote large and painted in colors. Their F looked different from ours today, but we still use it the way they wrote it, for our bass clef.

The next clef sign the monks used represented middle C. Nowadays the C clef is used only in music written for orchestras or other groups of instruments. The viola, larger than the violin and lower in pitch, plays the C clef. To us today the sign does not look much like a C.

Then came the G clef, and this is the most familiar, because it is our treble clef and we use it in writing music for the right hand on the piano and also in music for songs and most instruments.

How the Notes Got Their Names

Even while he was adding lines to the staff to help the choir singers sing the melodies accurately, the hard-working monk Guido was not satisfied. He wanted a better way than the letters of the alphabet to help the choir boys recognize the notes and remember them. And it came to him that there was a certain hymn which every choir boy knew. This hymn was always sung to the notes of the scale going up, each line sung on a single note.

Before we can see what Guido did with this hymn, we have to mention something we have not said before. The Church, you remember, was founded in Rome, when the Roman Emperor, Constantine, became a Christian. Since the language of the Romans was Latin, all the words of the church service from that time on were Latin. In the Roman Catholic Church they still are. In Guido's time, and for many years afterward, the churchmen and scholars knew Latin as well as they did their own languages.

So when Guido was looking for a new way to help the choir boys learn the notes, the hymn he chose, which was sung like a scale, was of course in Latin. Here it is:

UT queant laxis
RE sonare fibris
MI ra gestorum
FA muli tuorum   (It is a prayer to St. John the Baptist
SOL ve polluti   asking him to wash away the wicked-
LA bii reatum   ness of the worshippers so that they
SA ncte Johannes   may be good enough to sing his praises).

Guido chose the first syllable of each of the hymn's seven lines for the name of a note of the scale. The first one, UT, was later changed to DO, because that was an easier sound to sing. The seventh became SI (or TI). The eighth, of course, was UT, or DO, again, because the eighth note of the octave is the same as the first, only higher. In the dictionary you may still find the word UT as the lowest or the highest note of Guido's scale.

Have you discovered the names Guido gave to the notes? They are the friendly familiar DO RE MI FA SOL LA TI DO!

How to Read Music

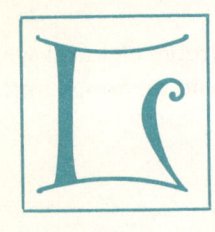

LEARNING to read music was much easier in Guido's time than it is today. All Guido's choir boys had to learn was the name of each note and where each one came on the staff, like this:

DO RE MI FA SOL LA TI DO RE MI FA SOL

Suppose we take a song we all know today, and see how it would look on a page of music like Guido's. Here are the first notes of *Three Blind Mice,* with Guido's names for the notes. Can you sing the notes?

MI RE DO MI RE DO SOL FA FA MI SOL FA FA MI

Three blind mice, Three blind mice, See how they run! See how they run!

There came a time when the early musicians found that music writing had to show something more than just the notes of the melody. They had to invent a way to show *how long* each note had to be held. This is called showing the *time-value* of the note.

Let's see what this means. When you sing the words, "Three blind mice," you sing the notes MI RE DO. The notes MI and RE in the song are equal in time-value. That is, each of them is held the same length of time. But when you sing the words, "See how they run!" SOL FA FA MI, the notes are not all equal. The two notes FA FA are sung more quickly

HOW WE USE THE CLEFS

Here are the three clefs and the notes of the scale that can be written on them:

As you see, the main curlicue of the big curving G in the G clef curls around the second line from the bottom, and this is where we write the note G on this clef. The other notes of the scale go up and down from that G.

In the C clef, the sign looks like two C's written backward, one on top of the other. Where they meet, on the center line, is the place where the note C is written on this clef.

In the third, the F clef, the sign resembles the outline of an F written backwards and without the little line at its middle. The sign begins with a little curl on the line next to the top of the staff, and that is the line for the note F on this clef.

The notes on the three clefs overlap, but each one covers nearly an octave and a half, and with little extra lines written in above or below, called "leger lines", it can show still more notes.

If we want to show notes still higher or lower, there is another sign, 8va... written above or below the staff, meaning that the notes are to be played a whole octave above or below the place on the staff where they are written.

Here is the treble or G clef again, with leger lines for notes below and above, and the octave sign above:

From C, on the leger line below the staff, to C on the third space from the bottom, is one octave. Can you count how many octaves altogether are written on this staff? (There are three).

than the other two. If you count it out—1–2–3–4—you will find that you have to count 3–4 on DO ("mice") the first and second times, and on MI ("run") the third and fourth times. You will also find that FA-FA both come together on the count of 2, like this:

```
MI  RE  DO    MI  RE  DO    SOL FA-FA MI   SOL FA-FA MI
1   2   3-4   1   2   3-4   1    2   3-4   1    2   3-4
Three blind mice, three blind mice, See how they run! See how they run!
```

When you are singing alone, or even if you are singing with others, when you all know the song, the notes don't need to show time-value. But if you don't know the music and you are reading it from the notes, there has to be a way to show you that the notes FA-FA in this part of the song are not held as long as the other notes. In fact, each FA is only half as long as the other notes, and it takes both of them together to equal one of the others. If you don't know this, the song will come out wrong.

You also have to be able to *keep time* as you sing. This is what you did when you counted 1–2–3–4, 1–2–3–4. Music has a regular rhythm, or time, and music writing has to show you what that rhythm or time is for this particular song.

The early musicians gradually worked out a system for all this. So today we have notes that show their time-values. We have whole notes, half-notes, quarter-notes, and so on.

This is a whole note, a plain oval, like an egg: o

A half-note is the same oval with a stem on it: ♩ The stem may go up or down, but that is just a convenience to fit it on the lines of the staff, and it doesn't change the note: The half-note is held *one-half* as long as the whole note.

The quarter-note is an oval with a stem, too, but the oval is filled in, so that it is solid black, and it is also a little smaller: ♩ The quarter-note is held *one-quarter* as long as the whole note.

An eighth-note has a fin added to the stem or tail: ♪ When two eighth-notes come together, their fins can be connected: ♫ Sometimes the fin is written curved, like a hook: ♪ An eighth-note is held *one-eighth* as long as a whole note. Two eighth-notes together have the same time-value as one quarter-note: ♫=♩

We can also write a sixteenth-note, by adding another fin: ♬ Two sixteenth-notes together can be connected by making their double fins into a double line: ♬ A sixteenth-note is quite fast. It takes two of them to equal an eighth-note, four to equal a quarter-note, eight to equal a half-note, and sixteen for a whole note.

Some music has to have still faster notes. By adding another fin, we can write a thirty-second note: ♬ With still another fin, we write a sixty-fourth note: ♬ This is the fastest note used in our music today.

To give the rhythm, or *time*, of the music, there are *bar lines* to mark off each *bar* of the music, and there is a *time signature* to tell how many beats there are to each bar. For instance, marching time is four-four time. This means that there are four beats to each bar: 1–2–3–4, 1–2–3–4. And each beat is for a quarter-note (a ¼ note, when you write it in numbers). Four-four time has a time-signature written like this: $\frac{4}{4}$. The top 4 means there are four beats to a bar. The bottom 4 means each quarter-note gets one beat. Marching time can also be in $\frac{2}{4}$ time, with two beats to each bar.

Waltz time is three-quarter time: $\frac{3}{4}$. The 3 means there are three beats to a bar, and the 4 means, again, that each quarter-note gets one beat.

Waltz time can also be written in $\frac{6}{8}$ time. This means that there are *six* beats to a bar, and each *eighth-note* gets a whole beat.

Here is marching time: | $\frac{4}{4}$ ♩ ♩ ♩ ♩ | or | $\frac{2}{4}$ ♩ ♩ | ♩ ♩ |
                               1 2 3 4   1 2   1 2

Here is waltz time: | $\frac{3}{4}$ ♩ ♩ ♩ | And here is waltz time in | $\frac{6}{8}$ ♪ ♪ ♪ ♪ ♪ ♪ |
                                                                                        1 2 3 4 5 6

In 4-4 time, each bar has four quarter-notes. But in any piece of music, some notes are longer than quarter-notes, and some are shorter. An eighth-note is only half as long as a quarter-note, so we will need two eighth-notes to make one beat, and we will need eight eighth-notes to make four beats to a bar of four-four time. A half-note is twice as long as a quarter-note, so each half-note gets two beats and we can have two of them in a bar. A whole note is four times as long as a quarter-note, so one whole note gets all four beats, a whole bar to itself:

              1   2   3   4   1   2   3   4   1   2   3   4   1 2 3 4
            8 Eighth Notes   4 Quarter Notes   2 Half Notes   1 Whole Note

We can also combine notes of *different time-values* in the same bar, as long as we come out with the right number of beats to the bar. For instance, we can have two quarter-notes (2 beats) and one half-note (2 beats) in one bar (4 beats). Or one quarter-note (1 beat), two eighth-notes (1 beat) and a half-note (2 beats) adding up to 4 beats to the bar.

Now let's see how *Three Blind Mice* looks with a time signature, bar lines, and notes that have time-value. It is in 4/4 time, so each of the first two bars has two quarter-notes and a half-note (4 beats, and each of the last two has a quarter-note, two eighth-notes and a half-note (4 beats). Tap 1–2–3–4 for each bar, and remember to keep the beat even.

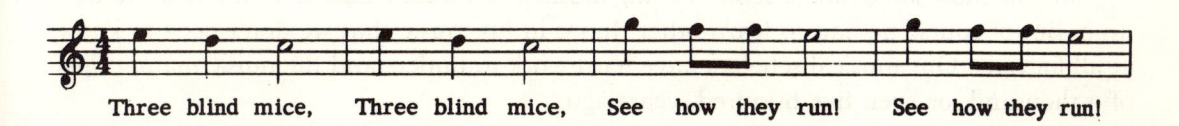

Three blind mice,   Three blind mice,   See how they run!   See how they run!

From Key to Key

Up to now we have been singing in the key of C, which does not need sharps or flats. But we can sing the same song in another key and see how the sharps and flats are written.

Here is *Three Blind Mice* in the key of F, which means that our scale begins with F and goes to the next F above. Another way of saying it is that in this key, DO comes on the note F. Now the key of F has one flat, and that one is B flat. If you will go to the piano, you will see why you need a B flat to play the scale beginning with F. Remember that the scale has a half-step between MI and FA, so that with MI falling on the note A, you have to lower the next note a half-step. So you don't use B, but B flat (the black piano key between A and B). And that takes care of the next step, which calls for a whole tone between FA and SOL. Can you see why?

On our staff, now, we put the sign for a *flat* on the line that stands for B on our treble clef. Our song now looks like this:

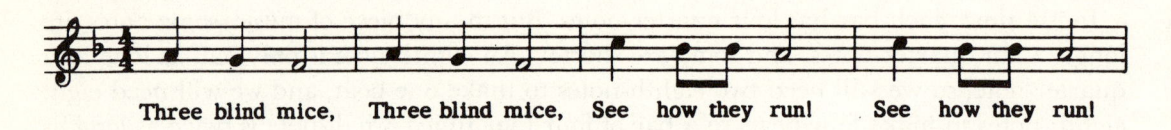

Now let's try the key of G, which has one sharp, F sharp. Can you tell why? You can see it on the piano. In the key of G, DO comes on the note G. Now everything goes smoothly on the white keys until you come to LA TI DO. From LA to TI you need a whole step, but from TI to DO only a half. F sharp takes care of both.

And here is our song again, with the *sharp* sign written on the line that stands for F. That shows us that we are singing in the key that has one sharp—F sharp. That is the key of G.

If you have a piano, you can try playing *Three Blind Mice* in all the other major keys, putting the sharps or flats on the staff where they belong. It's a good game, but you may need someone to play it with you. It is not easy to remember just where the whole steps and half steps must go in each key, especially if you have just been learning all this for the first time.

Now you know some things about reading music that would puzzle a choir boy of Guido's time. But of course he had to learn other things in his music that we don't need to know at all for ours. Our musical scholars have hard work to understand the music manuscripts of a thousand, or even five hundred, years ago.

Of course there are more signs on a piece of music than we have just worked out, and there are also words that mean something about the way the music should be performed. We will look at some of those later on.

Right now let's see what else was going on in music in Guido's day.

Songs the People Sang Long Ago

WHILE the Church musicians like Guido were working out the system of musical writing that we use today, other people of the time were singing and playing music of their own.

Not all the religious music was sung in Church. Some of the religious teachers, like St. Francis of Assisi, encouraged the people to sing hymns at home as well as in Church. And at fairs, and in the village squares, traveling players would act out stories from the Bible in the form of plays with music. These were called masques or miracle plays. There were also songs for pilgrims to sing while they were walking the long way to Rome and other holy places.

Then, too, people made up their own songs to sing, and to dance to on May Day and other holidays. They did not write down the words or the music of their songs and dances, because very few people could read or write in those days. They passed on their songs by singing them, father to son, mother to daughter, neighbor to neighbor. Sometimes the person learning the song did not remember it perfectly, and sometimes he thought he could improve upon it. And so these songs of the people, which we call *folk songs,* kept being changed. That is why we sometimes find different tunes for the same words, or different words telling the same folk song story. Of course the people sang their songs in their own languages—French or German or Italian or Spanish or English—not in Latin as they did in Church.

The music of the Church was slow and dignified and solemn. But the people's tunes were often lively and gay, and fast enough to dance to. These lively tunes kept creeping into the Church service, and now and then the Church musicians wrote songs for the people to sing. The oldest song in English is just such a song. It was written by John of Fornsete, a monk who kept the records of the abbey in Reading, England. It is a happy song for spring, a *canon* or *round,* to be sung by four tenor and two bass voices. In a round the voices follow one another, each one beginning after the singer ahead has finished the first line, and repeating the song as many times as the singers like. Perhaps you have sung *Three Blind Mice* as a round, and you remember that the first singer has already sung, "Three blind mice, three blind mice," and is beginning to sing, "See how they run!" when the second singer begins, "Three blind mice." A song sung like that is called a round, because it goes just that way, around and around among the singers.

John of Fornsete's song is sung the same way. This is how it looks as he wrote it down, in Reading Abbey about the year 1226: SUMER IS ICUMEN IN

The words look strange because they are written in the English of more than seven centuries ago. We would write the first few lines this way:

>   Summer is a-coming in,
>   Loud sings (the) cuckoo.
>   The seed grows and the mead blows
>   And the wood springs anew.

The Merry Minstrels and the Troubadours

There were other musicians at that time who made music to entertain the people, and especially to entertain Kings and noblemen. This was the time of knights in armor, about whom there are so many stories of adventure and gallant deeds. It was also the time of the Crusades, when Kings led their armies on the long march to Palestine to fight for the Holy Land and the city of Jerusalem.

When they were not fighting or hunting, or competing in fighting games with swords and lances at the tournaments, the Kings and noblemen and their knights liked to be entertained. And so there were musicians to sing to them of the adventures and exploits of famous knights. The musicians went from town to town and from castle to castle, carrying their lutes or harps. They could always get dinner and a place to sleep in return for a few songs. In England they were called *minstrels,* in Germany they were called *minnesingers,* and in France they were called *troubadours* or sometimes *trouvères.*

The troubadours of France were of knightly rank at least and were highly respected. A French King who invaded England gave to his court troubadour the honor of striking the first blow in the battle. King Richard the Lion-Hearted, King of England at a later time, was a celebrated troubadour, as well as a leader of the Crusades. One of his famous songs tells how he was captured and held for ransom by a rival King, when he was on his way back from a Crusade.

The troubadours sang long story-songs about heroes and battles. They sang songs about the beauty of nature. "I tune my voice to the key of summer," is the way one of these songs begins. Most of all, they sang songs of love. One of their love-songs, a famous one, goes like this:

>   The sweet glance of my lady
>   Makes me hope for mercy.
>   God keep her gentle self from harm.
>   The sweet glance of my lady—
>   I have never seen, by my soul,
>   A lady more pleasing than she.
>   The sweet glance of my lady
>   Makes me hope for mercy.

In this song the words are repeated in a regular way. You see how the first line of the poem comes back as the fourth line, and the first two lines are repeated at the end. A poem in this style is called a *rondeau*. The troubadours were skillful at inventing many charming forms of poetry. Adam de la Halle, who wrote this rondeau six hundred years ago, was a learned musician, too. He wrote down the music of some of his songs and that is how the music of this pretty song has been preserved through the centuries, as well as the words. Of course his music is quite hard for us to read today, and only musicians especially trained in the music of olden times can sing and play it.

As time went on, the wandering minstrels became less respectable. Queen Elizabeth passed laws against them, calling them "rogues and vagabonds."

In Germany the musicians organized themselves into guilds, which were like trade unions. They took young boys as their helpers or *apprentices,* and taught them. The best musicians were called *master-singers.* In one of Richard Wagner's operas, *Die Meistersinger von Nüremberg, (The Mastersingers of Nuremberg),* the leading character is Hans Sachs, a shoemaker, who was a famous master-singer.

Wagner used many of the melodies of the master-singers' songs in his operas, too. Here is the beginning of the song that wins a prize in his opera about Hans Sachs and the singers of the old German city of Nuremberg. It is known as the "Prize Song."

Music of Many Melodies

Up to this time in the story of music, the words of songs had the important place, and the music followed the words. Now we are coming to a time when music began to be important for itself. Composers were no longer satisfied to write only a single melody for all the voices of a choir to sing in octaves or even in intervals of fifths and fourths, in the kind of music called *organum* (we talked about this, when we were talking about early Church music). The composers began to write a different melody for each group of voices and to weave the different melodies together. This music of several melodies together is called *counterpoint,* a word which means "note against note."

Some of the early composers, writing for large Church choirs, became very skillful at counterpoint, weaving the melodies together into interesting and beautiful sounds. But some of this music grew so complicated that the Church fathers began to complain. They said that with so many voices singing different notes and different words at the same moment—sometimes even in different languages!—the people of the congregation could not hear the words of the service.

A choirmaster of the Pope's palace in Rome, named Palestrina, undertook to write Church music in counterpoint that did *not* confuse the words of the service. His music for the great choirs, which sang without any instrument to accompany them in the huge Cathedrals of those days, is some of our most beautiful and stirring music. Palestrina lived a long and busy life in Rome, leading choirs in the Churches of that city, until he died.

When Everybody Made Music

Palestrina and other composers of that time also wrote music of many melodies—music in counterpoint—for everybody to sing. These songs were called *madrigals*. The madrigals had parts for two, three, four, five or even more voices. In the madrigals, as in the big Church choruses, the composer showed his skill in the way he wove his melodies from one voice to another, and also in the way he made the music express the feelings of the words, which were often lovely poems. Madrigals were written about the pleasures of the country, about the beauties of nature, and about love.

Madrigal singing became a most popular pastime, all over Europe and especially in England. People would gather in each other's homes in the evening, just to sing madrigals. Queen Elizabeth I, who was Queen of England at that time, was very fond of these songs, and her court organist, William Byrd, wrote some of the loveliest madrigals of all. Writing Church music was still the main task of composers at that time, as it had been through the centuries of the Dark Ages, and so Byrd and the other composers wrote many beautiful Masses and other works for Church services. When madrigals became so popular they also wrote *motets,* which were songs like madrigals only with hymn words suitable for singing in Church.

That was a time when everybody made music. In the same way that mothers today put recipes for a new cake or a new soup in their recipe books, so ladies in those days copied madrigals, rounds, and other songs into their music books.

Musical Instruments of Shakespeare's Time

Besides singing madrigals, many people of those days liked to play them together on the favorite instruments of the time. Just as today we have a piano, a radio, a phonograph, or a television set in our homes, a family living in the sixteenth or seventeenth century had a *chest of viols* or a set of *recorders,* for members of the family and friends to play together.

The *viol* is a kind of grandfather of the violin. In playing, the viol is held downward, resting on the knee of the player and against his shoulder, and it is played with a curved bow. In those days there were usually six viols in a set, ranging from high to low like a group of voices. The largest were the bass viols, and they rested on the floor like a modern 'cello. A set of viols was called a chest of viols because the instruments were actually kept in a chest or cupboard especially designed to hold them.

The *recorder* is a wooden flute, with the mouthpiece at one end instead of at the side as it is in a modern flute. Recorders, too, used to come in sets, usually four: the small high soprano recorder, the alto, the tenor, and the bass. Queen Elizabeth's father, King Henry VIII, loved to play the recorder and had seventy-six of them in his collection. (He liked flutes, too, and had seventy-eight of those.) Recorders are mentioned by Shakespeare in his plays and by other writers of the time.

Nowadays many people have become interested in the music people sang and played in their homes in the sixteenth and seventeenth centuries, and many of them get together in madrigal groups and recorder groups. In some music schools, children learn to play the recorder before they learn any other instrument, because it is simple to learn and makes a gentle sweet tone, very much like the human voice. Naturally the songs of that time sound best when they are played on the instruments of the time, and it is fun to play them on those instruments, too.

Great Music Begins

THE TIME of Queen Elizabeth I, when so many people sang madrigals, was a time of great changes going on in the world. We can see that there had already been many changes since the Dark Ages when only Church scholars could read and write. By the late sixteenth century many people were able to read and write music as well as words. People had begun to travel at about the time of the Crusades in the 1100's and 1200's, and merchants of the Italian cities on the Mediterranean Sea began bringing spices and rich fabrics by ship from Eastern lands. An adventurous young Italian, Marco Polo, traveled all the way to China, which was then called Cathay, and came back to tell marvelous tales of inventions that had not yet been made in Europe, such as printing and gunpowder.

During the centuries that followed, people began to travel among the cities and towns of England and Europe and some even traveled across the ocean. Columbus discovered America in the famous year of 1492. In the 1500's, explorers were going back and forth across the Atlantic to North and South America, and one of them, Magellan, sailed around the world. In the 1600's people were sailing across the ocean to live in the New World. The first English colony was settled at Jamestown, Virginia, in 1607, and in 1620 the Pilgrims landed at Plymouth in Massachusetts and founded the first colony in New England.

To people living in those days, the world they knew was growing larger all the time. It was already quite a different world to live in from the little villages of a few centuries before when people had to huddle close to a nobleman's castle for protection from the private armies of other noblemen. The invention of printing had also made a great difference in their lives. The first printed Bible was produced by Johann Gutenberg and his apprentices in Germany in 1456, and by the 1600's people were accustomed to reading books and pamphlets about what was going on in the world. They could also buy music by famous composers in faraway cities.

All this was exciting to people's imaginations. The new times had already had an effect in the other arts, although music lagged a little behind. First a time of great painting and sculpture and architecture had begun in Italy and spread over the rest of Europe, as you have seen in the story of art in this book.

This time in history has a name. It is called the Renaissance, a word that means "rebirth." To people of today, looking back, it seems as though, after the narrow way of life during the thousand years since the Roman Empire fell, the world was really being re-born.

Let us see how music and musicians were getting on in these exciting new times. Music took a little longer to show the effects of so many changes. For one thing, new kinds of music could not be composed until there were new kinds of musical instruments. So let us first look at the instruments that were being invented in these new times.

From Organs to Pianos

It is strange to realize that until two hundred and fifty years ago, there was no such thing as a piano. But there were other *keyboard* instruments, and the oldest and most important of them was the organ.

Although through all the centuries composers had been writing music mainly for singing, with or without instruments to accompany the voices, the composers themselves were usually very fine performers on the instruments of their time, and especially on the organ. A famous Italian musician, Francesco Landino, although he was totally blind, was known everywhere as a marvelous organist who also played exceptionally well on the lute, the flute, and other instruments of those days. In his native city of Florence, the monument on his grave shows him playing his little portable organ.

For a long time there had been organs like Landino's, small enough to carry. There had also been great organs in the Churches. As far back as the tenth century, in Winchester Cathedral in England, there was an organ so large that it had to have two men to play it and seventy men to pump the air into the pipes. What a tremendous sound that organ must have made!

The organists had hard work, too. Each key was so broad and heavy that the musician could make it sound only if he struck it with his whole fist. Organists actually used to be called "organ-beaters." Luckily the music was extremely slow.

By the seventeenth century, organs were being made that were easier to play. The keys on the new organs could be played fairly rapidly with the fingers. In Germany the organ-builders also made pedals for the feet to play the great deep notes of the bass, and later this was copied in other countries.

In the time of Queen Elizabeth I another keyboard instrument became popular, one that could be played in the home. This was the *virginal,* and it was simply a box with strings, small enough to be put on the parlor table. At the front of the box was a row of keys. When a key was struck, it raised a strip of wood inside the box, and on the end of the strip was a quill, which plucked the string for that note and made it sound. Young ladies used to play the virginal just as many girls learn to play the piano today. Queen Elizabeth herself played this early kind of piano.

From the virginal came the spinet, a larger instrument that generally stood on its own legs, and from the spinet came the harpsichord. The harpsichord looks like a small piano, often with two keyboards, one above the other. But it has a very different sound and its mechanism is quite different from that of the piano. In the piano, when the keys are played, little hammers *strike* the strings inside the instrument. In the harpsichord, as in the spinet and virginal, a quill or a point of leather *plucks* the string to sound the note. The plucked string makes a light, delicate, twanging sound.

The harpsichord was considered a most important part of the furniture in a home of those days. It was usually made of the finest wood, and often it was beautifully carved or painted. It was a delicate instrument that needed frequent tuning and often had to have its quills replaced. In many London homes the harpsichord tuner came regularly once a week. To save money and time, most composers did their own tuning and re-quilling, and became quite skillful at it. An American gentleman, Francis Hopkinson of Philadelphia, who helped to write the Declaration of Independence, was also famous as the inventor of an efficient system of tuning and re-quilling harpsichords.

In spite of needing so much care, the harpsichord became a popular home instrument and a favorite with professional performers, who were as famous in their time as great pianists are today. Leading composers wrote especially for the harpsichord, and some of their compositions are so beautiful and interesting that, in order not to miss hearing them altogether, musicians nowadays play them on the piano. But some musicians have brought the harpsichord back into use to hear harpsichord music just as the composers intended it to sound.

It was when the harpsichord was most popular that the true piano was being designed. There was already a keyboard instrument with the hammer mechanism, called the *clavichord*. This was a small instrument, a box without legs that looked something like the virginal. The clavichord at its loudest could not make a very great sound but it could be played either loud or soft, as the harpsichord could not.

About the year 1709, an Italian inventor, Cristofori, designed an instrument that could make a bigger sound than the clavichord and could also make the sound loud or soft. He called it "a harpsichord with soft and loud." In Italian the word for "soft" is *piano,* and the word for "loud" is *forte.* So the instrument came to be called the *pianoforte,* and then, simply, the *piano,* and this is the name by which our most familiar musical instrument is known everywhere today.

Two of Cristofori's original pianos have lasted down to modern times, although they are no longer played. One is in a German museum, and the other is in the Metropolitan Museum in New York City.

The Violin-Makers of Cremona

A hundred and fifty years before Cristofori made his "pianoforte," three famous families living in the northern Italian city of Cremona were making a new kind of stringed instrument to be played with a bow, a great improvement over the viol. Perhaps you have heard the names of these violin-makers. They were the Amati, the Guarneri, and the Stradivari families.

The instrument these Italian craftsmen made had a deep rounded back that gave a much fuller, richer tone than the old flat-backed viol. There were other differences in design that made it possible for a performer to play with more variety of tone and greater skill. Like the "chest of viols" in different sizes, the violin was made in different sizes, too. There is the *violin* itself, the smallest of this family of instruments, with its high, sweet tone, which quickly became a favorite solo instrument; then the somewhat larger *viola;* the much larger violoncello, whose name has been shortened to *'cello;* and finally the largest "violin" of all, the *double-bass.*

As we shall see when we come to talk about the instruments, there are more instruments of the violin family in a symphony orchestra than any other kind of instrument. But the violin, viola, and 'cello are also sometimes played alone, as *solo* instruments, usually with a piano to accompany them, and they are often combined with other instruments in groups of various sizes. Great composers have written some of their finest music for the *string quartet,* a group composed of two violins, a viola, and a 'cello.

For two hundred years, from about the middle 1500's, the sons, grandsons, and great-grandsons of the three Cremona families made the finest violins, violas, and 'cellos in the world. Nobody has ever been able to explain why their violins were so much finer than those that were made in other countries later on. Experts still argue over whether it was the kind of wood they used, the careful workmanship, or the varnish! Even today, violinists would rather have one of Cremona's old instruments than any new one, and some of those which still exist are more expensive than the finest grand piano. It is true that stringed instruments, especially good ones, are supposed to improve with age. But besides this, the ones the violin-makers of Cremona made through the generations have never been equalled for the beauty of their tone.

The Beginning of Opera and the Ballet

The time of new organs, harpsichords, clavichords, and violins (though not yet of pianos) in the 1500's and 1600's was an exciting time for composers. With so many new and interesting instruments to write for, they began to write music for instruments alone, without voices. At the same time they began to write a new kind of music for voices, too. The year 1600 is remembered as the year when *opera* began.

Italy is famous not only as the birthplace of the violin and the piano, but also as the land of beautiful voices. More great opera singers have come from Italy than from any other country. Perhaps there is something about that sunny land that makes its people want to sing. Perhaps that is why opera was born in Italy in the first place. Whatever the reason, the way opera began is in itself an interesting story.

In the city of Florence, around the court of the Duke of Mantua, there was a little group of Italian gentlemen who liked to play and sing, and to compose music, too. (One of them happened to be the father of the astronomer Galileo.) These gentlemen became interested in the ancient Greek stage dramas, which used to be spoken to music. So they began to write musical plays, taking their stories from old Greek myths, with the actors and actresses singing their parts instead of merely speaking them. There was dancing in their plays, too, and that was the beginning of *ballet,* which came to be a wonderful new art and entertainment by itself later on.

The musical plays had an orchestra to accompany the singing, and as time went on there came to be an *overture* for the orchestra to play as a musical introduction to the stage drama. Also, during the performance, there often was a piece of music performed by the orchestra, called a *symphony*. This word merely means "sounding together," and it was used to refer to this small part of the music that was for the orchestra to play alone, during the course of the play. In these small beginnings, as we shall see, the musical gentlemen of Florence had a number of good ideas that led to great things in music later on.

Meanwhile a gifted composer from Cremona, Claudio Monteverdi, came to work for the Duke of Mantua as a court musician, and he liked the idea of the musical plays so much that he began to write them, too. Monteverdi's first opera, *Arianna,* told the story of Ariadne, the Princess of Crete, who fell in love with the Greek youth Theseus and helped him kill the sacred monster of Crete that fed on Greek youths and maidens. In the ancient Greek story Ariadne set sail with Theseus for Greece, but ungrateful Theseus left her on an island on the way. In Monteverdi's opera, the song he wrote for Ariadne to sing when she was left alone on the island was so moving that audiences wept when they heard it. A song like this, for a character in the opera to sing alone, was called an *aria,* the Italian word for "air" or melody.

Monteverdi and other composers wrote many more musical dramas. At first there was no name for this important new kind of music. It was called "the new musics" and "drama by means of music." But in time, musical dramas, performed by singers and an orchestra, came to be called *operas*.

The composers soon began to write musical dramas about Bible stories, to be performed in Church. But because a Church was not the place for plays with scenery and costumes, the Church singers simply sang the story without acting or wearing special costumes. This kind of composition is called a *cantata,* from the Italian word that means "something sung." Through the years that followed, some of our most beautiful and stirring music was written as cantatas for solo singers, chorus, and orchestra.

The Beginning of Harmony

MONTEVERDI and his fellow opera composers in Italy took another tremendous step with their new music. Instead of writing counterpoint, with separate melodies for the different voices or instruments in a group, they began to write music with a single melody, accompanied by *harmony*.

Let us see what this means. Have you ever sung a song while someone played a guitar or a ukelele as accompaniment? If you have, you know that the singer sings the melody, and the instrument plays *chords* to accompany the song. The *chords* are groups or clusters of notes that go with the melody as far as sound is concerned but *do not make separate melodies*. This is a simple example of the *harmony* that began with opera.

It is easy to understand why opera needed this kind of music with a single melody. In opera, the melody and its words *tell the story*. In an aria, for instance, the character who is singing tells what is happening and how he or she feels about it. An opera composer wants the audience to hear this one melody clearly. To weave other melodies together with it, as in a madrigal, could be beautiful and interesting but it would take attention from the melody that is telling the story. A harmony of chords does not take attention from the melody. It strengthens the sound of the melody and at the same time fills it out and makes it more beautiful to hear.

Here is another way to recognize harmony: Listen to two different recordings of a popular song, one by a dance band that plays sweet or swing music, the other by a band that plays Dixieland jazz. In sweet or swing music the melody is always there. You can hear it and sing along with it. In Dixieland jazz, no matter what tune the band is playing, each musician makes up his own melody around it, whether he is playing a solo bit or playing along with the others, and often you cannot hear the original melody at all. The Dixieland band is playing a kind of *counterpoint*. The swing band is playing *harmony*.

Of course there is a great difference between the dance band arrangements of a popular song and the music of the great composers. Jazz players make up their melodies as they go along. But the composer of serious music carefully works out his melodies and the way in which they weave in and out.

Here is an example of counterpoint in a simple form, by one of the world's greatest composers, Johann Sebastian Bach. It is the beginning of a composition for the piano that many piano students play, the *Two-Part Invention in F Major*. In this composition there are only two parts, or "voices," as the different parts in counterpoint are called. It was natural to call them "voices" since originally they were the actual voices of a choir or a chorus of singers. When counterpoint began to be written for instruments, the melody carried by each instrument was also called a "voice."

In this *Invention* by Bach, which is played on the piano, one voice is played by the right hand and the other voice by the left. The two voices have the same melody, but each voice follows the melody independently. This form in counterpoint is called a *canon*. A kind of canon that you have probably sung yourself is a *round*, like *Three Blind Mice*.

Just by looking at this little bit of Bach's composition, you can see how the melody begins with the right hand in the first measure, and begins with the left hand in the second measure. From there on, different parts of the same melody are being played by each hand at the same time, so that the melody is actually woven together with itself:

As an example of *harmony,* here is the beginning of the famous waltz, *The Beautiful Blue Danube,* by Johann Strauss. Here you can plainly see the *chords,* each chord looking like knobs on a stick standing upright. Each knob represents a note, and all the notes on a single stick or stem are played together. On the piano, the notes of a chord are played by the fingers of one hand or both hands, striking the keys all at the same time. In an orchestra, the notes of a chord are played by the different instruments, each playing different notes of the chord, but at the same time. In this bit of the beginning of Strauss's waltz, written here as piano music, you can follow the melody in the G or treble clef (the upper part of the music, for the right hand). The melody begins with the single quarter-notes, and goes on in the top note of each of the chords. The F or bass clef (the lower part of the music, for the left hand) accompanies the melody with more chords and also keeps the waltz rhythm of 1–2–3, 1–2–3:

Now compare the example of Bach's *counterpoint* with Strauss's example of *harmony*. Even if you cannot read the music, you can see the difference. In the Bach *Invention* the notes run along, one after the other. Each voice is separate and independent, and in each voice the melody marches along in a single line. In *The Beautiful Blue Danube,* there do not seem to be any separate voices at all. The melody marches along, sometimes in single notes, sometimes in clusters of notes strung together on an up-and-down stick, which means that they are sounded together as one note. Because of the difference in the way counterpoint and harmony look on a page of music, counterpoint is often called *horizontal* music, music that goes in a line from left to right, while harmony is called *vertical* music, or music that looks up-and-down.

Music Becomes Entertainment

ONE more important change was taking place in this exciting time in our story of music. Music was becoming a popular kind of *entertainment.*

Nowadays we think nothing of turning on the radio or the phonograph just to listen to music for pleasure. People go to opera and concert performances for entertainment as they go to the theatre or the motion pictures.

But this was not always so. As we have seen, through all the centuries, except for folk music and the songs of the minstrels and troubadours, all the music was composed for religious services and by church musicians. When music like the madrigals began to be composed for people to sing and play for pleasure, this music was also composed by church choirmasters or organists, who were also the composers of church music.

Gradually this was changing. Musicians began to be engaged by royalty and noblemen as *court musicians.* Dukes and Counts, Kings and Princes kept orchestras as part of the household. The Director of the orchestra was also a composer, who was expected to compose special music for every occasion, for a holiday or a party, the birth of a young Prince or Princess, a wedding, or the visit of another nobleman. He also had to present a whole evening's concert of new music or a brand-new opera at regular times, just for the pleasure of his employer. For this he composed all the music, rehearsed the orchestra, and conducted the performance.

When the noble employer went on a journey, the Director of music and all the musicians went with him. They were paid something like a salary, usually by the year instead of the week or month, and they were given food and lodging and clothes. They were dressed in uniforms or *livery* just like the grooms and coachmen and other servants, they ate in the servants' dining hall, and often the musicians were expected to do household tasks when they were not playing music. Even the Director was treated with hardly more respect than the cooks or the keepers of the royal horses.

How the composers liked this arrangement, and what kind of music they wrote for the noble employers and their guests, we shall soon see. But the new thing about music was that it was meant to *entertain*. After centuries when all music by professional composers was written for the Church, a new kind of music was being composed entirely for entertainment and pleasure.

The New Music in Many Lands

In Italy the new kinds of music were already flourishing in the 1600's. The first "opera house," a theatre where only opera was played and where people could pay to see a performance, was opened in Venice. In Naples, in the southern part of Italy, the composer Alessandro Scarlatti wrote and produced many operas, and other composers and performers, too, came from many parts of Europe to see his productions of opera and to study with him. His son, Domenico Scarlatti, also became a great musician, famous for his playing of the harpsichord and for his beautiful compositions for that charming keyboard instrument. Modern musicians play his harpsichord compositions on the piano. Domenico Scarlatti later became court musician to the King of Spain and music master to the Spanish Princesses. In many of his compositions we can hear the sounds of Spanish guitar music and the rhythms of Spanish dances. A charming composition of his, full of dance rhythms, is *The Good-Humored Ladies*.

The violin, too, was quickly becoming known, and pupils came from everywhere to study with Arcangelo Corelli, the first famous violinist, violin teacher, and composer for the violin family of instruments. Corelli came from the northern part of Italy but he spent much of his life in Rome. And in Venice there was Antonio Vivaldi, who wrote music for all the instruments and especially for the large groups of instruments of the violin family—violins, violas, and 'cellos—which made up the orchestras of that time. A favorite form of musical composition, for which Vivaldi was famous, was called the *concerto grosso,* for orchestra with solo parts for one instrument or for several small groupings of them. *The Four Seasons,* which we talked about at the beginning of our story, is a *concerto grosso* with a violin as solo instrument.

In France, at the magnificent court of King Louis XIV, the court composer and a special favorite of the King was Jean-Baptiste Lully, an Italian who had come to France as a boy. Lully composed operas, ballets, and music for the plays that were given at court, and he and the King too danced and acted in them.

In England, a young musician named Henry Purcell, who repaired instruments and played the organ in Westminster Abbey, also composed some of the most beautiful music ever written by an English composer. He wrote opera music, music for the theatre, and compositions for harpsichord, violin, and 'cello as well as older instruments. He also wrote a great deal of Church music, as many composers continued to do even when they had branched out into other forms of musical composition. Purcell was poorly paid and not really recognized as a great composer of his time until after his death at the youthful age of thirty-six. Many countries produced fine music in those days. But it was from Germany that the greatest music came.

Johann Sebastian Bach the Greatest of a Great Musical Family

O N A March day in 1685 there was born in a small town in Germany a boy who was to become one of the great composers of all time, although neither he nor anyone else thought he was anybody very special during his long and busy lifetime.

His name was Johann Sebastian Bach. For two hundred years before Johann Sebastian was born, the Bachs had been musicians. There had been so many musicians named Bach in that part of Germany that people used to call a man a Bach when they meant he was a musician, even though Bach was not his name at all.

Young Johann Sebastian wanted to become a musician, too. When he was ten both his parents died and he went to live with his older brother, who was the Church organist in the next town. This brother taught him music but he was very severe. He would not let the boy study from a certain valuable book of organ music which he kept locked in the book-case. At night when everyone was asleep, Johann Sebastian stole downstairs, squeezed his hand between the bars of the book-case door, got the book open, and began to copy the music by moonlight. He did this night after night, until he had copied all the music in the book. Then one day his brother discovered what he had done and punished him by taking his copy away from him.

When Johann Sebastian was fifteen his brother died and he set out for himself. He still had a good boy soprano voice and he was lucky enough to be taken into the choir of a

Church school. On vacations he would walk many miles to the big city of Hamburg, to hear a famous organist who played in the principal Church there.

On his way home from one of these trips, tired and hungry and with no money to buy his dinner, he sat down outside an inn to rest. Someone inside threw two herring heads through the window. Johann Sebastian, thinking he might as well nibble on them, picked them up—and found a coin inside each one. He used the money, not for dinner or to ride back to school, but to return to Hamburg and hear more music!

When he was nineteen he got his first job, as Church organist in the city of Arnstadt. As soon as he could, he asked to be allowed to visit another city near by to hear a famous organist and composer, Dietrich Buxtehude. He stayed away, not a few days or a few weeks, but three whole months! When he came back the angry authorities of the Church scolded him severely. There were other complaints, too. He kept surprising the congregation with new ways of harmonizing the familiar hymns when he played the organ. And he also allowed a strange young lady to sing in the Church.

Bach's lively answers to these complaints were not very pleasing to his employers. But he was such a fine organist that they did not dismiss him. He was soon offered a better position in another city. The "strange young lady" was really one of his cousins, with whom he had fallen in love, and when he moved to his new position they were married.

Johann Sebastian, who could play not only the organ but almost any instrument well, next became first violinist or *Concert Master* of the court orchestra of the Duke of Weimar. This Duke was interested in religious music, and so Johann Sebastian composed mostly Church cantatas and Church organ music during the nine years he held this position. He had become so well-known as an organist that he was invited to other cities to play Church concerts. On one of these trips his admirers persuaded him to challenge a visiting French organist to a competition. The Frenchman was successful and proud. He was not going to take any chances with his reputation. He secretly managed to hear Johann Sebastian playing before the contest was to be held, and on the day of the contest he was nowhere to be found! He had left the city by the earliest coach so that he would not have to compete with Johann Sebastian Bach.

Johann Sebastian continued to be the first violinist until there was a chance of becoming *Kapellmeister* or Musical Director. When the Duke did not promote him, he resigned from the Duke's orchestra. He was a man of spirit, and he had a growing family to support; so he wanted to look for a better position somewhere else. But for daring to resign, the Duke had him put into prison! Fortunately the young Prince Leopold of Cöthen wanted him as Kapellmeister for his court, and the Duke had to let him go.

Prince Leopold did not care for religious music but was very fond of *chamber music*. This is music composed for small groups of instruments, suitable for playing not in a Church or a large concert hall but in a room or chamber, as a nobleman's fine parlor or drawing room used to be called. So at Prince Leopold's court Johann Sebastian Bach composed many works for small orchestras and for various groups of instruments.

He and the musicians went on many journeys with the Prince. Coming back from one of these trips, Johann Sebastian found that his wife had become ill and died while he was away. In his grief he also had to plan how to take care of his seven children. In a year or so he was fortunate to find a lovely young girl, Anna Magdalena, who was kind and loving. She was also musical and had a beautiful soprano voice. With Anna Magdalena he began a second happy marriage. Together they had thirteen more children, making a family of twenty. Bach wrote some of the most inspired songs and solos in his cantatas for Anna Magdalena to sing. He also wrote many beautiful small pieces for her to play on the lute. These are now played on the piano. There is a whole collection of Bach compositions simple enough for young people to play, labeled "From Anna Magdalena's Notebook."

Johann Sebastian Bach, besides all his other musical abilities, was also teaching music to his children, and writing a great deal of it for them to study and practice. He decided that the children needed a better education than he could find for them at Cöthen, and so he took the position of Musical Director of St. Thomas's Church School in the big city of Leipzig. As a teacher, Bach was sometimes impatient with boys who were not really interested in music, but they had to be taught all the same. He was greatly respected by everyone, even by the city authorities who did not always appreciate his kind of Church music and who thought him too independent-minded. He stayed in Leipzig the rest of his life and wrote some of his greatest works there. During the last years of his life he became blind, and he died in 1750, when he was sixty-five years old.

Four of Johann Sebastian Bach's sons were musically talented, and two of them became famous. One of these, Karl Philipp Emanuel Bach, became court composer to King Frederick the Great of Prussia. Once the King invited the young composer's father to come and see him at his summer palace in Potsdam. For old Johann Sebastian this visit to the King, his son's royal employer, was one of the proudest moments of his life. The King had just bought fifteen of the newly invented pianos, and he had Bach play them all, as well as all the organs in the churches of Potsdam.

Another son, Johann Christian Bach, went to London and became successful there as an opera and concert director and music teacher of the family of King George III. Public concerts were a new idea. Until that time, only royal families had professional musicians to entertain them. The only places where ordinary people could hear music was in Church, or, if they played music themselves, in their own homes. Opera houses were the first places where people could buy tickets to enjoy music. Then came the idea of public concerts. Johann Christian Bach helped to organize concerts like these in London, and they were beginning in other important cities at about the same time.

The Kinds of Music Bach Wrote

During his lifetime Johann Sebastian Bach was not as well known as his sons were. Most people of that time, if they were asked whether they knew the musician Bach, would have said, "Oh, yes, you mean Mr. J. C. Bach, who is so famous in London! Or do you mean Mr. K. P. E. Bach who is at the court of King Frederick?" If they had heard of Johann Sebastian Bach at all, they would know of him only as an organist somewhere in Germany and the father of two famous musicians.

Old Johann Sebastian did not mind at all. He was proud of his sons, and he himself thought his music was old-fashioned. He was still writing counterpoint, while his sons were writing music with the new harmony.

But although his sons wrote beautiful music, and some of it is played nowadays, it is Johann Sebastian Bach whose music has come to be regarded as the greatest of all. Counterpoint was considered old-fashioned in his time, but most of the great composers who followed him used forms of counterpoint in their music, and especially some of the forms that he worked out so beautifully.

One of his favorite forms of counterpoint was the *fugue*. The name comes from an Italian word that means "flight," and when we listen to one of Bach's fugues it does seem like a flight of "voices" pursuing each other. In a fugue, the main melody, called the *subject,* is heard first in one voice, then the next, and so on until all the four voices are heard, each singing the melody by itself but combining with the others in wonderful harmonies. A fugue is something like a canon or round, but it is a much more elaborate composition in which the melody grows and changes as it is woven among the voices, and wonderful harmonies are heard. Bach was so skillful that he composed one fugue on a melody made out of the notes for the letters of his name, B-A-C-H (H is the name of a note in the German scale, although not in ours). Bach's last work was *The Art of the Fugue,* in which he composed seventeen different fugues on the same melody.

A great many of Bach's religious compositions were written for St. Thomas's Church in Leipzig. The Church needed fifty-nine cantatas a year for its services, and he wrote enough of these works for five years of Church services, 295 cantatas in all. He also wrote cantatas for other occasions such as celebrations, the visits of royalty, and one for a fellow-citizen because he had bought an estate in the country. He also wrote several choral works of a special kind, called *Passions,* for the Easter services. The *St. Matthew Passion* is still regularly performed in many Churches during Easter Week.

From **FUGUE IN C MAJOR** by *JOHANN SEBASTIAN BACH*

Here is the beginning of one of Bach's fugues for the piano, in which the subject is first heard in the alto voice, then the soprano, then the tenor, and finally the bass.

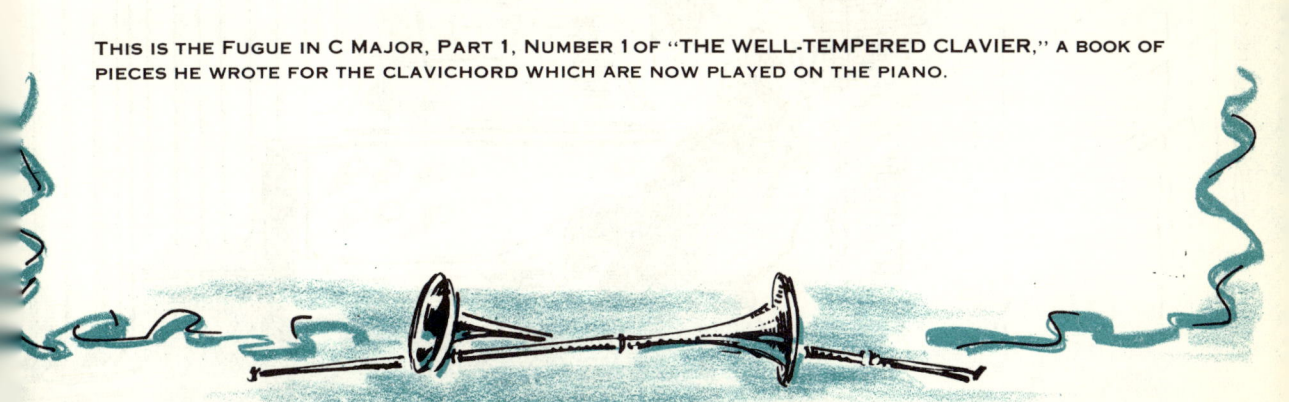

This is the Fugue in C Major, Part 1, Number 1 of "THE WELL-TEMPERED CLAVIER," a book of pieces he wrote for the clavichord which are now played on the piano.

Court composers had to write many dances for the noblemen and their guests to dance to, and often when they wrote music for instruments they followed the style of the court dances in these compositions too, even though they were not meant for dancing but for listening. Bach wrote many of these, and combined them in groups. A group of compositions of this kind was called a *suite*. Bach wrote a number of suites which he called English Suites and French Suites. Usually he wrote the different compositions of a suite in the same key, and put them in a particular order so that a gay and lively dance, like the *gavotte,* came after a *sarabande,* which was slow and dignified, and a courtly *minuet* came between a fast *bourrée* and a *gigue,* which was a rather elegant ancestor of today's jig.

Nowadays, when Bach is recognized as one of the world's greatest composers, it is almost impossible to believe that for nearly a hundred years his music was neglected and forgotten. Then another great composer in Germany, Felix Mendelssohn, began to play it and to urge others to play it, as we shall see when we come to Mendelssohn's story. Then musical scholars began studying Bach's compositions and putting them in collections and music books, and so this great music at last became known everywhere. The more difficult works are played by professional musicians and orchestras, and the smaller pieces, such as the ones he composed for his wife and children, are arranged so that young people learning to play an instrument can play and enjoy them.

By listening well to Johann Sebastian Bach's great music we learn to follow his melodies and to enjoy the marvelous variety and skill with which he used them. When we have listened to one of his compositions several times we appreciate the way he built a piece of music, with each part fitting into the rest like a well-told story or a well-built building. We come to share his deep understanding of joy or sadness, of holiness, and of many feelings for which there are no words. All these he expressed in his music. Hearing one of his great works, we feel as we might feel if we were standing in one of the great Churches of Bach's time, with his melodies and harmonies soaring like the arches far overhead and the sound swelling and filling the great spaces.

Mr. Handel of London Town

A MONTH before Johann Sebastian Bach was born in 1685, and in another German city not far away, another boy was born who was to become a great musician and composer. His name was George Frederick Handel. Although he was born in Germany, he became an English citizen and rose to be the leading musician of England. Handel was a great traveler and a worldly gentleman, very different from Bach who never left Germany and was unknown outside of the city of Leipzig. They never met, and Handel hardly knew of Bach, but Bach admired Handel's music and even copied some of his compositions by hand because he had none in printed form and he wanted to learn to play them.

The Handel family were not musicians. In those days, when there were no doctor-surgeons as there are today, the barbers were the surgeons, and George Frederick's father was a barber-surgeon. He wanted his son to be a lawyer and did not want him to study music. But a friend of the family helped the boy to hide a clavichord in the attic. On this small piano-like instrument, which has a tone so faint that it cannot be heard behind a closed door, George Frederick used to practise without his father's knowing about it.

One day, when the boy was seven, his father set off to visit an older son who was employed at the court of a Duke. Little George Frederick begged to go along, and when his father drove off he ran alongside the carriage so that his father had to stop and take him. At the Duke's palace George Frederick made friends with the court musicians. He cleverly managed to be practising at the organ when the Duke himself would be sure to hear. The Duke recognized the boy's talent and spoke seriously to his father. The result was that when they returned home the Church organist was hired to give the boy lessons.

Before his eleventh birthday George Frederick Handel had already composed a great deal of music. He had to write a new motet each week for his music lesson, and he composed other music too just for his own pleasure. When he was twelve, he was offered a position as a court musician in Berlin. But his father still wanted him to be a lawyer. A few years later his father died. George Frederick dutifully tried to carry out his father's wishes. He went to the University and studied law for a year. Meanwhile he was also employed as the Church organist. After a year his longing to be a musician finally won, and he went to the great musical city of Hamburg.

Bach as a schoolboy had walked to Hamburg to hear a famous Church organist there. Handel, now a tall youth of eighteen, when straight to the opera house and got a job in the orchestra as a violinist. He was quickly promoted to harpsichordist. This was the most important position in the orchestras of that time. The harpsichordist usually also conducted the orchestra.

Handel made friends with another young composer whose name was Matheson. Together the two lively young men went to another city to try for the position of organist from which the great Danish musician Buxtehude was retiring at the age of ninety. Bach had also gone to this city to hear Buxtehude, as we have already seen, and he got into trouble by staying too long. Young Handel and Matheson had a good time on their trip, but they did not compete for the position after all, because they found that whoever won the position would have to marry the old organist's daughter!

Back in Hamburg, an opera written by Matheson was produced at the opera house and led to a quarrel that nearly ended Handel's life then and there. Matheson conducted the orchestra for the performance, but he also sang one of the parts, and when it was time for him to go on the stage to sing, he gave the conducting over to Handel. When Matheson finished singing and came back to conduct again, Handel refused to give up the conductor's place. As soon as the performance was over, the two friends went outside the opera house and fought a duel. Matheson was very angry, and made a terrible thrust with his sword right at Handel's heart. But a large button on Handel's coat turned the sword aside, and he was not hurt. After that the friends made up, and remained friends.

Soon afterward Handel decided to travel to Italy, the great land of opera. Several noblemen offered to pay for his journey, but he had an independent mind and he had saved his money so that he had enough to support his mother at home and also to travel. In Italy he had three wonderful years. The Italian composers and the music-loving Italian noblemen made a great fuss about the big, energetic young German. He made friends with Alessandro Scarlatti, the leading Italian opera composer, and with his son, Domenico, the harpsichordist. In Rome the composer Corelli, who was famous throughout Europe as a violinist, was playing a violin part in one of Handel's compositions, and found it too hard. Young Handel rudely snatched the violin and showed him how to play it. The dignified composer, who was nearly twice Handel's age, was not angry, but only said gently, "My dear Handel, this music is in the French style, which I do not understand."

While he was still in Italy, Handel was invited to become Court Musical Director at Hanover in Germany. His new employer gave him permission to go to London, where Italian opera was very fashionable at the time.

And in London he stayed, writing operas and other music. He forgot all about his royal employer in Hanover. Then, to his great embarrassment, that same Prince came from Hanover to London as the new King of England, George I.

Knowing that the new King had good reason to be very angry with him, Handel did not know what to do. But his skill as a composer saved him. A friend told him that the King was planning a great party on the Thames River, and Handel set to work to compose special music for it. The orchestra sat in a barge on the river, playing to the King and his guests across the water in the royal barge. King George was so pleased with the music that he forgave Handel completely, awarded him a generous salary, and later appointed him music master to the two Princesses. The composition that pleased the King so much is called the *Water Music Suite* and it is often played on symphony concert programs today.

Handel became an English citizen. He was a huge man, handsome and imposing in the fine brocaded coats, frilled cuffs, and flowing white wigs of that time. He was a favorite with the nobility and with the English people, and he continued to be honored at Court. He wrote and produced many operas, and also a great deal of beautiful music for orchestra, harpsichord, and other instruments. His most important works are his compositions for solo singers, chorus, and orchestra, called *oratorios*. These are like the Church cantatas, in which the solo singers are characters telling a Bible story. But they are larger works and for more voices and instruments than the cantatas. When Handel's greatest oratorio, *The Messiah,* was performed, George II, who was then the King of England was in the audience. In this work there is a hymn of praise, called the *Hallelujah*. When the chorus sang this hymn, King George was so stirred by the splendid music that he stood up. The whole audience stood up, too. Since then, whenever *The Messiah* is performed, it is the custom for the audience to stand up for the *Hallelujah*.

Handel's music, especially for the voice, is so full of beautiful melody that many parts of his operas and oratorios are played separately by orchestra or individual instruments. A famous composition of his is the beautiful, serene *Largo*. This was actually an *aria* or solo song in one of his operas. The song was sung by one of the characters, the Persian King, Xerxes. In it he thanked a plane tree for its shade, under which he had rested.

Like Bach, Handel became blind in his late years. His sight failed as he was writing a chorus for one of his oratorios, with the words, "How dark, O Lord, are Thy decrees . . . all our joys to sorrow turning . . . as the night succeeds the day." But even when he was blind, Handel went right on with his work. He played the harpsichord and conducted at concerts, and continued to compose music, with a devoted secretary writing it down for him. He went to a performance of his own oratorio, *The Messiah,* a week before he died, at the age of seventy-four. He was buried with great honor in Westminster Abbey, and the English have held great musical festivals in his memory ever since.

How a Simple Melody Becomes a Great Symphony

WE HAVE seen how great changes in music began with the opera in Italy and spread to France, England, and Germany. After the middle of the eighteenth century these changes led to such a new kind of music that the great works of Bach and Handel in the old style were nearly forgotten for a long time. For it was at this time, after 1750, that the symphony and other important forms of musical composition were born.

Great events were taking place everywhere during those years. In 1775 the American Colonies began to fight for their independence from England, and in 1789 George Washington was elected the first President of the United States. In that same year of 1789 the French began their Revolution and overthrew their King.

During the same years, between 1750 and 1800, many new kinds of machinery were invented, such as the steam engine and the spinning jenny. Factories were built, and many people gave up farming and moved to the cities to work in the factories.

These events had their effect in the world of music, too. As the cities grew larger there were more people to enjoy musical entertainment. Concerts and operas became more popular. Noblemen tried to outdo each other with their private orchestras and with the fame of the conductors and composers they employed.

In Germany and Austria especially, the people were enthusiastic about musical entertainment. Almost every town had its own orchestra, and ordinary people who were not professional musicians met in each other's homes to play the new music just for pleasure.

The old city of Vienna, the capital of Austria, was a center of musical activity. The city was full of the fine palaces of noblemen, and all had their private orchestras. Today we usually like music better as we become familiar with it, but in those days people liked to have a constant supply of *new* music. The noblemen ordered new music from composers the way a housekeeper orders eggs from the grocer, by the dozens or half-dozens. For example, a Count would order a half-dozen new symphonies or six new quartets.

All this gave great encouragement to composers. The opportunities in Vienna brought many composers and performers to that lively musical city. One wonderful result was that three of the world's great composers came from other parts of Austria and Germany to Vienna, and there they did their finest work.

The three great men were Haydn, Mozart, and Beethoven. They were as different as could be from each other, but each one made his special contribution to the growth of music, and all of them wrote music that we enjoy today.

From Haydn, Mozart, and Beethoven came the first important *symphonies, sonatas, quartets,* and *concertos.* Their work inspired all the composers who came after them. Before we tell the stories of these three great men of Vienna, let us see what these new *forms* in musical compositions were, and how they came about.

How New Forms in Musical Composition Came About

As we know, music is made up of melodies. When there are words to a melody, we have a song. In a song we can repeat the same melody over and over without becoming tired of it, because we can change the words. Story-songs and ballads keep repeating the same tune, but each time with a different verse. Take, for example, the old song *Clementine:*

[Musical notation for "Clementine" with lyrics:
In a cav-ern in a can-yon ex-ca-vat-ing for a mine, Dwelt a min-er, for-ty-nin-er, And his daught-er Clem-en-tine. Oh my dar-ling, Oh my dar-ling, Oh my dar-ling Clem-en-tine, Thou art lost and gone for-ev-er. Dread-ful sor-ry, Clem-en-tine.
Chorus (Oh my)...]

That is the first verse and the chorus. Perhaps you know the second verse, which begins, "Light she was and like a fairy, and her shoes were number nine." The third verse tells how Clementine, driving ducklings to the water, "fell into the foaming brine." And so the song goes on, with six verses and a chorus, all to the same tune. Other ballads, such as *Barbara Allen* or *Lord Randall My Son,* have eight or ten verses or even more, as many verses as it takes to tell the story. Like these folk songs and ballads, our popular songs today usually have a chorus that repeats the same words each time, but the verses change and so there is enough variety to keep us interested.

Now one of the ways that the early composers found to make their music interesting was to write several different melodies together, in counterpoint, as we have already learned. Then, in the time of Bach and Handel, composers took over the forms of court dances, and to make their compositions still longer and more interesting, they grouped these dance forms together in suites, as we mentioned when we talked about Johann Sebastian Bach.

Still another way that the composers found useful was to write their music for instruments in the same way that they composed a song. For instance, the melody of a song usually has either two parts or three parts. This is true even of a very simple song. *America*, for instance, is a two-part song:

[Musical notation for "America" with lyrics: "My country, 'tis of thee, Sweet land of liberty, Of thee I sing. Land where my fathers died, Land of the Pilgrims' pride, From ev'ry mountainside let freedom ring." with A and B sections marked]

The first part of the melody goes from the beginning to the words, "Of thee I sing." The second part goes from "Land where my fathers died" to the end. For convenience we will call the first part *A* and the second part *B*, and we can call a two-part song an *AB* song. If you will hum the melody without the words, you can catch the difference between the two parts, A and B. The first part seems like one complete sentence, and the second part seems like another complete sentence.

In some AB songs, the first part, A, seems like a question, and the second part, B, seems like an answer, as in the Kentucky mountain song, *On Top of Old Smoky*. (You may know this tune with words of the ballad about an Indian maid, *The Little Mohee*.)

[Musical notation for "On Top of Old Smoky" with lyrics: "1. On top of Old Smoky, All cover'd with snow, I lost my true lover, Come a-courtin' too slow. 2. A courtin's a pleasure, A flirtin's a grief, A false-hearted lover, Is worse than a thief." with A and B sections marked]

There are also three-part songs. The old English song, *Drink To Me Only With Thine Eyes*, is a three-part song, with an A part, a B part, and then the A part again, ending the song. This is called the ABA form. In many songs like this, the A part or the B part may be sung twice before the melody goes on to the next part. In this one, the A part is sung twice at the beginning:

Oh, Susanna is another ABA or three-part song:

In this one, too, A is sung twice before the melody goes on to B. But in this song, A has a slightly different ending each time. The first time the A part ends with an unfinished sound, because the melody is going to repeat this part. This ending is like a comma in a sentence. The second time, A really ends, with a finished sound like the period in the sentence. Then comes the B part of the melody, "Oh Susanna, don't you cry for me." And then comes A again, the last line of the song, and it ends with a period as we might expect, because this is the end of the song. An ending in music is called a *cadence*.

The chorus of most popular songs is written in the ABA or three-part form. Hum your favorite Hit-Parade song and you will see that this is so. The separate parts are usually repeated, and they are not always repeated exactly. They often have different endings and sometimes they change in other little ways. But you will usually find the three parts: A, the *statement* of the melody; B an *answering or contrasting* part of the melody; then A again, a *reminder* of the original melody.

When the composers began to write larger and more elaborate compositions for instruments, this form—A, B, A—is what they took for their outline. This is the outline of the great musical works that we enjoy today. Knowing our ABA is our greatest help in enjoying those wonderful compositions that do not tell a story or paint a picture, but express the composer's feelings and ideas entirely in music.

The first works for instruments that used the ABA outline were the sonatas. A *sonata* is a composition for one or two instruments. The word *sonata* is Italian, and it means something *sounded,* just as *cantata* means something *sung*. Musicians usually call the ABA form the *sonata form,* just because it was first used in sonatas. Next the form came to be used for other kinds of compositions, and especially for *symphonies*.

Now a symphony is a really big work, for the whole orchestra, and so with the symphony the ABA form became more elaborate. Instead of presenting only one melody in the A part, a composer writing a symphony introduced first one melody and then a second melody, perhaps a third and even a fourth. In the B part he would weave these together, or use them to contrast with each other. He would change the rhythm of a melody, bring it in with different groups of instruments, make it go from one key to another, and vary its harmonies in many ways. All these ways of using his melodies were called *developing* the melodies, and so the B part came to be called the *development*. Finally, when the melodies had gone through all these changes, the A part would be repeated, to remind us of the melodies as we first heard them.

We can listen to the great symphonies that were written in this way as we listen to a story. First the melodies are introduced, just as in a story the characters and the situation are introduced. The composer seems to be saying in his music, "Once upon a time, there was . . ." only instead of meeting characters we meet the melodies.

Then, in a story, the characters go through their adventures and experiences. In a musical composition, this is the B part, in which the melodies go through *their* adventures and experiences—that is, the many changes that the composer has worked out with them.

Then, in a story, comes the ending, in which we are told how it all comes out so that the characters "lived happily ever after." In the musical composition, this is the A part repeated, the reminder, in which we hear the melodies again as they were in the beginning. Sometimes they return a little changed, as the characters in a story might be changed by their adventures. But even though they may be slightly changed, we recognize them and we are satisfied at hearing them again. The A part at the end of the composition is like the happy ending of a story.

Sometimes a composition begins with an introduction before the A part. This is like a pianist striking a few chords on the piano before he begins his concert, or like the orchestra conductor tapping his music stand with his baton, to signal to the musicians and the audience that he is ready to begin.

Also, there may be a special ending to a composition, after the A that repeats the melodies. A special ending is called a *coda,* an Italian word that actually means "tail." In some compositions the coda is quite long and elaborate. It may sum up all the melodies or the one or two melodies that are most important, or it may only be the composer's way of winding it all up with a flourish.

When we listen to a sonata, a symphony, or a quartet, we discover that each of these compositions is written in four sections, called *movements.* The *movements* of a composition are like the *acts* of a play. This was another way the composers had of making their musical works more interesting. Each movement has its own themes and its own form. The ABA is the usual form for the first movement. The other movements sometimes have this form, or they may follow a dance form, or they may follow the form of a theme with variations. They are arranged in such a way as to give variety. The first movement is usually fairly fast. The second movement is slow and song-like. The third movement is most often dance-like. The fourth movement is very fast and spirited, or it may be only fairly fast but big-sounding and impressive.

This is how, with the help of the ABA or sonata form, composers since Haydn's time have made little melodies grow into great symphonies. Haydn was the first to use this form, and he used it so skillfully and with so much variety that, for nearly a century, composers followed his example.

"Papa" Haydn and the Symphony

FRANZ JOSEPH HAYDN was born in a little Austrian village in 1732. He was one of twelve children, and he learned music as a choir boy in the Cathedral in Vienna. When he was dismissed from the choir school at the age of nineteen, although he was alone and without money in the big city, he determined to stay and continue his music studies. He found an attic room to live in and an old clavichord to practice on. There was a fashion in Vienna just then, of engaging musicians to play serenades at night outside the house of a lady or of a friend to whom one wished to pay a compliment. Young Josef got a job playing the violin for serenades like these. By teaching a few music pupils besides, he managed to earn enough money to pay for his room and food. Meanwhile he worked hard at his music. Altogether he worked about sixteen hours a day. He got too little sleep, but he made himself a thoroughly trained musician.

Then he had a stroke of luck. He was invited to the country house of a gentleman who liked to give musical house-parties. In a short time Josef composed eighteen musical works for this gentleman. One of these was his First Symphony and another was his First String Quartet, the two kinds of compositions for which he was to become known throughout Europe.

Soon Haydn was noticed by the nobleman who had the finest orchestra in Austria, Prince Paul Esterhazy, who hired him as conductor and composer. Haydn spent the next thirty years with this noble family who were famous for their music. When Prince Paul died, his brother Nicholas became Haydn's employer. Prince Nicholas was called the Magnificent. He gave splendid parties for which Haydn wrote every kind of music.

Meanwhile he became known all over Europe. His compositions were performed everywhere. With Prince Nicholas's permission he composed Masses and other religious music for Cathedrals and Churches in other cities, and he wrote symphonies and other compositions for Kings and noblemen in other countries and for public concerts in Paris and London.

In Vienna he became friends with young Mozart. Later Beethoven as a youth came to Vienna to study with Haydn. But Beethoven was not easy to get along with, even for sweet-tempered "Papa" Haydn, and the rebellious young man went his own way.

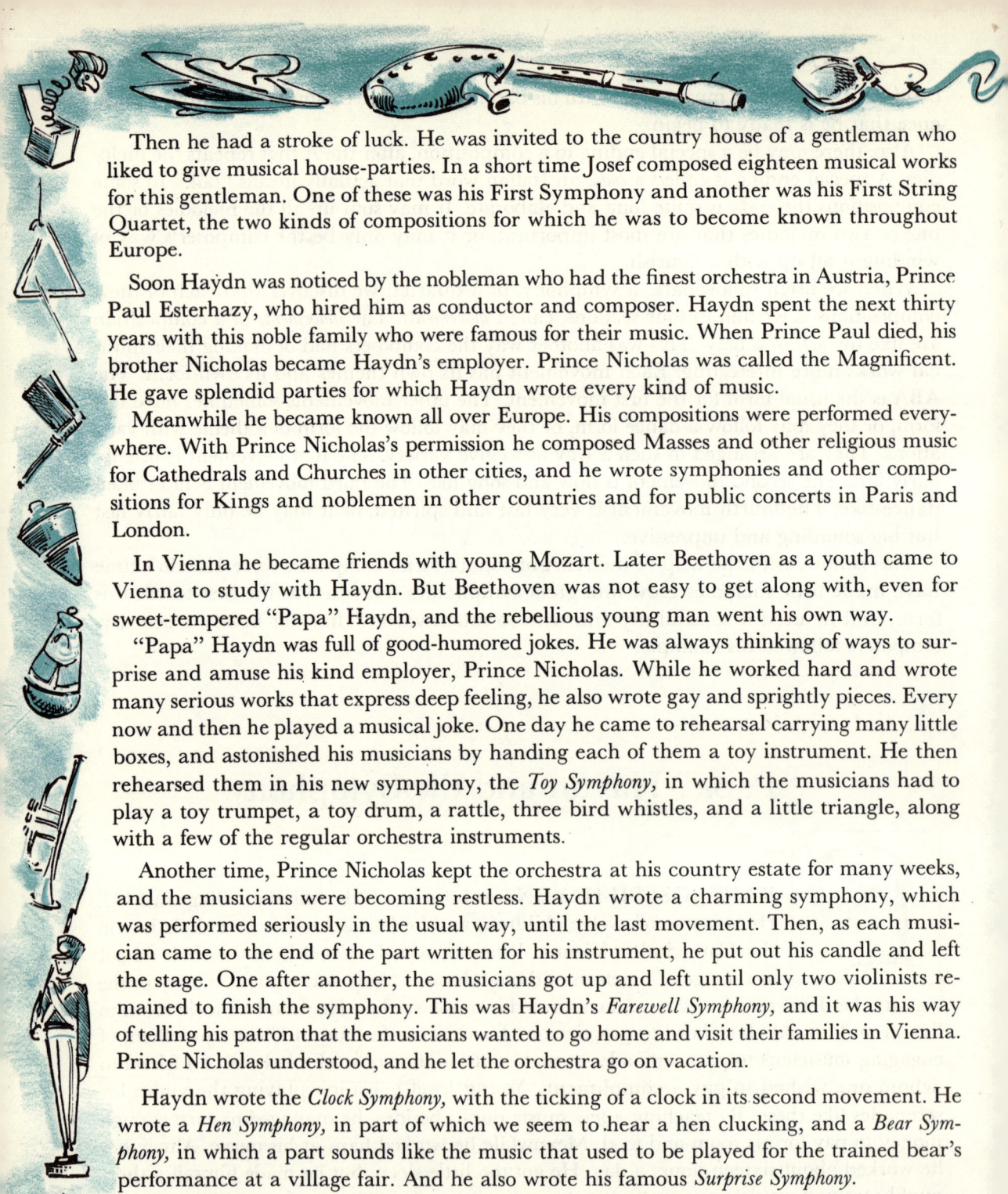

"Papa" Haydn was full of good-humored jokes. He was always thinking of ways to surprise and amuse his kind employer, Prince Nicholas. While he worked hard and wrote many serious works that express deep feeling, he also wrote gay and sprightly pieces. Every now and then he played a musical joke. One day he came to rehearsal carrying many little boxes, and astonished his musicians by handing each of them a toy instrument. He then rehearsed them in his new symphony, the *Toy Symphony*, in which the musicians had to play a toy trumpet, a toy drum, a rattle, three bird whistles, and a little triangle, along with a few of the regular orchestra instruments.

Another time, Prince Nicholas kept the orchestra at his country estate for many weeks, and the musicians were becoming restless. Haydn wrote a charming symphony, which was performed seriously in the usual way, until the last movement. Then, as each musician came to the end of the part written for his instrument, he put out his candle and left the stage. One after another, the musicians got up and left until only two violinists remained to finish the symphony. This was Haydn's *Farewell Symphony*, and it was his way of telling his patron that the musicians wanted to go home and visit their families in Vienna. Prince Nicholas understood, and he let the orchestra go on vacation.

Haydn wrote the *Clock Symphony*, with the ticking of a clock in its second movement. He wrote a *Hen Symphony*, in part of which we seem to hear a hen clucking, and a *Bear Symphony*, in which a part sounds like the music that used to be played for the trained bear's performance at a village fair. And he also wrote his famous *Surprise Symphony*.

Besides his other works, Haydn composed 104 symphonies in all. Favorite ones nowadays, besides the *Surprise Symphony*, which is Number 94, and the *Clock Symphony*, which is

Number 101, are the Symphony Number 88, which he wrote for his Paris concerts, the Symphony Number 103, which has a roll of the drums in it and is called the *Drum-Roll Symphony,* and the *London Symphony,* Number 104. This last one was actually the seventh of the twelve symphonies he composed for the London concerts.

On his two visits to London Haydn was given a royal welcome. There were dinners in his honor, and Oxford University conferred on him the honorary degree of Doctor of Music. In celebration of this event, one of his London symphonies is named the *Oxford Symphony.* Haydn was impressed with the fine choral singing for which England is famous, and when he returned to Vienna he composed two oratorios, *The Creation* and *The Seasons.*

Haydn spent his old age living quietly in Vienna. Musicians came from everywhere to visit "Papa" Haydn. He was made an honorary citizen of Vienna, was elected to many honorary societies, and was presented with many medals and decorations. He died in 1809, at the age of seventy-seven.

Besides his great work in establishing the form of the symphony, as well as the quartet and other important musical forms, Haydn also worked out the first modern orchestra. Until his time an orchestra was any fairly large grouping of instruments, with the harpsichord filling in many parts of the music. The harpsichord was so important that the harpsichordist was usually also the conductor of the orchestra, as we saw in the story of Handel.

Haydn put together his orchestra out of regular groups of instruments: the strings, the wind instruments, and the percussion instruments. He used the different instruments of his orchestra so well, both in writing music for them and in conducting them, that the harpsichord was no longer needed to fill in. Since his time the orchestra has become larger, but it has not really changed. So Haydn was not only the father of the symphony; he was also the father of the symphony orchestra.

THE SURPRISE OF HAYDN'S "SURPRISE SYMPHONY" COMES IN THE SECOND MOVEMENT WHICH BEGINS WITH A GENTLE LITTLE FOLK TUNE:

THIS IS PLAYED AGAIN, VERY SOFTLY. AND THEN, SUDDENLY, THERE IS A LOUD CHORD, LIKE A BIG MUSICAL BANG! IN WHICH EVERY INSTRUMENT IN THE ORCHESTRA SOUNDS ITS LOUDEST. HAYDN EXPLAINED THAT THIS WAS "TO WAKE THE AUDIENCE UP." BUT THAT WAS JUST ONE OF HIS JOKES, BECAUSE AUDIENCES LISTENING TO HAYDN'S MUSIC NEVER FELL ASLEEP. THE "SURPRISE" WAS ONE OF OF TWELVE SYMPHONIES HE COMPOSED FOR CONCERTS HE CONDUCTED IN LONDON. AT EACH CONCERT HE CONDUCTED A NEW SYMPHONY. THE ENGLISH AUDIENCES WERE SO ENTHUSIASTIC THAT AT EVERY CONCERT THEY INSISTED ON ENCORES. SO WE CAN BE SURE THEY NEVER HAD TO BE WAKED UP!

Marvelous Mozart

WHEN Wolfgang Amadeus Mozart became Haydn's friend in Vienna he was only twenty-six years old, but he already had a long career in music behind him and he was world-famous. He was a great composer and had been a most remarkable child. When he was only three years old he could play the harpsichord, and before he was five he was composing little pieces.

Mozart was born in 1756 in the Austrian city of Salzburg. His father was a violinist and court composer for the Archbishop of Salzburg, and he taught the astonishing little boy. He was a kind and sympathetic father, and did everything he could to encourage his little boy's great talent. Wolfgang's sister Marianne, four years older than he, was also a gifted child, who played the harpsichord with the skill of a grown-up musician.

When Wolfgang was seven, the father took his two remarkable children on a tour of the capital cities of Europe. In Vienna the Emperor of Austria sat beside the little boy while he played and called him his "little magician." One day, while running across the polished floor of the palace, little Wolfgang slipped and fell. He was lifted up by the Princess Marie Antoinette. This was the same Marie Antoinette who later became the Queen of France and died in the French Revolution. The little boy said to the lovely Princess when she picked him up, "You are very kind. When I grow up I will marry you."

On this and other journeys that he made with his father, little Wolfgang played for Kings and Queens and famous composers everywhere in Europe. On a visit to Italy he was taken to hear the music in the famous Sistine Chapel in Rome. It was a long and complicated service, sung by two choirs. After hearing it only once, the little boy sat down and wrote out all the music from memory.

Wolfgang's father had hoped that when the boy reached manhood his fame would bring him a good position at the court of one of the Kings or noblemen who had admired him so much as a child. Sadly, this did not come to pass. When Mozart grew up he went to Vienna, and the rest of his life was a continual struggle with poverty.

Mozart married Constanze Weber, the daughter of the family in whose house he had been living. Even though he wrote a great number of successful musical works of all kinds, his music never brought him enough money to support his family. Sometimes, when there was no firewood or coal to heat the house, Mozart and his wife danced together to keep warm.

Through all these struggles he wrote the most delightful, charming music. He wrote witty comic operas and graceful compositions for all instruments and combinations of instruments. He wrote wonderful symphonies, concertos, and quartets, as well as Masses and other Church music.

One of his lovely light compositions often appears on concert programs today. Its German name, *Eine Kleine Nachtmusik,* means *A Little Serenade,* and it was one of the most popular compositions in Vienna at that time.

At a time when he was terribly poor, Mozart gave a series of concerts in Vienna in the hope of paying his debts. For these concerts Mozart wrote fifteen concertos for the piano, which was quickly becoming very popular and replacing the harpsichord.

Several of the concertos he wrote at this time of trouble are among the finest of Mozart's works, and they are played by leading musicians today. One of them, the Piano Concerto Number 20, in D Minor, was Beethoven's favorite. He played it after Mozart's death, in a concert given for the benefit of the young widow.

Mozart himself was pleased with his Vienna concertos. He wrote to his father, "The concertos are neither too easy nor too difficult; they are very brilliant and pleasant to the ear." Mozart was actually the first musician to play a concerto for that new instrument, the piano, in a public concert in Vienna.

Mozart was so gifted that with all his wonderful works for orchestra and various instruments, he also wrote brilliant and witty operas. For his first operas Mozart took stories from ancient times, as the early Italian opera composers used to do. Later his taste in stories became gayer and more in tune with his own times. The wealth and glamor of the Eastern countries, especially Turkey, were a fashionable subject of the day, and so one of Mozart's operas is called *The Abduction from the Seraglio.* Another opera, *Cosi Fan Tutte* (So Do They All), is a witty story about the fickleness of ladies who are trying to win rich husbands.

One of Mozart's most popular operas, called *The Marriage of Figaro,* is taken froma play by a French writer, Beaumarchais, who dared to write about the love affair of a nobleman's servant at a time when only noblemen were considered worth writing about, not their servants. This play was written just before the French Revolution, and the King of France tried to keep it from being performed because he thought it was too democratic! Mozart made it a delightful comedy, poking a little fun at the nobility but not more than they could enjoy.

Don Giovanni is Mozart's most dramatic opera. It tells the story of a handsome and heartless Spanish nobleman, Don Juan. Mozart's last opera, *The Magic Flute*, is a lovely melodic fairy tale. All these operas are still performed in leading American and European opera houses.

All of Mozart's operas were successes in their time, but jealous rivals gave him a great deal of trouble. Meanwhile his money worries and overwork combined to ruin his health. At the age of thirty-six he became ill and did not recover. There was no money to pay for a proper funeral, and his grave was unmarked. But friends and music-lovers mourned for him. His widow, Constanze, later married a man who wrote a book on Mozart's life, which was published as the first biography of Mozart. He also tried to make a collection of Mozart's compositions so that they should not be lost to the world. But Mozart had composed so many works, of so many kinds, that it was a task of many years to list them all. Years later, a German musical scholar named Koechel devoted himself to making a complete catalogue of Mozart's compositions. A title of one of Mozart's works usually has the letter K. or sometimes K.V., and a number after it. This refers to the way it is listed in Koechel's complete catalogue.

Some of Mozart's music for piano and other instruments requires great skill and can be played only by highly trained musicians. The concertos that he wrote for his own concert performances are for great pianists such as he was himself. But he wrote charming piano sonatas when he was very young, and young pianists of today play and enjoy them as boys and girls have done since Mozart's time.

Beethoven, the Unhappy Genius

LUDWIG VAN BEETHOVEN was an unhappy genius. He was rebellious and impatient, and he had deep feelings that he could not express in words. He found the way to express these feelings in music, and this led to a new kind of music that is *expressive*. We shall see what this means as we go on with the story of this great composer.

Beethoven was born in the German city of Bonn, in 1770. His father was a singer in the Church choir, and he soon saw that Ludwig had musical ability. The father thought that Ludwig might be another wonder-child, like Mozart, and that he would make the family's name and fortune. He forced the little boy to practice long hours on the violin. Mozart's father had been kind, but Beethoven's father was impatient and often rough with him. Also, Beethoven's father was not reliable in earning a living for his family.

As young Ludwig grew up he had to take a great deal of responsibility. When he was fifteen, and was working in the Church as assistant organist, Ludwig was practically supporting the family. But he had kind teachers and some good friends, and he was lucky enough to get a position playing the viola in the opera orchestra in Bonn. There he became familiar with the operas of Mozart and other composers, and he learned a great deal about the instruments of the orchestra and how they played together. This was to be valuable to him later in his own composing.

When he decided to go to Vienna to study, the Archbishop at Bonn paid for his journey and other friends gave him letters to noblemen in Vienna. Beethoven was a very fine **pi**anist, besides being able to play the violin and other stringed instruments. The Viennese music-lovers quickly adopted him as a favorite concert performer. They liked his playing more than they did his musical compositions. They criticized every new work of Beethoven's because it was too different from the kind of music to which they were accustomed. But the Viennese soon realized that they had an extraordinary genius living among them, and they made every effort to keep him. When Beethoven had an offer to go to another city as an orchestra conductor, three noblemen of Vienna banded together to pay him a regular income every year if he would stay with them. He stayed, and went on composing his big, powerful symphonies, concertos, piano sonatas, and many other works.

But except for his music, Beethoven was not a happy man. Before he was thirty, he began to grow deaf. This was a terrible misfortune for a musician. His deafness came slowly and he was able to continue playing concerts until he was forty-four. But ten years later, when his great Ninth Symphony was performed for the first time, he could not hear at all. He was sitting on the stage at the performance, watching the conductor, and he had his back to the audience. One of the singers turned him around so that he could *see* the audience enthusiastically applauding this tremendous symphony.

Beethoven was a lonely man. Although he had fallen in love several times, he never married. His deafness made him still more lonely, for he would not go out in public at all. But he rose above his loneliness and his deafness through his music. He went on playing and composing at the piano long after he could not hear ordinary conversation. Even when he was totally deaf, he went on creating music that he could not hear except in his mind, expressing all the feelings he could not express to anyone in words. This was the time when he composed some of his most important music.

Beethoven would not go out to see people, but admirers came from far and near to see him. They carried on conversations with him in writing. Music-lovers sent him many presents. From England he received a gift of a fine grand piano, and another gift of the complete works of Handel. His adopted city of Vienna made him an honorary citizen.

During his last years, until he died in 1827 at the age of fifty-seven, Beethoven worked steadily at his music. He wrote his most important string quartets, a big religious choral composition called the *Missa Solemnis,* and the Ninth Symphony, which was unusual not only for the music itself but because for the first time a symphony for orchestra also had a chorus of voices.

Beethoven kept sketch-books in which he carefully worked out his compositions. These sketch-books, and the conversation books in which he carried on conversations with his visitors, have given musical scholars wonderful information about how the great composer worked, and about thoughts and ideas he had during those years when he lived and worked alone, hearing no sounds but the music in his mind.

The New Spirit Beethoven Brought to Music

Beethoven's music is different from all the music that had been written up to his time. It expresses troubled moods, stormy moods, and calm and thoughtful moods. It expresses great sorrow and great joy. During the years when he was growing up, music was not written to express such strong feelings. We must go back for a moment to the time of Haydn and Mozart to see just what this important difference is.

When Beethoven was a young man, gentlemen still wore rich brocaded coats with rows of ruffles at their cuffs, and they wore powdered wigs and hats with great plumes on them. Fine clothes and fine manners were important because they were the style of nobility. The nobility also set the style in music and the other arts, such as painting and literature. The *form* of a musical composition was important, and a composer was admired for his skill in carrying out the form of a piece of music in a graceful and polished way. A composer was not expected to express his serious thoughts or deep feelings in his music.

There were many composers of the time who had great success in writing elegant formal music. But their music is no longer interesting to us because it was nothing more than elegant and graceful.

Today we still enjoy the music of Mozart and Haydn not only because it is so graceful in its form and style but also because it is *expressive.* Mozart's operas, and the symphonies and other works of both Mozart and Haydn that we love today tell us a great deal about the kind of person the composer was and how he felt.

When Beethoven began composing, he wrote in the popular style of the day. His First Symphony, for instance, sounds very much like the symphonies of Mozart or Haydn. But as he went on, his music expressed more of himself. He followed the forms of the symphony, the sonata, the quartet, and the concerto that Haydn and Mozart had established, but his feelings were so strong that they could not have been expressed in the old elegant and graceful style. During Beethoven's lifetime, many of his admirers were shocked and disturbed by the turn his music was taking. Some of it was so stormy and troubled, and all of it was so powerful, that many people were puzzled on hearing his works for the first time.

We can hear how some of Beethoven's strong feelings are expressed, for example, in the famous *Moonlight Sonata*. This great piano sonata tells us of Beethoven's deep unhappiness and also of some serene and beautiful moments he experienced.

Beethoven had a fierce love of freedom. When the French Revolution began and Napoleon became the head of the French Army and saved his country, Beethoven wrote his Third Symphony in honor of Napoleon. But when Napoleon became a dictator and set out to conquer all of Europe, Beethoven angrily scratched Napoleon's name from the manuscript of his symphony and named it the *Eroica,* or the Heroic Symphony.

To write a symphony about an event of the times was a new thing to do. Composers of earlier times wrote a great deal of music to *celebrate* an event, such as a royal wedding or a nobleman's birthday. But Beethoven did not write his *Eroica* to celebrate anything. He wrote it to *express his feelings* about freedom and about the champion of freedom that he thought Napoleon was going to be. This symphony is not graceful music, but it is music with great power and feeling.

Beethoven's music has inspired people everywhere to have courage in time of trouble. His Fifth Symphony especially was an inspiration during World War II. The first four notes of this symphony were played by orchestras and bands at concerts and celebrations. In addition to their stirring sound, these four notes—three short and one long—have the same rhythm as the signal for the letter V (*dot, dot, dot, DASH*) in the telegraph code. Also, this was Beethoven's *Fifth Symphony,* or Symphony Number 5, and the Roman numeral 5 is V. So the great theme with which the *Fifth Symphony* begins came to be a signal that meant "V for Victory" and it made people think of and hope for the victorious end of the war.

The Opening Bars of **BEETHOVEN'S FIFTH SYMPHONY**

TWO CLARINETS AND ALL THE VIOLINS, VIOLAS, AND DOUBLE-BASSES, PLAYING THE SAME NOTES, LOUD.

SOFTLY NOW, ONE GROUP AT A TIME, 2ND VIOLINS—VIOLAS—1ST VIOLINS —REPEAT THE KNOCKING.

This startling theme is like the sound of someone knocking loudly at a door. Beethoven himself said that it meant Fate knocking at the door. Even if he had not said so, as we listen to this symphony we feel that the music tells of a great struggle, the struggle of human beings against Fate. The knocking theme is heard again and again, as other melodies strive to overcome it. At last man triumphs over Fate, and the music swells to a victorious end. In this symphony, with thrilling melodies and great sweeps of sound, Beethoven expressed his faith in the triumph of man's spirit.

Beethoven's courage in rising above sorrow is expressed in many of his works, and especially in his Ninth Symphony, the last one he wrote. When he was writing this symphony, he was so inspired by a poem, *Ode to Joy,* written by Friedrich Schiller, a leading German poet of the time, that he composed a magnificent chorus with the words of this poem for the fourth movement of his symphony. Not all of Beethoven's music gives us serious thoughts. A great deal of it is happy and gay. At the beginning of this story of music we talked about his Sixth Symphony, the *Pastorale,* which expresses his happy feelings and experiences in the country, with bird songs and the sound of brooks and the merry songs and dances of the country people. Beethoven also wrote many short compositions for the piano which are charming and gay, and simple enough for beginning pianists to play and enjoy. Some of his piano sonatas have been collected for more advanced students, and there are three sets of delightful pieces that he named *Bagatelles,* which is French for "trifles." The more we play or listen to Beethoven, the more we enjoy his music, for there is always a new treasure of meaning and beauty to be found in it.

There is also a great deal to be learned about music itself from the symphonies and other orchestral works of Beethoven, such as his overtures and concertos. Until Beethoven, no one had made such big and stunning music come from an orchestra or used so many changes and contrasts of sound to express the feelings of man.

The Exciting World of Romantic Music

BEETHOVEN'S thrilling, expressive music was music of the new century that was just beginning, the nineteenth century. The time of Haydn and Mozart, in the eighteenth century, is called the *classical* period in music, and the time of Beethoven and after, in the nineteenth century, is called the *romantic* period.

We often use the words *classical music* to mean all serious music or music that lasts from century to century, compared with *popular music* that lasts a season or two. In the story of music and other arts, *classical* can also mean a particular time and style. In music it means the time when composers paid great attention to the forms of music, when music followed many rules, as we have seen in the music of Haydn and Mozart.

The word *romantic* also has other meanings. We ordinarily talk of a story of love or adventure as *romantic*. In the story of music and the other arts, a work is described as *romantic* when it expresses the personality, the feelings, and the ideas of the composer or artist himself. This is what the music of Beethoven did.

Let us see how some of the composers who followed Beethoven expressed themselves in their music.

The spirit of freedom that Beethoven brought into music was part of a new spirit in all the arts during the nineteenth century. Painters, poets, and the writers of stories and plays were inspired by the new democratic ideas. They felt that every human being was important and his feelings and experiences were worth paying attention to, even though he might not be a king or a nobleman but just an ordinary man.

Painters, writers, and composers, too, were looking for new ways in which to express themselves. Many composers rebelled at the old forms, even those in which Beethoven expressed himself. They experimented with the various tones of the instruments in the orchestra to create a musical picture or a musical mood, to express the idea of a poem, or to tell a story.

They often wrote an explanation in words to go with their music, to explain the idea they meant to express. An explanation of this kind was called a *program* for the music, and music that told a story or described a scene came to be called *program music*.

Composers wrote music for the poems and stories of their own time, and also for great poems and stories of the past. They were attracted by the fairy tales and old legends that were being written by the brothers Grimm and other writers of the time. They liked the old stories of lovers and conspirators, of strange happenings in mysterious castles and dark forests. Often the same famous story was used over and over again by different composers. Thus it came about that Shakespeare's beautiful love story, *Romeo and Juliet,* was used for a number of operas and symphonic poems, all by different composers. Another favorite story was the legend of Faust, an old philosopher who sold his soul to the Devil in order to be young again.

These years of the nineteenth century, the *romantic* century, were a time of great musical excitement. Writers wrote about music as "the language of the emotions." Musicians and music critics carried on long discussions in letters and in articles for the magazines. They often quarreled and called each other rude names when they disagreed. Many composers took to writing in order to express their ideas about how music should be composed, and what was good or bad in music. Furious arguments went on in the coffee shops where musicians gathered to drink coffee and gossip about this fascinating subject.

Meanwhile in Germany three great romantic composers were following in Beethoven's footsteps. They were Schubert, Mendelssohn, and Schumann.

Franz Schubert's Lovely Songs and Symphonies

WHILE Beethoven was still alive, there was a shabby young schoolteacher who often came to the Vienna coffee shops. He was too shy and modest to take much part in the arguments, but he liked to be with people and especially with musicians. He was so poor that he rarely could afford to have heat in his room, and he went to the coffee shops to keep warm. He sat jotting down on old pieces of paper the many lovely melodies that came to his mind. This was Franz Schubert.

Schubert was born in a suburb of the great musical city of Vienna just before the end of the eighteenth century, in 1797. His father was a poor schoolmaster, and Franz was one of a large family that loved music. His father taught him to play the violin, and one of his older brothers gave him piano lessons. Like so many composers, he became a choirboy and was given the rest of his education in the choir school of the Austrian Emperor's own private Church. Franz played violin and viola in the school orchestra and came to know and love the symphonies of Haydn, Mozart, and Beethoven. Meanwhile a friendly young carpenter used to take him to a piano warehouse, where Franz could practice on a better piano than the family had at home.

Franz's father thought schoolteaching a more dependable career than music, and got Franz a position teaching in his own school. But Franz was not suited for teaching. He had been composing since he was thirteen, writing quartets that he played with his father and brothers at home on Sundays. He had also written a symphony, an opera, Church music, a cantata for his father's name-day, and the first of his many beautiful songs. Music came easily to Franz. He wrote fifteen songs in two days, at the same time as he was teaching school and studying musical composition. He was nearsighted, and he used to sleep with his eyeglasses on so that he would not waste a moment in the morning but could get right to work at his composing as soon as he woke up.

Young Franz was terribly poor, but he was a happy warm-hearted youth and he was rich in friends. When he was a boy his school-friends spent their own pocket money to keep him supplied with music paper for his compositions. Later, while he was teaching school, one of these friends who was a law student suggested that Franz should come to live with him as his guest, so that he could compose without having to worry about money.

From then on, Franz was almost entirely supported by his good friends. A poet, a singer, and several students made up the gay young group. They ate their meals together, and whoever happened to have enough money paid for the food. Franz lived first with one and then with another of them. They had "Schubert Evenings" at which they entertained their guests with the music of their beloved Franz and tried to get people interested in him.

One summer Schubert had the position of music master to the famous Esterhazy family who had been Haydn's patrons. For a while he was hopelessly in love with his pupil, the young Countess. Occasionally one of his friends would take him on a vacation trip to the country. Wherever he was, Franz composed music in his mind and wrote it down the moment he could.

He had many disappointments. His friends persuaded music publishers to print his compositions, but the publishers were not enthusiastic and paid him very little money. He wrote several operas, and they were not successful. In spite of his disappointments, beautiful music kept streaming from his pen.

Still, it grieved Schubert that his music was not appreciated, and he did not like to live on the generosity of his friends. His health began to fail, and when he was not quite thirty-two years old he became ill with typhus fever and died.

Shy lovable Schubert was so modest that he thought little of his own compositions. He left many of them lying about, or gave them away. Some, like his wonderful *Unfinished Symphony,* he never completed. After his death a few smaller compositions were published, but his important works were neglected until other composers came to search for them.

Ten years after Schubert's death, another composer, Robert Schumann, found the dusty manuscript of one of Schubert's fine symphonies in Vienna, and took it back to Leipzig, where Felix Mendelssohn conducted a performance of it.

Forty years more had passed before Schubert's music was discovered again. Then two Englishmen came to Vienna on a holiday trip. One of them was Sir Arthur Sullivan, the composer of *Onward, Christian Soldiers* and many other hymns, and also of the wonderful Gilbert and Sullivan comic operas such as *The Mikado* and *H.M.S. Pinafore.* Sir Arthur and his friend, who was a musical scholar, rescued a great deal of Schubert's music. They were so excited about their discovery that they made people pay attention to this neglected music, and a leading publisher at last made a collection and published it. Thus most of Schubert's music was saved from being lost forever.

Schubert was a poet in music. He wrote more than 600 songs, and some of them are familiar to us all, such as his *Serenade* and his *Ave Maria.* Schubert also wrote the music for the well-known songs *Hark! Hark! the Lark* and *Who Is Sylvia?* from Shakespeare's plays. The music he wrote for great poems tells the story along with the words.

One of his most famous songs, *The Elf-King,* was written to a poem by the great German writer Goethe. It tells a fairy tale about how a little boy, riding home with his father on a dark night, was stolen away by the King of the Elves. In Schubert's music for this song, we can hear the rhythm of the horse's hoofs and feel the darkness and loneliness of the night, and we can hear the voice of the Elf-King coaxing the boy to come with him to fairyland. In another song, *The Trout,* the music is bright and quick and makes us think of the darting of the bright little fish through the sparkling waters of a brook. Schubert also used this lovely melody in a composition for string quartet and piano, *The Trout Quintet.*

Another of his dramatic songs, *Death and the Maiden,* has the same melody as one of his beautiful quartets for string instruments. Schubert also sometimes wrote several songs connected with each other by the same idea. One of these, which concert singers often sing, is called *The Winter Journey.*

Schubert's compositions for instruments are as beautiful and melodious as his songs. Like Beethoven, Schubert wrote nine symphonies. The early ones are not often performed, but the Eighth and Ninth Symphonies are favorites on concert programs.

The Eighth Symphony is the *Unfinished Symphony.* A complete symphony consists of four movements, but Schubert finished only two for this symphony. They are very beautiful, and their themes are especially familiar because a popular composer, Sigmund Romberg, wrote a musical play about Schubert, *Blossom Time,* and he used themes from the *Unfinished Symphony* for songs in the play.

Schubert's Ninth Symphony is also full of beautiful melodies, and it is like Beethoven's symphonies in its harmonies and the skill with which Schubert worked out the forms. Schubert was the first of the *romantic* composers who followed Beethoven in the nineteenth century.

Mendelssohn
the Boy Who Wrote Fairyland Music

FELIX MENDELSSOHN, the next romantic composer after Schubert, was as different as possible from the poor young schoolteacher. Born in 1809, Mendelssohn was the child of a rich and cultured family. The Mendelssohn home in Berlin was a gathering place for famous musicians, poets, and the most celebrated men and women of the time.

Young Felix began to compose as a child. He used to sit on a high stool and conduct while his sisters and brother, and famous musicians who were his father's guests, played

348

his music. He wrote symphonies, operas, and charming trios and quartets for various instruments. When he was only seventeen he composed the famous Overture to Shakespeare's fairy-tale play, *A Midsummers Night's Dream.* Some years later he went on to write more music for this play. One of the compositions in this suite is the *Wedding March,* which has been played at weddings ever since. Felix also played his first piano concert when he was nine years old, and went on to become famous all over Europe as a concert pianist.

All this good fortune and admiration did not spoil the gifted boy. From childhood on, he worked hard for the sake of music and did a great deal to help and encourage other composers and musicians. He was only a young boy when one day in the library he read the music of Bach's *St. Matthew Passion.* This great choral work, together with all of Bach's music, had been neglected since the old master's death, seventy-five years before. When Felix discovered it, he could not rest until it was performed. At last, when he was twenty, he conducted a chorus of 350 voices in this great work. Later he became a friend of Robert Schumann, and these two, with a third musician friend, established a famous school of music, the Leipzig Conservatory. In that city, where Bach had taught and composed for so many years, Mendelssohn succeeded in having a monument put up in honor of the old master, and he paid almost all the expenses himself.

Mendelssohn traveled through Europe and England constantly, playing and conducting concerts of his own works and the works of composers he admired and wanted to make famous. He was greatly loved by his English audiences and was a favorite with Queen Victoria. When he was in England he wrote the rest of his *Midsummer Night's Dream* music as accompaniment to performances of the Shakespeare play. A visit to Scotland inspired him to write his *Scotch Symphony* and the overture, *Fingal's Cave,* with its magical atmosphere. The fine choral singing for which England is famous led him to compose two oratorios, *Elijah* and *St. Paul.* Another time, after a trip to Italy, he composed his gay *Italian Symphony.* He wrote songs, and he composed a great many lovely piano pieces that he called *Songs Without Words.* A familiar piano composition is Mendelssohn's *Spring Song.*

He had an extraordinary memory for music, and he was one of the first musicians to play a concerto without using the notes. But he did not like to show off. Once, when he was playing a trio with two other musicians, his copy of the music was mislaid. He put another book upside down on his music stand and asked someone to turn the pages, because he did not want people to see that he was playing by heart when the other musicians were playing from the notes. After the first London performance of his *Midsummer Night's Dream* Overture, a friend left the music in a cab. Mendelssohn wrote out the whole overture again from memory.

Mendelssohn was not physically strong, and he did not spare himself in his efforts to spread a love of music. Right after a wonderful first performance of his oratorio *Elijah,* in England, he was told of the sudden death of his beloved sister Fanny. He collapsed from the shock, and although he recovered enough to write several more fine musical works, he died when he was only thirty-eight years old, in 1847.

Mendelssohn's music expresses his gentle character and his personality as a graceful, cultured gentleman. He established new forms of music with his poetic *Songs Without Words* and with his overtures, which were meant to be played not as introductions to a play or an opera but as concert music. Other composers followed him in using these forms, and in using the tones of the different instruments in the orchestra to express a mood or describe a scene by means of music. No other music has such delicate grace as Mendelssohn's fairyland music.

Mendelssohn is also honored for his unselfish work in spreading a love and appreciation of music, and especially in re-discovering one of the world's great treasures, the music of Bach.

Schumann Wrote Music of Childhood

ROBERT SCHUMANN, Mendelssohn's friend, was the enthusiastic friend and teacher of many younger composers, and especially of the great Johannes Brahms, who followed him. He was also the first composer to write not only music for children to play, as Bach had done for his own children, but also music about children and the experiences of childhood.

Schumann was an intense, sensitive man who might have been a fine writer if he had not been a composer. He was born near Leipzig in 1810, a year after Mendelssohn. His father was an editor and publisher and wanted his son to become a lawyer. Robert obediently studied law, but he wanted to be a pianist. In his impatience he used a mechanical device to exercise and strengthen his fingers. The instrument injured one of his fingers permanently so that he could never become a concert pianist.

He had been composing music and writing literary works even in childhood. After injuring his finger he devoted himself to composing, and he went on writing, too. When he was twenty-four, he and a group of musicians and writers in Leipzig founded a musical magazine. He created imaginary characters to express different points of view about music, and he signed their names to the articles he wrote for the magazine. He also invented an imaginary club, to promote good music and the other arts and to defend them against unappreciative people. In the Bible, David fought the Philistines, and so Schumann called his club the League of David, and he called the unappreciative people Philistines. This name has stuck through the years, and we still speak of people who care more for money and success than for music, literature, and other arts as Philistines.

At about this time Schumann fell ardently in love. His piano teacher's daughter, Clara, had been in love with him since she was a little girl of twelve, but he had never noticed her while he was a pupil of her father's. Now she had become a young lady and a brilliant pianist. Clara's father would not hear of her marrying the struggling young com-

HOW SCHUMANN WROTE ABOUT CHILDREN IN HIS MUSIC

ROBERT SCHUMANN LOVED CHILDREN, AND HE AND HIS WIFE CLARA HAD A LARGE HAPPY FAMILY. EVEN BEFORE HE WAS MARRIED HE COMPOSED HIS GROUP OF PIANO PIECES "SCENES FROM CHILDHOOD" DESCRIBING THE EXPERIENCES AND FEELINGS OF LITTLE BOYS AND GIRLS. HERE ARE THE MELODIES OF SOME OF THEM:

"ABOUT STRANGE LANDS AND PEOPLE"—DREAMY AND FARAWAY MUSIC.

"BLINDMAN'S BUFF"—A RUNNING, RACING TUNE FOR A LIVELY GAME.

"REVERIE (TRAUMEREI)"—THIS IS THE MOST FAMOUS ONE.

PERHAPS YOU RECOGNIZE THE LAST MELODY. OTHERS ARE "CURIOUS STORY," "PERFECTLY CONTENTED," "CHILD FALLING ASLEEP," "THE KNIGHT OF THE ROCKING HORSE." SCHUMANN WROTE THESE ABOUT CHILDREN BUT FOR ADVANCED PIANISTS TO PLAY. CLARA SCHUMANN PLAYED THEM AT HER CONCERTS. WHEN THEIR FIRST BOY WAS BORN SCHUMANN BEGAN WRITING THE "ALBUM FOR THE YOUNG," FOR CHILDREN TO PLAY AND ENJOY THEMSELVES. HERE ARE SOME OF THE TUNES:

"SOLDIERS' MARCH"—A QUICK TUNE IN MARCHING TIME.

"THE WILD HORSEMAN"—FOR A CHILD GALLOPING ON AN IMAGINARY HORSE.

"THE HAPPY FARMER"—A CHEERFUL COUNTRY SONG.

THE MELODY OF THIS ONE IS IN THE LEFT HAND. SCHUMANN WROTE A "HUNTING SONG," A "REAPER'S SONG," AND OTHER SONG-LIKE PIECES IN THIS GROUP. HE ALSO WROTE PIECES FOR SPRING, HARVEST, WINTER; SAD PIECES FOR TIMES WHEN A CHILD FEELS SAD, AND MANY GAY ONES FOR HAPPY MOODS.

poser-writer. But after four years of asking, the determined Robert finally forced him to consent to the marriage.

Robert and Clara Schumann had a story-book life together, full of love and understanding. In his happiness Robert composed more beautiful music than ever. During the first year of his marriage he wrote a hundred and fifty love songs for Clara.

When his children came along, Schumann composed music for them. In his two famous groups of piano pieces, *Scenes from Childhood* and *Album for the Young,* Schumann expressed the feelings and experiences of childhood. Children through the years have played his energetic *Knight Rupert, The Wild Horseman,* and *The Happy Farmer,* and gentler pieces like *First Loss* and *May, Sweet May. Scenes From Childhood* include such charming pieces as *About Strange Lands and People, Child Falling Asleep, Frightening, Perfectly Contented,* and the lovely *Reverie* (Traumerei). These pieces are not very hard to play, but they are so tender and true to childhood that professional pianists often play them as a group on concert programs, and they have been recorded by leading musicians.

Schumann's ideal happiness at home was not matched by happiness in his musical life. He was too intense and emotional to be a good teacher or a good orchestra conductor. He had spells of depression, and he seemed to hear the single note A, to which orchestra instruments are tuned, continually sounding in his ears. When he was forty-four he became so gloomy that he threw himself into the icy waters of the Rhine River. He was rescued, but he was put in a mental hospital where he remained until he died two years later, in 1856.

Clara Schumann went back to her concert career after her husband's death. Until she was a very old lady she devoted herself to playing his compositions and making them known. Schumann wrote four symphonies, a 'cello concerto, and other orchestral music. He also wrote a piano concerto and a great many short piano compositions besides a number of more ambitious works for piano solo. One that is most frequently played, and was made into a ballet, is *Carnaval.* This is a charming fantasy of a masked carnival. Its characters are storybook people like Pierrot, Columbine, and Harlequin, along with the imaginary characters that Schumann invented for his musical magazine, including the League of David and the Philistines.

Schumann is also remembered for a prediction he made in his magazine. When he met Johannes Brahms he predicted that this young man would become one of the world's greatest composers, and his prophecy came true.

Brahms, the Third of the Three Great B's

IN MUSIC we often talk of the Three B's, meaning the three great composers: Bach, Beethoven, and Brahms.

The third one, Johannes Brahms, was born in Hamburg in 1833. His father played the double-bass, the big bass viol, in the theater orchestra, and he taught the boy to play the violin, the 'cello, and the horn. Young Johannes helped earn money for the family by playing at dances. He began to study the piano when he was seven, and when he was ten his teacher persuaded a more famous teacher of the time to take the boy as his pupil. This teacher set Johannes hard at work studying Bach and Beethoven. When he was fifteen, young Brahms played his first piano concert. On his program was one of Bach's fugues.

Until he was twenty Brahms earned a living in Hamburg by continuing to play at dances, giving lessons, and doing other musical odd jobs. Then he played the piano accompaniment for a visiting Hungarian concert violinist, and the violinist took him along on his concert tour. Through his friendship with this violinst, Brahms met Robert and Clara Schumann, and his whole life changed. With their encouragement he settled down to composing. Robert persuaded the leading German music publishers to publish the young man's music, and Clara helped Brahms get an appointment at the court of a nobleman near Hamburg so that he did not need to worry any more about money.

After Robert Schumann's death Brahms continued to be a devoted friend to Clara. He sent her many of his compositions to criticize and wrote her beautiful letters. He had other friends, but his friendship for Clara Schumann was the most important of his life.

Brahms lived quietly in Hamburg and afterward in Vienna, where he spent the greater part of his long life. An angry feud was going on during these years between the followers of Richard Wagner, the opera composer, and the followers of music in the older tradition of Beethoven. The Beethoven followers adopted Brahms as their ideal, but Brahms himself did not take part in the quarrel. He was busy conducting choral groups, going on long concert tours, and composing.

Like the careful craftsman he was, Brahms practiced composing for orchestra before he wrote his first symphony. His graceful melodious *Serenades* were actually some of his practice pieces. At last, when he was forty-three years old, his First Symphony was performed. The Second Symphony followed in the next year, and within the next ten years he finished two more symphonies and three of his concertos, besides other compositions. When he was given an honorary University degree, he composed his light-hearted *Academic Festival Overture* out of student songs, and conducted it at the University. Brahms was sixty-four years old and at the height of his success when he died in 1897. His grave is in Vienna, close to the graves of Beethoven and Schubert.

Brahms was like Beethoven in his ways as well as in his music. He lived alone and worked diligently, rewriting and polishing a piece of music until he was satisfied with it. He was gruff with strangers, but with his friends he was charming, witty, and loyal. He did not like public show, and he was so modest about his own works that it embarrassed him to have a fuss made about his music. In portraits he is pictured as a genial, grandfather-like old man with a flowing beard, smoking a cigar.

Brahms wrote every kind of music except opera. His symphonies and concertos have the greatness of form and expression that Beethoven first brought to orchestral music. Besides the strength of his music, his melodies have great sweetness, and his harmonies are rich and beautiful. Brahms also wrote tender songs and a number of great choral works. He wrote quartets and other chamber music, and many charming small pieces for the piano and other instruments. Many of his piano compositions, such as the Intermezzi, Waltzes, and Fantasias, can be played by moderately advanced piano students. He wrote his lively *Hungarian Dances* as a result of his friendship with the Hungarian violinist who had taken him along on a concert tour when he was a young man. His songs are full of lovely melody. One that is familiar to all of us is his *Cradle Song*.

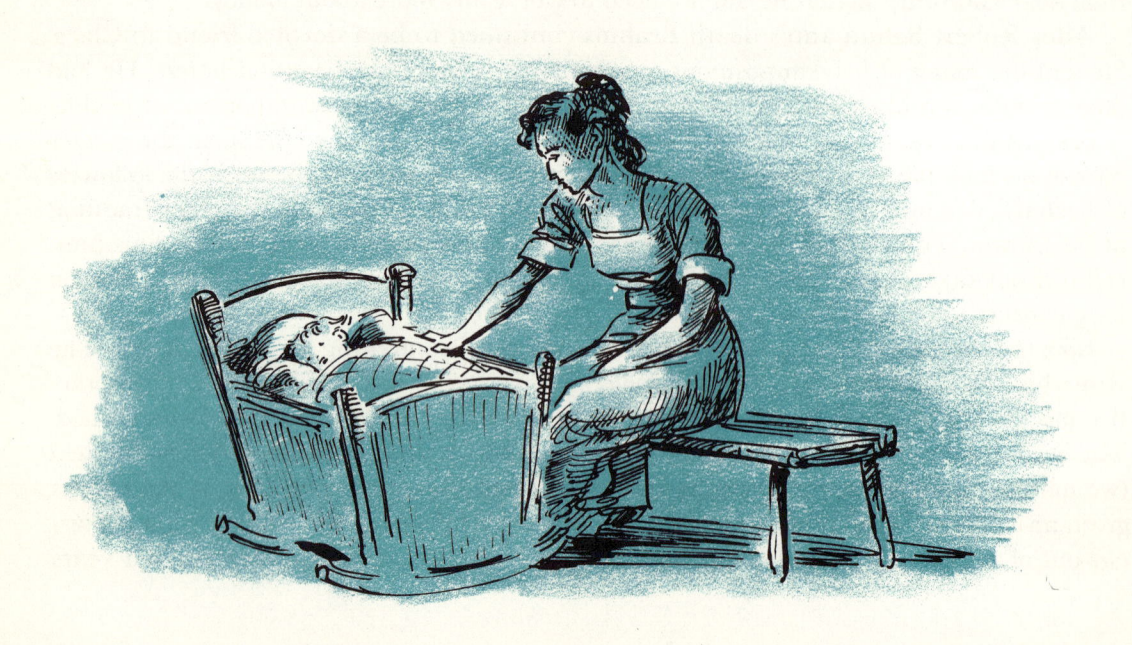

Tenderly
p

Lul - la - by and good night! With ros - es be - dight,

Music of Far Lands and People

EVERY country has its own language and customs, its own holidays and ways of celebrating them, its own fairy tales and folk tales, and its own folk music. In the nineteenth century, many composers turned to the folk songs and dances of their native lands for inspiration. Love of country —patriotism—was one of the strong emotions they wanted to express. They wanted to describe in their music the atmosphere and spirit of their homeland and its people, and they even wanted to paint musical pictures of how the country looked.

Franz Liszt was one of the first of the patriotic composers. He used the folk tunes and rhythms of his country, Hungary, in much of his music, and he encouraged other composers to do the same. Many of the nineteenth century composers followed his example.

Franz Liszt, the Prince of Pianists

Franz Liszt was a Hungarian, and the *Hungarian Rhapsodies* he composed are most familiar to us. These compositions, plus Liszt's teaching and encouragement, inspired many composers to write of their own countries, as we shall see.

Liszt composed a great deal of music in many forms. He was one of the greatest pianists the world has ever known, and of course he wrote music for the piano. He also wrote symphonies, choral works, and many charming songs.

All the same, Liszt is remembered today chiefly for the encouragement he gave to other composers and for his efforts to make people appreciate great music. He dared to play the music of Beethoven in his concerts at a time when the newer romantic music was more popular. He played whole symphonies of Beethoven on the piano, and he wrote out Beethoven's great Ninth Symphony so that it could be played on two pianos. He insisted that a statue should be put up in Beethoven's native city of Bonn, and he paid most of the expense and conducted a festival of Beethoven's music when the statue was completed. Liszt also wrote articles about the works of Robert Schumann and he composed a sonata in honor of Schumann. He would have been a friend to Brahms too, but Brahms as a young man did not like the crowd of admirers around Liszt. Liszt fought for Richard Wagner's new kind of opera. His daughter Cosima became Wagner's wife.

Liszt's whole life was romantic and glamorous. He was born in 1811, the son of a clerk employed by the famous Esterhazy family. A group of rich Hungarians paid for the gifted boy's education. He grew up to be a handsome, dashing gentleman, and his success as a pianist made him rich. He was as generous with money as with his time and effort in helping other composers. When he was thirty-seven years old he suddenly gave up playing in public, and went to live on his princely estate in Weimar, Germany, which became a musical center for musicians and composers from all over Europe. He continued to teach, never taking payment, until he died in 1886, an honored old man of seventy-five.

Great Music from a Small Country

A great deal of wonderful music expressing love of country came from one of the small countries that made up the Empire of Austria-Hungary. This land became part of Czechoslovakia after the First World War, but in the nineteenth century and for centuries before, it was called Bohemia. A Bohemian composer, Bedrich Smetana, wrote one of the first folk operas about his own country, using folk tunes and folk dances. This gay opera, *The Bartered Bride,* is often performed in opera houses and its overture is played on concert programs. Smetana also wrote a group of symphonic poems which he called *My Country.* A favorite composition in this group is *The Moldau,* a musical picture of the great River Moldau that runs past the city of Prague. The composition begins with rippling music like the swift mountain springs that run together to form the river at its source, and then the music swells into a broad flowing melody like the broad smooth current of the river itself. The music also pictures the scenes through which the river flows. At one place there is a village wedding going on, and in the music we hear the sounds of celebration and the tune of a merry peasant polka

Antonin Dvorák, another Bohemian, is best known in this country for his symphony about America, the *New World Symphony.* Dvorák spent four years in New York as Director of a music school, and he encouraged his American pupils to become interested in American folk music. He himself was inspired to write not only his famous symphony but *The American Quartet* and other works about this country. His *New World Symphony* has some of the rhythms and feeling of American Indian and Negro music, and one theme is very much like a Negro spiritual. Words have been written to this theme for a song called *Going Home.* Dvorák also wrote a good deal of lovely music out of love of his own country.

HERE IS THE SLOW SONG-LIKE THEME, THE BOHEMIAN COMPOSER'S IMPRESSION OF A SAD PLANTATION SONG. IT IS SOMETIMES SUNG AS A NEGRO SPIRITUAL CALLED "GOING HOME."

As a young man he was inspired by Brahms to write his *Slavonic Dances,* which are well known and often performed. He wrote many piano compositions and songs. A favorite song of his is called *Songs My Mother Taught Me.*

Bartók Discovered Different Folk Music

Another part of Austria-Hungary, which later became Yugoslavia, was the birthplace of an important composer of the twentieth century, Béla Bartók. Bartók spent his later years in the United States, but it was only after he died in 1945 that American music-lovers realized what an unusual genius had been living among them, unappreciated and in poverty.

As a young man Bartók traveled through his own country, into distant villages, over rough forest and mountain roads, and he collected thousands of folk melodies. Many of these were very different from the sweet melodies that earlier composers had used for their music. He found wild and primitive songs and dances among people who had been great warriors in times past, and who still lived a rugged life as hunters in the mountain villages.

The wild rhythms and harmonies of these melodies, and the sounds of the lonely woods and mountains where he traveled, inspired Bartók to write a new kind of music of his own. Right after his death, his music began to be played everywhere by concert artists and symphony orchestras, and some of his concertos, piano works, and string quartets are now frequently heard and admired. Much of Bartók's music is hard to listen to at first because it is new and different. But when we listen to one composition several times, we come to appreciate its strange beauty and expressiveness.

Not all of Bartók's music is strange. Out of the thousands of folk songs and dances that he discovered he composed many beautiful little piano pieces which are played and loved by children. Their titles tell something about the kind of music they are: *Sun, Come Out!, Dearie, Dearie, Do You Have a Daughter?, A Hawk Flew on the Branch, Old Maid's Song, The Grasshopper's Wedding, Do Not Come to My Garden!*—and there are many more.

Music from the Far North

One of the many young composers whom Franz Liszt encouraged was the Norwegian, Edvard Grieg. Grieg was born in 1843 and lived into the twentieth century, to 1907. He began composing as a schoolboy and was sent to Germany to study music. When he went back to Norway he organized an orchestra and devoted himself to his country's music. His beautiful Piano Concerto is a favorite on concert programs. So is his *Peer Gynt Suite,* a group of compositions inspired by stories of the Norwegian fairy tale hero, Peer Gynt. Young pianists often play *Anitra's Dance* from this suite. Another familiar part is *In the Hall of the Mountain King.* Many of Grieg's songs and piano compositions have been popular, and he was honored in his lifetime as Norway's leading composer.

Another twentieth century composer from a far northern country is Jan Sibelius of Finland. Sibelius was born in 1865 and lived to a very old age. His music belongs mostly to the twentieth century. He studied in Germany and Austria, and went home to write music about his native land. The hero legends and folk tales of Finland, its folk music, and especially the atmosphere of that northern country with its long dark winters and its sudden beautiful summers—all this is the inspiration of Sibelius's music. He is a national hero of Finland and his birthdays have been celebrated all over the world. Most familiar among his many great compositions are the stirring symphonic poem, *Finlandia,* and the sadly beautiful *Swan of Tuonela.*

Frederick Chopin, a Poet of the Piano

Frederick Chopin spent half of his short life in Paris, but from boyhood he loved the folk dances of his country, Poland, and they inspired some of his finest piano compositions. Chopin wrote two piano concertos and some chamber music compositions, but all the rest of his music was for the piano alone. In his writing for the piano, he found new ways to bring out richer tones and harmonies and more varied effects than had been known before.

Chopin was born in 1810 and grew up in the Polish capital, Warsaw. He was a gentle, sensitive boy who would burst into tears over a beautiful melody. He played his first concert when he was eight and published his first compositions when he was fifteen. When he was twenty he left Poland on a concert tour. In Paris he liked it so well and was so enthusiastically welcomed that he remained there for the rest of his life, composing, teaching, and playing for his friends at fashionable gatherings. He had many friends, among them Franz Liszt, and he also had a romantic friendship with the famous French woman writer who was known as George Sand. Chopin's health was delicate, and when he was only thirty-nine years old he died of tuberculosis. A little jar of Polish earth that he had brought with him from home, twenty years before, was buried with him.

Chopin's piano compositions were popular during his lifetime and are played and loved everywhere. Some are short and not too difficult for students, and others are only for very fine pianists. He wrote a great many kinds of piano music, among them waltzes, *mazurkas*, and *polonaises*. The *mazurka* is a lively Polish peasant dance, and the *polonaise* is a dignified, ceremonial court procession of noblemen from the time when Poland was a kingdom.

Many of Chopin's compositions are called simply *Etudes*. This is the French word for *studies,* or exercise pieces, but in spite of that bare title the *études* often express the composer's deepest feelings. A famous one is the *Revolutionary Etude*. Poland at that time was divided into three parts, ruled by three different countries, Russia, Germany, and Austria, and the Polish people longed to have a free and united country. Chopin wrote this composition out of unhappy patriotism, at a time when part of Poland had flared up in one of many unsuccessful rebellions against the foreign rulers.

Some of Chopin's compositions are strong and stirring. Others are like graceful dances, and a group of them has been made into the ballet, *Les Sylphides*. Still others are dreamy and poetic, with lovely song-like melodies.

Music from the Russian Steppes and Villages

When the Russian composers became interested in their country's folk music, they uncovered a rich treasure. The Russian Czar ruled over many different peoples. Along the great rivers, in the mountains, and on the vast prairie lands of the steppes, there were thatched villages of the peasants and there were tent camps of fierce wandering tribes. There was music of many different kinds: sad songs of loneliness and longing, dance tunes with the energetic rhythms of Russian peasant dances, as well as songs and dances that had an Oriental strangeness and mystery.

For many centuries, Russians had had little to do with Western Europe. In the eighteenth century, under the rule of Catherine the Great, Russian noblemen began to travel in Europe, and they brought back an interest in European music. Italian opera composers were invited to Russia to produce their operas. The nobility, following the fashion in

Europe, engaged household musicians. Music of Haydn and Mozart was played at parties. The famous Razoumovsky Quartets by Beethoven were actually ordered by a Russian nobleman, Count Razoumovsky, who was the Russian Ambassador in Vienna in Beethoven's time.

In the nineteenth century, Russian composers began to write their own operas, with Russian folk stories and music based on Russian folk melodies. Michael Glinka was one of these composers, and the overture to his opera, *Russlan and Ludmilla,* is played on symphony programs. In about the year 1860, in the capital city which was then called St. Petersburg, five young gentlemen got together with the intention of composing truly Russian music. Only one of them, Mily Balakireff, had had much musical training, and he taught the others. He was a good teacher but his pupils were the better composers. All four of them wrote music that became famous in Europe.

César Cui, an artillery officer in the Czar's Army, wrote several operas, but only one composition of his is played nowadays, a violin piece called *Orientale.* The other three composers were Modeste Moussorgsky, Alexander Borodin, and Nicholas Rimski-Korsakov.

Moussorgsky's Famous Musical Pictures

Modeste Moussorgsky was a young guardsman in the Army. He had grown up on his family's estate in the country, and he knew a good deal about the life of the poor peasants and their music. His biggest work is the opera, *Boris Godounov,* with a story out of Russian history about an ambitious man who committed a murder to make himself the Czar. It is full of folk themes and folk beliefs, and it has impressive musical effects. Music from a colorful folk opera *Khovantchina,* and a symphonic poem with the sounds of witches and spirits, *Night on Bald Mountain,* are played on orchestra programs.

A favorite composition by Moussorgsky is a suite of piano pieces, *Pictures at an Exhibition,* in which the music describes an exhibition of paintings by an artist friend of the composer. Some of the pictures are: a scene of old women chattering at a village market, a ballet of unhatched chickens, and a Russian fairy tale about a witch whose house in the woods turns around and around on chicken legs. There is also a musical description of the composer himself walking around the picture gallery, looking at the pictures. This fine composition is often played by concert pianists, and it is also played by orchestras in a wonderful arrangement that was made by the modern French composer, Maurice Ravel. Moussorgsky loved children, and he wrote a group of delightful children's songs. One of them, called *No, You Don't, Pussy!,* is a child's story of how the cat tried to get into the bird cage.

Borodin, Wrote of Mysterious Eastern Lands

Alexander Borodin was a medical doctor and a professor of chemistry. He helped to establish a medical college for women and he taught there, and he also wrote scientific articles. With all this professional work, he found time to play the piano and the 'cello, and to compose two symphonies, two string quartets, some songs and short compositions, and an opera, *Prince Igor*. A suite of the wildly exciting dances from *Prince Igor* is played by symphony orchestras and it is also the music of a famous ballet. Borodin's music has the mysterious haunting flavor of Eastern lands. It suggests vast spaces, savage huntsmen riding, and lovely veiled girls dancing.

Rimski-Korsakov and the Arabian Nights

Nicholas Rimski-Korsakov became the most generally popular of the Russian Five. He composed the well-known suite for orchestra, *Scheherazade*. This is the name of the young Queen in the *Arabian Nights* fairy tales, who was condemned to death and managed to postpone her execution by telling the Sultan a new story every night for one thousand and one nights. In the end, of course, the Sultan forgave her and she did not die. In his suite about the wonderful story-telling Queen, Rimski-Korsakov painted a series of musical pictures of far places and marvelous adventures. His music describes a procession in the streets of Bagdad, the stormy experiences of Sinbad the Sailor, and the charming love story of the Young Prince and the Young Princess. There is also a delicate theme, played by a solo violin in the orchestra, that represents clever Scheherazade herself, beginning each story with "Once upon a time . . ." This suite was made into a ballet.

Rimski-Korsakov also wrote other orchestral works, and he wrote several operas, all with Russian folk and fairy tale stories. He became interested in music while he was an officer in the Russian Imperial Navy. At one time his ship visited the United States. He studied music diligently, and when he was appointed an inspector of the Navy's bands, he took the opportunity to become familiar with the instruments, especially the wind instruments that make up the largest part of a band. He taught himself so well that he became a fine composer and was eventually appointed a professor at the St. Petersburg Conservatory of Music. Here he taught many young composers who later became famous. He also finished and arranged for orchestra some of the compositions by his friends, who did not have enough musical training to work out their own ideas.

Rimski-Korsakov's music is full of melody, and it is also exciting for the rich musical coloring and the picturesque effects that he was able to achieve with the different sounds of the instruments and the harmonies of an orchestra.

Tchaikovsky Expressed His Sadness in Music

Peter Ilitch Tchaikovsky was the first Russian composer to become world-famous outside of Russia during his lifetime. He was born in 1840 in a small town, and was in training as a young lawyer when, at the age of twenty-three, he gave up his career and began to study music. For his graduation from the St. Petersburg Conservatory he wrote a cantata on the same poem that Beethoven had used in his Ninth Symphony, Schiller's *Ode to Joy*.

In his musical life Tchaikovsky was a fairly fortunate man. Although his first works were not appreciated, a wealthy Russian widow became interested in him and paid him a yearly allowance so that he could compose without having to worry about money. He never saw his patroness, because she made it a rule that they were never to meet, but he carried on a friendship with her in letters for thirteen years. He had been composing steadily, in spite of disappointments in his work and an unhappy marriage. With the help and interest of his unseen patroness, he was encouraged to go on. From this time he wrote music that won him invitations to conduct in Europe and the United States. He conducted in Carnegie Hall in New York City when the famous concert hall opened for its first season, in 1891.

In spite of his success, Tchaikovsky was a deeply unhappy man, and he expressed his unhappiness in some of his greatest music. Tchaikovsky's song, *None But the Lonely Heart*, tells his sadness, and many themes in his symphonies have the same quality of grieving and longing. His Sixth Symphony, which was his last work, is called the *Pathetic Symphony* because it is so full of this sadness. In his Fifth Symphony, there is a theme that suggests Fate, just as there is in Beethoven's Fifth Symphony. But as we saw in Beethoven's story, the great German composer found the strength and courage to rise against Fate, and his music expresses his belief that human beings can triumph over Fate. But Tchaikovsky felt defeated and unable to conquer his sadness, and we feel this in his music.

But there is also gayety and even high spirits in Tchaikovsky's music, and excitement, too, especially when he chose lively Russian folk music to use for his themes. He did not make a point of using his country's folk music and folk tales in his compositions. But all the same his music is full of the colorful background and the rich melodies of his native land. His Fourth Symphony is big-sounding and spirited, and it is full of folk melodies and folk-dance rhythms. In his *1812 Overture,* which is a musical description of Napoleon's defeat by Russia, the music roars and shouts with patriotic joy.

Besides his six symphonies, Tchaikovsky wrote two beautiful piano concertos, two symphonic poems, an opera, and many songs and short compositions. He wrote two fairy-tale ballets, *Swan Lake* and *The Sleeping Beauty. The Nutcracker Suite* is a group of delightful dances from the *Nutcracker* ballet. In it, toys and fairy-tale characters come to life. A theme from his symphonic poem, *Romeo and Juliet,* has been made into a popular song.

Tchaikovsky died in 1893, in a cholera epidemic in St. Petersburg, when he was fifty-three.

Two Famous Pupils of Rimski-Korsakov

Two of Rimski-Korsakov's pupils who became world-famous composers in the twentieth century were Igor Stravinsky and Serge Prokofieff. Both these men traveled in Europe and came to the United States in their youth, but Stravinsky later came to live in America and Prokofieff returned to his native land.

Stravinsky was born in 1882, the son of an opera singer, and like so many other composers, he set out to become a lawyer. His first great fame came when he composed the music for two fairy-tale ballets, *The Fire Bird* and *Petrushka. The Fire Bird* tells an old Russian tale of an enchanted garden and a magic bird that helped a young Prince kill an ogre and rescue a lovely Princess. *Petrushka* is also a folk legend, about what happened at a village fair when a marionette, a little dancing clown made of wood and rags, came to life and fell in love. These ballets were performed all over Europe and America and the music for them was made into orchestra suites to be played on concert programs.

Stravinsky went on to write more ballets as well as symphonies, concertos, and many other works. He experimented with new harmonies and rhythms, and later he experimented with music in the style and forms of Bach and earlier composers. He became an

American citizen and a celebrated conductor as well as a composer. When he was past the age of seventy he was still actively writing and conducting music.

Prokofieff was born in 1891 and began composing as a child. By the time he was thirteen and studying at the St. Petersburg Conservatory, he had written a symphony, three operas, and quite a few piano compositions. He was witty and original in his music, and he liked to write for young people. He wrote a famous piece for children, *Peter and the Wolf,* which tells the story of how a little boy, Peter, captures a wolf. In the music there is a special little melody for each character, and each melody is played by a certain instrument of the orchestra. Prokofieff originally wrote this piece to teach children to recognize the sounds of the instruments, but children and grown-ups, too, came to love the charming music for itself, whether or not they learned the instruments from it.

Prokofieff wrote many important and beautiful works, among them an opera on Shakespeare's play, *Romeo and Juliet,* another opera called *The Love for Three Oranges,* music for motion pictures, symphonies, concertos, and chamber music.

He also wrote a group of delightful piano compositions, *Music for Children,* which he intended children to play as well as listen to. The music goes through a child's day, beginning with *Morning,* ending with *Evening* and *The Moon Goes Over the Meadows,* and with a walk, a fairy tale, a game of tag, rain and the rainbow, and other musical adventures in between. Like Robert Schumann's *Scenes from Childhood,* these compositions are so charming and true that grown-up pianists like to play them, too.

Prokofieff was inspired to write his great Fifth Symphony and the opera, *War and Peace,* during the Nazi invasion of his country in World War II. His sixtieth birthday in 1951 was celebrated with a great concert in Moscow, although several times the Soviet Government had criticized his music unfavorably. He died in 1953 when he was sixty-two.

HOW PETER CAUGHT A WOLF

The Russian composer Serge Prokofieff wrote the music story "Peter and the Wolf," to help children learn the instruments of the orchestra. Each character is represented by a different instrument.

Peter (violin)

Here's Peter coming out to the meadow, a happy skipping tune played by the string quartet (first and second violin, viola, and 'cello) with the first violin carrying the melody.

The Bird (flute)   Allegro

Peter's friend, the Bird, up in a tree, trills a welcome. The voice is the flute's, playing an octave higher than shown here.

The Duck (oboe)   Andantino

The Duck, complaining a little (the oboe sounds mournful) waddles down to the pond.

The Cat (clarinet)   Moderato

Now the Cat, in the clarinet's smooth silky voice (playing an octave lower than this) glides through the grass, eyeing the Bird.

Grandfather (bassoon)   Andante

Grandfather rumbles out, looking for Peter, scolding and bouncing along with big thumping bassoon sounds—a Wolf might come into the meadow!

The Wolf (three horns)   Andante molto

And the Wolf does come—three horns playing loud brassy chords—look out, Peter! In the story the Wolf catches the Duck, but Peter, with the Bird's help, catches the Wolf.

The Hunters Shooting   (The Kettledrum - -

- - And the big Bass   Drum)

The Hunters come out of the woods (the kettledrum and the big bass drum make the sound of shooting) in time to help Peter take the Wolf to the Zoo, in a joyful procession.

Richard Wagner and the Opera Revolution

MUCH of the excitement in the lively musical world of the nineteenth century swirled around Richard Wagner and his revolution in opera. For a long time, as we know, opera had been tremendously popular, especially Italian opera. Handel had written opera in the Italian style, and so had Mozart. But even then, the German composers had been rebellious about Italian operas and Italian opera singers, who invented trills and runs and high notes, until a composer could hardly recognize the music he had written. When Handel was producing opera in London, he once held a lady opera singer out of the window and threatened to drop her to the street unless she promised to sing the music as it was written.

After Handel came Christoph Willibald Gluck, a German composer who succeeded in writing and producing operas that the singers could not spoil. A lovely aria from one of his operas is sung by concert singers today. It is the song of Orpheus, who in the old Greek myth played the flute so beautifully that he charmed the wild beasts. In the story of Gluck's opera, Orpheus went under the earth into the kingdom of the dead, hoping his music would bring Eurydice, his dead wife, back to life.

After Gluck came Carl Maria von Weber, a composer and conductor, who devoted his whole life to encouraging German composers to compose operas out of German folk tales and folk tunes. His famous opera was called *Der Freischutz.* This title means "the free-shooter" or someone who shoots with magic bullets. The story of the opera is an old German folk tale about a young man who gets a magic bullet from an evil spirit and nearly kills his own sweetheart with it. The overture to this opera is often performed, but at the time he wrote it Weber was an unhappy man because his efforts to encourage German opera were not successful.

All this was before Richard Wagner's great opera revolution. Young Richard admired Weber; but he himself wanted to be a writer, not a composer. One day he heard a performance of a Beethoven symphony, and that inspired him to study music. He became a good conductor, though at first not much of a composer. He almost starved in Paris until one of his operas, *Rienzi,* was performed in Germany. Then Wagner became the conductor in the same German city where his idol, Weber, had suffered so many disappointments. He was successful there until a little rebellion began against the ruler of that part of Germany, and Wagner took part in it. He escaped and hid in Franz Liszt's home for a while, and then he fled to Switzerland. There, during eleven years of exile from Germany, he wrote the dramatic poems of his group of great hero operas, called *The Ring of the Nibelungs,* which was to have such an effect in the musical world. He also wrote an opera with a tragic love story, *Tristan and Isolde,* at this time. And he wrote the comic opera, *Die Meistersinger von Nuremberg* (The Mastersingers of Nuremberg). This was a failure with the fashionable audience in Paris because it did not have a ballet! Later all of Wagner's operas became successful even though there was no ballet in any of them.

But soon Wagner's disappointments ended. The young King of Bavaria heard one of his operas and took the composer under his protection. Wagner's music was so revolutionary that furious arguments went on about it for many years. He himself wrote many articles and letters defending his own music and attacking other kinds. Everywhere in Europe, musicians and music-lovers were either for Wagner or against him.

People felt so strongly about Wagner's music that they contributed money for a special theater, which was built in the little mountain town of Bayreuth, in the Alps of southern Germany. There his cycle of four operas, *The Ring of the Nibelungs,* was performed in 1876, and people came from everywhere to the performances. When his son was born, Wagner named the baby Siegfried, the name of the hero of his Ring operas, and he wrote a tender musical poem, *The Siegfried Idyll,* which is frequently performed on symphony programs.

Wagner's idea of opera was different from any that had been written before. He called his operas *music dramas* because there are no arias and no ballets in them to interrupt the story. The story is told continuously in the dramatic music he wrote for the performers to sing. He wrote big-sounding music for a large orchestra and for singers with powerful voices. The story of his *Ring* opera is written from German legends about gods and heroes, with a magic ring, magic fires, giants and dwarfs and dragons. For each of his main characters Wagner wrote a special theme which is heard in the music whenever that character appears in the story.

Wagner's music and his idea of opera as a musical drama had a great influence on composers everywhere and did much to change the kind of music that was written during his lifetime and afterward. His last opera was *Parsifal,* a religious opera about a young knight of King Arthur's Round Table who searched for the Holy Grail. This opera is regularly performed in Europe and America at Easter time. Wagner died in 1883, when he was seventy years old. Festivals were held at Bayreuth in his honor for many years.

German Followers of Wagner

The fairy-tale opera, *Hansel and Gretel,* which children and grown-ups have loved for many years, was written by one of Wagner's pupils, Engelbert Humperdinck. This German composer was famous as a teacher. He wrote several operas that were successful in his time but are not performed nowadays. He died in 1921.

Richard Strauss, the most important German composer since Wagner, was born in 1864, and he carried on Wagner's idea of opera into the twentieth century. Strauss did not write great hero operas, but his operas are like Wagner's in the way he uses the music and words together to tell the story, without arias or ballets. Strauss also wrote for a large orchestra. He wrote interesting new harmonies, and in his works the orchestra sometimes makes sounds that we do not expect from musical instruments, such as the bleating of a herd of sheep.

Several of Strauss's operas are regularly performed in the modern opera houses, and especially one witty opera with charming music, *The Rose Cavalier* (in German, *Der Rosenkavalier*). Strauss is equally famous for his poetic songs, and for his big symphonic poems, which he called *tone-poems*. A favorite one is *Till Eulenspiegel's Merry Pranks*. This tells about a mischievous sprite, known in German folk tales as Till Eulenspiegel, and how he upset the good people of a whole town with his tricks.

Richard Strauss lived to enjoy a great celebration in his honor on his eighty-fifth birthday, and died in 1949.

Another composer named Strauss was Johann Strauss, the "waltz king" of Vienna who composed *The Beautiful Blue Danube* and many other lilting waltzes. Johann Strauss was not related to Richard Strauss in any way, but he was the son of another Johann Strauss who was also a waltz king. The younger Johann became much more famous than his father. He was a composer of popular music, but he wrote with such skill and originality that serious composers like Brahms and Wagner admired his music. In his time, Vienna, which had been the center of serious music for so long, became the gay waltz capital of the world. Johann Strauss lived from 1825 to 1899, and one of his delightful comic operas, *Die Fledermaus (The Bat)* is regularly performed at the Metropolitan Opera House in New York, and other opera houses.

Romantic Operas of France and Italy

IN PARIS at the beginning of the nineteenth century, fashionable opera audiences were enjoying the comic operas of the Italian, Gioacchino Rossini, the most successful opera composer in Europe. Rossini wrote so many operas, and wrote them so fast, that even Beethoven made a joke about him, saying that any German composer would work for years to compose an opera that Rossini could finish in a few weeks. Rossini actually composed his most important opera, *The Barber of Seville*, in two weeks. This work is in the same Italian style as Mozart's comic opera, *The Marriage of Figaro*. In fact, the story of Rossini's opera is taken from another play by the same French author, Beaumarchais, and it has some of the same characters. Rossini's merry barber is the same Figaro as the hero of Mozart's opera. Later, Rossini wrote a dramatic historical opera, *William Tell*, about the brave Swiss hero who was forced to shoot an apple from his little son's head to prove his marksmanship. The overture to this opera is often performed by symphony orchestras.

The next opera favorite in Paris was Jacques Offenbach. Offenbach was born in Germany, but because he was so gifted the Paris Conservatory broke its own rule against taking foreign students and accepted him when he was fourteen. For many years his sparkling comic operas were the hits of Paris, London, and New York. Offenbach himself came to America and had great success as a conductor. His most important opera was *The Tales of Hoffmann*, the story of a romantic young man and his adventures in love. In one of the scenes the youth falls in love with a singing, dancing doll. Offenbach's lovely *Barcarolle* is from this opera. Other music of his has been made into successful ballets, and we often hear the music of one of these, *Gaieté Parisienne*, performed on symphony programs.

Meanwhile, French opera composers were struggling to be recognized. One French opera was successful during this time: *La Juive (The Jewess)*, a story of the Middle Ages, by Jacques Halévy. But two operas which have since become favorites everywhere were failures when they were first performed in Paris. The first of these was *Faust*, the legend of the old philosopher who bargained with the Devil for his youth. Charles Gounod, who composed this opera, also wrote another fine opera on a great story of the past, *Romeo and Juliet*. The other failure in Paris was Georges Bizet's truly great opera about the fiery Spanish cigarette girl, *Carmen*. This is the opera with the famous *Toreador* song.

At last, late in the century, these operas and some by other French romantic composers became successful. *Thaïs*, by Jules Massenet, tells the story of a beautiful Egyptian woman in the days of the early Christians. The *Meditation* from this opera is a famous violin solo. *Samson and Delilah*, by Camille Saint-Saëns, is about the strong man of the Bible, Samson, and the beautiful Delilah who cut off his hair while he slept and made him lose his strength.

The first opera about modern times was first performed as the new century began, in the year 1900. This was *Louise,* the charming story of a young girl of Paris who worked in a dressmaker's shop, and her love for a poor painter. This opera was the only important work of Gustave Charpentier, who wrote both the story and the music. It was immediately successful all over Europe and later in America, and in Paris it was performed more than 1,000 times. In 1950, when he was ninety years old, the composer conducted a scene from his one great work at the Paris Opera House.

Another famous French opera is *Pelléas and Mélisande,* by Claude Debussy. When this dream-like opera was first performed, in 1902, it made audiences almost as angry as Wagner's operas had made them twenty-five years before. Debussy had admired Wagner's music dramas, but his opera is nothing like Wagner's big-sounding hero operas. Debussy's story of Mélisande, the child-like maiden with long golden hair, and her unhappy love for her husband's younger brother Pelléas, is like a musical poem acted out on the opera stage. It was the only opera this interesting composer wrote. We shall talk more about Debussy's music later in our story.

A New Kind of Italian Opera

With all the changes going on in opera, the Italian opera style was changing, too. The excitement of the other romantic composers about story-telling in music was nothing new to the Italian composers, since their operas had always told a story. But during this romantic century the Italian operas became more emotional and dramatic than they had been. Happenings on the stage were often violent and bloody, and the story usually ended with the leading characters dying, in long and touching musical death scenes.

One of the great Italian opera composers was Giuseppe Verdi. He was born in 1813 in a little town where his father kept a tavern. The people of the town were so impressed with the boy's talent that they got together to pay the expense of sending him to the big city of Milan to study. He wrote twenty-six operas, with many beautiful melodies that are full of feeling and are also easy to remember. A famous opera of his is *Aïda,* a story of ancient Egypt, in which a Princess and a beautiful slave girl are rivals for the love of a handsome soldier. Another of Verdi's operas, *Rigoletto,* tells the story of a hunchbacked jester and his young daughter.

A later Italian composer whose operas are great favorites was Giacomo Puccini. Puccini's family were Church musicians, and he was helped along in his musical studies with money from the Queen of Italy. His operas are not so big and dramatic as Verdi's, but they are charming and full of lovely arias. One of his operas is *Madame Butterfly,* the story of a Japanese girl who fell in love with a Lieutenant in the American Navy. Another is *La Bohème,* an opera about life among the artists in Paris. Puccini came to America to conduct his operas, and he wrote an American opera, *The Girl of the Golden West,* which was a great success in its time. He died in 1924.

Musical Poets and Painters of Europe

THROUGH the centuries, France has been the country most friendly to the arts; but for many years the French were not very appreciative of their own composers. From the days of King Louis XIV, who danced in the ballets composed for his court by the Italian composer Lully, the most successful composers in France were Italians or Germans.

Hector Berlioz, First Music Story-Teller of France

The French neglected their first important composer of the romantic nineteenth century, Hector Berlioz, and this interesting composer often went cold and hungry for the sake of music. He was born in a small town in France in 1803, the son of a country doctor. His father sent him to Paris to study medicine, but music was his real interest. He was an intense, emotional young man who was always in and out of love. One night at the theater he saw an English actress, Henrietta Smithson, in one of Shakespeare's plays, and she became the love of his life.

The poor unknown composer had no way to meet the successful actress. Finally he rented a room next to hers in the same lodging house, only to learn that she was leaving Paris. In his unhappiness he wrote one of his finest works, *The Fantastic Symphony.* This story-symphony tells the strange dream adventures of a poet searching for the girl he loves. Like Henrietta in the composer's own life, the girl in the symphony whom Berlioz named "The Beloved," appears again and again and the poet can never attract her attention. Berlioz wrote a beautiful melody for his Beloved, which keeps returning in the music, a little changed each time. Franz Liszt heard the symphony performed in Paris and he admired it so much that he became a devoted friend of Berlioz. As for Henrietta, the real Beloved, Berlioz at last managed to meet her years later, and they were married. It was an unhappy marriage for both of them. But when Henrietta grew old and ill Berlioz took tender care of her until she died.

Berlioz became much appreciated in Germany. But his own country did not honor him, and he died a disappointed man in 1868, at the age of sixty-five. Years afterward he was recognized as one of France's important composers, and his *Fantastic Symphony,* his *Romeo and Juliet Symphony,* and the elf-like will-o'-the-wisp music from his Faust opera, as well as other works, are often performed. His musical story-telling and his expressive orchestration were an inspiration to the French composers who followed him.

Some French Impressionists

With the work of Berlioz, Paris began to be the center of his poetic kind of new music. It was already a center for the new kind of painting and poetry of the time. French poets were creating dream-like moods and effects with words, and the painters were painting the same effects with colors, light, and shade. The painters were called the Impressionists, because they painted their impressions of things and not the actual things themselves.

Soon the composers, too, were creating poetic moods and delicate pictures with new harmonies and rhythms and the tone shadings of the different instruments. César Franck, a Belgian organist and composer, and Gabriel Fauré, who was also a great teacher, were two of these poetic composers.

French Wit in Music

Sometimes the moods and pictures the French composers created with their music were witty, to make people laugh and think at the same time. Camille Saint-Saëns, who wrote serious operas and beautiful symphonies and concertos in the romantic style, also wrote the amusing *Carnival of Animals,* which makes us laugh at the animals and at ourselves. Paul Dukas, a professor at the Paris Conservatory, wrote *The Sorcerer's Apprentice,* telling the story of the boy who was an assistant to a magician, and who got into trouble when he began a spell and forgot the words to end it.

Erik Satie was a very daring composer. He played the piano in a nightclub for a living, and wrote music so original and disrespectful of all the old ways that people were provoked with him and would not take him seriously. He gave his compositions ridiculous titles such as *Flabby Preludes for a Dog,* and he wrote instructions on how his music should be played, for instance: "to be played dry as a cuckoo, light as an egg," and "like a nightingale with a toothache." But he was really more serious than he sounded, because he was trying to get away from the big showy compositions by Wagner and other German composers whose works were all the fashion. For all his peculiarities, Satie had a great influence toward making music simpler and more meaningful. His influence was particularly strong with one of the greatest of all French composers, Claude Debussy, who became his friend. Satie was so far ahead of his time that he wrote a jazz ballet, called *Parade,* as long ago as 1917. A real typewriter is used in the orchestra for a sound effect in this composition.

Debussy the Dreamer

Claude Debussy was both a poet and a painter in his music, and he was the first of the musical Impressionists. He was born near Paris in 1862, and his family was so poor that an aunt took over his education. Even while he was a student at the Conservatory, the harmonies and rhythms he used to create his imaginative effects were so new that his teachers did not approve of him at all. But he was so talented that they had to give him prizes for his compositions. He wrote a great many lovely, delicate piano compositions, which described places and people of his imagination, and his titles give the idea of these works, such as *The Girl With the Flaxen Hair,* and *The Cathedral in the Mist.* Many of the ideas about which he wrote music could be ideas for Impressionist paintings, too: *Clouds,*

Sails, Dead Leaves, Footprints in the Snow, Gardens in the Rain, Reflections on the Water, Goldfish. One of Debussy's famous orchestral compositions is *Afternoon of a Faun,* which was made into a ballet. Another is *Fêtes,* which gives a marvelous musical picture of a carnival parade. Debussy was a careful and patient worker. He spent ten years on his opera, *Pelléas and Mélisande.* He was interested in children, and wrote a delightful group of piano pieces called *The Children's Corner.* One of the famous pieces in this group is *The Golliwog's Cakewalk* which children particularly love. Debussy died in 1918.

There Were Arguments about Ravel

Maurice Ravel followed closely after Debussy in his music. Like Debussy, Ravel was impressed with the originality of Erik Satie, and imitated him at first. But he soon began to compose in an original style of his own. One of his first famous compositions was the *Pavane for a Dead Princess.* A *pavane* is a slow, stately court dance of old Spain, and this was the first of Ravel's many compositions in the Spanish style. It also became the melody of an American popular song, *The Lights Are Low.* Later Ravel wrote his *Spanish Rhapsody* and the fascinating *Bolero* which is played all over the world. Ravel loved children and animals, as we know from his charming *Mother Goose Suite.*

There were many arguments about Ravel's music. People who did not like it accused him of stealing melodies and harmonies from Debussy for his compositions. His friends defended him, and he went on to show by his fine original work that his friends were right. He came to be recognized as the leading French composer of his time, and he was invited to the United States in 1928 to perform and conduct his own works. Ravel died in 1937 as a result of a taxicab accident.

The Glamorous Music of Spain

Spanish folk music is rich and exciting, and in the nineteenth century Spanish composers began to explore this treasure. Isadore Albeniz was one of the first of these Spanish patriotic composers. Born in 1860, he was a brilliant child pianist. But he loved adventure, and instead of going on with his musical studies he traveled about in Spain. For a future composer this was probably the best education he could have had. He met a Spanish musical scholar, Felipe Pedrell, who aroused his enthusiasm for Spanish folk songs and dances. When the King of Spain gave him a scholarship for study he went to Paris, and then to Germany to study with Franz Liszt. With Liszt's encouragement, Albeniz returned to Spain, to compose many beautiful works with Spanish melodies and rhythms. His suite for the piano, *Iberia,* is especially famous.

Manuel De Falla also began as a pianist and was also inspired by the scholar, Felipe Pedrell. He was born in Cadiz, Spain, in 1876, and was taught at first by his mother. He studied in Madrid and then in Paris, and learned a great deal from the exciting French composers. He came home to travel through his own country, studying its music and folk tales, and wrote operas and ballets to tell these stories. His ballets, *Love the Sorcerer* and *The Three-Cornered Hat,* and the suite for piano and orchestra, *Nights in the Gardens of Spain,* express the glamor and romance of Spain. After the Spanish Civil War, De Falla left Spain because he was unsympathetic to the new government. He lived in Argentina until his death in 1946.

Respighi, a Tone-Poet of Rome

Italian composers were mostly too busy writing operas to compose other kinds of music, but one important composer, Respighi, wrote opera and also wrote poetic and picture-painting music. Ottorino Respighi was born in the northern city of Bologna in Italy, in 1879, and after studying in his own country he made the long journey to St. Petersburg to work with the inspiring Russian composer and teacher, Rimski-Korsakov. With his teacher's encouragement, he returned home to write of his own country. He wrote several fine operas and orchestral works, and he became famous for his symphonic poems about Rome. In these three works, *The Pines of Rome, The Fountains of Rome,* and *The Festivals of Rome,* he created a colorful musical picture of that centuries-old city with its ancient monuments, its palaces and gardens, and its spirited people.

For many years Respighi was a respected teacher of other composers in Rome. He visited the United States several times, and died in Rome in 1936.

Delius, an English Composer in a Florida Orange Grove

The most unusual composer, during this interesting time in the late nineteenth century and the beginning of the twentieth, was the Englishman, Frederick Delius. Delius was born in 1862, the son of a wool merchant in the north of England. His father sent him on a tour of Europe to learn the wool business, but all young Frederick was interested in was music. His father, trying to win him away from such an impractical career, then thought of a more attractive business. In faraway Florida in the United States, Delius's father bought an orange grove and gave it to young Frederick to manage. Frederick liked

Florida, but he stayed in the plantation house practicing the piano while the ripe oranges fell to the ground and spoiled. One day his brother came up the river to visit him. Frederick joyfully handed over the orange grove to his brother, and went traveling up the coast of the United States. He taught and studied in several cities, and played the violin at a concert he gave in New York. Then he went back to Europe.

But he did not return to England. He studied a while with the composer Edvard Grieg. Then he married, and settled down in a little house with a garden in a village in France. There he stayed for the rest of his life, writing his lovely music. Nobody except a few enthusiastic German musicians paid much attention to his compositions until Sir Thomas Beecham, the English conductor, discovered this interesting English composer and began to play his works on concert programs in England. Sir Thomas had hard work at first, because Delius's poetic music was so different from what audiences were accustomed to that they did not like it. But gradually Delius began to be appreciated in his own country and soon in the rest of the musical world as well.

During his last years Delius was blind and totally paralyzed, but he went on writing music, sitting in his French garden and dictating to a devoted young musician who acted as his secretary. He went back to England only once, in 1929, when Sir Thomas Beecham had him brought in a wheel chair to London to attend a festival of concerts of his works that lasted a whole week. He died in 1934.

Some of Delius's sensitive and lovely tone-poems are *On Hearing the First Cuckoo in Spring, Over the Hills and Far Away, A Song of the High Hills,* and an orchestral suite from his opera, *A Village Romeo and Juliet.*

English and American Composers of the Twentieth Century

A GOOD deal of experimenting has gone on in music in the twentieth century. Composers have been trying out new harmonies, new rhythms, and even new arrangements of notes in a scale. Some have turned back to the counterpoint and the many-voiced music of Bach and composers before Bach's time, and some have tried out modes like those of the old Church music.

Composers have also experimented with new ways of making musical sounds. They have brought telephone bells, fire sirens, lead pipes, and other unusual sound-makers into the orchestra. Now and then they use a phonograph record of a sound they cannot get in any other way. They have written music that needs new sounds from the old instruments, too. Sometimes a composer wants the music to sound harsh and rough for his effects, instead of smooth and pleasing. Or a composer writes music to be played on the piano with the fists instead of the fingers, or by reaching into the piano to pluck and brush the strings, as one plays the strings of a harp, and make a ghostly music.

But modern music is not all strange and not all of it is experimental. Many modern composers who write some music that is hard to understand also write music that is charming, poetic, witty, and meant for everyone to enjoy.

The English composer, Ralph Vaughan Williams for example, has written seven symphonies and several concertos for different solo instruments. Some of them are not easy to follow. But he has also composed *Old King Cole,* a merry ballet suite; and a suite of English Folk Songs. And on the theme of one familiar old song he has written his very lovely *Fantasia on Greensleeves.*

Benjamin Britten, another English composer of our time, has written modern music of all kinds, including the tragic opera, *Peter Grimes.* But he has also taken a theme from the early composer Henry Purcell and written *The Young Person's Guide to the Orchestra* to introduce the instruments of a modern symphony orchestra to boys and girls. In this composition each group of instruments plays a delightful variation on the original theme.

Just before the twentieth century, there was Sir Arthur Sullivan. He composed a great deal of serious music including such hymn tunes as *The Lost Chord* and *Onward, Christian Soldiers.* But he is most famous for the comic operas he composed with Sir William S. Gilbert, who wrote the words. Have you ever heard the song "The Flowers That Bloom in the Spring, Tra-La"? That is from Gilbert and Sullivan's opera *The Mikado.* And you surely know some of the rollicking tunes from *Pinafore, Iolanthe,* and *The Pirates of Penzance.*

The merry operas that Gilbert and Sullivan wrote in the 1870's and 1880's are still making audiences laugh especially where the English language is understood.

Here is a line from their famous operetta, *Pinafore*.

We— sail the o-cean blue, and our sau-cy ship's a beau-ty;

After Purcell, far back in the 1600's, England had no really important composers until nearly the twentieth century. But today the English can boast of several. We have already told the unusual story of Frederick Delius. Besides Delius, Vaughan Williams, and Britten, other modern English composers whose music you are likely to hear are Sir Edward Elgar and William Walton.

The United States is a young country, and Americans have not had a part in the story of music through the centuries of the past. But today Americans are making an exciting and original contribution to music. Jazz, the modern American folk music, is now enjoyed and respected for itself, and it has a strong influence on serious composers of both America and Europe.

Many modern American composers also use the older folk music of America, the square dance tunes and jigs, the ballads and spirituals and mountain songs and cowboy songs that Americans made for themselves when there were no phonographs or radios to play music for them.

You can hear some of these old tunes in music like Aaron Copland's ballets, *Rodeo, Billy the Kid,* and *Appalachian Spring,* and in his music for motion pictures like *The Plough That Broke the Plains* and *The Red Pony*. You can hear jazz tunes in Leonard Bernstein's ballet about three sailors, *Fancy Free*.

Modern American composers like these write music for everything from big orchestras to solo voices. They also write for the ballet and modern dance, for motion pictures, radio, and television. They write operas and folk operas and Broadway shows.

You may have heard *Amahl and the Night Visitors* performed on television at Christmastime. This is the lovely old legend about a little crippled boy and the three Kings of the East made into a beautiful short opera by the modern American composer Gian-Carlo Menotti.

George Gershwin wrote the music and his brother Ira Gershwin wrote the words of the beautiful folk opera *Porgy and Bess.* "Summertime," "I Got Plenty o' Nuttin'," and "It Ain't Necessarily So" are favorite songs from this opera.

Oklahoma!, Carousel, and many other musical plays composed by Richard Rodgers, with words by Oscar Hammerstein, have been great theatrical and motion picture successes. And certainly no one complains that the wonderful music of such modern American composers is hard to listen to!

Meet the Musical Instruments of Today

THE MUSICAL instruments all have different voices, just as all the people you know have different voices. Part of the fun of listening to music is in recognizing the voices of the different instruments, and enjoying the special quality of each of them. One way to get to know the instruments is to see and hear them on parade, in the symphony orchestra.

There are from seventy to a hundred musicians in a modern symphony orchestra, but they do not play a hundred different instruments. The instruments are grouped in four *sections:* strings, woodwinds, brasses, and percussion instruments. These are the names by which the four sections of the orchestra are known. Within each section there are several different instruments, and they are related to each other the way the members of a family are related to each other. Let's see now what the families of instruments and their separate members are like.

Here Are the Strings

The *strings* make up more than half the orchestra. Except for the harp, they are all instruments of the violin family: the violin, viola, 'cello, and double-bass. All four have the same shape, with four strings stretched from pegs, down the narrow finger-board and over the fat body which is the sounding box. All are played with one hand on the finger-board to press down the strings for the different notes, and the other hand drawing the bow across the strings to make them sound. A little bridge holds the strings away from the body so that they can vibrate freely.

First in the string section are the *violins,* the largest group in the orchestra. They are divided into *first violins* and *second violins,* with a few more first violins. Music is often written with separate parts for these two groups to play. The violins, with their high sweet voices, are the sopranos of the orchestra. In a full-sized symphony orchestra there may be as many as thirty-four first and second violins together. In many works the first violins carry the melody, and there are also famous violin solos in orchestra compositions, like the solo for the first violin in *Scheherazade* by Nicholas Rimski-Korsakov. This solo can be heard again and again through the music, like the "Once upon a time" of a fairy tale, because this music is written about the Arabian fairy tales that Queen Scheherazade told her husband, the Sultan, in the *Thousand and One Nights.*

Next in the string section of the orchestra come the *violas,* usually ten of them. A viola looks like a violin and is held the same way to be played, but it is a little larger and it has a deeper richer voice, sometimes rather a sad voice. In the *Caucasian Sketches* composed by Alexander Borodin, the violas play a melody that gives the feeling of space and loneliness around a little village, set among great mountains and wide plateaus in the Caucasus, a wild part of southern Russia.

The next larger members of the string section are the *'cellos,* and there are usually ten of them. The name 'cello is short for *violoncello.* A 'cello is held downward between the seated player's knees, and has a short rod or end-pin at its lower end that rests on the floor. The 'cello has deep strong low tones and rich sweet middle and high tones. It can be played quite high and quite low, and its warm velvety voice can be made to express great feeling. The composer Saint-Saëns used the 'cello for his beautiful sad melody, "The Swan," in his composition, *Carnival of the Animals.*

Last in the string section are the big *double-basses,* eight or ten. They are also called the bass viols, contra-basses, string basses or, simply, basses. They are so tall that they are ranged around the back of the orchestra, with the players standing up to play them. The double-bass has a heavy rumbling voice, and it cannot be played very rapidly because the strings are too long and thick to sound separate quick notes. The double-basses give depth to the sound of the orchestra and they also mark the rhythm. In some jazz bands a double-bass is used as a rhythm instrument. Saint-Saëns, in his *Carnival of the Animals,* wrote the "Dance of the Elephants" as a solo melody for the double-basses to play.

The *harp* is the one instrument in the string section that is not a member of the violin family. The shining gilded head of the harp's tall post stands out above the orchestra and is easily seen. It has forty-seven strings and seven pedals. The player sits down to play the harp, with his feet on the pedals and his hands free to pluck or sweep the strings. There is usually only one harp in an orchestra, and for many compositions no harp is needed at all. We hear the liquid notes of the harp together with the 'cello in Saint-Saëns' melody for "The Swan," and we also hear the harp in the "Waltz of the Flowers" in Tchaikovsky's *Nutcracker Suite.*

The Woodwinds Are Expressive

The *woodwind* section has a most interesting variety of voices. It is made up of groups of four instruments, all related to each other and yet each one having its own special char-

How the Instruments Are Generally Placed In a Full Symphony Orchestra

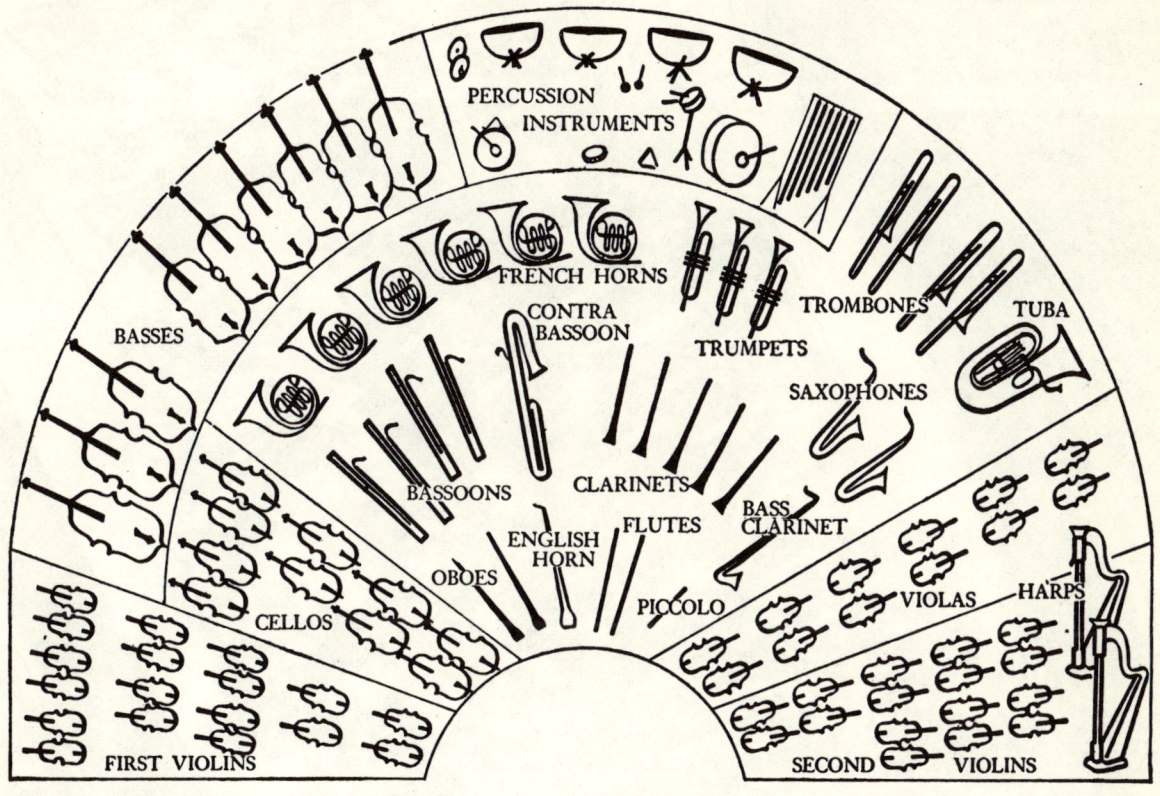

Illustration by Ava Morgan in *From These Comes Music*, by Hope Stoddard. Thomas Y. Crowell Company, New York.

It is the privilege of every professional conductor to make changes in the placing of his players and their instruments. But every conductor knows that there is a basic position for all the instruments. When he makes changes he does so for what he thinks will be better musical results in a particular performance or a particular symphony.

It is a good thing to understand the basic positions of instruments in a full symphony orchestra. It makes a concert more interesting to know where the various musical sounds come from.

There are about a hundred instruments in a standard symphony orchestra, and the orchestra is divided into four general groups of instruments, as follows.

Strings—about 60 players
Woodwinds—about 15 players
Brasses—about 15 players
Percussion Instruments—about 10 players

Boston Symphony Orchestra with Conductor

Wide World Photos

Heckscher Children's Symphony Orchestra
with Young Conductor

Wide World Photos

The Musical Instruments by Sections

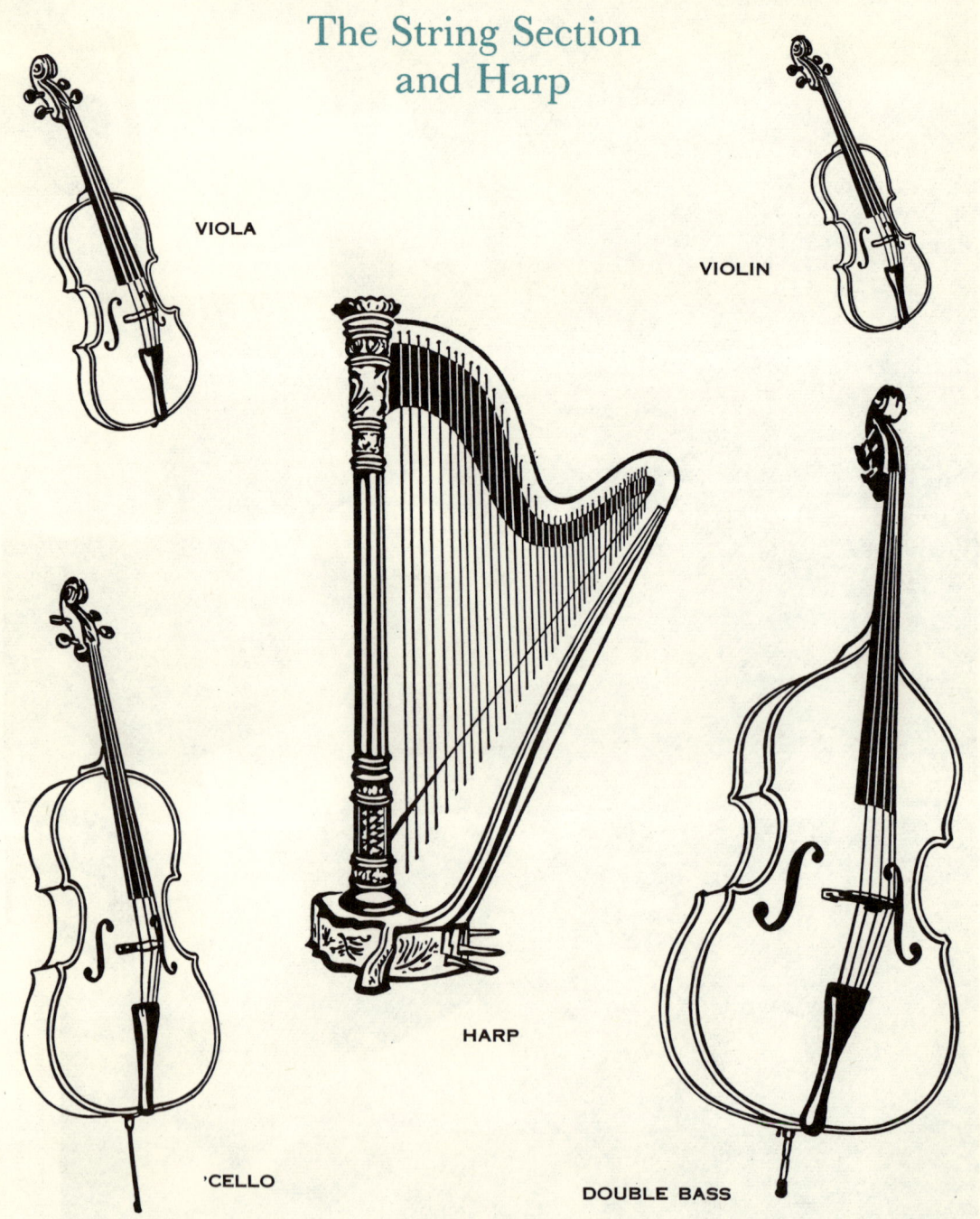

The String Section and Harp

VIOLA

VIOLIN

'CELLO

HARP

DOUBLE BASS

The illustrations on this page and the following four pages are from *The Enjoyment of Music* by Joseph Machlis. Copyright 1955 and 1957 by W. W. Norton & Company, Inc.

The Woodwind Section

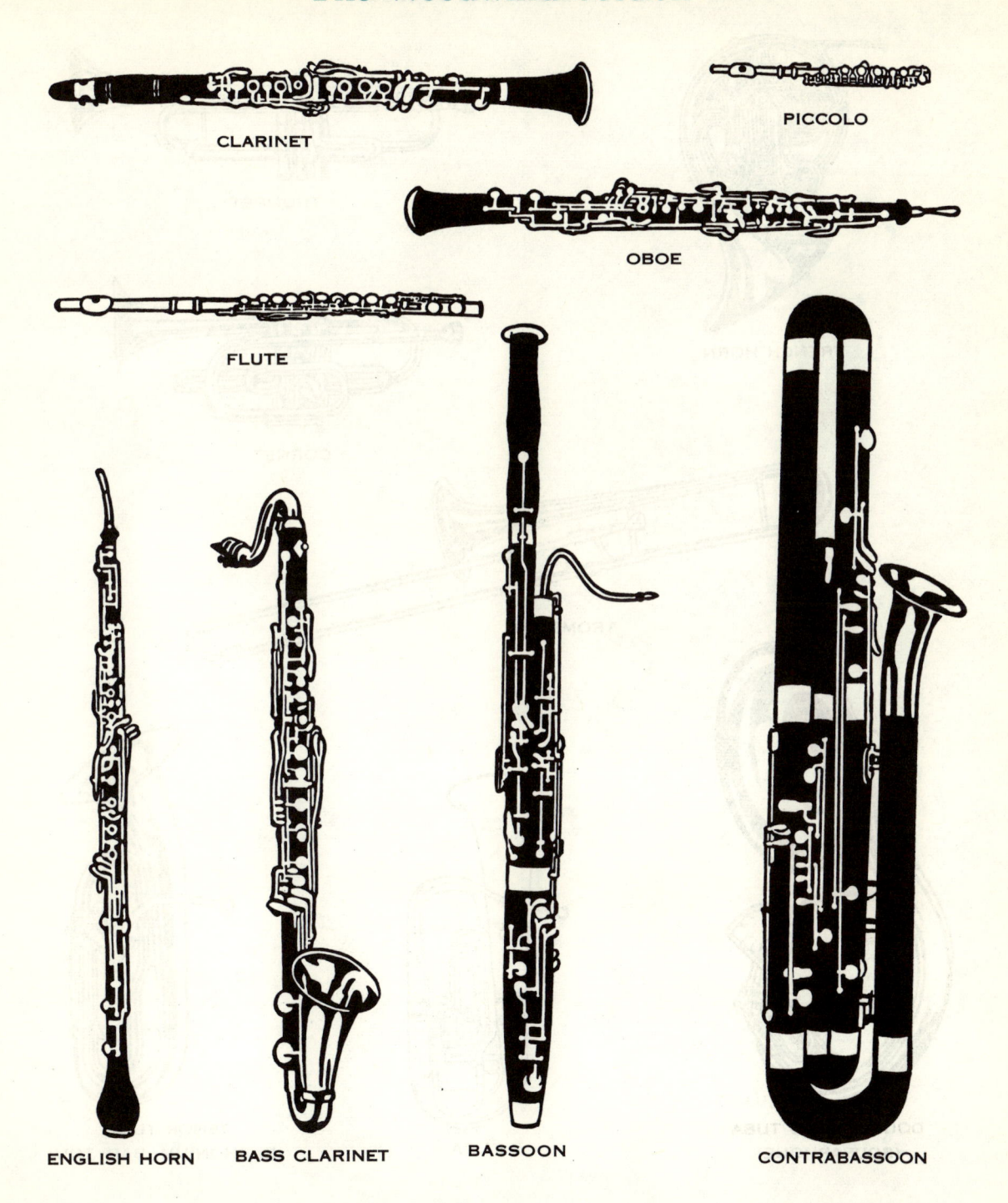

CLARINET

PICCOLO

OBOE

FLUTE

ENGLISH HORN

BASS CLARINET

BASSOON

CONTRABASSOON

The Brass Section

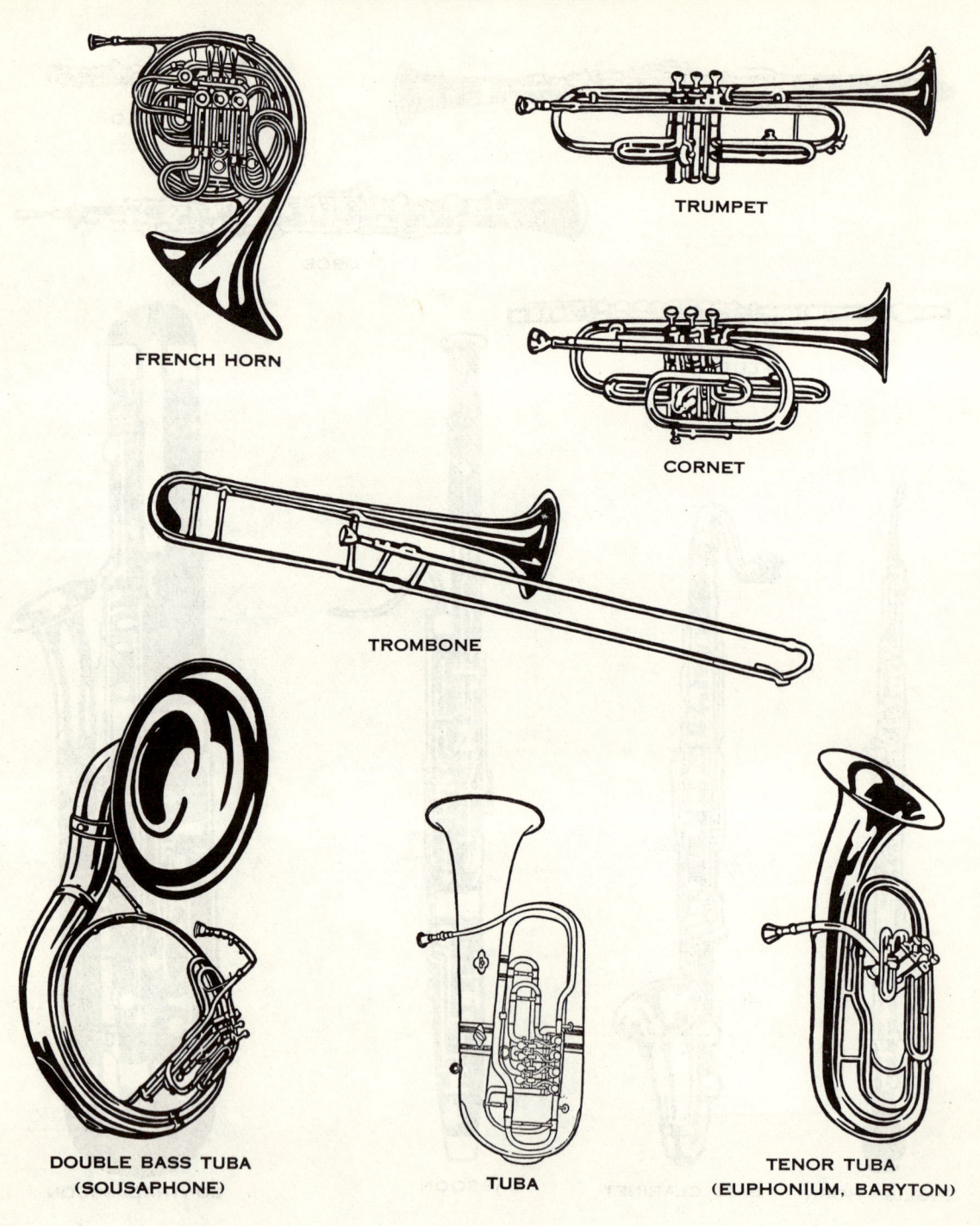

FRENCH HORN

TRUMPET

CORNET

TROMBONE

DOUBLE BASS TUBA
(SOUSAPHONE)

TUBA

TENOR TUBA
(EUPHONIUM, BARYTON)

The Percussion Instruments

TENOR DRUM

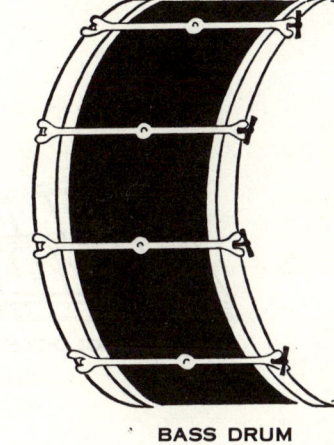

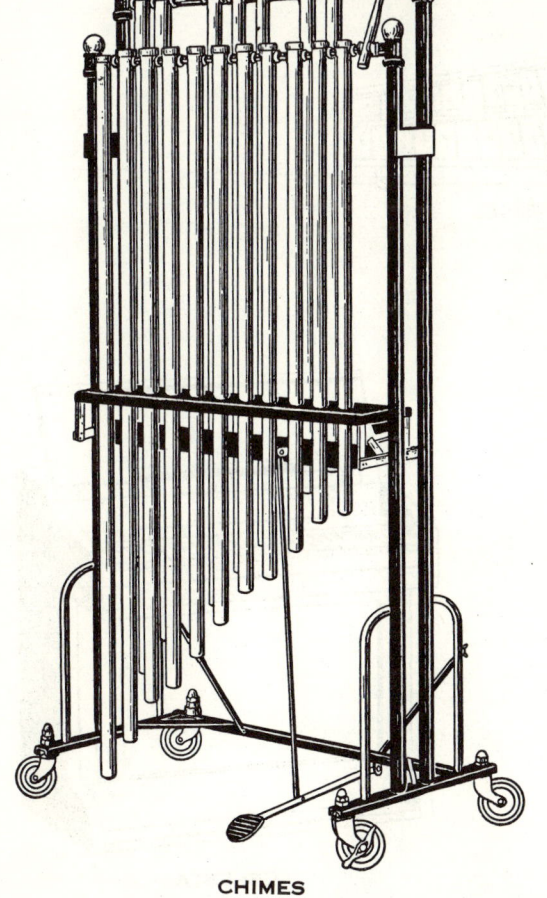

SNARE DRUM

BASS DRUM

CHIMES

KETTLEDRUM

The Percussion Instruments

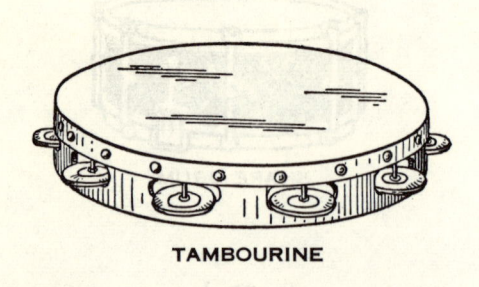

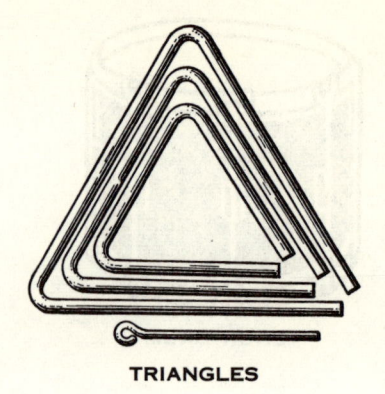

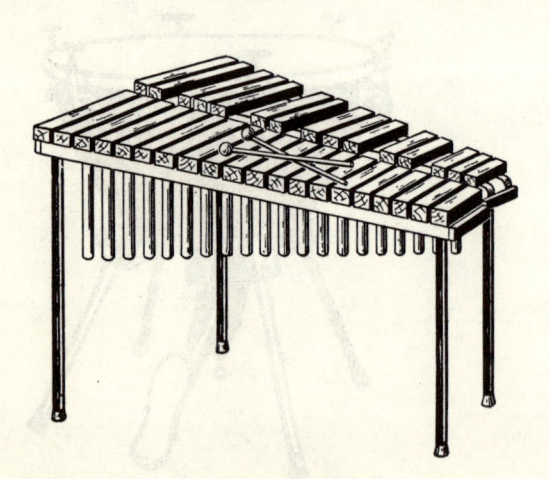

TAMBOURINE

TRIANGLES

GLOCKENSPIEL

XYLOPHONE

CELESTA

acter. The woodwinds are the flutes, oboes, clarinets, and bassoons, usually three of each in the orchestra. Except the flute, they are usually made of wood, and in all of them the player blows into the instrument to make it sound, and his fingers play the notes by stopping holes along the length of the instrument.

The *flute* is a very high voice among the woodwinds, and it is different from the others in several ways. Instead of wood, it is generally made of silver, sometimes of gold. Instead of being held lengthwise and blown from one end, it is held sideways and the mouthpiece is an opening in the side. The flute has a light cool clear voice, and a good flutist can play the notes wonderfully fast. A swift run of notes on the flute sounds like a shower of silvery tones. You hear three flutes together playing the melody in the "Danse des Mirlitons" (Dance of the Flutes) in Tchaikovsky's *Nutcracker Suite*. The flutes with their light notes, like cool crystal-clear drops of water, help to create the mood of nymphs playing in a forest, in Debussy's *Afternoon of a Faun*.

The *piccolo* is a little brother to the flute. Its voice is higher than the flute's, and so shrill and penetrating that it can be heard above all the voices of the orchestra if the composer wants it to be played loudly. One of the flute players plays the piccolo when it is called for. You hear the lively, saucy sound of the piccolo in Sousa's march, *The Stars and Stripes Forever*.

The other three woodwinds are *reed* instruments. A reed is a small thin piece of cane, like a fine sliver of wood, placed in the mouth opening of the instrument, and the sound is made by blowing on this reed and making it quiver.

The *oboe* is one of the ancient instruments in the orchestra. It is a double-reed instrument, with two bits of cane bound together. This double reed is so sensitive that the slightest breath will make it sound, and a good part of the oboe player's skill is in how well he can hold his breath back and control the strength of his blowing. He holds the double reed in his mouth and plays the notes with his fingers on finger keys that stop the holes along the length of the oboe. The oboe's voice is quite special in sound, thin and bittersweet and plaintive. Tchaikovsky wrote an Oriental melody for the oboe in the "Arabian Dance" of his *Nutcracker Suite,* and there is a lovely oboe solo in Haydn's *Surprise Symphony*.

A larger, deeper-voiced oboe is the *English Horn.* You hear the sad song-like tones of the English horn in *The Swan of Tuonela,* by the Finnish composer Sibelius. One of the oboists plays the English horn when it is needed.

The *clarinet* is a single-reed instrument, with its reed fitted against the mouthpiece. The clarinet's voice is full and rich, like a man's voice, and it can play quite high and quite low in the scale. There are several different clarinets, tuned to different notes in the scale. The largest one, the bass clarinet, looks different from its smaller brothers because its upper end curves downward to the mouthpiece and its lower end curves upward to the bell-shaped opening.

The clarinet is like an actor who can play many kinds of parts. It plays the tune of the mischievous sprite in *Till Eulenspiegel's Merry Pranks,* by Richard Strauss. It plays the mysterious Oriental melody of *Hymn to the Sun* by Rimski-Korsakov. And it also plays the famous blues of George Gershwin's *Rhapsody in Blue!* It is a star performer in the jazz world, and composers of symphonic music love it because it can do so many kinds of music so well.

The *bassoon* is the bass voice of the woodwinds. It is a double-reed instrument like the oboe, and it is even more difficult to play than its smaller cousin. It looks like two poles fastened together, with the thin curved metal tube of the mouthpiece coming out at the top of the shorter pole. The bassoon has a deep hollow-sounding voice. It can be dignified and solemn, or it can bounce its big tones and make us think of a clown or a dancing bear. One of the bassoon players plays the double-bassoon, which has the lowest voice of all the woodwinds. The bassoon and the double-bassoon together play the music of the magic broomsticks fetching water in *The Sorcerer's Apprentice* by Paul Dukas. The bassoon also plays a solo in Rimski-Korsakov's *Scheherazade,* in the charming story of "The Young Prince and the Young Princess."

A newcomer to the woodwind section is the *saxophone,* a modern reed instrument. The saxophone is familiar in jazz orchestras, but composers also use it now and then in symphony music. Georges Bizet, who composed the opera *Carmen,* wrote a part for the saxophone in his *Arlésienne Suite,* and Maurice Ravel wrote a solo for it in his famous *Bolero.*

The Bold Brasses

The *brass section,* like the woodwind section, is made up of wind instruments, but these are all made of brass, with bold brilliant voices that can be very loud. The brasses are both very old and very young. In their simplest forms they go back to ancient times, when the trumpet and the horn were nothing more than metal tubes of brass with a narrow end to blow into and a wider end for the sound to come out. The player had to make the different notes with his lips and the strength of his blowing. About a hundred years ago, valves were invented for these instruments so that they could be made to play certain notes more easily. A trumpet or horn without the valves is called a *natural* instrument. The bugle or cornet is this kind of simple or natural trumpet, and the hunting horn that we see in old pictures of hunting scenes is a natural horn. In the orchestra today the brasses are the improved kind with valves.

In the brass section we find three trumpets, four French horns, three trombones, and a tuba.

The *trumpet* is the smallest brass and has the highest voice. It can be shrill and piercing in tone, or noble, lordly, and commanding. You hear its voice in *The Poet and Peasant Overture* by Von Suppé, and there is a trumpet solo like a bugle call in the *Leonore Overture* by Ludwig van Beethoven.

The *French horn,* like its ancestor, the hunting horn, coils around in a circle from its mouthpiece to its big flaring bell-shaped opening. The valves are inside the circle of tubing where the player's fingers can reach them as he holds the horn to his lips. The French horn's smooth rich tones hardly sound like the voice of a brass instrument. It blends so well with the woodwinds that it often plays with them while its fellow brasses are silent.

Listen for the creamy tones of the French horn in Strauss's *Till Eulenspiegel*, and in the tender song-like melody of the second movement in Tchaikovsky's *Fifth Symphony*.

The *trombone* is the one brass that has no valves. It is a simple tube that winds back on itself, with a sliding part that the player slides in and out to make the different notes. Its voice is like the trumpet's voice, strong and bold, but lower and more dignified than the trumpet. There are two kinds of trombones in the orchestra, a tenor and a bass. The composer Richard Wagner wrote many important parts for the trombone in his music; listen for this instrument in the Overture to his opera, *Lohengrin*. You can also hear the trombone plainly in Ravel's *Bolero*.

The *tuba*, the lowest voice of the brasses, is also the biggest member of this family, with a thick coil of brass and a great bell pointing upward. The tuba's heavy, metallic voice is rarely heard alone but usually fills out the sound of the brasses in the same way that the big double-bass fills out the sound of the string section. Sometimes the tuba is used by a composer for a special character. Richard Wagner, for instance, wrote the music that represents the dragon in his *Ring* operas for the tuba to play. You can also hear the tuba's voice in the Overture to this composer's opera, *Die Meistersinger von Nüremberg (The Mastersingers of Nuremberg)*. One tuba is generally enough for the orchestra.

Drums, Bells, Chimes, and Odd Noisemakers

Finally we have the lively *percussion section*. Any odd noisemaker that a particular piece of music may need, from a cowbell to a taxi horn, may be found among the percussion instruments. But some of the percussion group are respectable musical instruments and regular members of the orchestra.

The *kettledrums* are the lords of the percussion section. They are the most musical of drums, because each of them can be tuned to play a note of the scale, and with several kettledrums the player can play an actual melody. A kettledrum is a big round copper pot like a witch's cauldron, with a calf-skin or sheep-skin stretched over the top and fastened down all around. There are screws around the edge of the drum which the drummer tightens or loosens in order to tune the drum. The tighter the skin is stretched, the higher the note the drum sounds. Some kettledrums have foot pedals that work a mechanism for quick tuning, because the notes of the kettledrums often have to be changed quickly several times in the course of the same musical composition.

The kettledrum player has to be a skillful musician. He must be able to tune his drums quietly and perfectly, no matter what the instruments around him are playing. He has to keep the most careful count of the music so that he will be sure to strike the right drum at the right moment. And he has to be able to make a great variety of sounds on his drums, from loud *booms* and rolls like echoing thunder to soft ripples and even whispers. The kettledrum's sound depends on how the player strikes it and whether the padded heads of his drumsticks are hard, medium, or soft. A composer sometimes takes the trouble to write down in the music just what kind of drumstick the drummer should use for a certain effect. One of the most impressive parts for the kettledrums is a long, threatening drumroll, at the end of the third movement in Beethoven's famous *Fifth Symphony*.

In the orchestra there is usually one player for the kettledrums and another to play the rest of the percussion instruments. More musicians may be needed when a particular piece of music calls for a great variety of percussion sounds and rhythms. Here are some of the instruments that make these many sounds:

Drums, besides the kettledrums, usually include the big *bass drum* and the *snare drum.* The snare drum is a small drum with wires—the "snares"—stretched against its underside. The snares add extra brittleness to the drum's rat-tat-tat. You hear the snare drum especially in Ravel's *Bolero,* as well as in marches and military music. Josef Haydn wrote the famous drumroll in his *Drumroll Symphony* for the bass drum. The medium-sized *tenor drum* is also needed sometimes in the orchestra.

The *cymbals* are two metal plates that are clashed together to make a ringing sound. Sometimes the pair of cymbals is fastened to the top of the bass drum or on a stand, and they are worked by a foot pedal or struck with a drumstick. Listen for the clash of cymbals in Tchaikovsky's *1812 Overture,* and at the end of *Finlandia* by Sibelius.

The *tambourine* is like the top slice of a small drum, just a skin stretched in a hoop, with little metal plates set in its round frame. The player strikes the tambourine with his knuckles to make a tap-and-jingle, or he shakes it or rubs his thumb over the skin to make a steady jingling. You hear the tap-and-jingle of the tambourine in gypsy music and in parts of many musical works that suggest folk dancing, for example in the peasant wedding on the riverbank that takes place in *The Moldau* by Smetana.

The *bells* in the orchestra are not really bells at all but large metal tubes of different lengths, hung from a bar. They are struck with a mallet to make the sound of church bells. They play the joyful sounds celebrating Russia's victory over Napoleon, at the end of Tchaikovsky's *1812 Overture.*

The *glockenspiel* is a row of small steel plates fastened to a wooden frame. The plates are of graduated sizes and play the notes of the scale. The player strikes them with a pair of small hard hammers to make bright metallic tones. In Wagner's opera, *Die Meistersinger von Nüremberg* the glockenspiel is played in the march of the apprentices, and it is also used in the magic fire music of the same composer's opera, *Die Valkyrie.*

The *celesta* is a box like a small organ, with a keyboard like a piano. Inside it has a row of steel plates like the glockenspiel, but a bit of wood is attached to each plate to make it sound a light crystal tone like the sound of soft chimes. The "Dance of the Sugarplum Fairy" in Tchaikovsky's *Nutcracker Suite* is played on the celesta.

The *xylophone* is another instrument with the same general idea as the glockenspiel, but instead of metal plates it has a row of wooden bars of different lengths, fastened to a frame that usually stands on legs. The player strikes the bars with hammers, and the notes have a soft dry sound.

The *triangle* is a steel bar bent into the three-cornered shape of a triangle. The player holds it up by a cord and strikes it with a small steel rod to make a tinkling sound. The triangle is not tuned to any note, but it has a way of sounding in harmony with whatever the orchestra is playing. Listen for the triangle in Haydn's *Toy Symphony*.

The *gong* is a big round brass plate with a turned-up edge, usually hung from a crossbar on a standing frame. It is struck with a padded stick, and it makes a big deep-voiced clang that can sound threatening or mournful. With a light touch, it gives a soft faraway sound like a mysterious echo. You may hear the mournful sound of the gong struck at the end of Tchaikovsky's *Sixth Symphony*, which is also called the *Pathetic Symphony*.

The *castanets* are pairs of small hollowed-out wooden clappers that a Spanish dancer clicks together in each hand. In the orchestra, castanets are fastened to the ends of a handle and the player shakes them to make a rhythmic clicking. Other clicking sounds are made by the *Chinese wood blocks,* a pair of blocks made of hardwood; the *jazzstick,* a stick with a wooden flap; the *rattle,* which is not like a baby's rattle but like the noisemakers we have at parties and on Hallowe'en, a little frame that revolves, with strips of wood that catch in the cogs of a little wheel. The rattle makes a good imitation of machine-gun firing.

The great keyboard instruments, the *piano* and the *organ,* are not regular members of the orchestra, although the piano has important parts in a number of orchestral works such as Saint-Saëns' *Carnival of the Animals* and the *First Symphony* of Shostakovich. The organ is almost never used with the orchestra because it makes the sounds of almost all the orchestra instruments, all by itself.

What's in a Band

Your school may or may not have an orchestra, but it probably has a *band*. A band, sometimes called a *symphonic band,* has all the orchestra instruments except the string section, and there are generally a few wind instruments added. One of them is the *baritone,* which looks like a small-sized tuba and sounds like a trombone. Another is the *alto horn,* which is like a small French horn. In a band the number of clarinets is greatly increased because they take the place of the strings.

A *marching band* is still another kind of band, the kind that leads the parade and plays at football games. The instruments in a marching band are woodwinds, brasses, and percussion, but only those that can be carried and played while the musician is marching. Bass drum and snare drums, for instance, go in a marching band but kettledrums do not, although in cavalry bands in the old days there were small kettledrums in pairs hung one on each side of a horse, and the drummer played his drums as he rode.

Several composers have written music that is enjoyable to listen to, and that teaches us the instruments of the orchestra while we listen. Here are three: *The Young Person's Guide to the Orchestra,* by the modern English composer Benjamin Britten; *Peter and the Wolf,* by Serge Prokofieff, with a story about a little boy who captures a wolf, in which the characters are played by different instruments; and *Tubby the Tuba,* by an American, George Kleinsinger, in which the tuba, tired of playing only *oom-pah, oom-pah* all the time, gets to play a real melody at last.

How the Composers Use the Instruments

A composer uses the sounds or tone qualities of the instruments in his music the way a painter uses his paints on a picture. When a composer writes a solo melody for one instrument alone, it is like a painter stroking in a single clear color at some spot on his canvas. And when the composer mixes the voices of certain instruments for a certain effect on the listener, he does it just as the painter mixes certain colors for the effect he wants to make on the viewer.

Besides this, the composer also has to know what each instrument can do. He has to know how high and how low it can sound in the scale, how loud and how soft, how quickly it can go from one note to another, how long it can hold a single note. Some instruments, for instance the strings, can play two or more notes at a time, making a chord. The piano can play as many notes as the player can reach with his fingers at one time, and the pedal holds the sound of some notes while he plays still more.

Some instruments can give a variety of effects by being played in different ways. The strings of a violin can be stroked with the bow, or they can be plucked for the effect called *pizzicato*. Strings, wind instruments, and even drums and gongs can be made to play a hushed or muffled sound with the use of little devices called *mutes;* each kind of instrument is muted in a different way. A composer does not have to be able to play all the instruments, although many composers can play several of them. But he does have to know what each musician can do with his instrument. If the composer wants some special effect, he writes it down on the *score*.

The *score* is the music written down. Each instrument or group of instruments has its own *part* written out separately, and each musician has the part for his instrument on the music-stand in front of him. The *conductor* has the complete score, with all the parts of all the instruments.

What the Conductor Does

When the orchestra plays, we see the conductor on his little platform, facing the musicians, his back to the audience. He may have the thick book of the score in front of him on the music stand, or he may not. Some conductors would rather remember the music than bother with a score.

The conductor taps his baton on his stand, raises it in the air—and the orchestra plays. The conductor meanwhile keeps time with his baton. From time to time he points to this or that section of the orchestra to remind the musicians there that in a moment it will be their turn to play their parts in the music. The conductor also reminds the musicians with his gestures and the expressions on his face when he wants them to play louder, softer, more lightly, more vigorously, or in whatever way the music should go.

By the time they are ready for a public performance, the musicians have already learned all this by having rehearsed their playing many times. In rehearsal, the conductor explains his understanding of the music. He tells his musicians how the music should sound, how fast it should go, how loud, and so on. He has the orchestra play the composition over and over, and he makes sure that each musician is playing his part correctly. He may have the orchestra go over one particular portion of the music again and again, or he may have a section of the orchestra play alone for him, until he is satisfied. The hardest part of the conductor's work is finished when the rehearsals are over.

The concert is the result of all this work. An orchestra of fine musicians, who have often played together under a fine conductor, can play the concert without the conductor if they have to. This has actually been done. All they really need is for someone to give the signal to begin, and the *concertmaster* can do that. The concertmaster is the leader of the first violins, and he must be an excellent violinist and an experienced orchestral musician as well. At the beginning of the concert all the players tune their instruments to his, and at the end they do not get up to leave the stage until he does.

But at the concert the conductor does more than start the orchestra and keep it playing in time. Enthusiasm, interest, and enjoyment are feelings that people catch from one another, and the conductor on the platform does more than lead his musicians. He also shares his feeling for the music with them as they play. This is how a fine conductor inspires his musicians to play their best. It has been said that the conductor "plays" the orchestra the way a musician plays his instrument, and the symphony orchestra is the greatest "instrument" that has ever been invented.

Listening to the Music of Our Time

ALL MUSIC is new and strange the first time we hear it, no matter how old the music itself may be. When we listen to a new piece of music, it helps our enjoyment to know something of the story of music of the past, to be familiar with the instruments, and to have an idea of how a composition is put together.

We can listen to music just for its pleasing or interesting sounds. We can listen for its rhythm, which may make us want to dance or march or may be soothing and quiet. We can listen to music for the thoughts and pictures it brings to our minds, for the story it tells, or for the feelings it stirs in us. We can listen to share the composer's feelings and ideas. We can listen for his melodies and follow the way he has worked them out. Whether music is old or new, it can be listened to in these many ways.

We do not have to *like* music any more than we like all the stories we read, or all the pictures or movies or plays we see. But in order to know what we like, we do have to listen. Usually it helps us to appreciate a new piece of music if we listen to it more than once before we decide whether we like it a great deal, a little, or not at all. Sometimes the music that we like best the first time is the music that we get tired of the soonest. Sometimes the very music that we find hard to understand at first becomes more and more interesting each time we hear it.

One thing is sure. Music is something to be *listened* to. Only by listening and understanding can we really hear all there is to hear in a piece of music. And only then can we really enjoy it.

Recommended Records for a Young Music-Lover's Collection

THE RECORDS listed here comprise a basic record library of good music selected with the tastes of young music students in mind. In cases where different versions of a record are available, we have chosen the one we consider the best.

In some cases, several versions of the same work are listed. This is done where the composition appears on the back of a record recommended for what is on the other side. The collector can thus choose whichever combination appeals to him most.

Except where otherwise noted all records are 33⅓ RPM.

ORCHESTRAL AND INSTRUMENTAL RECORDINGS

BACH, JOHANN SEBASTIAN
Brandenburg Concertos, Nos. 2 and 3. One 10" record, London
Gavotte (from *Partita No. 3 in E*). One 10" record, Victor (78 RPM)

BEETHOVEN, LUDWIG VAN
Symphonies Nos. 5 and 6. Two 12" records, Victor

BIZET, GEORGES
Carmen. Three 12" records, Victor
L'Arlésienne Suite. One 12" record, Columbia

BRAHMS, JOHANNES
Hungarian Dances, Nos. 17, 1, 3, 10. One 10" record, Columbia

BRITTEN, BENJAMIN
Young Person's Guide to the Orchestra (with SAINT-SAËNS, *Carnival of the Animals*). One 12" record, Angel

CHOPIN, FREDERIC
Chopin Recital (piano). One 10" record, London
Les Sylphides. One 12" record, Victor

COPLAND, AARON
Rodeo (ballet). One 10" record, Victor

DEBUSSY, CLAUDE
Children's Corner Suite. One 12" record, Columbia
Prelude to the Afternoon of a Faun. One 12" record, Victor

DE FALLA, MANUEL
The Three-Cornered Hat. One 12" record, London

DUKAS, PAUL
The Sorceror's Apprentice (with PROKOFIEFF'S *Peter and the Wolf*). One 12" record, Victor

DVORÁK, ANTONIN
Symphony No. 5—From the New World. One 12" record, Victor

GERSHWIN, GEORGE
An American in Paris (with *Rhapsody in Blue*). One 12" record, Columbia

GRIEG, EDVARD
Peer Gynt Suites, Nos. 1 and 2. One 12" record, Columbia

GROFÉ, FERDE
Grand Canyon Suite. One 12" record, Columbia

HANDEL, GEORGE FREDERICK
Water Music and *Royal Fireworks Music.* One 12" record, London

HAYDN, FRANZ JOSEF
"Clock" Symphony No. 101 in D (with *Symphony No. 92 in G, "Oxford"*). One 12" record, Columbia
Toy Symphony (with MOZART'S *Eine Kleine Nachtmusik*). One 12" record, Columbia

HUMPERDINCK, ENGELBERT
Hansel and Gretel. Two 12" records, Angel

MACDOWELL, EDWARD
Woodland Sketches. One 12" record, Continental

MENDELSSOHN, FELIX
Midsummer Night's Dream, Incidental Music, Op. 61 (with SCHUBERT'S *Rosamunde*). One 12" record, London

MENOTTI, GIAN-CARLO
Amahl and the Night Visitors. One 12" record, Victor

MOZART, WOLFGANG AMADEUS
Eine Kleine Nachtmusik (with HAYDN'S *Symphony No. 92*. One 12" record, Victor
Country Dances. One Young People's Record (78 RPM)

MOUSSORGSKY, MODEST P.
Pictures at an Exhibition. One 12" record, Victor

OFFENBACH, JACQUES
Gaité Parisienne. One 12" record, Victor
Tales of Hoffmann. Three 12" records, London

PROKOFIEFF, SERGE
  Peter and the Wolf (with SAINT-SAËNS' *Carnival of the Animals*). One 12" record, Columbia
  Classical Symphony in D major. One 12" record, London
PUCCINI, GIACOMO
  La Bohème. Two 12" records, Columbia
  Madame Butterfly. Three 12" records, Columbia
RACHMANINOFF, SERGE
  Preludes. One 12" record, Continental
RAVEL, MAURICE
  Mother Goose Suite (with RAVEL'S *Bolero*). One 12" record, Victor
RIMSKI-KORSAKOV, NICOLAI
  Scheherazade. One 12" record, London
ROSSINI, GIOACCHINO
  William Tell Overture. One 12" record, Camden
SAINT-SAËNS, CAMILLE
  Carnival of the Animals (with RAVEL'S *Mother Goose Suite*). One 12" record, Columbia
SCHUBERT, FRANZ
  Symphony No. 8 in B minor ("Unfinished") with MOZART'S *Symphony No. 41*). One 12" record, Columbia
  Ballet Music from Rosamunde (with MENDELSSOHN'S *Midsummer Night's Dream*). One 10" record, London
  Quintet in A, Op. 114 ("Trout"). One 12" record, Westminster
SCHUMANN, ROBERT
  Album for the Young, Op. 68 (with TCHAIKOVSKY'S *Album; Seasons*). One 12" record, Victor
  Kinderscenen (with CHOPIN'S *Mazurkas*). One 12" record, Victor
SIBELIUS, JAN
  Finlandia (with *Swan of Tuonela*). One 10" record, Columbia
SMETANA, BEDRICH
  Bartered Bride (Excerpts). One 10" record, Decca
  The Moldau (with *From Bohemia's Meadows and Forests* and DVORÁK'S *Slavonic Dances*). One 12" record, Columbia
STRAUSS, JOHANN
  Waltzes (wide selection available). Victor, etc.
STRAUSS, RICHARD
  Till Eulenspiegel's Merry Pranks. One 12" record, Victor
STRAVINSKY, IGOR
  Firebird Suite (with MOUSSORGSKY'S *Pictures at an Exhibition*). One 12" record, Columbia
  Petrouchka. One 12" record, Columbia
SULLIVAN, SIR ARTHUR
  H.M.S. Pinafore. Two 12" records, London
  The Mikado. Two 12" records, London
  Pirates of Penzance. Two 12" records, London

TCHAIKOVSKY, PETER ILICH
  Marche Slave, Op. 31 (with *Overture 1812,* Op. 49). One 10" record, Columbia
  Nutcracker Suite (with DEBUSSY'S *Children's Corner*). One 12" record, Victor
  The Sleeping Beauty (Excerpts) with *Nutcracker Suite*). One 12" record, Columbia
  Swan Lake Ballet (with *Sleeping Beauty*). One 12" record, Angel
VERDI, GIUSEPPE
  Aida. Three 12" records, London
VILLA-LOBOS, HEITOR
  The Baby's Family. One 12" record, Westminster
VIVALDI, ANTONIO
  The Four Seasons. One 12" record, London
WAGNER, RICHARD
  Toscanini Plays Wagner. Two 12" records, Victor

SONGS (*Listed by Artists*)

DE LOS ANGELES, VICTORIA
  Spanish Folk Songs. One 12" record, Victor
IVES, BURL
  Animal Fair. One 12" record, Columbia
  Burl Ives Sings for Fun. One 12" record, Columbia
  The Wayfaring Stranger. One 12" record, Columbia
LUTHER, FRANK
  Songs of Stephen Foster. One 12" record, Columbia
MARAIS, JOSEF
  South African Folksongs. Three 10" records, Decca
MARAIS AND MIRANDA
  Ballads of Many Lands. One 10" record, Decca
  Songs of Many Lands. Four 10" records, Decca
  South African Folksongs. One 7" record, Columbia
MILLS, ALAN
  Folk Songs for Young Folks. Two 10" records, Folkways
  French Folk Songs for Children. One 10" record, Folkways
  More Songs to Grow On. One 10" record, Folkways
NEW YORK PRO MUSICA ANTIQUA
  Elizabethan Songbag for Young People. One 10" record, Esoteric
OBERNKIRCHEN CHILDREN'S CHOIR
  Happy Wanderer. One 10" record, Angel
  Little White Hen. One 10" record, Angel
SEEGER, PETER
  American Folksongs. One 10" record, Folkways
  Birds, Beasts, Bugs and Little Fishes.
  Birds, Beasts, Bugs and Bigger Fishes. Two 10" records, Folkways

Here are some Musical Terms
(with pronunciations)

A Capella (ah cap-EL-la)
  Group singing without the accompaniment of any instruments, like a choir in church
Adagio (a-DAHJ-ee-o) Quite slowly
Allegretto (al-leh-GRET-toe)
  A little slower than *Allegro*
Allegro (al-LEH-gro) Quick, lively
Allegro ma non troppo (al-LEH-gro mah non TROP-po) Lively, but not too fast
Andante (on-DON-teh) Quiet, peaceful, fairly slow
Andantino (on-don-TEE-no) A little faster than *Andante*
Appassionato (ap-PAHSS-ee-o-NAH-toe)
  With strong emotion
Aria (AH-ree-ah)
  In an opera or choral composition, a melody sung by one singer with orchestral accompaniment
Arpeggio (ar-PEDJ-ee-o)
  The notes of a chord played singly and rapidly from the lowest upward. Sometimes called *broken chord*
Bagatelle (bag-a-TEL) Short light piece of music
Ballad (BAL-led) Story-song
Ballet (BAL-lay)
  Combination of dancing and music that tells a story
Band
  Large group of instruments combined for specific purposes or kinds of music, such as a dance band, a brass band, a symphonic band, a military band
Barcarolle (BAR-ca-role) Boat song
Bass (BASE) Low, deep
Berceuse (bear-SEUZE) Cradle-song or lullaby
Bolero (bo-LEH-ro) Spanish dance in 3/4 time
Brasses
  The brass wind instruments of the orchestra, such as the horn, trumpet, trombone
Bravura (brah-VOO-rah) Boldness, brilliance
Brio (BREE-o)
  Fire, spirit. Written *con brio* in music
Cadenza
  Solo vocal or instrumental passage, usually just before the end of the composition
Cantabile (can-TAH-bee-lay) In a singing style
Cantata ((can-TAH-ta) Short oratorio
Canticle (CAN-tickle) Song of praise
Carillon (CA-ree-yon)
  Set of tuned bells played by means of a keyboard
Carol
  Song of praise usually sung at Christmas or Easter
Cello (CHEL-lo) Abbreviation of violoncello
Chaconne (sha-CUN)
  Slow dance in 3/4 time, originally a Spanish dance
Chamber Music
  Sonatas, trios, quartets, etc. suitable for performance in small rooms or halls
Choir (QUIRE) Company of Church singers
Choral (CO-ral) For a chorus
Chorale (co-RAHL)
  A musical work composed for a chorus
Chord (CORD)
  Combination of tones sounded together
Clavichord (CLAH-vik-kord)
  An early keyboard instrument with hammer mechanism like the piano—a favorite of Bach

Concertante (con-cher-TAHN-teh)
  A composition in which two or more parts have equal importance
Concerto (con-CHER-toe)
  A composition starring one or more solo instruments accompanied by others
Concerto Grosso (con-CHER-toe GRO-so)
  An early form of musical composition for orchestra, with groups of instruments playing solo parts
Contralto (con-TRAHL-toe)
  The lowest female voice, also called alto
Counterpoint
  The art or method of composing by weaving two or more melodies together
Crescendo (kresh-EN-doe)
  Sounding louder. Written *cresc* in music
Da capo (dah CAP-o)
  From the beginning, meaning "repeat" Written D.C. in music
Diminuendo (dim-in-u-EN-do)
  Sounding softer. Written *dim* in music
Divertimento (de-vair-to-MEN-toe)
  A pleasing light composition, usually for the piano or orchestra
Dolce (DOLE-cheh) Sweetly
Duet (due-ETT)
  A composition for 2 voices, instruments, or music
Elegy (EL-e-gee)
  A mournful poem, song, or piece of music in memory of the dead
Encore (ONG-core)
  A piece sung or played by a performer in addition to the regular program, in response to applause
Ensemble (on-SAHM-bl)
  All performers together, or a group of performers
Etude (AY-tude) Study piece
Fanfare (FAN-fair)
  Brilliant flourish or trumpet-call
Forte (FOR-teh)
  Loud and strong. Written F on music
Fortissimo (for-TISS-i-mo)
  Very loud. FF or FFF on music
Fugue (FEWG)
  A composition with the parts seeming to fly after each other, developed according to strict laws of counterpoint in a complicated structure
Gigue (JHEEG)
  A fast, lively dance (jig). One of the movements in a classical suite
Hallelujah (hal-le-LOO-yah)
  "Praise God." Part of a sacred musical work
Harmony The art of combining sounds musically
Harpsichord (HARP-see-cord)
  Ancient keyboard instrument in which sound is made by a plucking mechanism, thus differing from the piano with its hammer mechanism
Hymn (HIM) Musical setting for a religious poem
Impromptu (im-PROMP-tu)
  Piece of music played or composed on the spur of the moment, or one meant to sound spontaneous
Intermezzo (in-ter-METZ-so)
  Short movement connecting larger movements of a symphony or sonata, or a separate piece of music

Interval (IN-ter-val)
  Difference in pitch between two sounds
Key (KEE)
  The scale beginning with a given note, as "the key of C," in which a composition is written
Largo (LAR-go) Slow, stately
Legato (leg-AH-toe)
  Smoothly and evenly, with notes connected to each other in series
Lento (LEN-toe) Slow
Libretto (lib-RET-toe)
  Literally "little book." The words of an opera, oratorio, or musical show, or the story of a ballet
Lyric (LIR-ik)
  Poem or song especially meant to be sung lightly but with feeling
Lyrics (LIR-iks) The words of a song
Madrigal (MAD-rig-l)
  An unaccompanied song sung in several parts
Mass
  Music written for a part of the Roman Catholic communion service
Mazurka (ma-ZOOR-kah)
  A spirited, rhythmic Polish peasant dance
Metronome (MET-ro-nome)
  Mechanical device for beating time
Mezzo (MET-zo) Half
Mezzo-Soprano (MET-zo so-PRAH-no)
  Woman's medium high voice
Minuet (min-u-ET)
  Slow stately dance in 3/4 time, a movement in a classical suite, also sometimes part of a symphony movement
Modulation (mod-u-LA-shun)
  Change of key or tone or intensity of sound
Molto (MUL-toe) Very much
Motet (mo-TET)
  Composition for several voices sung like a madrigal but set to sacred words
Motif (mo-TEEF) Musical theme
Nocturne (NOK-turn)
  Quiet dreamy piece. Originally a piece to be played for night or evening
Octave (OK-tav)
  Interval of eight notes, as from DO to the next higher or lower DO
Opera (OPP-a-ruh)
  A play in which the actors sing, solo and in chorus, to orchestral accompaniment
Opus
  A musical work. Often written with a number to indicate the order in which a composer's works were written
Oratorio (ora-TOR-ee-oh)
  Musical work for solo singers and chorus, with orchestra, based on themes from sacred history
Orchestra (OR-kes-truh)
  Company of instrumentalists
Overture (OH-ver-ture)
  Musical prelude to an opera or other dramatic musical work, or a composition to be played as a concert number by the orchestra
Percussion instrument (per-CUSH-un)
  Any instrument on which the tone is produced by *striking*, such as drum, cymbal, triangle, etc.—thus differing from *string* and from *wind* instruments
Piano
  To be played softly. Written *P* in music
Pianissimo (pee-an-ISS-ee-mo)
  Very soft. Written *PP* or *PPP* in music

Pizzicato (PITZ-e-kah-toe)
  The plucking of the strings of a stringed instrument
Poco (PO-co) A little
Polonaise (Po-lo-NAYS)
  A dignified ancient Polish court dance
Polyphonic music (pol-lee-FON-ik)
  Music written with intermingling melodies (counterpoint), not with a single melody
Prelude (PRELL-ude)
  A short introductory composition
Program music
  Music written to tell a story or describe a scene
Quartet (quor-TET)
  Composition for four performers. There are string, piano, wind instrument, and vocal quartets
Quintet (quin-TET)
  The same for five performers
Recorder (re-CORD-er)
  An old type of wooden flute, blown from the end instead of the side, an instrument recently revived
Reprise (rep-REEZ)
  Repetition toward the end of a theme or song of a melody heard earlier
Requiem (REE-quee-em)
  Sacred musical setting to honor the dead
Rhythm (RITHM)
  The regular repetition of the beat or accent
Scale
  A succession of notes going up or down in pitch at fixed intervals
Scherzo (SCARE-tzo)
  A light fast movement of a symphony, quartet, or sonata. The word means "joke"
Serenade (sehr-an-ADE)
  Evening song. Used also to mean a pleasant light composition for voice or instruments
Solo (SO-low) Composition for one performer
Staccato (stak-KAH-toe)
  The sounding of each note sharply and separately
String Instruments
  Instruments in which the tone is made by the vibration of strings plucked by the fingers (harp, guitar, etc.), struck by a plectra or pick (mandolin, zither, etc.), vibrated by a bow (violin, viola, cello, etc.). In an orchestra, the violin family plus the harp
Symphony (SIM-pho-nee)
  Elaborate instrumental composition in four movements for full orchestra
Tempo (TEM-poe)
  Time, such as slow, moderate, fast
Timbre (TAMBR)
  Quality of tone, the sound of an instrument
Transcribe (tran-SKRIBE)
  To change or arrange a musical composition from one kind of voice or instrument or group of them, to another, such as transcribing an organ composition for piano or orchestra
Transpose (trans-POZE)
  To change a musical composition from one key to another
Treble (TREBB-L)
  The highest part in vocal music or the upper (right hand) part in piano music
Trio (TREE-oh)
  Composition for three voices or instruments
Vibrato (vee-BRAH-toe)
  Vibrating with strongly accented tone
Vivace (vee-VAH-cheh) Quick and lively
Wood-winds
  Wind instruments in the orchestra not made of brass, such as the flute, oboe, clarinet, and bassoon

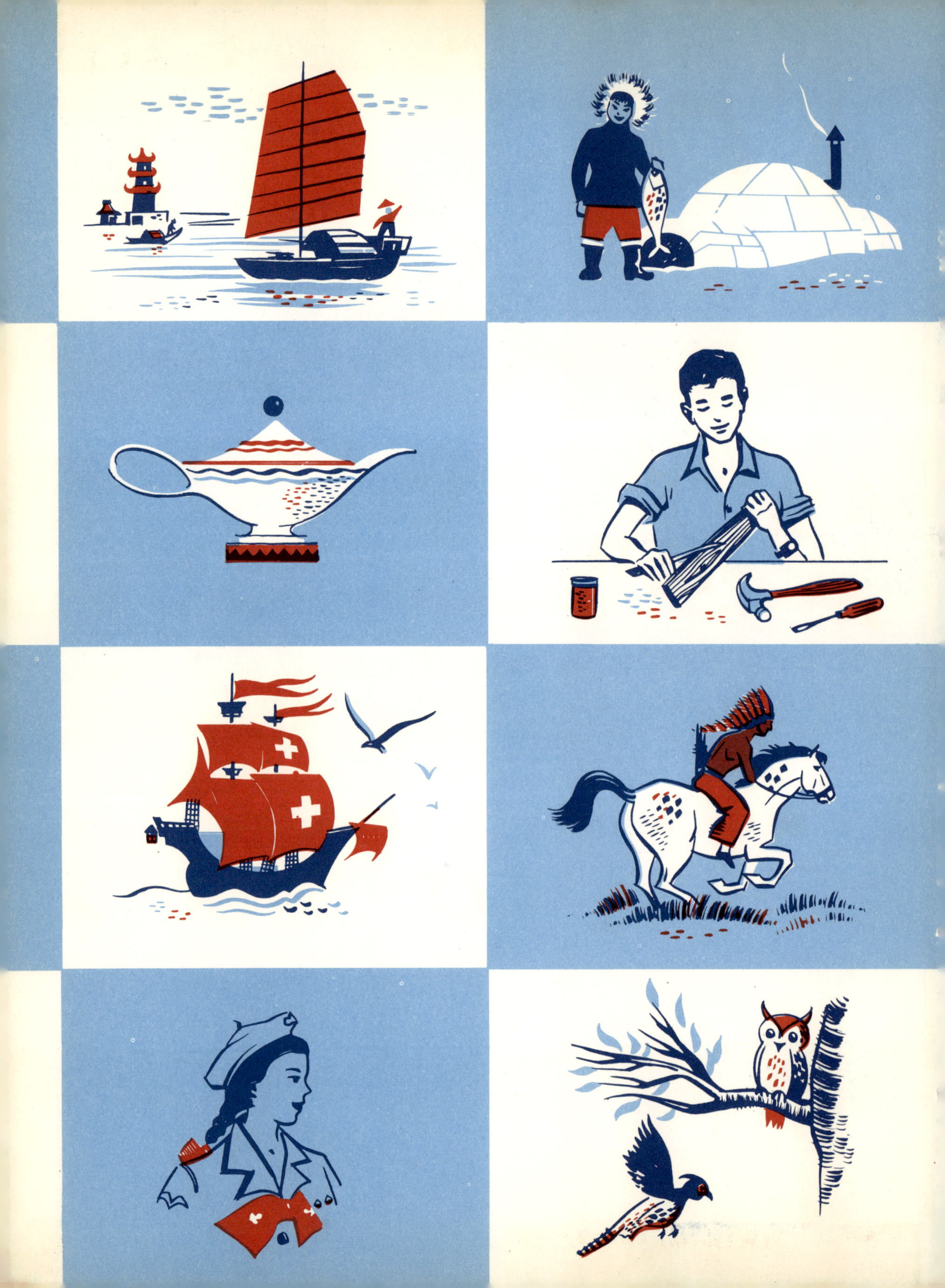